Software Quality Assurance
Principles and Practice

Nina S Godbole

Alpha Science International Ltd.
Pangbourne, U.K.

Nina S. Godbole
Quality-Assurance Manager
IBM Global Services (India) Pvt. Ltd.
Pune Export Division
Pune, India

Copyright © 2004

Alpha Science International Ltd.
P.O. Box 4067, Pangbourne RG8 8UT, U.K.

ISBN 1-84265-176-5

Printed in India

To My Family

Foreword

Engineering activities are, in general, process oriented, with most measurable design parameters being quantitative in nature. The field of software engineering is no exception. Software quality, like quality in any other aspect of human activity, often tends to be an illusive target to achieve, primarily because engineers find it so hard to understand quality in their conventional quantitative terms. On the other hand, complex and large software is increasingly being constructed and deployed in important and critical applications. It is thus essential to have a reasonable guarantee of the functionality and robustness of software in an observable, measurable, and controllable manner.

Software Quality Assurance has thus emerged as an important component of every software development activity. Standards have evolved which provide a holistic view of the entire quality process as opposed to emphasis on plain vanilla testing in the earlier years. Yet, there are not many books on this topic stressing this view. This book provides a very detailed coverage of all the important aspects of Software Quality Assurance.

What I liked most about the book is Nina's style of presentation, which is largely conversational. It permits readers to easily relate to the matter being discussed, thus obtaining a clearer understanding of issues involved. Organization of chapters provides a smooth transition from the holistic issues to the essential details. A separate chapter describing overall quality issues in products and processes preceding the chapter on software measurement and metrics is a good illustration of this style. The current version of ISO standard (9001:2000) is covered in sufficient details. This is important as this version attempts to bring in the notion of continuous improvement model, which has traditionally been the hallmark of CMM alone. The chapter on careers in quality is an interesting and unique feature. This should be a useful eye-opener to many professionals who wrongly regard QA to be a mundane activity synonymous with just routine testing and thus think of a QA job to be just a low level function. Nothing indeed could be farther from the truth.

While the book is meant for both practitioners and students, practitioners are likely to benefit more. This is because the student community, having no real world experience in development of large software, often relies upon a set of examples and questions to learn and consolidate conceptual understanding. I hope the next edition of the book provides examples and problems to help the student community to appreciate the concepts to a greater extent.

Nina was my student at IIT many years ago. More importantly, she herself is a practitioner rather than an academician, and books are traditionally written by academicians. Further, all of us in India are painfully aware of the larger demands that family life makes on working-women. To have found the time, energy and perseverance to undertake and successfully complete this task is indeed creditable. I thus take a special pride in writing this foreword.

Dr. Deepak B. Phatak
Subrao Nilekani Chair Professor
School of Information Technology (KReSIT)
IIT Bombay, Mumbai

Preface

Software Quality Assurance (SQA) as a professional domain is becoming increasingly important. A few years back they said, "SQA has a future"; now with a tight competition, we say—"There is no future for business without Software Quality Assurance practices built in". This book fulfills the long awaited need of the Information Technology/Software industry for a book on SOFTWARE QUALITY ASSURANCE.

There is no dearth of books on Software Engineering, which also cover the topic of Software Quality Assurance. But this book is entirely devoted to the topic of *Software Quality Assurance*. It starts with a discussion on importance of software quality assurance in the business of Information Technology. It covers key practices like Verification and Validation. It also discusses people issues and other barriers in successful implementation of Quality Management Systems in organization.

The basic premise here is that quality can be achieved through continuous process improvement and that product quality is possible through high quality of the processes used to produce the product. Thus, Quality Assurance, in its intent, is different than Quality Control (QC). While QC is an operational issue, Quality Assurance (QA) is a strategic issue requiring due attention from top management. QA is a proactive approach to ensure quality by establishing meaningful and adequate processes, to be followed throughout the life cycle. There are several definitions for the simple word "quality" – however, in reality it is not so simple when it comes to implementing it. My working experience as a quality professional (as well as a systems analyst and developer in earlier years) provided me opportunities to have a closer look at the quality scenario. This book is an attempt to explain the underlying quality assurance concepts in a way that would appeal to large diversity of readers.

A quality professional may successfully lead several cycles of verification and various types of quality audits and assessments. For me, too, my job responsibility provided an enriched experience through hands-on work in ISO audits, CMM Assessments, People CMM and also in the arena of the Integrated CMM. However, through and through, amidst these various implementations as part of organizational directives and initiatives, there was a growing conviction that quality is a "state of mind" a matter of "culture" and deep "institutionalization". As such, it needs to become a "way of life".

It looks like in its true sense; quality culture is yet to come in the software industry. The sheer change of designation from a "Programmer" to a "Software Engineer" or the mere shift in role responsibility from "coder" to "software design architect" may not bring in the right kind of mindset and mature attitude to quality in software development and service organizations. It is a thankless task that a true quality professional needs to take upon himself/herself to influence many non-believers of quality into strong believers in quality; the challenge lies in achieving this without going into conflicts or without creating abrasive situations.

Quality Management is an integral part of Project Management. However, Project Managers often fail to recognize/understand this. In the pursuit of acquiring quality certifications to flaunt them at the customers, one must not lose sight of quality. Quality Assurance has yet not earned its due place in software industry. There are reasons to believe that most Indian organizations go for quality certifications due to marketing/business pressures, and not much due to their firm belief in the concept of continuous process improvement as an on-going quest. It must be appreciated that Quality makes a business case and as such, it should be part of the strategic business plan.

The other motivation behind this work is the finding that there are not many titles on this subject by practicing quality professionals. Thus, there was a need for an Indian author to take this initiative towards writing a book on SQA that would serve a two-fold purpose; on one hand, it would serve as a rich source of SQA philosophy and discipline to champion the quality cause among the young students graduating out of engineering colleges and management schools, and on the other hand, a book rich with a practitioner's experience. It's with this strong conviction that this book-writing endeavor was taken up. It took two years to complete this work—whereas for a full-time writer perhaps, it'd have taken much less. Writing a book while holding a busy working schedule is not easy! Priority to the job often result in long hours at work.

Motivation for writing this book also came from the experience of imparting SQA skills to the aspirants of quality certification who joined the study circles devoted to this purpose. During this association, interactions with the working professionals from industry, threw open several eye-opening, mind-boggling questions. This provided an impetus to constant thinking and deep introspection.

The book is organized into 11 chapters and 3 appendices. It can be read cover-to-cover as well as in combinations of certain chapters. The first three chapters form a theme together to provide a *business context to Quality*. Chapter 4 and 5 should be read together as the topic of *measurements and metrics* is related to the notions of *product quality and process quality*. Reading chapter 8 and 9 together would form another cohesive theme on *process improvement*. Chapter 10 on *testing* is to satisfy the needs of those who are looking for a focus on *quality control*. Chapter 6 on *Walkthroughs and Inspection* along with the chapter on testing would form another coherent theme as these review techniques are considered "static testing". Chapter 11 helps paint a canvas in the light of the rest of discussion in the book, on career decisions. The three appendices are stand-alone references for providing allied information related to the topic of Software Quality Assurance.

One of the aims for this book is to spread the message that embedded quality practices can make a difference between lost revenues and improved profitability, between delayed release and speedier delivery, between poor product performance and true customer satisfaction. This book will have served its purpose if it motivates practitioners towards a process-oriented approach to establish Software Quality Assurance in their organization and if it can help create a conviction about the subject in the mind of quality professionals and finally if it creates many "quality champions" out of education campuses.

Nina Godbole

Acknowledgements

Book writing is a daunting task; it is a project and as such requires collaboration from a multitude of people apart from the author's own will and skill! At times, it may even seem that the efforts will never go through and that's when one needs a few encouraging words of support to keep up one's enthusiasm level.

The following individuals mattered for completing this book-writing project. All of them did their bit to help—either directly or indirectly: in one form or the other. Some provided valuable review comments; others offered to help or keep me company during the long hours of arduous proof reading. Some others helped co-ordinate meetings with various individuals who needed to be consulted during the two-year tenure of this endeavour. Some were a remote source of inspiration and role models as authors, while some just kept me going with their benign smiles. I was fortunate also to find the guidance and time of some very busy individuals, well known in the field of Information Technology. I take this opportunity to express my gratitude to all of them for their valuable support.

N.K. Mehra

Prabha Ananthanarayanan

Karunanidhi O. Aiyar

Gautam Modi

Ketaki Godbole

Dr. Sundeep Oberoi

Nitin Yeravadekar

Dr. Bhuvan Unhelkar

Dr. Shashikant Kelkar

Sagar Joshi

Dr. Asha Pachpande

Dr. D.B. Phatak

Narendra Barhate

Dr. Asha Goyal

Uday Panchpor

Sudhir Godbole

Gireendra Kasmalkar

Alok Mohgaonkar

Dr. Athula Ginige

Pramod Paranjpe

Vishwas Mahajan

Anupama Jauhry

CONTENTS

Foreword   v
Preface   vii
Acknowledgements   xi

Chapter 1:   Software Quality in Business Context   1
    1.1   The Meaning of "Quality": Defining Quality   1
    1.2   The Quality Challenge   2
    1.3   Why is Quality Important?   3
    1.4   Quality Control v/s Quality Assurance   7
    1.5   Quality Assurance at each Phase of SDLC   8
    1.6   Quality Assurance in Software Support Projects   18
    1.7   The SQA Function   19

Chapter 2:   Managing Software Quality in An Organization   25
    2.1   Quality Management System in An   25
         Organization
    2.2   Quality Management System: Various   31
         Expectations
    2.3   Quality Assurance: Some Diagnostic   38
         Questions
    2.4   The Need for the SQA Group in An   46
         Organization

Chapter 3:   Planning for Software Quality Assurance   55
    3.1   Software Quality Assurance Plans   55
    3.2   Software Quality Assurance: Organizational   67
         Level Initiatives
    3.3   Quality Planning—Some Interesting   76
         Dilemmas and Observations

Chapter 4:   Product Quality and Process Quality   80
    4.1   Introduction   80
    4.2   Software Systems Evolution   81
    4.3   Product Quality   82
    4.4   Models for Software Product Quality   84
    4.5   Process Quality   88

Chapter 5: **Software Measurement and Metrics** **96**
    5.1   Overview   96
    5.2   Introduction   97
    5.3   Measurement during Software Life   102
         Cycle Context
    5.4   Defect Metrics   106
    5.5   Metrics for Software Maintenance   110
    5.6   Classification of Software Metrics   114
    5.7   Requirements Related Metrics   115
    5.8   Measurements and Process Improvement   119
    5.9   Measurement Principles   120
    5.10 Identifying Appropriate Measures and   125
         Metrics for Projects
    5.11 Metrics Implementation in Projects   132
    5.12 Benefits of Measurement and Metrics for   135
         Project Tracking and Control
    5.13 Earned Value Analysis   137
    5.14 Planning for Metrics Program   141
    5.15 Issues in Software Measurements & Metrics   142
         Program Implementation
    5.16 Object Oriented Metrics: An Overview   146

Chapter 6: **Walkthroughs and Inspections** **155**
    6.1   Overview   155
    6.2   Introduction   155
    6.3   Structured Walkthroughs   156
    6.4   Inspections   158
    6.5   Various Roles and Responsibilities involved   159
         in Reviews/Inspections
    6.6   Some Psychological Aspects of Reviews   162
    6.7   Making Reviews and Inspections Effective   165
    6.8   Comparison of Review Techniques   167
    6.9   Inspection Related Checklists   169

Chapter 7: **Software Configuration Management** **173**
    7.1   Overview   173
    7.2   Configuration Management: Why and What   174
    7.3   Software Configuration Management   177
         Activities
    7.4   Standards for Configuration Audit Functions   192
    7.5   Personnel in SCM Activities   197
    7.6   Software Configuration Management: Some   197
         Pitfalls

Chapter 8: ISO 9001 **200**
  8.1   Overview   200
  8.2   What is ISO 9000   200
  8.3   The Origins of ISO 9000   201
  8.4   How Does ISO (as an organization)   202
        carry out its work?
  8.5   ISO Standards Development Process   203
  8.6   How the ISO 9000 Family of Standards Work   205
  8.7   ISO 9001:2000   205
  8.8   Why do Organizations Need ISO 9000?   207
  8.9   ISO Certification   208
  8.10 Assessment/Audit Preparation   212
  8.11 The Assessment Process   213
  8.12 Surveillance Audits/Re-Certification/   215
        Re-Assessment Audits
  8.13 ISO Consulting Services and Consultants   215
  8.14 ISO 9000: Some FAQs   221
  8.15 e-Business and ISO   222

Chapter 9: Software CMM and Other Process **224**
Improvement Models
  9.1   Overview   224
  9.2   The Capability Maturity Model for Software: 224
        An Overview
  9.3   Practices Followed at "Mature Organizations"   227
  9.4   CMM and ISO (A Comparative Analysis)   227
  9.5   Types of Capability Maturity Models (CMMs)   234
  9.6   The CMM-Integrated Model (CMM-I)   235
  9.7   Other Models for Software Process   244
        Improvement and Performance Excellence
  9.8   The People Maturity Model (P-CMM)   252

Chapter 10: Software Testing **257**
  10.1 Overview   257
  10.2 Purpose of Testing   258
  10.3 Differences Between Inspection and Testing   260
  10.4 Testing v/s Debugging   262
  10.5 Testing Life Cycle   264
  10.6 Roles and Responsibilities in Testing   266
  10.7 Test Artifacts   269
  10.8 The Test Plan   273
  10.9 The V-Model for Testing Phases   275
  10.10 Testing Techniques   279
  10.11 Test Metrics   289
  10.12 Risk-Based Testing   293
  10.13 Test Automation and Test Tool Selection   297
  10.14 Extreme Testing   300

10.15	Test Process Improvement Framework	301
10.16	Human Issues and Challenges in Testing	306
10.17	Software Testing Careers and Testing Competence Through Professional Certifications	308

Chapter 11: Careers in Quality — **311**
11.1	Overview	311
11.2	Introduction	311
11.3	P-CMM and Careers	312
11.4	Some important "People Issues"	312
11.5	Finding a Mentor to Shape Your Career	313
11.6	Roles for Quality Professionals	314
11.7	Quality Certifications	320

***Appendix A*: Process Improvement Related Miscellaneous Topics** — **325**
A.1	Some Basic Terms	325
A.2	High Maturity Organizations (those at SW CMM Level 4 or 5)	328
A.3	Strategic Planning for Software Process Improvement	334
A.4	Software CMM for Small Organizations	335
A.5	Mini Assessment Process	337
A.6	The Integrated Capability Maturity Model (CMM-I)	338

***Appendix B*: Indian Software Industry in Perspective** — **341**
B.1	Quality Certifications Scenario in India	341
B.2	The Indian Software Scenario in General	350
B.3	Cost and Quality Advantage: Indian Software Industry	351
B.4	The Indian Software Industry: Problems & Challenges	352

***Appendix C*: Quality Related Additional Topics** — **360**
C.1	Statistical Quality Control and Statistical Process Control	360
C.2	Software Maintenance Models: The Evolution	366
C.3	OO Maintainability	371
C.4	Maintenance in e-Business Era	372
C.5	Cyclomatic Complexity	383
C.6	Requirements	386
C.7	Principle of COUPLING and COHESION	388
C.8	Six Sigma	402

Index — 406

Chapter 1

SOFTWARE QUALITY IN BUSINESS CONTEXT

1.1 The Meaning of "Quality": Defining Quality

The term "Quality" is one of the most discussed terms but is often not defined crisply. All practitioners agree that "Quality" is a major business factor, a distinguisher that makes the difference and yet the term is extraordinarily difficult to define precisely. Quality is easy to see and is immediately apparent when encountered or missing! But when you try to pin it down or define what it is, you find that the concept is elusive. It is not the complexity, but the utter simplicity of quality that defies its explanation.

Here are several excerpts from views on this matter from various software quality specialists whom we refer to as the "Quality Gurus":

- Dr. Barry Boehm thinks of quality as "Achieving high levels of user satisfaction, portability, maintainability, robustness, and fitness for use
- Phil Crosby has created the definition with the widest currency because of its publication in his famous book "Quality is Free". He states that quality means "conformance to user requirements"
- Edwards Deming considers quality to be "striving for excellence" in reliability and functions by continuous improvement in the process of development, supported by statistical analysis of the causes of failure."
- Watts Humphrey, of the Software Engineering Institute (SEI), tends to speak of quality as "achieving excellent levels of fitness for use, conformance to requirements, reliability and maintainability."
- James Martin has asserted that software quality means being on time, within budget and meeting user needs.
- Tom McCabe, the software complexity specialist, defines quality as "high levels of user satisfaction and low defect levels, often associated with low complexity"

- John Musa of Bell Laboratories states that quality means combination of "low defect levels, adherence of software functions to users needs, and high reliability."
- Bill Perry, head of Quality Assurance Institute has defined quality as "high levels of user satisfaction and adherence to requirements".

Each of these definitions, individually, has its own merits and presents a view point on quality. Taken together, all these definitions resembles the "the blind men and the elephant" : each is a true aspect of quality. An end user's definition of quality would be "absence of defects that would make software either stop completely or produce unacceptable results". Defects can be traced to any stage in the Software Development Life Cycle (SDLC): requirements, design, code, documentation or to bad fixes of previous defects. Defects can range in severity levels. Thus, a working definition of quality must meet two important criteria:

- Quality must be measurable when it occurs
- Quality should be predictable when it occurs

Table 1 below lists the elements of quality definitions quoted above and indicates which elements meet both criteria.

Table 1: Elements of Quality Definition

Quality Factor	Predictable	Measurable
Defect Level	Yes	Yes
Defect Origins	Yes	Yes
Defect Severity	Yes	Yes
Defect Removal Efficiency	Yes	Yes
Product Complexity	Yes	Yes
Project reliability	Yes	Yes
Project maintainability	Yes	Yes
Project schedules	Yes	Yes
Project budgets	Yes	Yes
Portability	Yes	Yes
Conformance to Requirements	No	Yes
User Satisfaction	No	Yes
Fitness for Use	No	Yes
Robustness	No	No

1.2 The Quality Challenge

The goal of software quality is elusive in an actual project environment. The measures differ from project to project and organization to organization. Criteria vary as a function of the specific characteristics of the project, the needs of the users and stakeholders, and the application requirements of the system and software. Quality measures used for small systems may not be appropriate for the large ones. Criteria for quality applied to real-time applications are not always relevant when dealing with systems that are not real-time. Complex software requires different monitoring procedures than trivial applications. Quality criteria vary dramatically depending on the phase of the project at which the evaluation takes place (later in this chapter, quality assurance at each SDLC stage is discussed). The measures of quality must be specific to the project being evaluated and must assess the effectiveness of the entire development process, not just individual segments.

It is said that quality cannot be directly checked in the product; it must be planned right from the beginning. Thus, software quality must be planned into the project right from the initiation stage, engineered into the products of the software development project, and be monitored by assessing not only individual segments of the project or single data products but also by evaluating the interactions and interrelationships between them. Quality goals must be clearly defined, effectively monitored, and rigorously enforced. The project must focus on the quality issues of the project from the outset, ensuring that quality criteria are consistent with defined requirements. Throughout software development, the management of quality must be an overriding concern of all project personnel. Quality must be planned into the project structure, constantly evaluated, and corrections applied when deficiencies are identified.

1.3 Why is Quality Important?

Why do we need to bother with quality? Because today, quality is critical for survival and success. Customers demand it. Software is now a global business and organizations will not succeed in this global market unless they produce quality products/services and unless the organizations are also perceived by customer to produce quality products and services. This is the first message of this chapter. It applies as much to software development and support as to any other product or service (ISO definition of product includes services as well). However, there is something very interesting when it comes to a discussion on the topic of "quality": everybody seems to understand it, everybody wants it and yet everyone has a different perception of quality. Earlier in this chapter we had provided various definitions of quality, as originated from various quality gurus; essentially quality means satisfying customer. A happy customer will get you repeat business and business houses agree that the cost of getting a new customer is much higher; so much that businesses would like to focus on getting more and more business from the same customers. The entire CRM world (Customer Relationship Management) harps on this aspect. Thus, there are several reasons why businesses should be concerned with quality:

- Quality is a competitive issue now
- Quality is a must for survival
- Quality gives you the global reach
- Quality is cost effective
- Quality helps retain customers and increase profits
- Quality is the hallmark of world-class business

Now let us discuss each of these arguments.

1.3.1 *Quality: A Competitive Issue*

Several years back, software was considered to be only a technical business, in which functionality was the key determinant of success. Today, you can no longer rely on functionality alone of your products to be a winner. Your competitors can match your functionality relatively quickly and easily. The only way to differentiate your product from those of your competitors, in the long run, is by its quality, and the quality of support that goes with it.

As the software market matures, customers want to be assured of quality. They no longer accept your claims at face value; they expect you to demonstrate quality at each step of their business relationship or interaction with them. Certification to international quality standards is becoming a pre-requisite for getting business.

This does not apply only to the products developed for the external customers; it applies equally well to in-house information systems development. Internal customers also want quality assurance (for example the Help Desk function established in organizations' Information System department goes to prove this point). Increasingly, there are discussions whether the work should be carried out in-house or outsourced to external suppliers. Even while selecting these suppliers, businesses would give a prime consideration to the fact that they are certified in quality or not.

1.3.2 *Quality: An Issue for Survival*

As said earlier, customers are demanding demonstrable quality. If you cannot deliver it, your ability to survive in a higher competitive and rapidly changing market is in doubt. More and more large organizations are deciding to reduce the number of suppliers they deal with. In the drive to improve their own quality, they want to work closely with their few key suppliers, whom they treat as business partners. They often use quality certification as a way of selecting suppliers.

1.3.3 *Quality: For Entry into International Markets*

Software is a global business now where players can enter notwithstanding their organization size. The ability to demonstrate quality gives even a smaller company the credibility to enter an export market. Today, there are many Indian companies in the global market; some of them very small in size in terms of employee numbers but they are dealing with software giants like Microsoft. Although, most of the Indian software houses took quality certification only from the point of entry into international business, today it has become a way of working. Thus, the game of quality works both ways—your home market is vulnerable to quality foreign imports unless you can compete on quality.

1.3.4 Quality is Cost-effective

An effective quality system leads to increased productivity and permanently reduced costs, because it enables management to reduce defect correction costs by emphasizing prevention. Everyone in the software industry knows that the cost of correcting defects in software late in development life cycle can be orders of magnitude greater than the cost of correcting them early. Preventing defects in the first place can save even more. It is possible to achieve this. Leading companies, are aiming at "6 Sigma" quality in the near future.

The scope for reducing costs can be demonstrated by applying the "cost of poor quality" technique. This is a way of analyzing business processes to identify targets for improving initiatives. It is applicable to a software organization as to any other business. Organization's costs can be broken down into the following categories:

- Basic costs inherent in doing the work
- The cost of low quality, comprising:
  - Prevention costs, incurred to prevent defects from occurring, for example training or corrective action aimed at eliminating the causes of failure
  - appraisal costs, incurred for example reviewing work-products, testing software to ensure it meets requirements
  - failure costs, incurred in correcting defects found by appraisals, or by customer after delivery (post delivery defects or customer reported defects)

The cost of low quality can amount to more than 50% of total costs in software organizations. Large savings can be made by analyzing these costs. Large savings are possible by analysis of these costs, and targeting resources to reduce them. Typically, this will be achieved by redirecting resources towards prevention as illustrated in the figure 1. This applies as much to in-house information systems departments as to commercial software organizations.

The initial costs of establishing a quality system are more than compensated for subsequently, and significant return on investment can be

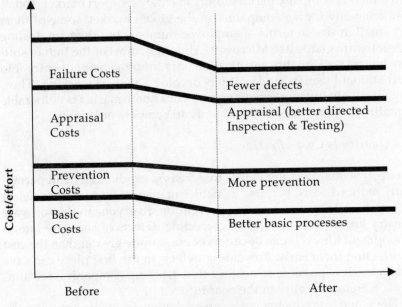

Figure 1: Costs of Poor Quality

expected. For example, there are reports saying that a well known engineering equipment division was able to reduce failure costs over a three year period from about 45% to 15%, and the cost of low quality by 20%, by improving their software engineering process. The savings in the cost of low quality flow straight through to a firm's bottom line, and can dramatically increase profits.

1.3.5 Quality for Retaining Customers and Increasing Profits

Poor quality often costs customers much more than it costs suppliers. Most customers will not tolerate this and will place their business elsewhere. It is said that a silent customer is more dangerous than a complaining customer; you will never know when you lost him ! Better quality leads to improved customer satisfaction, delightful customer relationship, and ultimately results in year-on-year retention of existing customers.

As said earlier, the sales cost of attracting a new customer is high. Studies from management consulting firms show that for a software company a 5% increase in customer retention increased profits by 35%.

1.3.6 Quality as the Hallmark of Global Business

World-class businesses place a strategic emphasis on quality. This enables them to grow their business and outperform their competitors.

The reason for this is illustrated in figure 2 below. It shows the "chain reaction" advocated by Deming, one of the quality gurus.

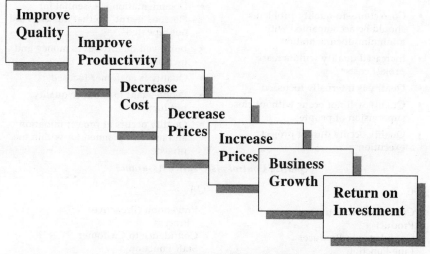

Figure 2:Deming's Chain Reaction

Today, view towards quality has drastically changed. Figure 3 below shows how the scenario stands now.

Changing Views of Quality

Past

- Quality is the responsibility of blue collar workers and direct labour employees working on the product
- Quality defects should be hidden from the customers and management
- Quality problems lead to blame, faulty justification and excuses

Present

- Quality is everyone's responsibility, including white-collar workers, the indirect labour force and the overhead staff
- Defects should be highlighted and brought to the surface for corrective action
- Quality problems lead to co-operative solutions

Figure 3

1.4 Quality Control v/s Quality Assurance

Often, this issue is confused. The two approaches are complementary to each other but different. Whereas QC is corrective, QA is a preventive approach. Quality Control is the operational techniques and activities that are used to fulfill requirements for quality. It includes the processes & methods used to monitor work and observe whether requirements/standards are met. On the other hand, Quality Assurance is all those planned and systematic activities implemented within the quality system and demonstrated as needed to provide adequate confidence that a work product will fulfill requirements for quality.

Changing Views of Quality

Past

- Corrections-to-quality problems should be accompanied with minimum documentation
- Increased quality will increase project costs
- Quality is internally focussed
- Quality will not occur without close supervision of people
- Quality occurs during project execution

Present

- Documentation is essential for "lessons learnt" so that mistakes are not repeated
- Improved quality saves money and increases business
- Quality is customer focused
- People want to produce quality products
- Quality occurs at project initiation and must be planned for within the project

Quality Control v/s Quality Assurance

QC

Correction (Reactive)
Product
Confidence to Producer
Line Function
Find Defects

QA

Prevention (Proactive)
Process
Confidence to Customer
Staff Function
Prevent Defects

Examples

- Walkthrough
- Testing
- Inspection
- Checkpoint review

- Defining Processes
- Quality Audit
- Selection of Tools
- Training

Figure 3

Figure 3 above makes the difference clear.

1.5 Quality Assurance at each Phase of SDLC

Quality during ANALYSIS

There are three major activities that foster quality during the Requirements Analysis phase of a software development project: (1) measurement of process attributes (2) Verification and validation, and (3) management. In fact, these themes will be followed throughout each of the succeeding life cycle stages

We are in a paradoxical situation when we try to measure accuracy, completeness and rationality, the attributes of analysis. We really will not know how well analysis has succeeded until the end of the project. It will be very useful, however, if we compare the predicted schedule, cost, feasibility and market acceptance, staffing needs and so forth with actual figures. This can be done as part of the project debriefing and any variances between planning and actuality can be fed back into the analysis methodologies.

Here, it is important to mention two important terms: VERIFICA-TION and VALIDATION. Verification refers to the set of activities that ensure that software that software correctly implements a specific function. Validation refers to a different set of activities that ensure that the software that has been built is traceable to customer requirements. In other words:

Verification: "Are we building the product right?"
Validation: "Are we building the right product?"

Verification during analysis can be performed by making sure that functional and non-functional requirements and constraints, as in the requirements specification document are traceable to customer requests that were determined during systems analysis. It is also important to verify risk analysis, cost estimation, strategy and model selection and so on, by comparing them with the results of previous projects. Validation can be performed by allowing users to review the project plan and experiment with prototypes.

Managing quality in the analysis stage is a challenge because requirements may not be very clear at this state. It is at this point that the most important management decisions for the rest of the project will be made. The major management deficiencies in most software development projects seem to be incorrect schedules, incorrect cost estimates, inadequate project accountability procedures, inadequate quality assurance procedures and imprecise goals and success criteria—all products of the ANALYSIS stage

What is a Requirement?

A requirement is a specification of what a system/application must do—the things about the system users can observe. Good requirements have three primary characteristics:

1. They are precise, with no room for misinterpretation by users or implementors.
2. They specify just what the system must do, not how to do it. They avoid specifying implementation details.
3. They show conceptual integrity, building on a simple set of facilities that interact well with each other.

From the user's point of view, the last property is the most important. Conceptual integrity is the key to making a system users can understand. If it has too many features or if each facility has its own peculiarities, the user has an enormous task to understand the system. The key to conceptual integrity is to have one architect or at most a few architects. More than about three people can hardly agree when to meet, let alone what to do!

While defining systems requirements, one may also define constraints and goals for the system. Constraints can also be referred to as "nonfunctional requirements". A constraint is a limitation on possible implementation of the system. For example, a customer may require a particular implementation language, a particular search algorithm say for product search feature of the on-line catalogue module of a web application, or a particular format for a database table etc. in a way not visible to the end users. It is often in our interest to negotiate away constraints since they limit implementation freedom. However, since the customers are paying for the product, they normally succeed in imposing constraints if they really want them.

A goal is a statement that guides tradeoffs among design decisions; For example, a customer may care a lot about maintainability of the software, but not care much about efficiency. A goal may become a requirement if you find a way to quantify it, which in turn allows introduction of measure for improvement. For example, "high throughput" is a goal but "at least 53 transactions per second" is a requirement.

Since requirements are specifications of the observable behaviour of the system, an "implementation detail" is any property of the system that should not be visible to users. Some people use "requirement" to mean any property of the system they care about, and "implementation detail" to mean any property they don't care about. This can lead to confusion. It is better to use taxonomy of this terminology to promote clarity for communication with the users/client during the analysis stage of a software project. Table 2 shows a way of distinguishing among these various terms discussed so far (goal, constraint, requirement).

Using the terminology depicted in above table, an implementation detail the customer cares about is a constraint. A requirement the customer does not care about is simply a requirement that is likely to change. If you list several alternatives, the customer may choose one, or at least reject a few. If the customer still does not care what choice you make, you may discover after delivering the system that the users are unhappy with your choice. Subsequently, during the system design stage, one should try to minimize the consequences of changing this particular requirement.

Quality during DESIGN

Design is pivotal activity in a software development project. A lack of quality in the design process can invalidate an otherwise good requirements specification and can make correct implementation impossible. For this reason, we must take special care to ensure that the design process is carried out correctly.

We'll now discuss the term "metrics" as described in SEI Curriculum Module SEI-CM-12-1.1. (A more detailed discussion will be

Table 2: A Taxonomy of Requirements Terminology

	Customer Doesn't care	Customer Cares	
		Measurable	Un-measurable
Observable to Users	Requirements likely to change	Requirement	
			Goal
Not observable to Users	Implementation detail	Constraint	

undertaken in the chapter on Software Metrics) As per this published report of December 1988, essentially, SOFTWARE METRICS deals with the measurement of the software PRODUCT and PROCESS by which it is developed. Software metrics may be broadly classified as either PRODUCT METRICS or PROCESS METRICS. Product Metrics include SIZE METRICS (Lines of Code or Function Points) and Complexity Metrics, QUALITY METRICS (Defect Metrics, Reliability Metrics, Maintainability Metrics). Process Metrics, on the other hand, are measures of the development process such as development time, type of methodologies used, or the average level of experience of the programming staff. There are other metrics, too, apart from the ones mention in the SEI literature.

To evaluate design, it is necessary to choose a set of design attributes that will be measured along with some objective metrics, which can be applied in a procedural way to the design. There should also be a procedure for combining individual metrics to evaluate overall design quality. There are several metrics that can be used during the design stage: cyclomatic complexity of a software module (McCabe), the notion of Coupling & Cohesion. One of the fundamental principles of Structured Design is that a large system should be partitioned into manageable modules. However, it is vital that this partitioning should be carried out in such a way that the modules are as "independent" as possible—this is the criterion of COUPLING. Design should ensure that each module carries out a single, problem related function—this is the criterion of COHESION. Readers should make a note that the difficulty of understanding a program is largely determined by the complexity of the control graph for that program.

In an object-oriented design paradigm, the visibility of an object can be taken as a measure of the degree to which it is global to the entire system (Public and Private Access Designations). Generally, a high level of visibility is desirable for more than few objects in the design, and then only those most central to the software (principle of data hiding in object oriented methodology). Industry practice shows that use of checklist during design helps improve design quality. We have provided below one example of such a checklist.

Checklist for Software Design Description

- *Have we addressed all the requirements mentioned in the SRS ?*
- *Has the SRS been put under document control ?*
- *Have the requirements related to the following features been addressed during the design?*
  - *performance*
  - *security*
  - *concurrency*
  - *usability*
  - *portability*
  - *testability*
  - *language/DB/OS/hardware requirement*
  - *development environment*
  - *compatibility (backward/existing products)*
  - *adherence to industry standards*
  - *scalability/expandability*
  - *exception handling*
- *Is the design methodology chosen appropriate for the type of software project to be developed?*

a) Clarity
- Is the design documentation clear/unambiguous?
- Can the design be technically justified?

b) Compatibility with existing software (if applicable)
- Have the effects of this design on existing software been identified? Have we done the impact analysis?
- Does this design rely on the side effects of other software? Does this design have any dependency on any other related designs?

c) Component level
- Are the interfaces well defined? (have we taken care of *coupling* and *cohesion* principles?)
- Are the main data structures defined?
- Are the main algorithms defined?
- Is the data/control flow defined?

d) Data structures and algorithms
- Are the data structures defined?
- Are the access methods to the data structures defined?
- Are the algorithms defined?
- Do the data structures and algorithms solve the problem?

e) Error/exception handling
- Are data type errors handled?
- Does the software validate user input?

- Does the software give explicit, non-threatening messages if error occurs? (Quality of error messages)
- Can the software be restarted from any point after an error?
- Does the software gracefully handle exception conditions such as access violations and floating point errors?
- Is the error handling consistent?

f) Procedure interfaces

- Does the number of actual parameters match the number of formal parameters?
- Do the type and size of actual parameters match the type and size of formal parameters?
- Have we specified the local and global functions correctly?
- Are global variables defined and used consistently across modules?
- Is all communication documented (i.e. parameters and shared data)?

g) Procedure level

- Does the procedure do something very similar to an existing procedure?
- Is there a library procedure that will do the same thing?
- Is the procedure excessively complex?
- Could the procedure be broken into separate, more logical pieces?
- Is the procedure of acceptable size?
- Does the procedure do only one logical thing? (Principle of COHESION)
- Does the procedure rely on procedure scope static variables?
- Is the procedure easily maintained and correctly referenced?
- Can the procedure be easily tested?
- Are the side-effects described?

h) Quality

- Are the goals of design stated (reliability, flexibility, maintainability, performance etc.)?
- Does the design satisfy its stated goals? (Traceability to REQUIREMENTS)
- Is there evidence that more than one design option was considered?
- Are several design options listed along with the reason for their adoption or rejection?
- Are the design assumptions stated?
- Are the design trade-offs stated?
- Is the design efficient?
- Is the design maintainable?
- Is the design portable?
- Can the design handle changes to the external environment with minimum modifications?
- Is the design parameter driven or are the values hard coded in the programs?

i) Requirements
- Does the design satisfy every requirement?
- Is there traceability between the design and the system specifications?
- Can the design meet development cost requirements?
- Can the design be completed in the given time frame?
- Does the design stay within the required memory constraint?
- Does the design stay within the required disk usage constraint?
- Does the design satisfy the response time requirement?
- Will the design handle the expected rate of transactions?
- Will the design handle the expected data flow volumes?

j) Reuse
- Does this functionality exist within another procedure or library function?
- Is this functionality sufficiently general purpose that a library function should be created?

k) System level
- Can this design be implemented on the given hardware platform and operating system?
- Can this design be easily ported to other hardware platforms and operating systems?
- Does this platform handle the required terminals, workstations, PCs and printers?
- Does the design allow outputs on a variety of printers?
- Will the design allow for easy installation and configuration?
- Does the design have full international capabilities? Does it handle:
  - Translated text and error messages.
  - Date/time formats and separators.
  - Numeric separators.
  - Sorting sequences.
  - Input/recognition of accented characters etc.

l) User interface
- Had the user interface been prototyped in collaboration with the users?
- Is the software intuitive, consistent, and predictable?
- Does it cater to the various kinds of users—from beginners through experts?
- Can commands be abbreviated?
- Does the program provide sensible defaults to avoid redundant typing?
- Does the software provide context sensitive help?
- Is there detailed help information available on each command?
- Can users cancel time-consuming operations?

- Is the menu hierarchy logical and simple?
- Can the users perform more than one action while in a particular screen or do they have to exit and back up a menu hierarchy?
- Is it easy to back out, wherever the user may be in the program?
- Is it obvious what format to enter information/date in?

Quality during Specification

As the technical foundation of software development, the specification work products should exhibit the highest quality possible. Unfortunately, this is not so. Attention to specifications often gets less focus than other developmental stages. Hence, not much can be said about metrics, verification & validation, and management as they apply specifically to the specification stage in the life cycle of a software project. The irony is that, since all other work products are formally verified against the specifications, it is appropriate to consider here the groundwork necessary for future verification of design and code against specifications.

Quality Indicators for Specification

First, let us explain the difference between the two terms MEASURE and METRICS. MEASURE(ment)—a NUMBER with a DIMENSION—for example: "5 defects" is a MEASURE. METRIC is two related MEASURES—for example: "6 Defects/KLOC is a METRIC. (This is explained in great details in the chapter devoted to Metrics and Measurement)

There are a few measures that are used for indicating the Software Requirements Specification. The first measure is simply whether it conforms to the standard that has been accepted by the software organization. This requires a simple check-off procedure to determine whether each part of the document required by the standard is actually present, whether standards in notation and style are met and so on.

The most obvious attributes for specifications are listed below:

- Correct
- Consistent
- Complete
- Unambiguous
- Minimal
- Formal
- Verifiable
- Transformable
- Modifiable
- Traceable

The quality of the Software Requirements Specification (A good reference for this is : IEEE Guide to Requirements Specification 830) can be evaluated with regard to several different attributes. The level of these attributes in a given specification will determine its appropriateness and usefulness for the task. Let us now discuss each of the above attributes.

The first, and by far the most important attribute is correctness of requirements important to the customer and that are stated in the Software Requirements Specification (SRS) The SRS should have backward traceability to the Contract/Document of Understanding and the SoW—Statement of Work) must appear in correct form in the Software Requirements Specification. Unfortunately, since the customer's requirements were probably stated in an informal language or because may be he was not articulate enough, there are no formal method for verifying the correctness of the SRS (Refer Table 1). This specification can, however be validated by allowing the user to exercise the means of a prototype.

Consistent, Complete and Unambiguous are the attributes that can be logically grouped together. Consistency means we are sure that requirements which are correct in isolation can still be achieved when taken together. Completeness guarantees that no important requirement specification has been left out. Use of checklist helps in this. Unambiguous means that everyone on the project (all stakeholders included) will agree on the exact meaning of the specification..

Minimal means we must guard against over specifying software at this point of time. This further means that the specifications should be "functional" (The functional requirements need to be tested down the project stream). Another kind of minimality is obtained by use of a notation that supports us in saying just what we want, with no additional, redundant, or distracting verbiage. Verbose SRS do not gel well with software engineers—they would not want to spend a lot of time wading through superfluity. Redundancy can only add confusion and not certainty to the SRS document.

Verifiability is the capacity of determining that requirements are met at each stage of development. It depends on precise, unambiguous and concrete statements of constraints, exceptions and software functions. Unfortunately, verifying that design and code follow from specifications (SRS) is easier when specifications are procedural rather than functional. This puts a constant tension between the attributes of minimality and verifiability.

Transformability describes the characteristics of specifications that provide for a smooth processing to create a design, the working product of the next stage of the development life cycle. This smooth transition will minimize the amount of "rework" and adjustment needed to prepare for the design process (Effort on rework can be found by logging the time spent on the correcting the defects in the design document). For this reason, specification notation should be compatible with the methodology and tools used during design.

Modifiability refers first to the ease with which changes can be made to the specifications themselves. Modifiability is also promoted by modularity in the specification with minimum cross-connections and dependencies between different requirements.

Traceability is the inclusion of sufficient pointers, cross indexes, references etc to allow us to go forward from a requirement to find those part of a subsequent work product to satisfy the requirement or backward from a portion of the work product to find the requirements that give rise to it. Traceability also refers to our ability to correlate the specifications backward to the requirements analysis as shown in Figure 1 below.

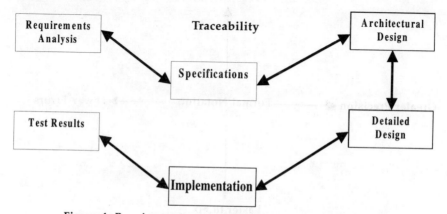

Figure 4: Requirements traceability to other work products

Formality, as indicated in the figure 4 above, is the key to much of the specification process. Software engineers often resent the time spent on documented specification, believing that it simply delays their "real" work i.e. coding. However, most of the essential attributes of good specification can be supported. SRS should be written in a language that is minimal—they include nothing that is not needed. A specification written using formal specification language is supposed to be characterized by the following:

- Appropriateness
- Cleanliness
- Constructability
- Structuring
- Ease of access
- Precision
- Lack of ambiguity
- Completeness
- Consistency

- Analyzability
- Formality
- Testability
- Traceability
- Executability
- Tolerance of incompleteness
- Adaptability
- Economy of expression
- Modifiability

Thus, the advantages of Formal Notation can be summarized as indicated below.

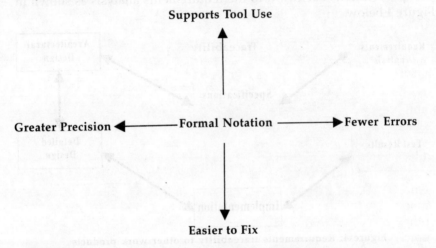

1.6 Quality Assurance in Software Support Projects

So far, we have discussed quality in the context of developing software products, but it is vital for software developers to recognize that the quality of support for a product is normally as important to customers as that of the quality of the product itself. Delivering software technical support has quickly grown into a big business. Today, software support is a business in its own right. Software support operations are not there because they want to be. They exist because they fill a vital void in the software industry; helping customers use the computer systems in front of them, a job that is getting more and more difficult. There is a phenomenal increase in the number of people who use their computers for "mission critical" applications. This puts extra pressure on the software support groups in organizations. We discussed the concept of "complexity measure" in the previous section. During maintenance phase of a software project, the complexity metrics can be used to track and control the complexity level of modified module/routines.

In this scenario, the software developer must ensure that the customer's support requirements are identified, and must design and engineer the business and technical infrastructure from which the product will be supported. This applies equally to those businesses producing software packages and to in-house information systems departments. Support for software can be complex and may include:

- User documentation, including on-line help text
- Packaging and distribution arrangements
- Implementation and customization services and/or consulting
- Product Training
- Help desk assistance
- Error reporting and correction
- Enhancement

For an application installed on a single site, the support requirement may be simply to provide telephone and assign a staff member to receive and follow up queries. For a shrink-wrapped product, it may mean providing localization and world-wide distribution facilities, and implementing major administrative computer systems to support global help-desk services.

1.7 The SQA Function

One of the critical challenges for any quality program is to devise a mechanism for enabling independent reviews of the work done by others. The need is to focus on those SQA methods that permits development work to be reviewed by people who are not primarily developers. As per S/w CMM (Capability Maturity Model) version 1.1, Software Quality Assurance includes activities like AUDITING, REVIEWS etc. in addition to performing WALKTHROUGHS, PROCESS CHECKS etc. These could be performed by different sets of persons. A Person performing this role is called the "Software Quality Analyst". Thus, the acronym "SQA" is used in both senses of the terms (the role as well as the function in an organization). The role of a Software Quality Analyst is to monitor the methods and standards the software developers use and to verify that they have properly applied these methods to their work products. Quality Assurance as a function is a valid discipline in its own right. People can be quality assurance experts without being software design experts. This expertise and commitment of Quality Assurance function is what is required to establish a strong quality program in an organization. It includes knowledge of statistical methods, quality control principles, the software process, and an ability to deal effectively with people in contentious situations.

A key management axiom says that:" What is not tracked is not done." In software there are so many things that need to be done but the manager can't possibly track them all. Since effective management of software project requires that thousands of activities are done precisely right, some mechanism is needed to do the tracking. This is the role of Software Quality Assurance function. Before establishing an SQA function it is essential to first decide how important software quality is to the organization, is it, for example, more important than meeting a critical delivery schedule? Just how much "quality" is important? Is it looked upon merely as a means to woo customers? Should the product be delayed to fix 1 more bug, or 10 more, or 100 more or…?

As long as software quality is treated as a matter of faith, no formal actions are required. Incantations about the need to believe in quality will change nothing. If management's commitment to software quality does not come down to day-to-day actions, no consistent improvement is likely.

Similarly, if management views the mere act of setting up a Quality Assurance just to show the presence of such group, then, it will have wasted a lot of money, established another bureaucratic bottleneck, and probably used to be effective. The prime benefit of establishing a dedicated Quality group is the assurance it provides management in showing that the officially established process is actually being implemented. More specifically, establishing a Quality Assurance program in an organization ensures that:

- An Appropriate development methodology is in place.
- The projects use standards and procedures in their work.
- Independent reviews and audits are conducted.
- Documentation is produced to support maintenance and enhancement.
- The documentation is produced during and not after development.
- Mechanisms are in place and used to control changes (Configuration Management).
- Testing emphasizes all the high-risk product areas.
- Each software task is satisfactorily completed before the succeeding one is begun. (Phase-end Inspections)
- Deviations from standards and procedures are exposed as soon as possible. (Waivers and Deviations)
- The quality control work is itself performed against establishment standards.
- The SQA plan and the software development plan are compatible.

1.7.1 The Benefits of SQA Function

The reasons for concern about software quality are compelling. Especially, these days, in the face of the American WTC tragedy, everyone who travels in an airplane agrees on the importance of quality software for air traffic control and the quality of security measures employed on airports. Similarly, a payroll processing software should not have errors, nor should the software that controls air defenses, flies aircraft, steer ships, runs banking systems forecasts weather, directs police, and so on. Software has an enormous impact on almost everything we do, and this impact will only increase in the future.

"SQA" is used in two contexts; as a role (Software Quality Analyst) and a function (Software Quality Assurance). Beyond logical arguments on the need for SQA, experience also provides a useful guide. In a study, aimed at studying software managers' views of the reasons for project success or failure, it was found that while the value of quality Assurance was not explicitly addressed, when the project management standards were enforced, 76 percent of the projects were successful, as opposed to only 60 percent when no standards were followed.

The experience with IBM system/360 and 370 software development also demonstrate the value of SQA in enforcing development standards. IBM reported software quality improvements of three to five times over an eight-year period. While this was due to many factors, SQA was an important part of their project. Many project managers feel that it is found increasingly advantageous, from both product quality and cost-effectiveness standpoints, to have an explicit quality standards enforced on their software projects. Thus SQA has significantly increased ability to predictably engineer reliable systems.

1.7.2 The Need for Software Quality Assurance Function

It is hard for anyone to be objective about auditors- this is a normal human psychology. People feel that they do their jobs pretty carefully and as such they resent any contrary implication. The need for "outside" review, however, is a matter of perspective. Suppose you had just packed a parachute and were about to take a jump. The odds are you would be happy to have a qualified inspector monitor your every step to make sure you did it just right. Similarly, when quality is a vital business issue, some independent checks are necessary, not because people are not trustworthy but because they are human. There is a well-known saying that "to err is human". The issues with software are not whether checks are needed, but who does them and how. The people employed in the Quality Assurance function perform this independent check.

In very small organization it is often possible for the software managers to monitor the work so closely that no SQA activity is needed. As the size of the staff grows, the managers become involved with other duties, and they quickly lose touch with the day to day technical work. This is when they need to do one of the following;

- Find some way to handle their own workload so that they can monitor more closely their people's work.
- Hire someone to do the audit work.
- Motivate the people to monitor each others' work

From technical, economic, and moral viewpoint, the last alternative is generally the most desirable. Unfortunately, as software organizations grow beyond a few dozen people, these "buddy systems" break down. This is when management must resort to establishing the Software Quality Assurance function.

1.7.3 *The Objectives for Software Quality Assurance Function*

Broadly stated, the goals of SQA function are:

- To improve software quality by appropriately monitoring both the software and the development process that produces it.
- To ensure full compliance with the established standards and produces for the software and the software process.
- To ensure that any inadequacies in the product, the process, or the standards are brought to management's attention so these inadequacies can be fixed.

It is important to understand that the SQA function is not responsible for producing quality products or for making quality plans—these are the responsibilities of project managers. SQA as a function is responsible for auditing the quality actions of the line organization and for drawing management's attention to any deviations or predictable defects. There are two styles in which the SQA role can be deployed. Either an independent responsibility can be given to an individual as a team member of the project, who then, reports to the project manager in the capacity of an SQA (Software Quality Analyst) or there can be an independent SQA function from where the Software Quality Analysts are assigned to an organization's software projects. They will typically review the assigned project with a pre-determined frequency to ensure that organization's software processes are being adhered to. In this latter mode of SQA function deployment, the head of the SQA group will typically report to the apex responsibility in quality say the Vice President—Quality or Corporate Head or Director for Quality. In either case, what is important is that the Quality Assurance function objectively maintains its independence of duty, working as eyes and ears of management, providing visibility to the senior management into the product realization activity. Quality Assurance function should not be affected by any external influences and vested interests.

To be effective, Quality Assurance function needs to work closely with development group. Software Quality Analysts in this function need to understand life cycles of software projects, and ensure that the project plans are in line with this, verify their execution, and monitor the performance of the individual tasks against the stated quality goals. If the development people view SQA as the enemy, it will be hard for them to be effective. Persons performing the role of Software Quality Analyst need to have an attitude of cooperation and support. If they

are arbitrary, antagonistic, or nit picking to the extent of being impractical, no amount of management support can make them effective.

1.7.4 The SQA Role

Readers should note that the acronym (SQA) is used to denote both the
person playing the role of Software Quality Analyst or the function
Software Quality Assurance. The meaning of the term is to be interpreted depending on the context in which is it being discussed. As said
earlier, the people executing the software projects are the only ones
who can be responsible for quality. The role of SQA is to monitor the
way these groups perform their responsibilities. In doing this, there are
several potential pitfalls to watch for:

- It is a mistake to assume that the SQA people themselves can do
  anything about "enforcing" quality.
- The existence of an SQA function does not ensure that the standards and procedures are followed.
- Unless management periodically demonstrates its support for SQA
  by following their recommendations, SQA will be ineffective.
- Unless line management requires that SQA try to resolve their
  issues with project management before escalation, SQA and development will not work together effectively.
- All SQA can do is alert management to deviations from established
  standards and Management must then insist that the quality problems be fixed before the product is shipped; otherwise SQA becomes
  an expensive bureaucratic exercise.

1.7.5 SQA Responsibilities

Software Quality Assurance function can be effective when people
working in the function are allowed to report through an independent
management chain, when they are properly staffed with competent
professionals with appropriate skills and dedication, and when they
see their role as supporting the development and maintenance personnel in improving product quality. This requires that they be given the
following responsibilities:

- Review all development and quality plans for completeness
- Participate as inspection moderators in design and code inspections
- Review all test plans for adherence to standards
- Review a significant sample of all test results to determine adher-
  ence to plan
- Periodically audit SCM (Software Configuration Management)
  performance to determine adherence to standards
- Participate in all projects quarterly and phase reviews and register

nonoccurrence if the appropriate standards and procedures have not been reasonably met.

• If SQA fulfills its responsibilities and if senior management refuses to allow line management to commit and to ship products until the SQA issues have been addressed, then the SQA can help management improve product quality. Items typically brought under SQA review are shown in Table 3.

Table 3: Example of Items under SQA Review

1. ***requirements traceability matrix*** *to show that the product specifications cover the requirements asked for by the customer*
2. ***implementation traceability matrix*** *or similar tool used to show that the product specifications are implemented in the design*
3. ***documentation samples***
4. *Samples of **development records***
5. ***Software Configuration Mangement activities*** *as per practices stated in the **configuration management plan, change control board***
6. ***Sub-contractor's quality assurance function*** *(important when outsourcing part of or entire development work)*
7. *All **plans** prepared during the tenure of software projects*
8. ***Peer Reviews*** *and **Testing** related activities*
9. ***Reviews of design, documentation and code*** *to see adherence to organization's standards*

Since the potential workload is enormous, some of these reviews are generally done on statistically selected sample of the work. Next chapters deal specifically with other areas and aspects of software quality assurance.

REFERENCES

[1] *Software Engineering: A Practitioner's Approach*—Roger S. Pressman (McGraw-HILL Publication)
[2] *Software Quality Assurance & Management*—Michael W. Evans, John J. Marciniak (John Wiley & Sons)

Chapter 2

MANAGING SOFTWARE QUALITY IN AN ORGANIZATION

2.1 Quality Management System in an Organization

In chapter 1, we discussed importance of quality and how quality can be brought out at each level of the software systems development life cycle. In this chapter, our focus will be on understanding quality management in an organizational context. We'll discuss the details of a quality management system, contents of a Software Quality Assurance Plan and roles and responsibilities of the Software Quality Assurance (SQA) group in an organization that has committed itself to quality system.

Applying the principles of quality to the software process is the beginning of organization's commitment to quality. An organization expresses its commitment to Quality through an apex document known as the 'Quality Policy'. The term QMS (Quality Management System) is used internationally to describe a process, which ensures and demonstrates the quality of the products and services provided by the organization. QMS is a set of procedures/processes, which as a whole form the basis for executing organization's product/service delivery mechanisms. Typically, the Quality Manual begins with a Vision and Mission Statement of the organization committing itself to quality; for example, a vision statement can read like" *To be the leader and most respected e-Solutions Company in India*", or say *"Providing best of the breed CRM solutions to our customers"*. Organization's Vision is followed by its Mission Statement. Figure 1 shows the Quality Pyramid with the terms mentioned above.

An example of a mission statement could be *"We are in the business of Providing Value to our customers through CRM solutions with a commitment to quality of solutions providing. Making our organization a winner in the Global e-Business Market with solutions that are cost effective and with requisite quality"*. Having decided on the Vision and Mission for the business, an organization must, next, device a mechanism that helps deliver the solution with the commitment made. QMS, which is a set of well thought out and well defined processes helps to do this.

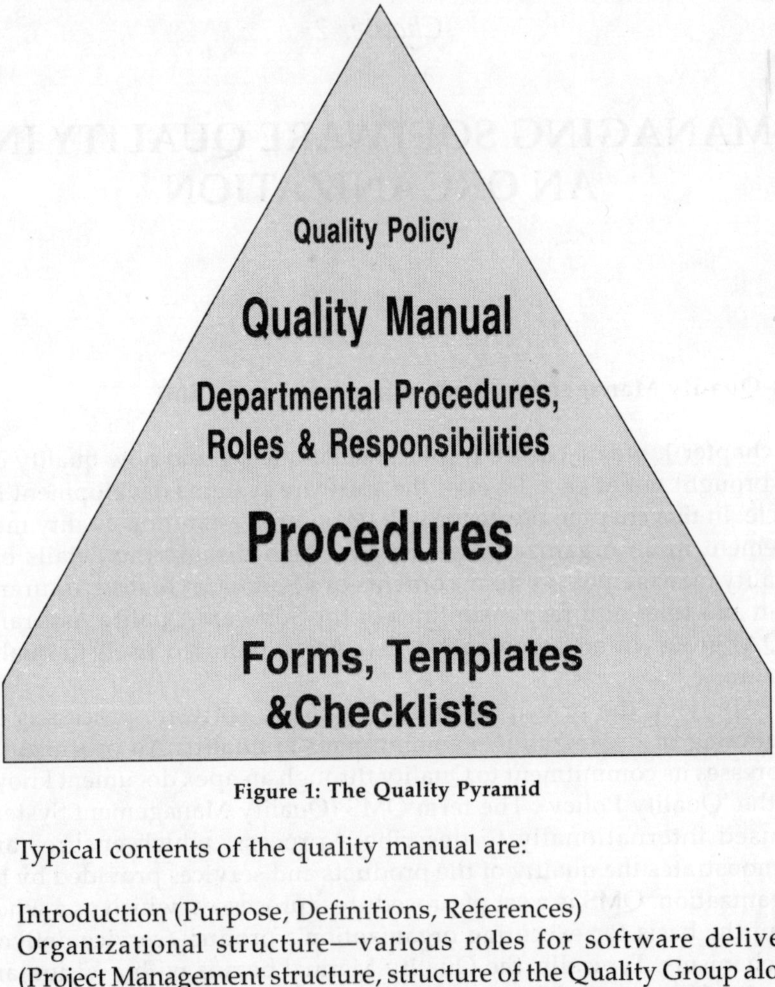

Figure 1: The Quality Pyramid

Typical contents of the quality manual are:

- Introduction (Purpose, Definitions, References)
- Organizational structure—various roles for software delivery (Project Management structure, structure of the Quality Group along with the descriptions of various sub-groups within it such as—
  - Process Engineering Group (PEG)
  - Software Quality Assurance (SQA)
  - Measurements Assurance (MA)
  - Defect Prevention (DP)
  - Technology Change Management Group (TCMG)
  - Quality Systems Requirements (Quality Policy, Quality System Procedures, Approach to Quality Planning along with Quality Objectives
  - Software product/services realization mechanism deployed in the organization

2.1.1 What is QMS

The ISO 9001-2000 is one of the International Standards, which, defines and describe what is required of a satisfactory quality system. It specifies requirements for a Quality Management System (QMS) where an organization:

a) Needs to demonstrate its ability to consistently provide the product that meets customer and applicable regulatory requirements, and
b) Aims to enhance customer satisfaction through the effective application of the system, including processes for continual improvement of the system and the assurance of conformity to customer and applicable regulatory requirements

(ISO 9001-2000 Clause 1 Scope—In this international standard, the term "product" applies to product or service intended for, or required by, a customer)

Apart from ISO, many other industries, national and international bodies have evolved standards, which describe quality systems to be applied to software development and support. These are discussed later in this chapter. (In addition to this, we have devoted a separate chapter on ISO 9001:2000 and also a separate chapter on other Software Process Improvement frameworks)

The term 'quality system' is sometimes used instead of 'quality management system (QMS). This emphasizes the need for the quality process to be actively managed to ensure that it continues to be effective and efficient. Software development organizations must keep the practices and tool they use under constant review and make changes in a controlled way. This helps to ensure that the QMS is effective in the face of continuously changing business environment.

Just as important as the practices and tools are the organization's employees who use them. They need to be properly trained (through awareness programs etc.) in usage of the QMS. Training plays a very important part in quality related activities of an organization. It is essential that a quality professional has the mindset and skills for imparting training within his/her area of responsibility. The onus goes to the quality system as well. QMS must ensure that the employees have the right skills to do their jobs in a professional way. If they need training, they should receive it (with proper metrics to evaluate effectiveness of training imparted). QMS must also ensure that employees understand their responsibilities and how their work relates to that of others.

Successful QMS gives great emphasis to early corrective action. It is much cheaper for the software developer to correct errors early in development life cycle (We discussed 'cost of quality'in Chapter 1).

It is also worth realizing that an error might cost the customer much more than it costs the developer. The aim must be to inculcate 'right first time' attitude throughout the organization. Quality Control activities such as *Inspection* and *Testing* are therefore to be built at every stage to detect errors as early as possible before moving on to the next stage of building the product. (Inspection and Testing is also separately discussed in chapters devoted to these topics).

It is always better to avoid making errors in the first place. Successful QMS include ways to analyze records and errors to determine their causes and make action plans to prevent errors by eliminating their causes (*Root Cause Analysis*). QMS must assure customers and developers that software products and services developed by adhering to the QMS will be of good quality.

QMS should be auditable. This means that the development process must be well documented and quality records including suitable measurements must be generated throughout the software development process. Quality Record is a record kept as part of QMS—It is a document, which furnishes objective evidence of activities performed or results achieved. For example; review record of a Project Plan, Code Review results, Test Execution Report etc. Quality records help demonstrate the achievement of quality and the effective operation of the quality management system. Many persons and organizations resist to QMS implementation because they feel it leads to paper factory. However, this is a misconception. The overheads of such record keeping need not be excessive (it depends how practically the QMS is designed) if the quality system is carefully designed. The improvement in quality more than compensates for the costs and efforts involved.

As per ISO 9001:2000, general requirements from Quality Management system are that the organization shall establish, document, implement and maintain a quality management system and continually improve its effectiveness. In particular, ISO requires that the organization shall

a) Identify the processes needed for the quality management system and their application throughout the organization
b) Determine the sequence and interaction of these processes
c) Determine criteria and methods needed to ensure that both the operation and control of these processes are effective,
d) Ensure the availability of resources and information necessary to support the operation and monitoring of these processes,
e) Monitor, measure and analyze these processes, and
f) Implement actions necessary to achieve planned results and continual improvement of these processes.

Processes needed for the QMS referred to above should include processes for management activities, provision of resources, product realization and measurement. Figure 3 depicts this concept.

Software development can be exceedingly complex and there are often many alternative ways to perform the various tasks involved in the software development lifecycle. A defined process can help guide the software professionals through these choices in an orderly way. Need for Process Standards and Definitions can be put forth as follows:

- Process standardization helps to reduce the problems of training, review, and tool support
- With standard processes/procedures and methods, each project's experiences can contribute to overall process improvement
- Process standards and definitions provide the basis for process and quality measurements
- Since process definition takes time and effort to produce, it is impractical to produce new ones for each software development project.

The conflicting needs for customization and standardization can often be resolved by establishing a process architecture, which consists of a standard set of process steps with rules for describing and relating them. Customization is then achieved through appropriate interconnections of these standard elements into tailored process models.

Thus, the philosophy underlining successful QMS is that the continuous improvement of every aspect of the software process. The quality records and measurements are analyzed and used for this purpose. (For example comparing defects per KLOC – Kilo Lines of Code of a project with that of the organizational standard and seeing if the performance lies within the upper and lower control limits defined). In the light of this analysis, senior management must regularly review (through periodically repeated audits and assessments) the effectiveness and efficiency of the quality management system, and ensure that action is taken to improve it.

In summary, a QMS is a set of procedures. Procedures are at the heart of the quality system. They are the documents, which tell staff how to follow a quality system, day to day, in their work. QMS is management's means to establish a uniform and consistent approach to product realization/providing services. The quality system is the complete work process, including policies, procedures, tools and resources, both human and technological as shown in Figure 2.

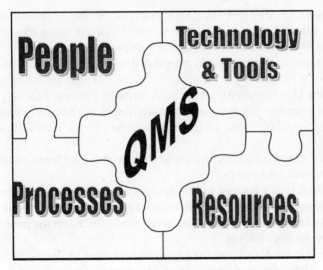

Figure 2: Components of a Quality Management System

2.1.2 *Quality Policy*

Quality Policy is a document that states the overall intentions and direction of an organization with regard to quality as formally expressed by top management. Clause 5.3 of ISO 9001:2000 says that

> *Top Management shall ensure that quality policy*
>
> a) *is appropriate to the purpose of the organization (i.e. Suitable for the business conducted by the organization)*
> b) *includes a commitment to comply with requirements and to continually improve the effectiveness of the quality management system,*
> c) *provides a framework for establishing and reviewing quality objectives,*
> d) *is communicated and understood within the organization, and*
> e) *is reviewed for continuing suitability*

The implied meaning of this requirement is that Quality policy must be documented. Quality policy does not have to include objectives but should create a framework for establishing them. Quality policy has to be assessed at its merit in relation to Management Commitment and Continual Improvement. Figure 3 illustrates a model for process based QMS.

Top management should begin the quality program by forming a quality policy. Quality Policy should be a clear statement of the organization's commitment to quality, and management's expectations of the quality program. The Quality Policy should be published, and communicated to the employees so that it understood and implemented at all levels in the organization.

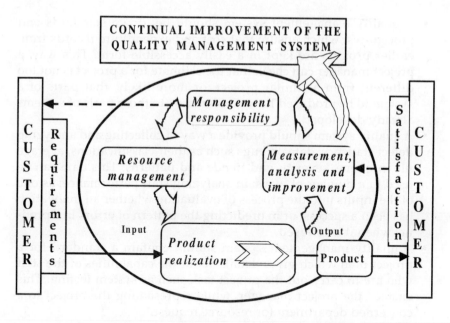

Figure 3: Model of a process-based quality management system

2.2 Quality Management System: Various Expectations

A quality management system is used by a number of users within and outside the organization: Senior Management, Project Mangers, Programmers, Application Systems Designers, Analysts, and Staffing department, Testers, Marketing Department. Each of them has certain expectations from the Quality Management System deployed in the organization.

2.2.1 The Project Manager

Project manager, in this, book, is referred to as the member of staff who has day-to-day control of a software project. He is the person armed with responsibilities of monitoring the project by checking its progress, innovating by introducing new methods of working; represent his or her team while dealing with the customer. Here are some of the ways in which, a Quality Management System is expected to support these functions of a Project Manager:

- A quality system should provide facilities whereby a project manager can consider the vast majority of possible risks, which could affect a project.
- A quality system should specify standards, which will enable staff to report on their activities in a uniform way (formats for monthly status reporting). Such reports should be able to be easily processed by a project manager.

- A quality management system should lay down standards and procedures, which ensure that cost and expenditure records from earlier projects are kept in a easily accessible form. This way, a project manager can check that the estimate for a project is not too different from a similar project, or more likely, that parts of a system to be produced have similar costs to those parts of systems already developed.
- A quality system should provide a way of collecting and analyzing defect statistics; data on bugs such as their classifications, average life in queue, severity, and trends and patterns. This data can be used in a number of ways: in analyzing staff performance; as one of the inputs into the process of evaluating whether an innovation has been a success; or in predicting the pattern of errors in a product when it is released.
- A quality management system should contain a standard for a project plan which gives details about the capabilities of the staff who are to carry out the project task such as system testing. This enables the project manager, while representing the project to a concerned department for resource request.

This is just a subset and not an exhaustive list of the facilities that should be provided by a quality management system.

2.2.2 The Programmer/Developer

Programmer or Developer is a member of staff who is given a specification for a chunk of software and who then has to produce program code, which is taken through unit testing. Most programmers also carry out modification to the code as requirements keep evolving. Some of help that a quality system should provide to the developer is:

- The quality system should set coding standards, which determine the way that a software program is to be constructed. Use of coding standards, guidelines make testing and debugging easier
- It should provide directions to the developer to store away test data and test outcomes in files. This way, re-programming becomes easier. The developer can retrieve test data, modify it in response to, say a requirements change, and then apply it again.
- It should provide a standard which insists that the names of the software chunks, which have been produced by a developer, have a correspondence to the files used to store the source code, object code, test data and test outcomes for the software. In other words, the QMS should guide the developers and the configuration manger towards organizing the entire software project repository. Typically, the items in a project repository are the following:

- Software Requirements Specification Document (SRS document)
- Design/Application Architecture Document
- Change Requests
- Coding Standards
- Quality Documents
- Test Procedures
- Test Cases and Test Scripts
- Test logs
- Source Files
- Binary Files
- Model files, Property Files

2.2.3 The Application System Designer

A systems designer is responsible for preparing a description of the software application/system that is to be produced. He/she is the design architect and in this role his/her job is to prepare the requirements specification or use the given requirements specification to produce the system design. He/she provides architecture which implements the functionality demanded by the customer. A number of the facilities that a good quality system should offer the system designer are shown below:

- It should provide a standard, which describes how the process architecture and data architecture are to be written. A good standard should enable the designer to check that the system, which has been, designed actually implements the functions described in the requirements specification.
- It should also specify standards, which lead to a system that should be easily maintainable. For example, a good standard for design is high cohesion and low coupling. (Cohesion means insisting that each module in a system carries out one function—an only one function.. Reducing the coupling between modules means, in effect, reducing the complexity of the connection(s) between the modules as much as possible.) For details of this fundamental design principle, reader is referred to Ref [1] Design based on high cohesion and low coupling principles tend to be easier to maintain than a system consisting of modules that carry out a large set of functions.
- It should provide standards, which lead to a good requirements specification. For a system designer, the word 'good' implies that the requirements specification should contain no ambiguities, contradictions or platitudes, and that constraints such as response time are directly cross-referenced to the functions to which they apply.

2.2.4 *The Analyst*

An analyst is a member of staff who maintains a liaison with a customer to produce requirements specification which is used by system designer to produce a blue print for carrying out the functionality intended by the customer. The analyst's need is centered around the requirements specification. Some examples of how a good quality system can help him toward this is shown below:

- It should provide a standard for the requirement specification, which, among other concerns, specifies an organization of the requirements specification in which related functions are contextually close to each other. For example, in a stock control system, the descriptions of the functions associated with querying database information about products, which are out of stock, should be physically close to each other. This makes it easier for the analyst to check for contradictions.
- It should provide a number of checklists, which enable the analyst to ensure that features or issues associated with a software system that is to be developed are not forgotten. Such checklists are usually general.
- It should provide a description of the processes involved when an analyst liaisons with a customer; for example, specifying the way in which functions in the requirements specification are checked against the customers requirements.

2.2.5 *Senior Management*

Senior management comprise of the members of the organization who work at the next level of the management structure above project managers. They are also called business mangers or program managers, and usually supervise a number of projects. Senior management members will require the quality system to provide a number of facilities; some of which are enumerated below:

- It should provide senior mangers with reports of achievements against targets for each of their projects; for example, what tasks should have been completed by a certain date and what tasks have, in fact, been completed, what expenditure should have been incurred by a certain date and what expenditure has actually been incurred i.e. Earned Value Analysis (See the Vignette below).

> *"Earned value" is a management technique that relates resource planning to schedules and to technical cost and schedule requirements. All work is planned, budgeted, and scheduled in time-phased "planned value" increments constituting a cost and schedule measurement baseline. There are two major objectives of an earned value system: to encourage contractors to use effective internal cost and schedule management control systems; and to permit the customer to be able to rely on timely data produced by those systems for determining product-oriented contract status.*

- It should provide direction on the setting up of audit trail documentation. Such a trail might consist of memoranda, which have been generated by checklists; for example, when analysts in a project have queried a particular set of requirements with the customer. Such audit trails are useful for members of senior management; for example, when resolving some dispute about requirements, which has escalated out of a project to his or her level of responsibility.
- It should provide facilities whereby reports on defects discovered during development are issued regularly. Such reports are not only of value to the individual project manager, but are also useful for senior management. For example, where are senior manager is actively involved in a management team which is attempting to carry out some *process improvement*, diagrams showing where defects were introduced during development, and where they were discovered, would be a major input into the tasks of determining processes that need improvement. (Frameworks for "Process Improvements" are covered in a separate chapter devoted to this topic)

2.2.6 *Staffing Department*

Staffing department is a central function responsible for providing human resources to the projects. Sometimes, this department may also be entrusted with the responsibility of training. There are a number of ways in which a quality system could serve the interests of this department; for example:

- The standards for a project plan should insist that the skill level of the staff on the project is properly specified. This obviously helps the staffing department to allocate the right people to the project, and to specify requisite training if staff with the specified skills are not available. The sub-clause 6.2.2 of clause 6 (Resource Management) from ISO 9001:2000 specifying this requirement is quoted below.

6.2.2 Competence, awareness and training

The organization shall:

a) *determine the necessary competence for personnel performing work affecting product quality,*
b) *provide training or take other actions to satisfy these needs,*
c) *evaluate the effectiveness of the actions taken,*
d) *ensure that its personnel are aware of the relevance and importance of their activities and how they contribute to the achievement of the quality objectives, and*
e) *maintain appropriate records of education, training, skills and experience*

- The quality management system should provide instructions on the activities carried out when the project has been completed. ne activity relevant to a staffing department, which also has a personnel function, if for the project manager to produce a written report on the effectiveness of the staff on the project. After all, as a result of working on the project, the members do value addition to their profile. It is important that their updated resumes get submitted to organization's human resource database so that it is useful to the next project to which they are to be allocated. Quality Management System should provide a standard format for this report as well as for the resume.

2.2.7 The Customer

The customer is also the user of the quality management system of the supplier organization. The customer's concerns are rather different from those of the developer; for example, he or she is concerned that adequate means are going to be used to develop the software and to check that it meets requirements; that adequate reporting facilities are provided which enable the progress of the project to be monitored, and that adequate liaison occurs during the period in which the developer is demonstrating that the system actually meets user requirements. (They say "QFD—*Quality Function Deployment* is a technique to incorporate "customer's voice" into the design. Ref [3] has a discussion on this.) Some examples of the type of facilities that a quality system should provide for the customer are:

- It should provide directives which specify how progress meetings are to be organized: who should be invited from the developer's staff, when the meetings should be scheduled, what physical arrangement, such as the booking of a room, should be made, and how issues arising from a progress meeting are to be resolved.

- It should provide guidelines about how facilities provided are to be extracted and used as quality controls for a project. This list of controls would be specified in the quality plan. This is often a contractual document (also called Document of Understanding), or is at least signed off by the customer. This document should be complete description of the way in which the developer intends to check that the system meets customer requirement, and the role of the customer in this process.
- It should specify the format of reports that are to be sent to the customer concerning progress and how to determine the frequency with which these reports are sent.

The sub-clause 7.2.1 of clause 7.2 (Customer Related Processes) from ISO 9001:2000 is quite related to these customer concerns. It is quoted below.

7.2.1 Determination of requirements related to the product

a) *The organization shall determine requirements specified by the customer, including the requirements for delivery and post-delivery activities,*

b) *Requirements not stated by the customer but necessary for specified or intended use, where known,*

c) *Statutory and regulatory requirements related to the product, and*

d) *Any additional requirements determined by the organization*

2.2.8 The Testers

System Testing and Acceptance Testing (These terms are discussed in the chapter devoted to Testing) are the two critical activities in a software project. Either the development staff or people from quality assurance department derive a series of test cases from the requirements specification. The intention is to check that the system, which has been developed, meets customer requirements. Such staff would expect a number of facilities from a quality system:

- It should ensure that the *requirements specifications* are constructed in such a way that system tests can be easily derived and related back to the functions they test. Quality Management System should also ensure that procedures and associated checklists are in place to enable test data and test outcomes to be stored in a project repository. This is called the "Re-Use Pack". The test files in the Re-Use Pack can easily retrieved when re-testing takes place.
- QMS should ensure that procedure exists to ensure that those responsible for test planning can check that adequate resources are available during the test phase; for example, that during the

development of a software system integration, software and hardware required for simulating the test environment are actually available.

2.2.9 The Marketing Department

The job of the marketing department is to sell the software systems and applications prepared by the organization. In an organization, which is in the business of developing one-off or tailor made systems for the customers, the effectiveness of the marketing department will determine the profit levels. A quality system is expected to offer facilities to staff involved in marketing. For example, as part of the project debriefing process, every project should produce a list of sub-systems and modules, which can be used in the next project. Based on this list, in the next bid, the marketing department, along with the project staff may be able to produce estimates to the client. Being backed by the strong learnings and re-usable components, in the next project, the organization is likely to be more productive and smarter in bidding and thus it can have edge over its competitors. A Quality System should encourage the projects to document their "lessons learnt" by providing a repository, mandating metrics on project productivity (Effort logs), schedule slippage data etc.

Thus, in this section, we have discussed examples of how various users in the organization expect the Quality Management System to help them. In summary, every one in the organization is the user of the QMS, and hence in a software company, every one is responsible for quality assurance.

2.3 Quality Assurance: Some Diagnostic Questions

Given such wide range of expectations from the Quality Management System, it must get evaluated for its effectiveness. One of things expected from a Quality System Auditor is to visit a client organization and evaluate its quality system for adequacy (this is known as "Adequacy Audit"). Before embarking upon the final audits by an third party auditing organization, it is important to know whether the company wishing to go for quality certification has an adequate quality system in place. There are few typical questions, which pinpoint problems in quality. Most of them are directed at the software developers of the client organization. There are two aims in discussing these questions here: one is to make you appreciate how to evaluate your quality system and, second to have an introduction to the rest of the topics discussed in this book. These diagnostics questions are:

- Functional traceability
- Project monitoring

- Design validation
- Quality planning
- Quality system review
- Unit test records
- Planning for systems testing and acceptance testing
- Risk analysis
- Configuration management practices
- Training
- Intergration testing
- Project costing procedures
- Cost checking and tracking
- Early requirements checks
- Test data storage
- New technology impact analysis
- Traceability into testing
- Decision making rationale
- Standards and procedures for auditing
- Functional specification structure
- Defect data analysis
- Design guidelines
- Acceptance test failures
- Project debriefings

Let us now discuss each one of above points briefly.

2.3.1 Functional Traceability

This is one of the first few questions that concern traceability. Ask a developer to show some of the listings of the program code of a completed project. Indicate a module and ask him or her to explain which requirements (as stated in the Requirements Specification Document) that module has implemented. If they can point out to the functions/ specifications, then it is a good sign that probably the organization has a good quality system. If this takes a long time to answer, you can suspect that probably there is something wrong with the organization's quality system or it may even be non-existent.

2.3.2 Project Monitoring

It is a good idea to ask this to a project manager—"how do you monitor the progress of your project?" (i.e. in terms of tasks completed, tasks that slipped and the amount of resources expended at a certain point in a project as compared with the amount of resources planned at the start of the project.) If the project manager can point out to procedures, which enabled him or her to get this information easily, then the part of the quality system dealing with planning and project monitoring is in place.

It means that the planning is carried out at a task level, and there are good facilities for staff to report on task completion. This is a topic on its own—Project Planning and out of the scope of this book. Ref [4] indicated at the end of the book is one concise and good reference to Project Management that reader may like to refer.

2.3.3 Design Validation

It is worth asking a developer what efforts he or she takes to validate a design; i.e. what quality controls exist to provide assurance that a design meets its corresponding requirements specification—both functional and non-functional. If the answer you receive is that a senior staff member signs of the design, then it is not adequate. If the developer states that method such as *technical reviews* and *prototyping* are used and that standards and procedures exist for these activities, then it is an indication of quality system existing in the organization. Reviews and Inspection are discussed under chapter 6 of this book.

2.3.4 Quality Planning

A very relevant question to be asked to the developer is about the quality plan of his project. If the developer simply states that each project uses the quality manual of the organization, then it is a poor answer. The correct answer is that the organization has a quality manual, but that the elements of the manual relevant to a project are extracted after quality factors have been identified and a risk analysis has been carried out.

2.3.5 Quality System Review

Another useful question to developer is: how does the organization evaluate the effectiveness of the quality system and also, how does it evaluate the potential changes that new software development technology and business policy might have on the quality system? A quality system is an evolving entity, and it is important that mechanisms are in place to evaluate what degree of evolution should be. An organization should receive information such as project debriefing reports, error statistics, and project audits, or periodical project reviews. These should be used as input into the process of evaluating the effectiveness of the quality system. (Quality Systems Improvement)

2.3.6 Unit Test Records

An important question concerning *Unit Testing* is what is the entry point to begin unit testing and what records exist to prove that a programmer has actually carried out a test? Many quality systems do not provide enough standards for this part of the software project. If it is not obvious that a programmer has carried out testing, but that all that might have happened is that a clean-compiled module has been passed off to staff who carry out the integration, then one can say that there is a weakness in the quality system; it allows developers to pass untested modules to staff who carry out *System Testing* and *Acceptance Testing* at a later stage in the project.

2.3.7 Planning For Systems Testing And Acceptance Testing

Another revealing question to ask about system and acceptance testing is: when does your quality manual insist that you start planning and thinking about system and acceptance tests? If the answer is that this occurs during later stages of the System Development Life Cycle (SDLC), say, during coding, then it is not a good situation. The correct answer is that as soon as the requirements specification has been validated as being correct, the system tests and acceptance tests should be developed in outline.

2.3.8 Risk Analysis

Another question concerned with project planning is: what standards and procedures does your quality manual contain to deal with the identification of risk? All projects are risky, with a degree of variation from one to another. A good quality management system should provide standards and procedures, which direct the processes of organizing and planning a project based on an appraisal of the possible risks in the project. A quality manual should provide procedures for analyzing the risks in a particular project and guidelines, which provide advice on how to minimize the effect of risk.

2.3.9 Configuration Management Practices

It is worth investigating how the process of change is managed. A typical question that can be asked in this regard is: what happens when an error is discovered during operation and it necessities changes to the requirements specification, system design and program code. This is a question about configuration management; the process of documenting, appraising and implementing changes to a system. In an organization with a reasonably good QMS, the developer is expected to point to standards and procedures which describe how errors are notified to the software developer; how any proposed changes arising from the error are communicated to staff in charge of configuration management; how a decision to carry out the change is made, how the change is applied and validated; and finally, how staff who should know about the change have details communicated to them.

2.3.10 Training

A good project ensures that its members are qualified and experienced enough to carry out project tasks assigned to them, or at a minimum, they have been trained adequately in that task. If an organization does not keep adequate records of training, then a project manager is unable to access important information needed for planning. The question to ask in this case is: do you keep training records? Can they be evidenced? It is worth looking at these records to see what training is considered worth by the organization: if project team members are just being sent for courses in programming languages alone, then this is not a very good sign. However, if the project team members are sent on a variety of software engineering related courses on topics such as requirements specification, system design, project management, quality assurance and testing, then that is a much better sign.

2.3.11 Integration Testing

Integration testing is a term used to describe the process of validating a system as it is being built up incrementally, with coded modules being added a few at a time. Developing a system this way enables errors to be discovered more efficiently than if the system was not integrated and just collected together prior to system testing. A good question to ask is: have you got standards and procedures to describe the process of integration testing, which, for example, provide advice on integration strategies and describe the documentation to be generated from integration testing?

2.3.12 Project Costing Procedures

A good question to ask is: are there standardized procedures, which every project has to use to use in establishing a cost estimate? It is important that projects use the same costing technique, as the results from previous costing can be used for future projects. This may not seem to have much to do with quality; however, projects which make erroneous costs usually start running out of budget during testing and often have to cut corners on the testing process, thus delivering a poor quality product.

2.3.13 Cost Tracking

It is important that there are standards and procedures, which enable a project manager to check the estimated cost of a project. Probing questions should be asked about the existence of such standards and procedures. For example, are there mechanisms whereby a project manager can prepare the cost of part of a finished system which is similar to part of a proposed system by looking at historical data on costing, or even the actual amount of resources spent on the finished system?

2.3.14 Early Checks On Requirements

Another good question to ask an organization is: what is the earliest point in a software project at which a system and its documentation are checked against the customer requirements? The answer to this should be that the requirements specification is checked just before it is frozen, and the developer has clarity on it adequate enough to proceed with coding. The validation technique could be such as a requirements review or prototyping. Everyone knows that the earlier the errors get detected in a life cycle of a project, the cheaper it is to fix them.

2.3.15 Test Data Storage

There is a question you can ask to find out discover how serious an organization is about systems maintenance: do your standards insist that, as far as possible, test data for module, integration, system testing and acceptance testing should be stored? This is what we had referred to as the *"re-use pack"*. It ensures that if re-testing occurs, then little extra effort is expended in the re-developing old test data.

2.3.16 New Technology Impact Analysis

New technology can give rise to new demands on a quality system. The purpose of Technology Change Management is to establish procedures to identify, evaluate, select pilot and deploy newer technologies, which will foster quality process improvement. It is good question to ask the developers as to how the growth of new technology is monitored in their organization and how is it ascertained if the new technology threatens to affect quality system. One of the factors to be considered for quality systems improvement is its response to a number of factors; change of technology being one of them. You can also ask the developers if there is process in place for managing the changes in technology. For example, does the organization have guidelines for designing human-computer interface?

2.3.17 Traceability Into Testing

As an auditor, you can ask a question, which pinpoints problems in testing: can you easily trace from a function, expressed in your requirements specification, to the individual tests, which check out that function? In short, do you have a "requirements traceability matrix"; i.e. a two-dimensional grid chart that lists out the REQUIREMENTS on one hand and the FUNCTIONALITIES as the other dimension. If the organization can readily retrieve these tests from past project documentation, then there is a good chance that the part of the quality system concerned with testing is in good shape.

2.3.18 Decision Making Rationale

An important thing in a software project is that when a major decision is made, it should be made with a full justification; i.e. the responsible person provides a rationale, or set of reasons, for making the decision in the way that it was made. You can take the developer into confidence to find out if standards for project organization, application system design and module testing include a directive, which specifies that the staff carrying out these activities provide this rationale. For example, a designer can be asked to explain why a particular design was adopted for a system. By getting these explanations from the development staff, a quality system encourages them to think more deeply about a task. This is very important from the CMM-I requirement angle where "Decision Analysis and Resolution" (DAR) is one of the process areas.

2.3.19 Auditing Standards And Procedures

A question which often enables a quality consultant to find out how seriously an organization takes quality is: do you have explicit standards, procedures and guidelines which govern the process of checking that projects follow standards and procedures? In some organizations (mostly large organizations with 500 plus employees in a single location), this is achieved through monthly reviews of the projects with a focus on finding out if each project in the location is following the processes defined in the organization's QMS. If such procedures exist, then they cover the process of auditing, when to audit, how frequently to audit, what reports are generated from the auditing process, and what actions to are taken when a project fails an audit. It may so happen that the Quality Manual omits any mention of auditing but this is not desirable.

2.3.20 Functional Specification Structure

It is worth exploring the standards that a developer uses for the requirements specification. A good question to ask is whether the functional part of the requirements specification is structured in such a way that all functions, which are connected with each other, are physically adjacent. A requirements specification organized in such a manner is much easier to access by both software development staff and the customer and, hence would be prone to fewer errors.

2.3.21 *Defect Data Analysis*

Validation of software systems gives rise to defect data, which describes the errors that have occurred, and their classification. A good question to ask is what happens to this data? Is it, for example, used to improve the technical process employed by the software developer and also the quality system?

Watts S. Humphrey, in his classic book "Managing the Software Process" provides the following classification:

Errors *are human mistakes, and their quantification often depends on an understanding of the programmer's intentions. In the case of typographical or syntactic errors, their causes are generally clear, but the nature and cause of design errors is much harder to establish precisely.*

Defects *are improper program conditions that are generally the result of an error. Not all errors produce program defects, as with incorrect comment or some documentation errors. Conversely, a defect could result from such nonprogrammer cause as improper program packaging or exception handling*

Bugs *A bug (or fault) is a program defect that is encountered in operation, either under test or in use. Bugs result from defects, but all defects do not cause bugs (some are latent and never found). With widely used software, the defects may be found many times, resulting in duplicate or multiple bugs per defect.*

Failures *A failure is a malfunction of a user's installation. It may result from a bug, incorrect installation, or a communication line hit, a hardware failure, and so forth.*

Problems *are user-encountered difficulties. They may result from failures, misuse or misunderstandings. Problems are human events as opposed to failures, which are system events.*

2.3.22 *Design Guidelines*

Design can have a major effect on the amount of project resources expended during maintenance and the number of residual errors that occur during this process. A good quality system should provide design guidelines or checklist for reviewing the design at the higher level. A quality system, for example, might state that design containing multi-functional modules is to be discouraged (Design Principle; High COHESION). An auditor or a quality consultant should ask for these guidelines (if they exist in the organization visited) and read them thoroughly.

2.3.23 *Acceptance Test Failures*

Ask the testers in the organization what happens when an acceptance test fails. An undesirable answer is: we rectify the error, repeat the test and carry on. A desirable answer is: we rectify the error, repeat the test and the re-execute those tests, which exercise modules that had to be changed for rectifying the error(s). There is a high probability that a change necessitated by the discovery of an error will have caused further errors, which can only be discovered by re-running previous tests. The procedure for acceptance testing should ensure that this is a part of every acceptance test.

2.3.24 *Project De-Briefings*

Project de-briefings are a useful source of information used for improving the quality system. You should closely question the organization about the existence of standards and procedures governing the conduct of a de-briefing meeting and the associated documentation that is produced.

2.4 The Need for the SQA Group in an Organization

In an organization the Quality Policy, Quality Manual and Quality Management System form the 3-tier layer as shown in Figure 1. It should be noted that the terms SQA, depending on the context, might mean either the Software Quality Assurance as a function or Software Quality Analyst as a person. This should be kept in mind while reading the next few sections.

2.4.1 *Why Does an Organization Need a Software Quality Assurance Function*

This question is asked very often! People find it difficult to be objective about auditors. After all, people feel that if they are doing their jobs carefully, why do they need any "third party" telling them if they are doing it in a right fashion. It is a natural human psychology to feel this way. The need for an "outside" or "third party" intervention, however, is a matter of perspective and a sign of organizational maturity. All of us would agree that while selecting a parachute or for that matter even a car, it is better to buy one that has been through a "proper" (i.e. strict) inspection. However, this is not how people and most organizations think when it comes to Software Quality, which is so vital for business survival as discussed in Chapter 1. The issues with software are not whether checks are needed (they are indeed needed) but who performs these checks and how (i.e. with proper procedures in place rather in a new ad-hoc fashion every time).

How large the SQA function is and how it is organized really depends on the size of the organization where it is employed. In very small organizations, it may not be practical/feasible to have a full time dedicated Software Quality Analysts. Also it may not be feasible to assign an SQA per project.

As the size of project staff grows, however, managers become involved with other duties like client liaison, taking care of statutory and regulatory requirements, reporting to senior management etc. They, then quickly lose touch with the day-to-day technical work. This is when they need to do one of the following:

- Find some way to handle their other workload so they can monitor more closely the people issues
- Hire someone to do the audit work
- Motivate the people to monitor each other

Of the alternatives indicated above, the third one is economically and technically most viable and so also from the morale point of view for the project team. Unfortunately, it does not work out practically; as the size of organization as well as the size of software projects within the organization grows beyond a few dozen people, these home grown "buddy systems" break down. This is when management needs to seriously think about deploying a Software Quality Assurance Function.

Software Quality Analyst role can be organized in one of the following ways; each project has a full time embedded SQA—i.e. a billable team member performing this role or have a member of the SEPG (*Software Process Engineering Group*) visit the project once in a while (frequency as pre-determined and documented) to check on adherence to processes or procedures defined in the Quality Management System. A typical thinking seen in Indian scenario is to assign the SQA role to developers who do not seem to be doing well in that job or assigning it to young and not-so-experienced members of the project team! This is only unfortunate for the software industry as a whole. It is time we realize that SQA (Software Quality Analyst) is a very responsible role with independent reporting to and close interaction with the senior management of the organization. As such this role should be respected.

2.4.2 The Role SQA Function: Roles and Duties

Although, we may often hear a cliché "Quality is Everyone's Responsibility!", in practice, the people responsible for the software projects' execution (the practitioners) are the only ones who can influence the quality culture in the organization along with the support from top management. The role of the SQA (Software Quality Assurance) function is to monitor the way the practitioners fulfill their responsibilities towards quality commitment of the organization. The SQA function is the "Eyes and Ears of Management". In this context, a few common pitfalls are often noticed:

- You cannot assume that the SQAs (the Software Quality Analysts) themselves can do anything about quality
- The mere existence of an SQA function alone does not ensure that the standards and procedures are followed
- SQA will be not be effective unless the top management shows its commitment through able leadership and periodically demonstrates its support for the SQA function by following its recommendations
- SQA program in an organization will not work effectively unless line management makes it clear that SQA try to resolve their issues with the project management before taking the route of escalation.

Thus, all that the SQA function can do is to alert management whenever deviations from established standards and procedures and practices occur. This is the primary responsibility of the Software Quality Assurance function. SQA can be effective when they report through an independent management chain. It is essential that the SQA function is staffed with qualified, competent and motivated individuals who are very committed to their job of quality assurance. It is difficult to get such people to work. For the SQA function to really perform like the "eyes and ears of management" performing objectively, the function (SQA) and quality professionals working in the team (the Software Quality Analysts) should be respected and be given the following responsibilities:

- Review all development and quality plans for completeness. It is possible to achieve this to some extent by deploying checklists designed with the help of the SEPG (Software Engineering Process Group) in an organization.
- Participate as inspection moderators (More on this will be discussed in the chapter on INSPECTIONS AND REVIEWS) while reviewing work-products of software projects (Design documents, code, user documentation etc.)
- Review of all Test Plans for adherence to standards. (An organization QMS could be mapped to international standards like *ISO* and *CMM* (*Capability Maturity Model*—this is discussed in greater details in a separate chapter devoted to process improvement frameworks)
- Review a significant sample of all test results to determine adherence to plans. (More on this in the chapter on *TESTING*)
- Periodically audit Software Configuration Plan (SCM) and configuration audit records to determine adherence to standards

(There is a separate chapter for detailed discussion on Software Configuration Management)
- Participate in all internal audits, co-ordinate external audits and register non-conformances (if any), participate in phase-end reviews of the projects, any other special project reviews as required.

For the SQA function to really fulfill this role in its fullest sense, it is the responsibility of the senior management to give adequate authority to this function. For example, declaring that a product cannot be shipped to customer unless and until the SQA has given a green signal by conducting the final release check (also known as Product Certification). Table 1 below provides an example of items that should be under SQA review.

Table 1: Items Under SQA Review

Item No	What the SQA does
1	Ensuring that a *requirements traceability matrix* or similar tool is used to show that the product specification cover the requirements
2	Verifying that an *implementation traceability matrix* or similar tool is used to show that the product specifications are implemented in the design.
3	Reviewing *project documentation* to verify that they are produced and maintained according to standards
4	Checking appropriate samples of *development records* (Project Plans, design review records, code review records, Test execution reports etc) to ensure that they are properly maintained and adequately represent the software design
5	Periodically verifying that *Software Configuration Management* (SCM) maintains proper baseline control as well as full records of change requests received for Requirements, Design, Code, Test and Documentation
6	Certifying that all the *sub-contractors' SQA functions* are adequately monitoring the performance of their organizations
7	Reviewing all *Plans* (Main as well as auxiliary) to ensure they include the required contents
8	Selectively *monitoring the performance* of the development, documentation, and test activities to ensure consistency with the approved plans and standards
9	Verifying that all specified *tests and peer reviews* are properly conducted, that the required results and data are recorded, and that suitable *follow-up actions* are performed and that *issues* are tracked to closure.
10	Auditing the *Change Control Board procedures* to verify that they are effectively implemented and planned
11	Selectively reviewing the resulting *design, code, and documentation* to ensure that they adhere to standards

2.4.3 The Goals of Software Quality Assurance Function

Goals of the SQA function can be broadly stated as:
- Improving software quality by appropriately monitoring both the software (Product Quality issues) and the processes used to produce it
- Ensuring full compliance with the established standards (based on frameworks and model like ISO, IEEE or CMM etc) and procedures for the software and software processes

- Ensuring that any inadequacies in the product, the processes, or the standards are brought to management's attention so that the in-adequacies are fixed on time.

Since the SQA function has such a entwined role with software development staff, at times it becomes tempting for the SQA staff members to get into "advisory" capacity and pass judgements that may not be called for. Although a technical/development background would be helpful, person playing the SQA role is not expected to play the "expert" role even when he or she may have had adequate development background. Nor should a person walk into an SQA function by looking upon it as place for his or her unfulfilled "development dreams" i.e. the mind-set:"now that I could not be a developer or be successful as developer, I'll show them how to do their job!" The skill of an SQA role lies in performing this entwined role in an objective and at times, in a remote fashion. A point to be noted and understood by both SQA and Management is that the SQA group or department is not responsible for "producing" quality products or for preparing projects' quality plans; this is the responsibility of the software project team members. SQA is a support function responsible for auditing the quality actions of the line organization and for altering management to any deviations and waivers. It is essential that a person performing SQA function keeps this focus all the time to be effective, SQA needs to work closely with development. They need to understand the project plans, verify the execution of these plans, and monitor the performance of the individual project tasks.

2.4.4 Functions of SQA

The basic organizational framework conducive to Software Quality Assurance Function is:

- **Quality Assurance Practices:** Adequate and state-of-the-art development tools, techniques, methods and standards should be defined and available for use. They should also be under periodic review.
- **Software Project Planning Evaluation:** Quality practices should be planned well in advance so that they can be implemented.
- **Requirements Evaluation:** You need high quality requirements to develop high quality products. Therefore, the key is reviewing the requirements right from the beginning to see if they conformance to the established quality standards. (Section 2.3.14 has already stressed the importance of this)
- **Evaluation of the design Process:** This was discussed in section 1.3.3. There should be appropriate mechanisms to ensure that the organisation follows the planned methodologies, that it implements the requirements, and that the quality of the design itself is adequately reviewed.

- **Evaluation of coding practices:** Appropriate coding standards/ practices and guidelines must be established and used
- **Evaluating the software integration and test process:** A few remarks about this were made in sections 2.3.15 and 2.3.17. Testing should be performed (where possible) by an independent group that is both motivated and capable of finding defects. Test planning should begin early and the quality of the testing itself should be reviewed.
- **In-process evaluation of the management and project control process:** Sections 2.3.2, 2.3.8, 2.3.12, 2.3.13 and 2.3.18 had touched upon this. By ensuring that the management processes are working, SQA helps to see to it that the entire organization is focused on producing quality results.
- **Tailoring of Quality Assurance Procedures:** Guidelines must exist to tailor the QMS processes if required. The SQA plan should be tailored to the unique needs of each project and at times even to the needs of their customers. For example, in a situation where, adherence to customer's QA procedures is a part of contractual requirement, SQA should help do the mapping between the supplier organization's QMS and customer's QMS to avoid the need of duplication that may arise out of following both the sets of processes.

2.4.5 Who Should SQA Function Report To

Now that we have discussed the importance of the SQA function, the next logical question to discuss who should this function report to. Many differing practices will be found in organizations; some wrong, some right. Let's discuss here how the SQA reporting should be.

SQA function can be under a lot of flak from time to time both from the management as well as from the project staff. SQA role is tricky and it is easy for an SQA function to become ineffective. It is not a popular function in an organization since the job involves constantly telling people what is wrong! Without some motivating force and self drive, SQA people can degenerate to counting defects and arguing over petty and not so important matters (i.e. spelling mistakes and font selection in a project plan, for example!)

The one simple rule on SQA reporting is that it should not be under the software development manager. Projects face tight schedules and line mangers are not likely to "listen" sympathetically to reports of inadequate test-plans, missing quality goals, defects found before release etc. Given this, SQA should report to a high-enough management level so that there is some chance of influencing project priorities and obtaining the resources and time to fix the key problems.

Reporting level is a matter of trade-off between, organization size, available choices etc. There are pros and cons with each option. With lower-level reporting, working relationships with development groups/

teams are generally better, while the ability to influence priorities is reduced. There is no silver bullet; a specific reporting level decision should be made in the context of suitability and specific needs of an organization. There are, a few thumb rules, however:

- SQA should not report to the project manager
- SQA should report to somewhere within the local software labs or plant organization
- Typically, there should be no more than one management position between SQA and the senior location manager
- SQA should always have a "dotted-line" relationship to a senior corporate quality executive
- Wherever possible, SQA should report to someone who has a vested interest in software quality

2.4.6 Launching the SQA Function in an Organization

Quality mission cannot be accomplished without the solid support from the top management. Therefore, the first essential step in establishing an SQA function is to secure top management agreement on its goals. Since it is the senior management who ultimately helps resolve all escalated issues, it is important that their agreement is taken in advance on the basis for doing so. If this is not done, then SQA function is unlikely to get the support from the senior management in situations of disputes. In view of this, following are some important points to keep in mind while announcing and launching the SQA Function in an organization:

- Initiate the SQA Program
- Identify SQA issues well in advance
- Write the SQA Plan
- Establish standards
- Establish the SQA function
- Conduct training to create awareness about the SQA function and promote the SQA function
- Implement the SQA Plan
- Evaluate the SQA Program

2.4.7 Commitment By Top Management

In the previous section, we already started this discussion; we'll complete it in this section. By now, it would be clear that the cause of quality cannot be simply delegated to a 'quality champion' or project leaders. While all mangers and staff must own and take responsibility for day-to-day quality issues with their control, the quality endeavour must be supported, endorsed and enforced from the top, as part of "quality culture". Without this, attempts to improve quality will fail, since staff will feel demoralized in absence of solid support form top management. A quality champion can be appointed by all means to do this Herculean task but the role of such a champion is only to help top management fulfil their responsibility to quality. Top management can best fulfil this responsibility by:

- Treating quality as a strategic business issue (remember the discussion in Chapter 1)
- Developing a policy for quality; a policy that can be implemented
- Taking customers in confidence to take their buy-in, educating the customer about the importance of quality
- Ensuring the quality policy is communicated to all the employees and is understood by them
- Ensuring that the Quality policy is implemented throughout the organization
- Regularly reviewing the quality policy and its implementation

2.4.8 People Issues in Software Quality Assurance

Quality is a matter of the mind-set and "attitudes". In all the immediately preceding sections we've drawn attention to the people aspect of SQA. In this section, we'll specifically focus on this topic considering its importance. Successful SQA function implementation requires empowering employees. Staff will not be able to produce quality software and give their support to SQA function unless they have the necessary skills, knowledge, experience, and competence. In the first place, Management must select the right staff for the SQA job and must provide staff with the resources and training they need to give their best. This will motivate staff, and generate a commitment to excellence and continuous improvement. Under these circumstances, authority and decision making can be delegated to the appropriate level, where they can be exercised most effectively to respond promptly to customers' need.

In section 2.4.3, we also discussed, the skillfulness needed in performing the SQA role. People-handling skills along with adequate technical background is a combination that makes an SQA successful. Unfortunately, it is a rare combination to come by! Getting good people into SQA is one of the most difficult challenges faced by organizations. The practice of starting new hires or relatively junior employees in the SQA function can work to be effective only with adequate handholding and senior members' involvement in mentoring. Considering the speed of software deliveries today and the ever-shortening life cycles of software projects today, this seems unlikely. An organization can induct younger members into SQA function for grooming them further, provided there are already some seniors to do this noble job. At times, job-rotation schemes (whereby project members work as SQAs for a few months) can also be effective, but unfortunately, projects will have a penchant to generally transfer their poorer performers to the SQA function. Also, the ability of the SQA function to attract practitioners on job rotation basis will really depend upon the importance of the SQA function "perceived" by the employees. For getting respect for the SQA function only senior management is responsible. One solution that may work is to require that all new development managers be promoted from SQA. This would mean that potential managers would spend about six months to a year in SQA before being promoted into management back in their home departments. While this may look like an extreme measure, it can be effective.

2.4.9 Total Quality Management

A final thought before concluding this chapter; the approach to management of quality described in this chapter is often known as Total Quality Management (see the vignette below). Readers can also refer to [5] quoted at the end of this chapter.

> *Total Quality Management is a structured system for satisfying internal and external customers and suppliers by integrating the business environment, continuous improvement, and breakthroughs with development, improvement, and maintenance cycles while changing organizational culture.*

It encourages management to give as much attention to the quality culture of the organization as to its customers. If the internal customers' requirements are agreed and met, a chain of quality is made that reaches out to the external customer. To get people to identify the internal customers for the main output of the work group is to make a start at a total quality process and to sustain the spirit of "continuous improvement". This is important to touch off a dialogue between the "internal supplier" and the "internal customer" that leads them to agree customer requirements in the beginning of creating a "total quality culture". You'll never achieve quality externally until you have quality internally!

REFERENCES

[1] *The Practical Guide to Structured Systems Design*—Meilir Page-Jones (Prentice-Hall International Edition)
[2] *ISO 9000: Preparing for Registration*—James L. Lamprecht (ASQC Quality Press)
[3] *Quality Function Deployment*—Nina Godbole (Article in the August 2001 issue of the Information Technology Magazine
[4] *Effective Project Management*—Robert Wysocki (John Wiley & Sons)
[5] Management in a Quality Environment—David N.Griffiths (TATA McGraw-Hill)

Chapter 3

PLANNING FOR SOFTWARE QUALITY ASSURANCE

3.1 Software Quality Assurance Plans

3.1.1 Purpose of SQA Plan

In section 2.4.6 of Chapter 2, we discussed about launching the SQA function in an organization. In section 2.2 of Chapter 2, we talked about what the various organizational players expect from the Quality Management System. Users' expectation from software is usually more than the expectation that it will work. Software must pass the Acceptance Test. When custom software is built for the specific requirements of a particular customer, a series of *'acceptance tests'* are conducted to enable the customer to *validate* all requirements.

Failed software entails loss of time and the lost competitive advantage. Therefore, while placing the contract on the supplier, user is entitled to ask for an assurance that the software, when finished, will perform according to its specification. The public at large may be affected by the user's use of the software. The user's public liability for damages, should the public be harmed in some way by the malfunctioning of the software, reinforces the user's requirement that the software should be of suitable quality. Thus Quality Assurance does have a dimension of social commitment, too.

Quality is achieved by building it into the software all throughout the project lifecycle; it cannot be added at the end of software development. This implies that the relationship between software quality and the software development process is known and that, by proper engineering of this process, a product of the appropriate quality can be produced. Defining the standard software process is discussed in a later section of this chapter. The quality of the software as it is developed must be continually evaluated to ensure that it is satisfactory. This evaluation must be planned and documented and made known to those who execute the software development project. The planning of how quality is to be built in and also how it is to be evaluated is recorded in the *quality assurance plan.* Quality Plan should be produced very early in the life of the software development project. It has a bearing on the *quality objectives* of the organization. It may not exist as a separate document; it could be incorporated into project's software development plan. The software quality plan should provide confidence to the user that the software product or service will be of high quality (as agreed between the Customer and the Supplier).

3.1.2 Content of the Software Quality Assurance Plan

Each development and maintenance project should have a Software Quality Assurance Plan that specifies its goals, the SQA tasks to be performed, the standards against which the development work is to be measured, and the procedures and organizational structure.

The IEEE Standard for Software Quality Assurance Plans states that the plan should contain the following sections:

- Purpose
- Reference documents
- Management
- Documentation
- Standards, practices and conventions
- Reviews and Audits
- Configuration Management
- Problem reporting and corrective action
- Tools, techniques and methodologies
- Code Control
- Media Control
- Supplier Control
- Records collection, maintenance and retention

At the end of this section, we've illustrated how a quality objective section of a project plan would be written by showing an excerpt from a real life project.

3.1.2.1 Purpose

This states the specific purpose and scope of the SQA plan. It names the software products that it covers and describes the use to which they will be put.

3.1.2.2 Referenced documents

A complete list of the documents referenced in the plan.

3.1.2.3 Management

IEEE standard lays down three aspects that should be covered in this section of the Quality Assurance Plan: *organization, tasks* and *responsibilities*

Organization

This section is about the project organization, roles of team members, their hierarchy etc. It is important that the head of Software Quality Assurance (SQA) function in the organization has adequate authority to be able to perform independent verification that the processes (as laid down in the Quality Management System of the organization) are adhered to.

Tasks

Assuming the prior existence of a comprehensive set of company standards, the chronological sequence of tasks, which need to be performed, includes:

- Preparing preliminary software requirements specification; perhaps as a part of the development of a system involving hardware and software
- Preparation of a software configuration plan, a software quality assurance plan and a software development plan which may or may not include the other two documents
- Software requirements review
- Software design review
- Preparation of software requirements specification
- Conducting review of software requirements specification document
- Preparing a software test plan
- Preparing a top-level software design (Also known as High Level Design)
- Preparing a draft support documentation, e.g. user manuals etc.
- Top level software design review
- Preparing software test description
- Production of a detailed software design
- Detailed software design review
- Production of software test procedures
- Production of source code and object code for the code units
- Testing of code units
- Integration of software modules/units
- Testing of integrated software units
- Systems integration and systems integration testing
- Acceptance Testing

Responsibilities

The project manager and design/development teams have primary responsibility for the quality controls applied during the development of the software project. The quality manager will:

- Define the responsibilities of quality personnel in the form of quality assurance procedures applicable to the project (Refer section 2.3 of Chapter 2 for a discussion on what the auditor would look for)
- Agree to the quality plan with the project manager
- Approve the plan of audits for the project which are to be carried out by quality personnel
- Resolve any disagreement between the project manager and quality personnel on matters relating to quality (for example non-conformances raised during internal audits and reviews, classifications of the non-conformances raised, dates for implementing corrective actions etc.)
- Review the activities performed by project personnel to ensure that the requirements of the quality plan and quality procedures are being satisfied
- Review the contents of software standards, engineering codes of practice and quality procedures for adequacy and efficiency

Quality personnel will:

- Carry out planned internal audits of the project to assess compliance with quality objectives
- Agree on corrective action with the project manager for any discrepancies, non-conformities found and ensure that corrective action is taken
- Evaluate defect trends and take appropriate action
- Refer any unresolved discrepancies to the quality manager for resolution

In the section of the Software Quality Assurance Plan, one would be looking for a real commitment to quality on part of the company. (Refer section 2.4.7 of Chapter 2). Quality personnel must be seen to have authority and power (In reality, some actual issues come up on this. They are discussed in section 3.3 of this chapter). It is desirable that the quality personnel should be independent from the developers of the software. (Refer section 2.4.5 of Chapter 2 for a brief discussion on this) They should have sufficient resources, authority and technical expertise to perform quality evaluation activities objectively (Refer section 2.4.3 of Chapter 2 for a discussion on this) and initiate corrective actions, if required.

3.1.2.4 Documentation

The basic purpose of this section of the Software Quality Assurance Plan is to describe the documentation to be produced and how it is to be reviewed. All the documentation relating to the development, verification, use and maintenance of the software will be listed. This section will normally include the following:

- Software Requirements Specification (SRS)
- Software Design Description
- Software Verification Plan: this describes the methods used to verify whether the requirements in the SRS are implemented in the design and in the code, and that the code, when executed, meets the requirements expressed in the SRS. These methods will include Inspection, Reviews and Testing etc. (Refer separate chapters on "Reviews and Inspection" and "Testing")
- Software verification report: this describes the results of executing the software verification plan and includes the results of all reviews, audits, tests etc.
- Reference to Software Standards (ISO, CMM, IEEE etc) and procedures mentioned and defined as in the Quality Manual and Quality Management System respectively of the organization). In section 2.2 of Chapter 2, we discussed what expectations the organizational players have from the Quality Management System.
- User guides, operators' and programmers' manual (This section is optional). In this section you may provide pointers to these manuals instead of directly including them here.
- Configuration Management Plan (for details, see the separate chapter on Software Configuration Management.) If your project is very large with complex configuration management activities, then you can have a separate document on Software Configuration Management; here you may only provide a reference to that.
- Software Quality Objectives: In this section, you define the various measures and metrics for the quality objective suitable for you plan along with the Upper and Lower Control limits for this.

3.1.2.5 Standards, Practices and Conventions

This section of the Software Quality Assurance plan should contain at a minimum, the following:

- Documentation standards
- Logic structure standards
- Coding standards
- Commentary standards

The developer will have designed and documented the process by which the software will be built. This expresses the methodology adopted. Work will be undertaken according to defined *standards* and in defined ways. (This is what the procedures in the QMS explain). These standards will be written down and used by the development team. Quality personnel shall check that the work has been done in accordance with these standards. The standards encompassed in these documents will cover things as diverse as the contents and format of each of the documents produced during the development. (These could be as per the Templates provided in the QMS.) The standard could also mention the textual layout of the code, the reviews to be undertaken (QMS may define what kind of reviews are mandatory depending on the nature of the project i.e. full development project, or an enhancement project or a purely maintenance work project etc.), the composition of the review board, the design methodology to be used to produce the software design, configuration management and testing.

Thus, this section of the SQA plan will identify the standards, practices and conventions to be applied and state how it is proposed to ensure that the work is undertaken in accordance with these standards. The plan states that, at a minimum, there will be standards for documentation, algorithm description, coding and ways of adding comment lines in a software program.

3.1.2.6 Reviews and Audits

This section of the Software Quality Assurance plan will state which technical and managerial reviews will be undertaken and how they will be carried out. Project can separately keep a schedule of provisional dates for conducting these reviews. The ANSI standard (American National Standards Institute) suggests that the following would be a minimum set of reviews:

Software Requirements Specification Review

This review is held to approve the document defining the software requirements specification and it aims to check the adequacy of the requirements. At this review the project manager will be expected to state which evaluation activities have taken place during the preparation of the document. These evaluation activities will ensure that the preparation of the requirements specification was undertaken in accordance with the developers' codes of practice using the approved tools and techniques. The document will have been checked to ensure that it conforms to the appropriate organization standard. The technical adequacy of the specification should have been evaluated to ensure that it forms the basis from which software of the desired quality can be developed. The requirements specification document will have been checked for internal consistency, understandability and completeness.

(one good reference for standard practices in drawing requirements specification is the *IEEE Guide to Software Requirements Speciation – ANSI/ IEEE Std 830*)

It is being realized how important it is to ensure that the required quality aspects of the product are explicitly stated in the specification. It is not reasonable to hope that software of the required quality can be produced without proper analysis of the required quality and its formal explicit statement. The adequacy of the quality aspects can be evaluated once they have been stated. Proper recognition of the desired quality aspects at the earliest possible stages is in everyone's interest. To aid traceability, it is helpful if each requirement has a unique identifier. (Refer to discussion under section 1.5 of Chapter 1)

Preliminary Design Review

The purpose of this review is to approve formally, the software top-level design document. As part of this process a summary of the quality evaluation, activities undertaken during the top-level design will be reviewed. These will be included ensuring that:

- The design was produced in accordance with the development standards chosen to implement the selected methodology
- All the necessary tasks were undertaken (Joint Application Review, Proof of Concept etc)
- The top-level design is an adequate basis for future work
- The top-level design, when implemented, will satisfy any **sizing** and timing constraints
- The software top-level design document was produced in accordance with the organization's standard and is internally consistent, understandable, complete and appropriately detailed

The design document will be checked to ensure that each of the requirements in the requirements specification can be traced to a part of the design. Forward and backward traceability is extremely important. (In fact this concept of *Bi-directional Traceability* is emphasized by the CMM-Integrated) It should be possible to trace each requirement forward from the requirements specification and see how it is implemented at each stage of the development process. Similarly, it should be possible to take any part of the software product at any stage in the production process and trace the reason for its existence back to the implementation of a particular requirement.(Refer section 2.3.1 of Chapter2)

Critical Design Review

The purpose of this review is to approve the software detailed design document as a basis for further development work. As part of the process, a summary of the software evaluation activities undertaken during the detailed design phase will be reviewed. These will be included ensuring that:

- The design was undertaken in accordance with the organization's standards and is technically feasible
- All the necessary tasks have been undertaken (Application architecture, entity relationship diagrams, entity life history diagrams, state transition diagrams, principles of Coupling and Cohesion etc)
- The detailed design was internally consistent, understandable, complete and appropriately detailed
- Traceability is maintained through the top-level design to the software requirements specification
- Test cases for unit test and integration test have been prepared as part of the design and have been checked for consistency with the organization's standards

Software Verification Review

The purpose of this review if to approve the test plan. It is an evaluation of the adequacy and completeness of the methods described.

Functional Audit

This is held to verify that all the requirements in the software requirements specification have been met.

Physical Audit

This is held to verify that the software and its documentation are internally consistent prior to delivery to the user.

In-Process Audits

In-process audits of a sample design are held to verify the consistency of the design. Points, which will be checked, are consistency of code and documentation, consistency of design and functional requirements and consistency of functional requirements and test descriptions.

Management Reviews

It is important that the execution of the quality plan is evaluated and there will be one or more reviews of this. For example, if it is found that there is a slippage (i.e crossing of either the Upper Control Limit or the Lower Control Limit) of the agreed and documented goals of the project, then **causal analysis** must be done (Refer Figure 3.2 for an example) to find out the reasons for slippage, decide on an action plan to prevent this in future, inform the management and track the action plan (produced by the project team) to closure.

3.1.2.7 Configuration Management

We'll undertake detailed discussion about this in a separate chapter dedicated to this topic. This section of the Software Quality Assurance plan will cover **configuration identification, configuration control, configuration status accounting,** and **configuration auditing.** As said earlier, this section of the SQA plan may refer to a separately written configuration management plan in case of large complex software projects. Various forms, formats and templates in relation to configuration management will be discussed in the chapter on this topic.

3.1.2.8 Problem Reporting and Corrective Action

This section of the Software Quality Assurance plan will describe the system, which ensures that software problems are documented and resolved. It should be a closed-loop system. All the problems should be promptly reported/escalated at appropriate level, acted upon and resolved. Each problem should be capable of being tracked throughout life cycle of the software project. Each problem should be analyzed to determine its significance and causes and classified by category (such as requirements, design, coding etc.) and each problem must have severity level and a priority number (to enable action on it). Trends in the problems reported should be identified.

For each problem or adverse trend discovered, some corrective action and a target completion date should be identified. The appropriate level of management should be made aware of the problems and adverse trends. Corrective action will be authorized and the activities undertaken will be documented. The corrective action taken will be evaluated to ensure that it solved the problem without introducing any new problems. Management should monitor the status of all unresolved problems and be aware of any that have not been resolved by their target completion date.

3.1.2.9 Tools, Techniques and Methodologies

This section of the SQA plan should identify the special software tools, techniques and methodologies employed that support quality assurance, state their purposes and describe their uses.

3.1.2.10 Code Control

In a software project, this is likely to be implemented in conjunction with the *library function*. The library receives and maintains copies of all software tools and documentation. The library will issue all material and ensure that the most recently Authorized Version is the one routinely available. Access to code files is controlled to ensure that no unauthorized use or modification takes place. The library will ensure that the correct version of software is submitted for testing. A large project will require a full time library function to take care of distribution of the *configuration items* (more about this in the chapter on Software Configuration Management).

3.1.2.11 Media Control and Back Up

This section of the Software Quality Assurance Plan will describe how the media are to be protected from unauthorized access or damage. One would expect to see details of storage arrangements that protect the media from harmful environmental conditions. At least one back-up copy of the current configuration should be held safely in a remote off-site location. Actually, *Disaster Recovery Plan* is a much larger aspect of Media Control and back up. It is a very large topic on its own. Security threats to a software project come from the following environmental factors:

- Fire Damage
- Water Damage
- Energy Variations
- Structural Damage
- Pollution
- Unauthorized Intrusion
- Viruses and Worms
- Misuse of Software, Data and Services

The purpose of a disaster recovery plan is to enable the project or information systems function to restore operations in the event of some type of disasters (natural like storms, floods etc. or man-made). In some organizations, periodic surveys are conducted to assess the adequacy of their disaster recovery plan. A common recurring finding is that the quality of the disaster recovery plans— if at all an organization has one, often, it is low quality. In organizations that have extensive decentralization and distributed computing resources, disaster recovery planning will be an onerous activity. The minimum that an SQA plan expects is media control and a suitable scheme for back up as discussed above.

3.1.2.12 Supplier Control

This has relevance while outsourcing some components of a software project. It is important that externally developed software is of the appropriate quality. From the CMM-I angle, its importance comes from the fact that "Supplier Agreement Management" (SAM) is an all new process area under CMM-I.

> **Clause 7.4 of ISO 9001:2000** states that: (as part of the caluses)
>
> *The organization shall evaluate and select suppliers based on their ability to supply products and services in accordance with the organization's requirements. Criteria for selection, evaluation and re-evaluation shall be established. Records of the results of the evaluation of supplier and any necessary actions arising from the evaluation shall be maintained.*

This section of the SQA plan would state how it was supposed to ensure that this was the case. It would normally contain a form of words to the effect that sub-contractors will implement a quality assurance program to the satisfaction of the main contractor who would have the right to evaluate the system. Software received from the subcontractor will of course be tested and evaluated before it is accepted.

It must be acknowledged that there are some cases in which little can be done to influence the quality of bought-in software (re-usable objects, DLLs, Object brokers and similar other components). The classic case concerns operating systems. Anecdotal evidence suggests that in some cases the suppliers have been unwilling to provide any of the assurances concerning quality, support etc. that purchasers have required. Software is supplied on a "take it or leave it" basis, knowing that given the oligopolistic state of the market, the potential purchaser cannot leave it. This situation where the supplier is in the dominant economic position is very difficult to handle and problems that it creates appear incapable of easy resolution.

3.1.2.13 Records Collection, maintenance and Retention

Any successful project will undergo substantial maintenance over a long period. As such, it is important to ensure that all the documentation necessary to undertake this quickly, efficiently and cheaply is going to be available when required. This documentation must be produced during development. It will be retained. This section of the Software Quality Assurance Plan will identify who is responsible for ensuring that the appropriate documentation produced and stored, and under what conditions. Important clauses from ISO 9001:2000 pertaining to this are quoted below. This is followed by an illustration of quality assurance plan for a hypothetical project.

ISO 9001:2000 Clause 4.2.3 Control of Documents

A documented procedure shall be established to define the controls needed

a) *to approve documents for adequacy prior to issue,*
b) *to review and update as necessary and re-approve documents,*
c) *to ensure that changes and the current revision status of documents are identified*
d) *to ensure that relevant versions of applicable documents are available at points of use,*
e) *to ensure that documents remain legible and readily identifiable,*
f) *to ensure that documents of external origin are identified and their distribution controlled, and*
g) *to prevent the unintended use of obsolete documents, and to apply suitable identification to them if they are retained for any purpose*

ISO 9001:2000 Clause 4.2.4 Control of Records

Records shall be established and maintained to provide evidence of conformity to requirements and of the effective operation of the quality management system. Records shall be legible, readily identifiable and retrievable. A documented procedure shall be established to define the controls need for the identification, storage, protection, retrieval, retention time and disposition of records.

Illustration: Quality Assurance Plan of XYZ Project

Quality Objectives
XYZ Project will comply with the agreed quality objectives as given by the QMS. The quality objectives for the project is as follows:

Reviews
Project progress will be reviewed in every week and monthly status report as mentioned in the "Status Reporting section of this document.

Peer Review will be planned & scheduled for each internal or external deliverable as defined in the project plan or in Statement Of Work. Review records will also be maintained as per the approved template.

Test Plan
Test plan for the project is in the document called "Test Plan for XYZ Project". Please refer to the document ID D1003. Since deliverables of each service are documented in Statement Of Work, test plan will be reviewed and updated as and when any new Statement Of Work is being executed or any new service is being started.

Standards & Guidelines
Coding & other project's Standard/Guidelines are documented and kept in the specific area in the controlled space as mentioned in Configuration Management plan. Standard & Guidelines will have to be approved by the Project Manager.

Process Adherence
Project will be executed to comply with the process as defined in this project plan, Contract, Statement Of Work or Standard & Guidelines as mentioned above. It is possible that certain processes (as defined in Quality Management System) are tailored as per the requirement of XYZ project. Adherence to the defined processes should be reviewed in various project reviews and audits.

Document Control
Documents are being categorized in two categories Master Documents & Other Documents. List of all the Master Documents will be kept along with the Master Documents in the specific controlled area as mentioned in Configuration Management Plan. Each Master Document will be issued a running Document ID. Master Documents will be modified as per the process mentioned later in this document while other Documents will be modified as other Configuration Items of this project.

3.2 Software Quality Assurance: Organizational Level Initiatives

3.2.1 Managing the Software Process

3.2.1.1 Process Management

The organization's software process assets include the Standard Processes, Software Life cycles, Methodologies and Tools, Standards, Tailoring guidelines for project's software process and a library of Best Practices and Project Components. These are created, updated, maintained and made available to projects for use in developing, implementing, and maintaining the projects' defined software processes.

Software development can be extremely complex, with a choice for selecting an alternative from among those available for performing the same task. Organizations aim at reaching a process-oriented way of working rather than being "person dependent". A "defined software process" provides a framework within which the development staff can make choices in an orderly way rather than in an ad-hoc fashion. Such a framework improves communication between staff, allow them to be moved quickly and easily between projects, and makes planning for quality more reliable. At the same time, it needs to be appreciated that software engineering is not an activity that can be rigidly regimented and structured like a repetitive manufacturing process (although occasionally one hear a term like "software factory" Ref [3]. Therefore, there is a need to trade off the individual project's need for flexibility against the benefits of defined standards and procedures to the organization. In that sense, this organizational level activity is like a closed feedback loop. Its aim is to:

- Define a standard software process: You need a method to define the procedures, to develop and maintain process documentation and a usable set of software process assets.
- Ensure that each project uses an appropriate version of the standard process that has been tailored to its individual needs. For this *"tailoring guidelines"* need to be developed
- Use the results from projects to improve the standard process. For this a *metrics program* needs to be established. (A separate chapter is devoted to discussion on software measurements and metrics).

This is shown in the Figure 3.1. Functions must be established to manage the defined process, and in particular, to carry out process measurement, process improvement, process improvement and technology innovation activities. In large organizations, one or more dedicated teams may discharge these functions. In smaller organizations, a director may be nominated to take care of this; as and when required, teams may be formed to assist the director in this function.

3.2.1.2 Standard Process Definition

Organizations need to establish, document and maintain a standard software process. This standard process may be tailored to suit the need of individual projects as discussed above. It is important for staff and managers involved in the implementation process to participate in the definition of it and to be kept informed about it. Defining a standard software process is a significant task. So it is important to carry out the definition activities in accordance with a documented plan. This plan must set out the activities and schedule for defining the process, specify group and individual responsibilities for the activities, and identify the required resources. It is important for management to review and approve the plan before it is implemented.

The Process for Process Definition should typically address:

- Activities in Process Definition
  - Develop and maintain Organization's software process
  - Identify organization's software process
  - Define /Change Organization's software process
  - Document The Process

- Review and Approve the Process
- Release, Distribution and Retirement of QMS Document
- Identification and documentation of Software Life cycles, methods and tools
- Develop and Maintain Tailoring guidelines for projects
- Guidelines for Writing a Process Document
- Guidelines for creating a Release Notice for announcing the new/ modified processes
- Guidelines for reviewing new Process documents
- Guidelines on Process Release

It is important for the standard process to reflect any constraints on working practice that may be imposed by customers, and for it to incorporate up-to-date software engineering methods, and tools. It is also important to ensure that it makes provision for the collection of **project measures** (see section 3.2.1.3). The standard process describes and orders the software tasks that are common to all projects. It also contains guidelines for tailoring the standard process to the needs of different projects, so that each project has its own approved life cycle that defines:

- Required procedures, practices, methods and technologies
- Applicable process and product standards
- Responsibilities, authorities and staff interrelationships
- Required tools and resources
- Process dependencies and interfaces
- Process outputs and completion criteria
- Product and process measurements to be collected.

It is important to set and track quantitative, measurable goals for process improvement, and to direct these goals at increasing the quality of products and services as well as productivity. A process improvement program should be established that empowers staff and managers to improve their own working processes and participate in improvements made by others.

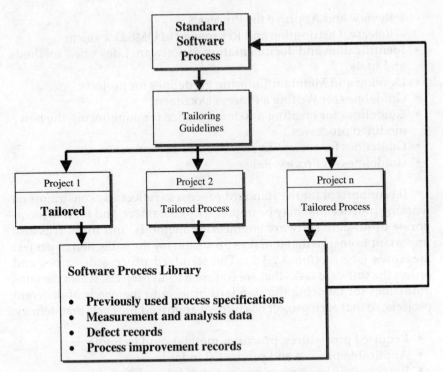

Figure 1: Process Management Activities

3.2.1.3 *Software Process Measurements*

In the chapter on Software Metrics, there will be a detailed discussion on this topic. Here, only an overview will be provided in the context of software process definition. It is said that you cannot "improve" something that you cannot "measure". Therefore, it is essential to take measurements of the performance of the standard software process, as applied to individual projects. Further, these measurements must be analyzed. (a detailed discussed on 'measurement' and related terms is undertaken in the chapter devoted to this subject.) This analysis should be used to adjust or tune the standard process, with a view to improving it and stabilizing its performance within acceptable limits.

It is important to drive process measurement and analysis activities from a documented and approved plan. The aim of the metrics program is to determine the various parameters to be monitored and measured, define a mechanism for assimilation of data from the implementation team for analysis at Project level as well as at Organization level. A process established for Measurements allows defining a mechanism for collecting various metrics from the projects. The objective is to define measures, to collect and analyze the various measures, to consolidate organizational metrics, monitor and verify process effectiveness, isolate problem areas and take appropriate actions to ensure that occurrence of such defects is not repeated (*Defect Prevention*) and occurrence of similar defects are minimized. The measurement plan (which is a part of the overall metrics program in the organization) should also describe and schedule the activities to be performed, identify groups and individuals responsible for the activities, specify the required resources, staffing and tools and identify the procedures to be followed.

In developing a metrics program, the following issues need to be resolved:

- "What" should be measured?
- "Why" it should be measured?
- "How" it should be measured?
- "Who" should measure it?
- "When" and "Where" in the process it should be measured

Most important thing is to have a linkage of these measurements to organization's ability to meet the requirements of its customers. If projects are not convinced about this, they are unlikely to provide their support to the organization's metrics program. The selected metrics should therefore:

- be linked to real customer requirements
- support the overall goals and objectives of the measurement program
- support predefined analysis activities
- be consistent across all projects
- cover the entire life cycle, including support and maintenance

Examples of specific measurements that can be used are:

- estimated versus actual SIZE, COST and SCHEDULE data
- quality measurements as defined in the quality plan (PRODUCTIVITY, EFFORT, DEFECT REMOVAL EFFICIENCY, PROCESS COMPLIANCE etc)
- Number and severity of defects in requirements, design and code
- Number and cost of changes to approved requirements and design specifications
- Number and turnaround time of customer requests and bug reports (customer reported bugs)

3.2.1.4 Defect Prevention

Defect prevention is concerned with ensuring that sources of defects that are inherent in the software process, or of defects that occur repeatedly, are identified and eliminated. Defect prevention activities should be defined and implemented at both organizational and project level. They should be well coordinated.

The objective of Defect prevention at Organizational level is to identify & prioritize defects, which have organization wide impact and prevent them from recurring in future. The defects are identified from following inputs:

- Project wind up reports
- Organizational metrics analysis
- Audit & Assessment reports
- Other organizational level meetings

Defects with organizational wide impact should be identified & prioritized for defect prevention. Root cause analysis should be carried out & recommended preventive actions should be arrived at. Measurements should be made to check the status of defect prevention activities & the status should be presented to senior management for review.

At the project level, it is essential to include defect prevention activities in the project development plan and schedule. One useful technique is to hold meetings during the development to identify defects and analyze their root causes. The defects can then be categorized by cause, such as inadequate training, breakdown of communications, oversight of important details, or manual errors. **Figure 3.2** shows an example of a root-cause analysis (also known as the fish bone diagram). The activity of finding out the causes for defects and classification of defects is known as *causal analysis*. (Causal Analysis & Resolution happens to be an important process area at level 5 of CMM-I).

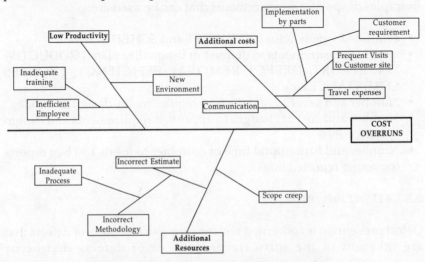

Figure 2: Root Cause Analysis (An Example)

When defects have been identified and classified, measures to prevent their recurrence can be developed and documented. Records of causal analysis meetings should be kept for use by the organization and by the future projects. A format for maintaining a record of Root Cause Analysis is suggested below.

Project Name :					Team Members Present :				
Project Code :					Meeting Date :				
Time Spent (Person Hrs)									

Trigger Where did the trigger occur?	Causes	Corrective Actions Identified	Preventive Action Identified	Impact of Not Preventing	Action Owner	Date for completing Action	Status (OPEN/ CLOSE)	Remarks

Note:

Stage where Trigger occurred:
 Planning
 Requirements
 Design
 Coding
 Testing
 Acceptance

Root Causes:
 P – Process/Methods
 C – Communication
 S – Skill/Training
 T – Tools
 L – Planning
 R – Resources

Impact of not Prev rocess changed.
Effort (Additional / Rework) or
Schedule delay / Post Delivery Defects

Recommendations:
 SP – Successful & PCR can be raised
 SN – Successful
 SF – Successful but needs further study
 PC – Project closed before implementation
 R   – Not Successful
 SLO– Successful and Learning Submitted to LDB/PAL,
 SLP – Successful and Learning logged in Project Learnings Document
 SPP – Successful and Project Process changed.

At the organizational level, it is essential to identify and document trends that indicate broad problems across several projects, and to take corrective action to eliminate them. It can be useful to record information on proposed defect prevention actions such as the following: (This is shown in the template shown above)

- description of the defect
- description of the cause
- category of the cause
- stage where the defect was identified
- description of the proposed action
- Whether the proposed action is feasible or not
- person responsible for implementing the action
- date by which the action is to be completed
- description of the areas affected by the corrective action
- individuals who are to be kept informed of the action's status
- date of the next status review
- rationale for key decision

3.2.1.5 Technology Innovation

In section 2.3.16 of Chapter 2 we had discussed about the importance of new technology impact analysis. Here, we discuss Technology Innovation at organizational level. Technology changes encompass a very broad spectrum of changes in the technological arena, in the context of the Quality Management System; it will focus on technology changes or introduction of new technologies that are likely to improve the capability of it. These changes:

- Enable the organization to achieve exacting quality standards resulting in decreases in defects
- Empower it to reduce process cycle times and increase process effectiveness, both of which would in turn improve productivity and quality
- Improve the capability of the organization's standard software processes

Technology change management should be integrated with process change management (the next section), and is compatible with the organizational business directives. Thus, it is essential to monitor and evaluate new technologies from time to time especially in the current era of rapid technology change and obsolescence. Appropriate technologies should be implemented in the organizations. It is therefore important for the organization to develop and maintain a plan for technology innovation. Technology (change) management plan of an organization should define the organization's long term technical strategy for automating and improving software process activities, and describe its plans for introducing new technologies.

It is essential that a regular feedback be given to staff and senior management on the status of new technologies and the results that have been achieved by their use, and that they are kept aware of relevant areas where new tools and technologies have been used successfully. In large organizations, a separate function/group is established entrusted with the responsibility of technology innovation, coordinating technology innovation activities, providing assistance to projects for piloting new technology etc. A suggested format for recording summary of Technology Pilot is indicated below. As indicated there, it helps to arrive at early estimate of training efforts that may be involved in imbibing the new technology. Various parameters that can be considered in evaluating the new technology are EASE OF AVAILABILITY, EFFORT REQUIRED TO IMPLEMENT TECHNOLOGY, ADDITIONAL EFFORT/ RESOURCES REQUIRED TO USE TECHNOLOGY, VENDOR SUPPORT, and TRAINING REQUIREMENTS.

Technology Pilot Results Summary

Technology piloted

Project Name

Expected Benefits

Cost

Platform on which evaluated

Evaluation period

Modules evaluated

Number of people involved in
  evaluation

Technology installation effort
  (person hours)

Training duration (hours/days)

Learning curve (days/months)

Average effort required to use
  technology during steady state

Benefits (preferably quantitative
  in terms of schedule, effort, etc.)

Issues/Problems Faced

Lessons Learned

Risks/Uncertainties in results

Recommendations for wider
  usage in the organization

Additional Comments

3.2.1.6 Process Change Management

Here, we discuss 'Process Change Management' at organizational level. Software CMM (*Capability Maturity Model* has this as *a key process area* at Level 5 of maturity) Organization's standard software process must be maintained under configuration management. For this, it is essential to document and review changes derived from various agencies from time to time. Sources of inputs for process change are:

- Findings and recommendations from Audits and Assessments
- Lessons learnt from monitoring process activities
- Change proposals from project staff and managers
- Analyzed and interpreted processes and product measurement data

A system must be established for employees to communicate the Process Change Request to the Process Engineering Group. The group will then evaluate the change request and accordingly reject or accept the request. The accepted change request will be closed when the changes asked for are incorporated in the process by modifying it and the new process is released. The format for Process Change request should include the following:

- Requester's Name
- Requester's contact no
- Ref to process in the Quality Management System for which change is requested
- Description of change requested
- Justification for the change suggested

For any meaningful process management activity, it is essential that all the accepted process change requests be analyzed to look for various trends. Trends could be - distribution of Process changes requests received from various projects business area wise, names of employees contributing highest change requests, nature of change requests (if there are too many change requests only asking for cosmetic changes like slight improvement to language, syntax etc, then perhaps not much thinking is 4happening). Too many Process Change Requests received could mean that the QMS processes are not stable or that they are defective.

3.3 Quality Planning—Some Interesting Dilemmas and Observations

It is well known that "quality" owes its origin to the manufacturing industry. Fine concepts like "Quality Circles"—Ref [4] etc. have their roots in the manufacturing industry. The notion of "root cause analysis" finds its origins in the industrial engineering discipline.

Software industry is relatively young in implementing these practices in the pursuit of bringing the fine practices of classical engineering into the business of "software engineering". Quality is a buzz word today; to many its like a nice healthy child; nice to admire from a distance but difficult to take the pains of bringing it up with a myriad of thankless tasks.

Through the discussion so far, is should be clear that the Software Quality Assurance Plan is a vehicle to put the quality policy in practice. It is a mechanism whereby the procedures/processes defined in the Quality Management System get implemented. We also know that senior management commitment to quality gets expressed through the Quality Plan. In reality, however, there are many interesting practices noticed. . At the time of proposal writing, practitioners will come running to the quality manager and ask - "can you tell me where can I find a "nice" write-up available in our organization? We'd like to include it in our proposal to the client." At this time, probably, the business manager/practitioner knows it fully well that there is no go without including this write-up, that the proposal cannot really be completed without this "nice" write-up on organization's "commitment" to quality. It'd woe the customer; it would help him fetch the contract, the much-needed feather in his/her cap.

In chapter two, we discussed the various expectations that organization players would have from the Quality Management System. When the project gets initiated as per organization's process, the quality goals get documented; it's the same manager who starts finding the QMS a "big nuisance". Attempts after the attempts are made to undo the "leash of QMS processes". The tirade begins between the project SQA and the Project Manager (who believes that, his/her job is to push the product out of door or deliver the services to client as long as it works that way). After all, he can always look at process compliance at the "end of the project" or write a "nice" paragraph about it in the project wind-up project; that too because "quality people" insisted on it. It could even be that half of these project managers could be certified project managers who, as a part of their certification preparation, vouched for "quality practices"; Wasn't it one the domains they had to study for their exam! And once they become certified project managers, don't they help their organizations by getting their "rates" up?

Consider one more scenario, when once in a while the (say quarterly or bi-annually; whatever the defined frequency) the reporting to management begins, the "circus" really starts. A "symbiotic being" is discovered once again. QA department goes on a talent scoot to look for best practices, to look for assets that can be submitted etc.

Yet another scenario; when a customer-visit is announced, projects would become very friendly with the Quality Department. They want the "impressive metrics" to be presented to the client to have the mesmerizing effect. The reality is that to collect periodic metrics from these same projects would probably be the worst nightmare for the quality team. Experience would not differ much if your were a quality consultant rather than a full time quality manager; at times your client's imagination about your "magic abilities" would range from expecting you to fudge the metrics to "creating" data on "actual efforts" for example.

In Chapter 1, we discussed about quality being a business issue. The reality is that having a "good quality department" for most Indian software organizations is like having a "smart enough" wife; she can cook well, do good English conversation in parties, enjoys a bit of drink with her husband, can dance a bit.. You name it and she can do it. And yet when the husband says, "shut up" she will be quiet until he allows her to speak again. With due consideration to the fact good exceptions do exist, it's a question worth an introspection to the Indian software industry-"do we dare to give enough authority to our quality department to put their foot down and stop the shipment of a product/services if it is not found to be worthy of release/shipment?" Are we capable of educating our clients right from the beginning that quality is a serious business issue and that we want to be married to it right from start to end of a project; focussed on long-term victory rather than being driven by some petty short-term goals? How many business managers would come to terms with this fact? Will the senior management get over the dilemma "how much quality" is the right amount of quality?" "How much process-suaveness is just enough and when to give it a back-seat?" At times, it is observed that even if the project manager is following all the processes 100% along with the readiness of his team members (and yet managing the project "successfully" from the client" point of view), his senior management would lament the fact that he/she is probably spending far too much time on "quality".

When a client tries to push a Change Request implementation "quickly" enough for us to be called a "co-operative" supplier; and you tell them that as per our QMS we need to get it through the Change Control Board, the client may frown. At this point of time, a question to ask ourselves is did we not "tame" our client on quality thinking right from the beginning? Did we give a realistic estimate to the client? Were we honest enough to tell our client that quality requires efforts? Or we took Phil Crosby so seriously that we created an impression to our client's mind that "quality is free", "effortless" i.e. that we're naïve enough to believe that commitment to quality comes without putting in any hard efforts"?

Of course, there is the other side of the coin too. Quality professionals need to have the "tact" of "selling" the QMS processes to the practitioners to see its realistic and yet meaningful implementation. Better, if they come from Project background; having burnt their fingers on "misguided estimates", having lost their hair in managing customer expectations. If a quality professional comes from project implementation background rather than either an academic or theoretical background, then there would a far more conviction in his/ her appeal to practitioners to follow the QMS processes. That is what we meant in the section 2.4.8 of Chapter 2 on "People issues in Software Quality Assurance.

REFERENCES

[1] *IEEE Guide to Software Requirements Speciation* —*ANSI/IEEE Std 830*
[2] *Software Engineering: A Practitioner's Approach*—Roger S. Pressman (McGraw-Hill International)
[3] *The Software Factory: Managing Software Development and Maintenance*—James R. Johnson (BPB Publications)
[4] *The Essence of Total Quality Management*—John Bank (Prentice Hall India)

Chapter 4

PRODUCT QUALITY AND PROCESS QUALITY

4.1 Introduction

In the first three chapters, we discussed about the business case for Software Quality Assurance, the role of the SQA function and how it should be organized, whom it should report to. Personality traits required in a Software Quality Analyst to succeed in his/her job in SQA function were also discussed. We further discussed how the quality managmemet system (QMS) gets deployed in the organization and the various expectations from it. We also discussed the typical items that are under SQA review. Our discussion in Chapter 3 was focussed on how to plan for Software Quality Assurance, typical contents of an Software Quality Assurance Plan etc.

With this background created, in this chapter we'll discuss two important concepts—"*Product Quality*" and "*Process Quality*". This will be done with the help of various models for software product quality and process quality. It is important to distinguish between PRODUCT QUALITY and PROCESS QUALITY because it has a bearing on how an organization in software business wants to organize its mechanism to reach the ultimate objective in gaining an edge in through quality. Although discussion of product quality and process quality is akin to the discussion of "measures and metrics", we have chosen to take it up in a separate chapter.

Software Engineering Institute (famously known as SEI) at Carnegie Melon University has done extensive work in this area known as "*Process Improvement*". It is a site well worth visiting (www.sei.cmu.edu). SEI also distinguishes between "product metrics" and "process metrics"; this is discussed in the chapter on "software metrics" (classification of software metrics). IEEE (Institute of Electrical and Electronic Engineers) also has an extensive number of standards (www.ieee.org). We'll start this chapter with a discussion on "Product Quality". We'll discuss

"Process Quality" next. The issue of "Process Quality" will be approached from the "maturity" viewpoint and at the end we'll discuss the relation between them. In addition to this, a separate chapter is devoted to provide an overview to SEI's Capability Maturity Model, which is basically a well-known framework for *continuous process improvement*. (Process Improvement frameworks are discussed in detail in a chapter devoted to the topic).

4.2 Software Systems Evolution

Much has happened since in the last 40 or so years of computer invention. If we look back, we realize that each era was characterized by focus on certain kinds of software systems. Table 1 below summarizes this.

Table 1: Software Systems Evolution

Name of the Era and the Period	Characteristics of the systems
The Early Era (1950—60's)	• Batch processing oriented systems • Limited Distribution •Customized Software
The Second Era (1960—70's)	• Multi-user Systems • Real Time Systems • Databases • Product Software
The Third Era (Mid 70's—Late 80's	• Distributed Systems • Embedded Software • Low cost Hardware • Consumer Impact
The Fourth Era (Late 80's to just before Millennium)	• Powerful Desktop Systems • Object Oriented Technologies • Expert Systems • Artificial Systems and Neural Networks • Parallel Computing • Network Computing
Current Era	• Pervasive Computing • Internet based systems • Growth in Intranets • E-Commerce • M-Commerce (mobile e-Commerce) and Wireless Computing

In each era, the problems and challenges faced by the producer software product have not changed much: (Interested readers are directed to ref [1] for an excellent discussion on this.)

- Why does it take so long to get the software product/project finished
- Why are software development costs so high

- Why can't we find all errors before we deliver the software to our customers
- Why do we face difficulties in measuring the progress of software product/service development

Software products, as compared to non-software products have certain characteristics:

- Software is "developed" or "engineered"; it is not "manufactured" in the classical sense
- Software does not "wear out"; it only deteriorates over a period of use—it needs "Enhancements"
- Most software today is assembled from re-usable components rather than being custom-built based on fresh requirements analysis

4.3 Product Quality

If we reflect on these points and look around for our own experiences during software product development, we realize that it is the project infrastructure, which provides the framework through which software quality is "built in" the software product. The framework is really the "process" aspect of software product development. The "attributes" and characteristics of the software products and the degree that they fulfill specific project needs provides an incremental measure of quality of the end product. Product attributes are defined, first, as attributes for each data product produced, as the software is developed and second, as attributes that must be integral to the software when delivered for system integration. Before moving on with our discussion on "product quality" let's consider some basic definitions (as in IEEE Std. 610.12 IEEE Standard Glossary of Software Engineering Technology). It defines *"Software Product" as (1) The complete set of computer programs, procedures, and possibly associated documentation and data designated for delivery to a user. (2) Any of the individual items in (1)*

4.3.1 Software Attributes

According to IEEE STD 983-1986, "Standards" are *Mandatory requirements employed and enforced to prescribe a disciplined uniform approach to software development, that is, mandatory conventions and practices are in fact standards.* In order to ensure that development product meet a defined quality standard when delivered, standards and practices must be defined early. They must be specific to the software products. There must be quality "gates" identified, which will monitor the quality of the software products being produced before they are used by the project. Without a means to measure conformance to standards, practices and conventions, quality of a software product cannot be monitored.

Standards, Practices and Conventions

As said above, IEEE standard 610.12 defines "Standard" to be Mandatory requirements employed and enforced to prescribe a disciplined uniform approach to software development, that is, mandatory conventions and practices are in fact standards.

Quality Assurance Institute (QAI) says that "**Standards**" are the measures used to evaluate products and identify nonconformance; a basis upon which adherence to policies is measured.

IEEE standard 610.12 defines "**Practices**" as Requirements employed to prescribe a disciplined uniform approach to the software development process.

Conventions (according to IEEE Std. 983) are requirements employed to prescribe a disciplined uniform approach to providing consistency in a software product, that is, uniform patterns or forms for arranging data.

"Quality" is really a composite of many characteristics—it is best to capture the notion of quality in a model that depicts these composite characteristics and their interrelationships. Sometimes, the distinction between "internal" and "external" attributes of software product becomes blur, making it difficult to understand exactly what software product quality is! Still, *Quality Models* are important because they tell us what people think is important and also help us to understand the commonalities of their views. In this section, we want to look at some very general models of software product quality that have gained acceptance within the software engineering community.

Several researchers have decomposed the notion of "*Software Product Quality*" into a number of features or characteristics. Such features typically include:

- **Reliability:** The ability of a system or component to perform its required functions under stated conditions for a specified period of time.
- **Usability:** A set of attributes that bear on the capability of software to maintain its level of performance under stated conditions for a stated period of time.
- **Functionality:** A set of attributes that bear on the existence of a set of functions and their specified properties. The functions are those that satisfy stated or implied needs.
- **Maintenability:** A set of attributes that bear on the effort needed to make specified modifications.

- **Correctness:** (1) The degree to which a system or component is free from faults in its specification, design, and implementation. (2) The degree to which software, documentation, or other items meet specified requirements. (3) The degree to which software, documentation, or other items meet user needs and expectations, whether specified or not.
- **Portability:** A set of attributes that bear on the ability of the software to be transferred from one operating environment to another.
- **Testability:** The effort required to test a program to ensure that if performs its intended functions.
- **Efficiency:** A set of attributes that bear on the effort needed to make specified modifications.

Perhaps, McCall, in the Factor-Criteria-Metric, gave the first definition of the characteristics of *software product quality*. Basili and Rombach and Boehm have done considerable work in the area of proposing models for Software Product Quality Ref [6]. A detailed discussion on this is taken up in the following sections.

4.3.2 Classification of Software Application Attributes

Specific attributes for software products and services are defined based on the requirements of the project. These attributes are specific to the application and fall into several categories:

1. *Performance Attributes*—attributes, which describe the execution characteristics of the software when, integrated into an operational configuration. (*Configuration is the arrangement of a computer system or components defined by the number, nature and interconnections of its constituent parts*)
2. *Form Attributes*—Those, which describe the form of the product and how it will appear when delivered (the look and feel). This is important from the view point of the end user
3. *Processing Attributes*—Those which describe processing characteristics of the software
4. *Functional Attributes*—Those, which describe the functionality of the system when, integrated into an operational configuration. (The chapter on TESTING will discuss various aspects of functional testing.)
5. *Operational Integrity*—Those, which describe the reliability, system control, and operational support characteristics of the software and the degree that the system supports the requirements of the application. (*"Reliability" is the ability of a system of component to perform its required functions under stated conditions for a specific period of time*)

6. *Maintainability*—Those which describe the ease with which the software may be updated to reflect changing system or operational needs to correct operational discrepancies. (In the chapter on Software Measurements and Metrics, measurement aspects relating to Maintenance are discussed)

4.4 Models for Software Product Quality

4.4.1 McCall's Factor-Criteria-Metric Model

This model assumes that there are a number of high-level quality factors of any software product (e.g. *usability*) and that these factors may be defined in terms of criteria (e.g. *modularity*). At the lowest level are the *metrics* (more on this in the chapter "Software Measurement and Metrics"), which indicate or measure the criteria. The purpose of McCall product quality model was to define the characteristics to be assessed and to suggest some measures to capture those characteristics. McCall has described quality using a decomposition approach, which is depicted in Table 2. Figure 1 presents Boehm's view of software product quality.

In models such as these, (McCall and Boehm) the focus is on the final product (usually executable code) and they identify key attributes of quality from the user's perspective. These key attributes, called *quality factors* are normally high-level external attributes like "reliability", "usability", and "maintainability". But they may also include several internal attributes; such as "testability" and "efficiency". Each of the models depicted above assumes that quality factors are still at too high

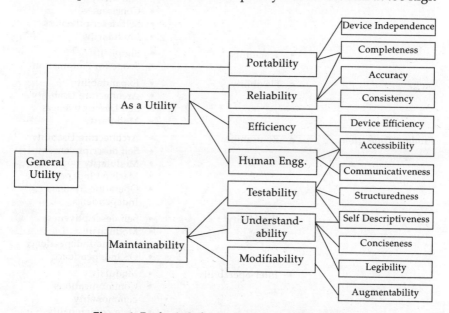

Figure 1: Boehm's Software Product Quality Model

a level to be meaningful or to be measurable directly. (Selection of the right kind of measures for various process and product attributes is discussed in the chapter on Software Measurements and Metrics.) When these high-level quality factors are decomposed into lower level attributes, we get *quality criteria*. The McCall model was originally developed for the US Air Force and its use is promoted within the US Department of Defense for evaluating software product quality.

Table 2: McCall's Software Product Quality Model

Use	Factor	Criteria
Product Operation	• Usability	• Operability • Training • Communicativeness • I/O Volume • I/O Rate
	• Integrity	• Access Control • Access Audit
	• Efficiency	• Storage requirement • Execution speed
	• Correctness	• Traceability • Completeness • Consistency
	• Reliability	• Accuracy • Error Tolerance • Consistency • Simplicity
Product Revision	• Maintainability	• Consistency • Simplicity • Conciseness • Self-descriptiveness • Modularity
	• Testability	• Simplicity • Scope for Automation
	• Flexibility	• Expandability • Architecture Usability • Self Descriptiveness • Modularity
Product Transition	• Re-usability	• Architecture Usability • Self descriptiveness • Modularity • Machine Independence • Operating Systems Independence
	• Portability	• Self descriptiveness • Modularity • Machine Independence • OS Independence
	• Inter-operability	• Modularity • Communications commonality • Data commonality

4.4.2 *The ISO 9126 Standard Quality Model*

For a long time, the user community was looking for a single model for depicting and expressing quality. A universal model makes it easier to compare one product with another. In 1992, a derivation of the McCall model was proposed as the basis for an international standard for software quality measurement. This is called *"Software Product Evaluation: Quality Characteristics and Guidelines for their Use"*. This standard is more commonly referenced by its assigned standard number, ISO 9126 (1991). As per this standard, software quality is defined to be: *" The totality of features and characteristics of a software product that bear on it ability to satisfy stated or implied needs"*. Quality is decomposed into six factors:

- Functionality
- Reliability
- Efficiency
- Usability
- Maintainability
- Portability

The standard claims that these six attributes of product quality are comprehensive; i.e. any component of software quality can be described in terms of some aspect of one or more of the six factors. In turn, each of the six is defined as a "set of attributes that bear" on a relevant aspect of software, and each can be refined through multiple levels of sub-characteristics.

4.4.3 *Other Models for Software Product Quality*

Goal-Question-Metric Model is another well-known model from Basili and Rombach. The other one is by Gilb; we'll discuss this a little later. The basic idea behind the work of Basili and Rombach is that metrics are derived from measurement goals (for which an organization committed to quality must have a well defined processes for quality planning and measurement) and questions, usually related to quality characteristics.

Gilb (and Kitchenham) have pioneered the "define-your-own-model" approach. This method can be thought of as "design by measurable objectives"; it complements his philosophy of *evolutionary development* (See the vignette below on *Evolutionary Models*) of the software product. Gils's approach is similar to work by others including McCall, in that high-level features of software product quality are decomposed into more measurable attributes. This is the philosophy underlying in Gilb's model/approach to software quality; the software engineer delivers the product incrementally to the user or market, based on the importance of the different kinds of functionality being provided. To assign priorities to the functions, the user identifies key software attributes in the product specification. These attributes are described in measurable terms, so the user can determine whether measurable objectives (in addition to the functional objectives) have been met. Figure 2 illustrates and example of this approach.

The COQUAMO (Constructive QUAlity Model) approach of Kitechenham and Walker extends Gilb's ideas and supports them with automated tools as part of an ESPRIT (European Community) project.

Evolutionary Software Models

There is a growing recognition that software systems typically are complex and as such they evolve over a period of time. Business product requirements often change as development proceeds. This makes it difficult to follow the linear sequential approach to software development. To accommodate the ever changing market requirements, tight market deadlines, a one shot release of software product is impossible. Instead, a limited version must be introduced to meet competitive or business pressure. In such cases, it becomes essential to adopt an "evolutionary approach" to software product development. Evolutionary models are iterative. They enable software engineers to develop increasingly more complex versions of the software product.

An important point to be noted that all product quality attributes may not go together; in fact some can be in direct conflict with others. This is illustrated in Table 3. The person eliciting software requirements must keep this in mind.

There is a significant amount of ongoing effort within the software industry, academia and government, directed towards developing the entire area of what is commonly called "Software Quality Metrics" – that is how to describe the overall characteristics of software, namely attributes, and the measurement of those attributes, namely metrics.

IEEE defines Quality Metric as (1) A quantitative measure of the degree to which an item possesses a given quality attribute. (2) A function whose inputs are software data and whose output is a single numerical value that can be interpreted as he degree to which the software possesses a given quality attribute.

4.5 Process Quality

A commonly used definition of software quality as defined in ISO 8402 international standard is:

Quality is the totality of features and characteristics of a product or service that bear on its ability to satisfy stated or implied needs.

Table 3: Relation among Software Attributes

Factors	Efficiency	Flexibility	Integrity	Inter-Operability	Maintain-ability	Port-ability	Reliab-ility
Efficiency							
Flexibility	X						
Integrity	X						
Inter-Operability	X	O	X				
Maintain-ability	X	O					
Portability	X			O			
Reliability	X			O			

X Factors Conflicts   **O** Factor Supports   Blank No Relation

(For a complete list of software factors, readers can refer to IEEE STD 1061)

Flexibility   *The ease with which a software system or component can be modified for use in applications or environments other than those for which it was specifically designed*

Interoperability   *The degree to which software can be connected easily to other systems in order to operate it*

Portability   *The effort required to transfer the software code from one hardware and/or software system environment to another*

Given this definition there would appear to be no such thing as "process quality"; although by implication a quality process is one, which leads to the production of a quality product. To evaluate the process it has to be made tangible. One way of doing this is to base the process on a standard or model against which conformance may be assessed. (In Europe, the prevalent approach is to base the process and any evaluation of it on a standard (ISO 9001 or similar) while in the United States the focus for process quality improvement and evaluation is a process 'maturity model'. (A detailed discussion on standard models will be taken up in chapters *Software Certifications and CMM Mode*)

But both approaches are discussed in brief in this section, bearing in mind that process evaluation only takes account of and is ultimately only as good as, the underlying standard or model used. The rationale is : A Process Approach implies that every activity in an organization has a defined start and finish and can be measured. (The topic of *Measurements and Metrics* is discussed in detailed in a separate chapter.)

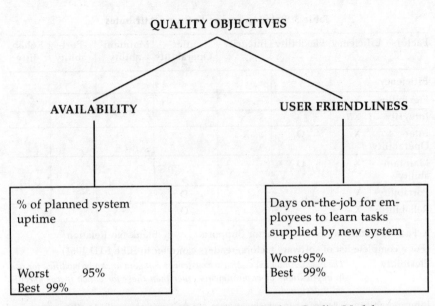

Figure 2: Gilb's Approach to Software Product Quality Model

4.5.1 ISO 9001 Quality Management for Process Quality Framework

One approach to the achievement of high quality is based on the use of an "adequate" predefined production process. At best, Quality Management Standards provide a baseline for an adequate production process by subjecting the processes to fulfill certain key requirements. In doing so, the attempt is to ensure the capability and commitment of organizations to produce quality products. The leading international Quality Management Standard (QMS) for software development is the International Standards Organization's generic 'Quality Systems' series of standards, ISO 9000 to 9004. When we refer to the ISO 9000 series, we will normally mean ISO 9001, which has been tailored for use in software environments by the addition of software-specific guidance documentation. ISO 9001 makes reference to "the process approach" to managing an organization. Figure 3 provides a graphic representation of what is famously known as the PDCA cycle (PLAN, DO, CHECK, ACT). In applying ISO 9001 to software it has to be recognized that software differs in a number of ways from other industrial products, and that the processes used to produce software are not typical industrial processes.

International Standard ISO 9000-3, *Guidelines for the Application of ISO 9001 to the Development, Supply and Maintenance of Software*, helps address some of these differences with references to the software lifecycle and supporting activities. The general framework of ISO 9000-3 includes sub-sections on management, quality system, internal audits and corrective actions. The standard assumes a lifecycle model of some

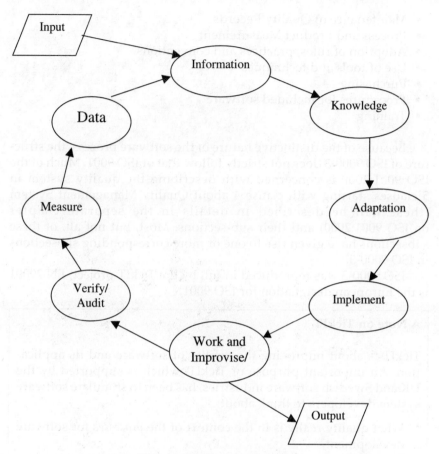

Figure 3: The Process Approach

type is used but does not prescribe any particular one. References to requirements, design, implementation and testing all appear in the standard. A number of plans are required by the standard, including:

- A development plan
- A quality plan
- A test plan
- A maintenance plan

A proposed structure of each of these plans is itemized. The emphasis throughout lifecycle selection is on the definition and control of the software process in accordance with established good practices in software production. Supporting activities in the ISO 9000-3 standard include:

- Configuration Management (there is a separate chapter about this)
- Document Control

- Maintenance of Quality Records
- Process and Product Measurement
- Adoption of rules, practices and conventions
- Use of tools and techniques
- Purchasing
- Procedures for included software
- Training

Because of the distinctive nature of the software process, the structure of ISO 9000-3 does not strictly follow that of ISO 9001. Much of the ISO 9001:2000 is concerned with describing the quality system in 5 clauses starting with clause 4 about Quality Management System (these will be described in details in the separate chapter on ISO 9001:2000) and their sub-sections. Most, but not all, of these subsections have given rise to one or more corresponding subsections in ISO 9000-3.

ISO 9000-3 was reproduced in full by the TickIT project. EN 29001 is the European designation for ISO 9001.

A Note on TickIT

TickIT is about improving the quality of software and its application. An important purpose of TickIT, which is supported by the UK and Swedish software industries, has been to stimulate software system developers to think about:

* What quality really is in the context of the *processes* for software development?
* How quality may be achieved, and
* How quality management systems may be continuously improved

---

4.5.1.1 Role of ISO 9001 in Evaluation of a software product

ISO 9001 was designed for use between two parties; the *purchaser* and the *supplier* involved in a contract for the development of a particular (software) product. However, the standard is now also used for independent assessment of a (software) *production process*, a purpose for which it was not originally intended. It should be noted, however, that QUALITY MANGEMENT SYSTEMs such as ISO 9001 are little more than very general guidelines, which help to ensure that all reasonable steps have been taken to encourage *process quality*. Although undoubtedly of value, there is little ground for supposing that their use inevitably leads to the manufacture of quality products. Among the reasons for this one is that quality management systems do not rigidly define the *development process* and their successful implementation is dependent on strict adherence and good workmanship (for software products, this would mean programming practices, coding guidelines,

GUI standards etc). For evaluating product quality through certification, an impact could be dependent on availability of widely recognized *process certificates*. For example, the availability of a comparatively cheap process certificate covering a number of software products may disincline organizations to opt for product certification for every product. Conversely, but to a lesser extent, the availability of such certificates may reduce certification costs by limiting the overhead of certifying different releases of the same product where it is felt that a re-evaluation is not necessary.

4.5.2 Maturity Models for Process Quality

We have a separate chapter dealing with the CMM (Capability Maturity Models). In this section we wish to provide only a brief overview of the CMM. For details, readers are directed to www.sei.cmu.edu.

The Software Engineering Institute (SEI), a federally funded research and development laboratory based at Carnegie Mellon University in the United States, has developed a model of the software development process known as the "Capability Maturity Model (CMM)". The model is used as the basis for *process improvement* and evaluation. Many documents relating to the model are kept in the public domain and are available for downloading at the site mentioned above.

The CMM is based on the quality principles first espoused by Walter Shewart in the 1930s and first cast into a 'maturity framework' by Philip Crosby (1979) [Ref 8]. Crosby discusses fourteen principles for a *quality improvement programme*. Shewarts principles were further refined and demonstrated during the 1980's by, among others, Edwards Deming (1982) , Juran (1988, 19889) and Ron Radice *et al.* (1985). At the time, Radice and colleagues were working at IBM under the direction of Watts Humphrey. Humphrey brought the concepts to the SEI and made this the foundation of the SEI's process maturity framework, with a view to assessing the software engineering capabilities of American Department of Defense (DoD) contractors.

Basically, the SEI framework identifies five 'maturity levels' (initial, repeatable, defined, managed and optimizing), on an ordinal scale (for discussion on various types of scales, readers can refer the chapter on metrics and measurements) which roughly corresponds to a progression of candidate (software) process from 'ad hoc' (unpredictable, poorly managed), through intuitive (basic project management practices and the ability to repeat previously mastered tasks), qualitative (well defined and institutionalized), quantitative (where the process is 'measured' and 'controlled'), up to the point where a process is in a continuous state of optimization based on measurement feedback.

The basis premise in this process improvement model is that if the quality of process for developing for a software product is good then there is a reasonable assurance that the quality of the end product is also likely to be good ('quality' as discussed in various sections of this book). For convenience, the practices that describe *key process areas* are grouped into the following '*common features*':

❖ Commitment to perform
❖ Ability to perform
❖ Activities performed
❖ Measurement and Analysis
❖ Verifying implementation

It may be noted that since the CMM, unlike ISO 9001, is software specific, there is not need for guidance in relating the model to software. SEI offers various training courses (mainly for assessors and for general awareness); the details can be found at the SEI mentioned earlier.

Conclusions

In this chapter, our aim was to give insights into 'product quality' vis-à-vis 'process quality' as this is the foundation for discussion software metrics and measurement. If an assessment of the (software) development process is to be a factor in evaluation and certification of a software product, it will be essential to establish some quantitative criteria as to the value of the process in relation to the quality of the product. To the best of author's knowledge, no such direct relationship exists—it is simply assumed that a well managed and disciplined (software) development process leads to a superior quality product. However, practical experience in the industry show that a 'good' process in itself is no guarantee of quality, especially if the process itself does not enforce good workmanship or adherence to well well-defined software development standards; coding guidelines, GUI standards etc. On the other hand, it is also true that a bad process is likely to engender good product quality; for example, lack of well defined and practiced process for peer reviews and inspection.

REFERENCES

[1] *After the Gold Rush*—Steve McConnell (Microsoft Press)
[2] *The Mythical Man-Month*—Frederick Brooks (Pearson Education)
[3] *Applied Software Measurement*—Capers Jones (McGraw Hill)
[4] *Software Metrics—A Rigorous & Practical Approach*—Norman Fenton and Shari Pfleeger (Thompson Books)
[5] *Software Quality Assurance & Management* —Michael Evans and John Marciniak (John Wiley and Sons)

[6] *Software Evaluation for Certification—Principles, Practice and Legal Liability—* Andrew Rae, Philippe Robert, Hans-Ludwig Hausen (McGraw Hill)
[7] *Microsoft Secrets—*Michael Cusumano and Richard Selby (Harper Collins)
[8] *Quality is Free—*Philip B. Crosby
[9] http://www.humanfactors.com/downloads/guistandards.pdf
[10] *The Goal Question Metric Approach—*Victor R. Basili 1 Gianluigi Caldiera 1 H. Dieter Rombach (Institute for Advanced Computer Studies, Department of Computer Science University Of Maryland—USA)

Chapter 5

SOFTWARE MEASURMENT AND METRICS

5.1 Overview

Some twenty to twenty-five hear ago, Software Metrics was a curiosity confined to a few university researchers and one or two industrial or commercial organizations. Today, Measurement is becoming increasingly accepted part of software engineering, but it is not always a well-understood one. Also, one of the problems facing the information technology (IT) industry today is the application of measurement-based techniques in a business environment. The world seems to be dichotomously divided between "measurement believers" and non-believers! It is said that we see what we want to see. In the software world, it is better to change this attitude to—"we'll see only if we measure".

A key element of any engineering process is "measurement" Measures help us to better understand the attributes of the software products or systems created and to assess the quality of those engineered products/systems. Measurement is the process by which numbers or symbols are assigned to the attributes of entities in the real world in such a way as to define them according to clearly defined rules.

While doing this, a distinction is to be made between "measures" as representations of observable attributes of objects or processes and prediction systems that combine measurements and parameters in order to make "quantitative predictions". This is an important distinction when validating measures. By recourse to measurement theory (a discussion on this out of the scope of this book), it can be determined whether the measure is proper in the sense of representing the attribute adequately. However, empirical validation of the engineering usefulness of a measure requires an explicit prediction system. Also, it is important to distinguish between the terms "measure" and "metrics"; whereas a measure is a pure number, metrics is most typically a ratio of two or more related measures. Figure 1 below illustrates this point about the difference between measurement and metric.

Figure 1: Definitions	
NUMBER	– an 'un-described' value ("5" is a NUMBER)
DIMENSION	– a descriptor "defects" is a DIMENSION
MEASURE(ment)	– a NUMBER with a DIMENSION "5 defects" is a MEASURE
METRIC	– two related MEASURES "6 Defects / KLOC is a METRIC
UNIT	– a target or area of measurement

In this chapter, we have covered:

- What is measurement and the need for measurement
- Role measurement in software development life cycle
- Defect Metrics
- Metrics for software maintenance
- Software metrics classification
- Requirements related metrics in view of Integrated CMM (CMM-I)
- Role of Metrics in process improvement
- Measurement principles
- Selecting appropriate metrics for projects and benefits of metrics for proactive project tracking
- Metrics Implementation
- Earned Value Analysis
- Planning for metrics program in an organization
- Metrics Program Implementation Issues
- Object Oriented Metrics

The next section will discuss each of above points briefly. We'll also provide a classification of Software Metrics. Toward the end of the chapter some planning issues are discussed along with the issues faced in reality while implementing a metrics program in an organization.

5.2 Introduction

5.2.1 What is Measurement?

This chapter is about measurements and metrics. It is therefore appropriate to do a brief discussion on what we mean by measurement. As said above, by its nature, engineering is a quantitative discipline. Engineers use numbers to help them design and assess the product to be built. It is essential that the same approach is adopted while designing software products. Also, measurement is such an everyday activity that we take it for granted. Measurement is defined as:

The process of assigning symbols, usually numbers, to represent an attribute of the entity of interest, by rule.

A definition of Software Metrics is [4]:

The continuous application of measurement-based techniques to the software development process and its products to supply meaningful and timely management information, together with the use of those techniques to improve that process and its products.

There are a number of points to note from this definition. First, the entity that we wish to measure can either be an object (for example, a person or a computer program) or it could be a process (for example, traveling from place A to place B or say debugging some code). Second, there must be some distinct attribute that we wish to measure; examples are: height, length, duration and cost. Third, typically, although not necessarily, we use numbers to represent the attribute being measured—for example length of a computer program could be represented by 315. Lastly, it must be noted that there is the requirement that the assignment of numbers, or whatever, must be according to some explicit rule.

Often, you may hear a term "indicator" in the literature on metrics. The term indicator is used to denote a representation of metric data that provides insight into an ongoing software development project or process improvement activity. Indicators are metrics in a form suitable for assessing project behavior or process improvement. For example, an indicator may be the behavior of a metric over time or the ratio of two metrics. Indicators may include the comparison of actual values versus the plan, project stability metrics, or quality metrics. Examples of indicators used on a project include actual versus planned task completions, actual versus planned staffing, number of trouble reports written and resolved over time, and number of requirements changes over time.

5.2.2 Why Measure?

We measure in order to answer questions—How large?, How maintenable? Does technique 'A' yield more productivity gains than technique 'B'? Will 'this' approach be more cost-effective than 'that'? What characterizes error-prone programs? How long will it take? Thus, if we have no questions, we have no need for measurement. Measurements inform our analysis and hone our critical faculties; it helps us to overcome subjectivity and provide a level of precision not otherwise possible. This does not mean that measurement is a panacea—misuse is all too possible—however, it has the potential to underpin computing as an observational science and software development as an engineering activity. From this, it should be possible to appreciate that the potential diversity of software engineering related measures, generally termed "software metrics" is vast. (Typically, whereas measure is a pure number as discussed above, metric is usually a ration of two or more measures—for example 30 defects v/s 30 defects per 1000 lines of code, or as another example—50 kilometers v/s 50 kilometers per hour)

Let us now discuss some examples for application of measurement. One example is to monitor software reliability over a period of time. Is it improving? If so, what is the rate? Another example could be to assess the maintainability of aging software systems and to direct re-engineering or re-structuring activities. As yet another example, consider software engineers applying measurement for early identification of a project going off the track. The idea of measurement as part of software development is not new. Right from the pioneering days of computers, people have been concerned with measurement related questions.

5.2.3 What are the Steps in Measurement?

Step 1

The first step in the measurement process is to identify the software measures and metrics that are "appropriate" for the representation of software that is being considered. Next, data required to derive the formulated metrics are collected. Once computed, appropriate metrics are analyzed based on a pre-established guidelines and data on past performance. The vignette on the next page illustrates how a project can make use of past data to set quality goals. Figure 2 shows the Control Chart for the same data based on hypothetical data on the acceptance test defects. For an excellent discussion on control charts and other analytical techniques for software measurement and metrics, reader is strongly urged to see [13] from the reference list at the end of this chapter.

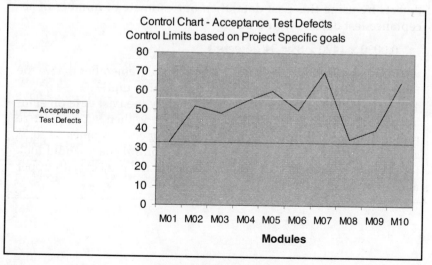

Figure 2: Control chart

Use of Past Performance Data: An Illustrative Example

Suppose 'Yojana' (Phase 2) is a project that involves two system components developed earlier, each handled as an independent project. Suppose these three projects (Yojana, Component 1 Project and Component 2 Project) are all similar in many respects (i.e. in terms of customer, development language and platform, end use domain, nature of the application etc.) Because of this similarity, the past data from two completed phases (development of Component 1 and Component 2) will be the best source of information for planning. Hence the data from earlier phases of Yojana (Component 1 and 2) is used. The Table below shows the acceptance test defects and total effort for the previous two projects.

Earlier Project	Effort Peron-Days	Defect detected during Acceptance Test	Integration/System Testing Defects
Component 1	528	17	54
Component 2	282	16	25
Total	810	33	79

Suppose, it is estimated that the effort for the current project (Yojana) is 1,420 person-days. Using *effort* as the basic predictor for defect levels, we obtain the estimated number of defects in *acceptance testing* for Yojana:

$$33 \times [1,420/810] = 58 \text{ defects}$$

Suppose the past data from *process capability baseline* shows 0.0030 defect per person-hour and if we were to estimate acceptance test defects by using this past data, then our estimate of number of acceptance test defects would be:

$$0.0030 \times 1420 \times 8 = 34 \text{ defects}$$

where an assumption of 8 Hrs per day is used (remember that in the table above the efforts are shown in person-day unit)

This value is lower than what is predicted by the past data on similar projects. The quality goal of this project is then set as a range rather than a fixed number. Thus the *quality goal* becomes *34 to 58 acceptance defects*. Figure 2 shows how the control chart would look for some hypothetical data from modules of the project with upper and lower control limits.

Step 2

As a next step, the results of the analysis are interpreted to gain insight into the quality of the software, and the results of the interpretation lead to modification of work products arising out of analysis, design, code or test. This is how the measurement program ties to the SDLC (Software/System Development Life Cycle). This aspect is discussed in section 5.3. As will be seen later, Figure 6 translates these steps in a diagrammatic form.

5.2.4 *Attributes of Effective Software Metrics*

Extensive work has been done in the area of software metrics. A wide variety of information sources on technical metrics and related subjects is available on the Internet [8]. Several hundreds of metrics have been proposed for computer software but all may not provide practical support to the software engineer. It is important to understand that metrics need to be innovatively designed to suit demands of each software project situation. In principle, the derived metrics and the measures should be:

- **An effective mechanism to enable high quality feedback:** the metric should provide a software engineer with information that can lead to a higher quality product.
- **Independent of the Programming language:** Metrics should be based on the phases of the life cycle model (Analysis, Design or structure of the program itself) but not dependent on the idiosyncracies of programming language constructs, syntax or semantics.
- **Simple and computable:** Simplicity is the essence of things! It should be relatively easy to learn how to derive the metric, and its computation should not demand inordinate effort or time.
- **Consistent and objective:** The metric should always yield results that are unambiguous. An independent third party should be able to derive the same metric value using the same information about the software.
- **Consistent in its use of units and dimensions:** The mathematical computation of the metric should use measures that do not lead to weird combinations of units (units of measure). For example, multiplying the number of people on the project teams by programming language variables in the program results in a spurious mix of units!
- **Empirically and intuitively persuasive:** This is a little esoteric but it is considered an important aspect—the metric should satisfy the software engineer's intuitive notions about the product or process attribute under consideration. For example, when schedule re-estimation done, depending on the past performance data, the band of allowed variance could tighten as compared to that with the first

estimation. This is because in the second attempt, one is expected to be in a better position to plan the schedule, as at this stage, more details are known about the project. For a detailed discussion on process variation etc reader should refer to [4] in the list of references listed at the end of this chapter

5.3 Measurement during Software Life Cycle Context

A project management measurement system is based on SCHEDULE, COST AND EFFORTS. Such a system adds value to all of the major phases of software life cycle. Figure 3 illustrates the major kinds of *measurements* associated with each phase starting from project initiation right up to the maintenance phase. Project accounting and configuration management shown in the figure are the umbrella activities in a software project in that, they encompass the entire project life cycle.

5.3.1 Measurement for Enhancement Phase

For projects that are *enhancements* (projects where the work involves extension of the existing functionality or the modules or components) or replacements or re-engineering of existing systems, the *structure*,

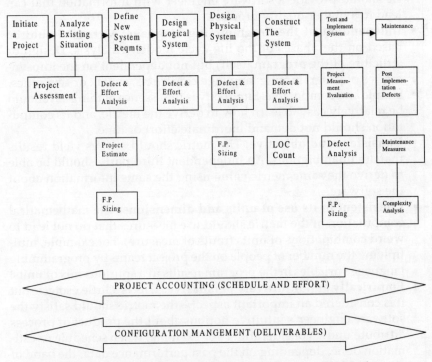

Figure 3: Measurement Activities and the Software Life Cycle

complexity and *defect injection rates* (Defect injection rate is defined as ratio of in-process and customer reported defects with respect to the Total size of Product in Line of Code or Function Point) of existing software should be analyzed. It is at this point that the normal project cost tracking system should be initialized for enhancements.

5.3.1.1 Measure for Product Size

The commonly known units for measuring the size of the software work product are either the lines of code (LOC) or the function points or feature points (FP). For the concept of function point and feature point see the vignette below.

Function Oriented Metrics—Function Points and Feature Points

For measuring the functionality delivered by the application, it makes sense to use function oriented software metrics. This is because "functionality" cannot be measured directly. Based on this concept, function point analysis (FPA) is a one of the popular method for estimating and measuring the size of an application. Function points quantify the functionality provided to the user based on the user's requirements and high-level logical design. Using the FPA method, the size of an application system's functionality is calculated in terms of Function Point count.

Function oriented metrics were first proposed by Allan Albrecht of IBM. He suggested a measure called the *function point*. Function points are derived using an empirical relationship based on countable (direct) measures of software's information domain and assessment of software complexity.

A slight variant over function point is "feature point". According to Capers Jones [1], for applications in which the number of algorithms is uncertain or in which algorithmic factors are not significant, *function points* would be the appropriate choice for a metric. Many business applications fall within this category—for example, accounting software, Sales Information Systems, Marketing Support Systems. For applications in which the number or algorithms is countable, and in which algorithmic factors are significant i.e. high algorithmic complexity, *feature points* would be appropriate choice for a metric. Many scientific, engineering, and real time systems application, process control systems and embedded software fall in this category.

For an easy to understand examples of how the function points are calculated, readers may like to see [14] in the list of references given at the end of this chapter.

For new projects, the requirements phase is the normal point at which the project cost tracking system should be initialized. It is also appropriate to initialize the project defect and quality tracking system, since requirements problems are often a major source of both expense and later troubles.

As the requirements are refined, the next aspect of measurement deals with whether the project should be in the form of a customer application or in the form of a package that is acquired and modified (make v/s buy decision). The risks and value of both approaches are considered.

5.3.2 Measurement during Construction Phase

If the decision is to construct the project, then, a second estimate should be prepared in conjunction with the logical design of the application. Since from this point on defect removal can be the most expensive element, it is imperative to utilize reviews and inspection (this is discussed in Chapter 6) and record defect data. A second and more rigorous cost estimate should be prepared at this time. During physical design, review and inspections are also valuable and defect data will continue to accumulate.

The coding or construction phase of a project can be either troublesome, or almost effortless depending upon the rigour of the preceding phases. A third formal cost estimate should be prepared; it will be very rigorous in accumulating costs to date and very accurate in estimating costs to the completion of the project. Defect and quality data recording should also be kept during code reviews or inspections. Complexity measures of the code itself can now be performed well.

5.3.3 Measurement during Testing Phase

The *testing* phase of a software development project can range from a simple unit test by an individual programmer to a full multi-state formal test suite that includes function test, integration test, stress test, regression test, independent test, field test, system test, and final acceptance test (also the alpha and beta tests—various types tests and test related measures are discussed in Chapter 10). Both the defect data and the cost data from the testing phase should be measured in detail and then analyzed for use in subsequent *defect prevention* activities (see the vignette below on Defect Prevention).

The Principles of Software Defect Prevention

The fundamental objective of software defect prevention is to ensure that defects, once identified and addressed, do not recur.
Everyone must be involved in defect prevention activities. Tenets
of defect prevention are:

- The programmers must evaluate their own errors (common tech-
niques are walkthroughs and inspection discussed in Chapter 6)
- Feedback is an essential part of defect prevention
- There is no panacea (single cure-all that will solve all the prob-
lem—an important activity is root-cause-analysis)
- Process improvement must be an integral part of the process
- Process improvement does not happen overnight—there is no sil-
ver bullet! It takes all the hard work to improve a process.

Major steps in implementing a defect prevention program are:

- Set up a defect reporting system
- Perform root-cause analysis
- Develop a focused action plan
- Implement the action plan
- Track performance improvement
- Take the lessons learnt and start the cycle all over again!

During the maintenance and enhancement phase, both *user satisfaction measures* and *defect measures* should be carried out. User
satisfaction is a basic metric for organizations that market software. It
is an important metric for internal information systems too. There are
various methods available for measuring user satisfaction; however a
discussion on that is not within the scope of this book. It is interesting
to note that industry data shows a strong observed co-relationship between defect levels and user satisfaction. From this point of view,
measuring software defect rates becomes important. However, before
we undertake this discussion, we wish to mention here that often, the
terms "bug", "error", "defect" get used interchangeably. Also, sometimes, these terms get used synonymously with other terms like
"failures" and "problems". Let us understand these terms before going
ahead with the discussion on defect metrics. Watts Humphrey, in his
famous book "Managing the Software Process" provides a good
discussion on this. The vignette below explains these terms. This discussion is only for the conceptual clarity. In this chapter we use the
term defect as the most general one.

Errors, Defects, Bugs, Fault, Failure, Problems

Errors – These are human mistakes. Their quantification would depend on an understanding of the programmer's intentions. (Examples: Typographical and syntactical errors)

Defects—These are improper program conditions that are generally the result of one or multiple errors. All errors *may not* produce software defects (Examples: incorrect comments or minor documentation errors). Conversely, a defect could result from such non-programmer causes like improper packaging or handling of the software product. A typical example would be error in the logo of the splash screen coming up on product start up!

Bugs—A bug or fault is program defect that in encountered while operating the product either under test or while in use. Point to note is that the operational condition or operating environment is often responsible for manifesting a bug which could otherwise have remained un-exposed! Thus, bugs result from defects but all defects do not cause bugs (some are latent and may never be found!) With widely used software (such as commercial off the shelf products) the defects may be found many times, resulting in duplicates or multiple bugs per defect.

Failures—A failure is a malfunction of a user's installation. It may result from a bug, incorrect installation, a communication line fault, a hardware failure, incorrect setting of environmental parameters for the software product etc.

Problems—Problems are user-encountered difficulties. They may result from failures, misuse, or at times, even from misunderstanding!

5.4 Defect Metrics

With this background as discussed above, various *defects measures* and *metrics* are indicated below:

5.4.1 Defect Density

Intrinsic product quality (Chapter 4 has a discussion on *product quality*) is usually measured by the number of "bugs" (functional defects) that a software product may have. Two metrics typically used in this context are *"mean time to failure"* (MTTF) and *defect density*. The MTTF metric is most commonly used with safety critical systems such as airline traffic control, avionics and weaponry applications in military. For example a specification such that air traffic control system *cannot be unavailable* for more than five seconds in a year (i.e. almost nil downtime required). In contrast, the defect density metric is typically used in commercial software system. Defect density is monitored at different stages as follows: (the terms system testing, acceptance test are explained in Chapter 10).

5.4.1.1 Defect Density (at System Testing Stage)

This is calculated as:

$$\frac{[\text{Total number of Defects identified during System Testing}]}{\text{Actual Size of the product}}$$

where size may be indicated by a suitable measure—most typically either as lines of code (LOC) or Function Points/Features Points (FP)

5.4.1.2 Defect Density (at Acceptances Testing Stage)

This is calculated as:

$$\frac{[\text{Total number of Defects reported at Acceptance Testing}]}{\text{Actual Size of the product}}$$

Though the two metrics (MTTF and Defect Density) are correlated, they are different enough to merit close attention. This is discussed below.

First of all, MTTF show the temporal dimension of the defect—i.e. it measures the *time* between successive failures, whereas, defect density measures the defects relative to the software *size* (lines of code, function points etc.). Secondly, although it is difficult to separate defects and failures in actual measurements and get the data tracked, "failures" and "defects" have different meanings (see the vignette at the end of section 5.3). However, for practical purposes, there is not difference between the two terms. Third, we usually, encounter the defects that cause higher failure rates. The probability of failure associated with a "latent defect" is called its size or "bug size". For missions critical applications (such as air traffic control systems) the operational profile and scenarios are better defined. As such, MTTF metrics is more appropriate here. Fourth, from the data gathering perspective, time between failure data is expensive. . To be useful, time between failure data requires a high degree of accuracy. Gathering such data requires special arrangements and that is not always easy. Finally, the *defect density metric* has another appeal for the development organization of commercial products. Study of such data gives them an opportunity to strengthen/improve their testing processes.

To sum up, regardless of their differences and similarities, MTTF and defect density are two key metrics for intrinsic product quality and as such they are among the most important defect metrics.

5.4.2 Defect Rate

The general, the concept of "defect rate" is the expected number of defects over a certain time period specified is important for cost and resource estimates of the maintenance phase of the software life cycle. It should be noted that "defect rate" and "defect injection rate" (discussed below) are not the same.

5.4.2.1 Defect Injection Rate

Defect injection rate (DIR) is defined as the ratio of in process and customer reported defects with respect to the total size of the product. Thus, DIR is:

$$\frac{[(\text{Number of In-process-defects}) + (\text{Number of Customer-reported Defects})]}{\text{Actual size of the product}}$$

There is an important point to note: *Unit Testing, Integration Testing, System Testing* are the tests carried out by the development organization before the product is shipped. In addition, the work product is reviewed prior to testing. Any defects found in either of these activities i.e. review and/or testing till the product is shipped by the development organization are called the *in process defects*. Once the product is shipped and enters into production stage for actual use, defects reported thereafter are known as the customer-reported defects.

5.4.3 Defect Removal Efficiency

Defect removal efficiency (DRE) is the efficiency of eliminating all defects before delivering the product to the customer. DRE includes all the defects identified and eliminated during review and testing phase (*Review* is discussed in Chapter 6 and *Testing* is discussed in Chapter 10).

DRE is calculated as follows:

$$\frac{\text{Number of defects identified up to System Testing (both during review and testing)}}{[(\text{Number of defects identified up to system testing}) + (\text{number of defects identified at Acceptance testing}) + (\text{number of defects identified during warranty support}) + (\text{Number of defects identified by customer during work product reviews})]}$$

5.4.4 Defect Removal Effectiveness

The discussion here is only for academic interest. In practical scenarios measuring "effectiveness" is almost impossible. However, we discuss some concepts here only for the sake of completeness of our definitions. The philosophical argument here is that whereas *efficiency* implies the element of time, *effectiveness* is related to the extent of impact and we may feel that the latter is more important.

To define defect removal effectiveness, we must first understand the activities in the development process that are related to *defect injections* (a defect being injected into a product though not intentionally) and *defect removals*. This is illustrated in Figure 4 below

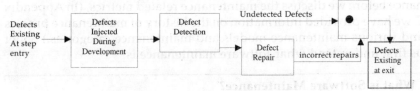

Figure 4: Defect Injection and Removal

Defects are injected (get introduced) into the product or intermediate deliverables of the product (for example, design document) at various phases of software project. It is a wrong assumption to make that all defects are injected at the beginning of the development phase. Before testing, the development activities themselves are subject to defect injection, and the reviews/inspections etc. at the end of the phase activities are the key vehicle for defect removal. For the testing phases, the testing itself is for detecting and reporting defects. When the problems found by testing are fixed incorrectly, this is another chance for error injection. In fact, even for the review/inspection steps, there are the chances for *bad fixes*. Figure 4 depicts the mechanics of defect injection and removal at each step of the development process. From the figure, defect removal effectiveness for each development step can be defined as:

$$\frac{\text{Number of Defects removed (at the step entry)}}{\text{(Number of Defects existing at step entry)} + \text{(Number of Defects injected during development}} \times 100$$

This is the conceptual definition. Note that the number of defects removed is equal to the number of defects detected minus the number of incorrect repairs. If an ideal system existed for defect tracking, all elements in figure 4 could be tracked and analyzed. However, in reality, it is extremely difficult to reliably track incorrect repairs. Assuming that the percentage of incorrect repair or bad fixes is not high, defects removed could be approximated by defects detected. If bad-fix percentage is high (greater than 2% as is the industry practice), one may want to adjust the *defect removal effectiveness* metric accordingly.

5.5 Metrics for Software Maintenance

5.5.1 *What is Software Maintenance*

Maintenance Projects are important. They are one of the most viable sources of business. It is of enormous importance to the Indian software business scenario where majority of work is in the maintenance and support area. Given that this is such an important area, it would be worthwhile to have a brief discussion on the topic of software maintenance before we discuss the maintenance related metrics. (In Appendix C we have provided information on the history of maintenance process and various maintenance models and maintenance categories.) So let us first understand what software maintenance is.

What is Software Maintenance?

Part of the confusion about software maintenance relates to its very definition. It is difficult to get people agree on a standard definition for "software maintenance". People often wonder what *really* happens during the maintenance phases of the life cycle. Another thing people wonder about is where does it fit into the system/software development life cycle? So let us look at some generally accepted traditional definitions of *software maintenance*:

1. *"......changes that have to be made to computer programs after they have been delivered to the customer or user."*

2. *"......the performance of those activities required to keep a software system operational and responsive after it is accepted and placed into production."*

3. *"Maintenance covers the life of a software system from the time it is installed until it is phased out."*

4. *"Modification of a software product after delivery to correct faults, to improve performance or other attributes, or to adapt the product to a modified operating environment."*

5. *"......software product undergoes modification to code and associated documentation due to a problem or the need for improvement. The objective is to modify existing software product while preserving its integrity."*

From this, one thing is clear: the common theme of above definitions is that *maintenance is an "after-the-fact" activity*. Based on these definitions, no maintenance activities occur during the software/system development effort. *Maintenance occurs after the product is in operation* (during the post delivery stage).

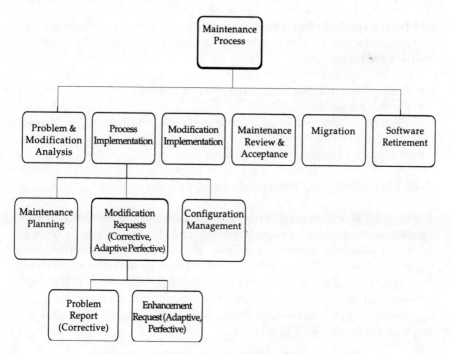

Figure 5: Maintenance Process Activities

5.5.2 Activities Involved in Software Maintenance

Having seen what software maintenance is, let us understand the activities involved in software maintenance. This will form a good background for the discussion on maintenance metrics. Figure 5 above depicts the activities involved in a software maintenance process.

5.5.3 Metrics for Software Maintenance

As seen in the light of discussion above, when a software product has completed its development and is released to the market, it enters into the maintenance phase of its life cycle. During this phase, the defect arrivals by time interval and customer problem calls (which may or may not be defects) are the de facto metrics. However, the roots of these defects or problems reported are in the development process prior to the maintenance phase. Not much can done to alter the quality of the product during the maintenance phase. Therefore, these two de facto metrics, while important, do not truly reflect the quality of software maintenance. All that can be done during the maintenance phase is to fix the defects at the earliest possible and with excellent fix quality (i.e. minimum Bad fix—this term will be explained later in this section). Such actions, although still not able to improve the defect rate (the term has been explained in section 5.4.2) of the product, can improve customer satisfaction to a large extent. From this perspective, the following metrics are important:

- Fix backlog and backlog management index
- Fix Response time
- Percent delinquent fixes (or the percentage adherence to the Service Level Adherence)
- Fix quality (as judged by "Bad Fix")

5.5.3.1 Fix Backlog and Backlog Management Index

Fix backlog is a workload statement for software maintenance. It is related to both the rate of defect arrivals and the rate at which fixes for reported problems become available. It is a simple count of reported problems that remain opened at the end of each period (month or week). By keeping the data in the form of trend charts, this metric can provide meaningful information for managing the maintenance process.

Another metric to manage the backlog of open problems is the backlog management index (BMI).

$$BMI = \frac{\text{Number of problems closed during the month}}{\text{Number of problem arrivals during the month}} \times 100$$

Since the BMI is a ratio as defined, a BMI larger than 100, it means the backlog is reduced. If BMI is less than 100, then backlog increases. The goal is always to strive for a BMI larger than 100.

5.5.3.2 Fix Response Time

For many organizations, guidelines are established on the time limit within which the fixes should be available for the reported defects. Usually the criteria are set in accordance with the severity of the problems:

1. (most severe) – Data loss, hardware damage, or a safety related failure
2.   – Loss of functionality *without* any reasonable workaround
3.   – Loss of data or functionality with a reasonable workaround
4.   – Partial loss of a function or a feature set
5. (least severe) – A cosmetic error

For "Crit-Sits (Critical Situations) where the customers' businesses are at risk due to the defects encountered in the software product, teams work round the clock to fix the problems. For less severe defects, for which workarounds are available, there are more relaxed *fix response time* requirements. The fix response time metric is usually calculated as follows for all problems as well as by severity level:

Mean time of all problems from open to close

If data points collected have extreme values, medians should be used instead of mean. Such cases could occur for less severe problems for which customers may be satisfied with the workaround and did not demand a final fix. Therefore the problem may remain open for a long time in the defect tracking report.

5.5.3.3 Percent Delinquent Fixes

Another measure for sensitive metric in maintenance phase is the percentage of delinquent fixes. For each fix, if the turnaround time exceeds the response time by severity, then it is classified as "delinquent":

Percent delinquent fixes =

$$\frac{\text{Number of fixes that exceeded the fix response time criteria by severity level}}{\text{Total number of fixes delivered in a specified time}} \times 100$$

This metric is related to the well known as the *percent adherence* to the SLA (service level agreement), which is defined only slightly differently:

$$\frac{\text{Number of fixes provided within the SLA time specified (as per the severity level)}}{\text{Total number of fixes delivered in a specified time}} \times 100$$

5.5.3.4 Fix Quality

Fix quality or the number of defective fixes is another important quality metric for the maintenance phase. From the customers' perspective, it is bad enough if they have to encounter functional defects when they are running their business using the software. It is even worse if the fixes have to be turned down due to some defect in them. As discussed earlier, for mission-critical software applications, defective fixes adversely affect customer satisfaction. The metric of percent defective fixes is simply the percentage of all fixes (in a given time interval) that turn out to be defective. A fix is defective if it did not fix the problem reported by the customer, or if it fixed the original problem but injected a new problem (that is why regression testing is so important. *Regression testing* is briefly discussed in Chapter 10).

"*Bad Fix*" or "*Defective Fix*" is the other commonly used term to express the quality of fix. Bad fixes include:

- Number of fixes rejected by the customer
- Bad fix injection

Bad fix injection(s) are the new defect(s) that are introduced when performing a service request (Fixing a problem). Bad fix percentage is calculated as:

% Bad Fix =

$$\frac{(\text{Number of Rejected Fixes}) + (\text{Number of New Defects introduced})}{(\text{Total Number of fixes delivered over a specified period of time})} \times 100$$

It is at this point that it becomes possible to carry out retrospective analyses of the *defect removal efficiencies* of each specific review, inspection and test and of the cumulative efficiency of the overall series of defect removal steps.

Figure 6 below summarizes application of measures for process management.

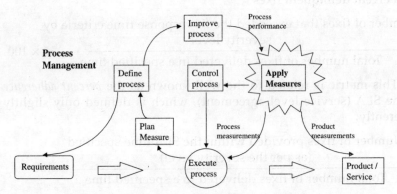

Figure 6 Applying Measures to Process Management

5.6 Classification of Software Metrics

According to the Software Engineering Institute (SEI—[2], software metrics may be broadly classified as either *product metrics* or *process metrics*. *Product metrics* are measures of the software product at any stage of its development, from requirements to installed system. Product metrics may measure the complexity of the software design, the size of the source code or the object code, or the number of pages of documentation produced. *Process metrics*, on the other hand, are measures of the software development process, such as overall development time, type of methodology used, the average level of experience of the development staff.

However, this is not the only way to classify metrics; i.e. further classification of Process Metrics and Product Metrics is possible. Both of them may be distinguished on their *objective* and from *subjective* properties. Generally speaking, objective metrics should always result in identical values for a given metric, as measured by two or more qualified observers. For subjective metrics, even qualified observers may measure different values for a given metric, since their subjective judgment is involved in arriving at the measured value. As an example of this—for the product metrics, the SIZE of the product measured in lines of code (LOC) is an objective measure. An example of a subjective product metric is the classification of the software as "organic", "semi-detached" or "embedded" as required in the COCOMO (Constructive Cost Model) cost estimation model proposed by Boehm. As another example—for process metrics, development time is an example of an objective measure, whereas the level of developer experience is likely to be a subjective measure.

Yet another way in which metrics can be categorized is a *primitive (or primary)* metrics or *computed (or derived)* metrics. Primitive (or Primary) metrics are those that can be directly observed (such as program size in LOC, number of defects observed in unit testing or total development time for the project). Computed (or Derived) metrics are those that cannot be directly observed but are computed in some manner from other metrics. For example—metrics commonly used for productivity, such as LOC produced per person-month (LOC/person-month), or for product quality, such as the number of defects per thousand lines of code (defects/KLOC). Computed metrics are combination of other metric values and thus are often more valuable in understanding or evaluating the software process than are simple metrics.

Having discussed classification of metrics, the next section, is devoted to requirements related metrics.

5.7 Requirements Related Metrics

Readers may wonder why the topic of *"Requirements related metrics"* is discussed as a separate section. There are two good reasons for this. First of all, requirements have an all-encompassing relationship to other project processes as depicted in figure 7 below. It shows the linkage between functional requirements to the software products including design and code. As you'll see later in this section, the requirements related metrics help us report on the percentage of requirements traced.

The second reason comes from the fact that the new Integrated Capability Maturity Model (known as the CMM-I) focuses on this as shown in the vignette on the next page. (In Chapter 9, the CMM-I model has been discussed as among other process improvement frameworks). The Integrated CMM Model expects what is known as 'bi-directional traceability" of requirements.

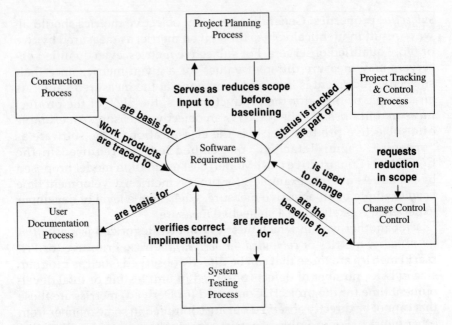

Figure 7: Relationship of requirements to other project processes

---

Requirements Related Metrics: the CMM Integrated Perspective

Level 2: Process Area-REQUIREMENTS MANAGEMENT

The CMM Integrated model expects that the organization is able to:

Monitor and control the requirements management process against the plan for performing the process and take appropriate corrective action.

Level 3: Process Area-REQUIREMENTS DEVELOPMENT

The CMM Integrated model expects that the organization is able to:

Monitor and control the requirements development process against the plan for performing the process and take appropriate corrective action.

This means that a good amount of control on requirements is expected. For this, there should be requirements related metrics in place. *Requirements metrics* pertain to specification, translation and volatility of requirements. The two well-known requirements metrics are—*Requirements Traceability* and *Requirements Stability Index*. Both of them pertain to *functional requirements*. The vignette on the next page explains what functional requirements are. Next, we discuss further details on requirements related metrics.

> **Levels of Requirements**
>
> Software requirements include three distinct levels of requirements: business requirements, user requirements and functional requirements.
>
> *Business requirements* represent high-level objectives of the organization or customer requesting the system or product.
>
> *User requirements* describe the tasks the user must be able to accomplish with the product.
>
> *Functional requirements* define the software functionality the developers must build into the product to enable users to accomplish their tasks thereby satisfying the business requirements.

5.7.1 Requirements Traceability

This traces the linkage between functional requirements and the software product including design & code and reports on the percentage of requirements traced from the function to the test case. The table below shows recommended items for requirements traceability metric tracking.

Table 1: Recommended items for requirements traceability metric tracking

From	To	Backward trace also ?
User requirements (mission)	User requirements (system)	Yes
User requirements (system)	System requirements	Yes
System requirements	Software requirements	Yes
Software requirements (SRS)	Software design high level	Optional
Software requirements (SRS)	Software design detailed	Optional
Software requirements (SRS)	Code	Optional
Software requirements (SRS)	Software qualification test cases	Optional

Note: SRS is Software Requirements Specification

5.7.2 Requirements Stability Index

This tracks changes to the functional requirements and plots the cumulative number of changes requests over time against the number of requests that have been resolved. Thus, a requirement stability index (RSI) is a metric used to organize, control, and track changes to the originally specified requirements for a new system project or product.

Typically, a project begins, after consultation with customers or clients and research into their needs, with the creation of a *requirements document*. The document expresses what the customer or client needs and expects and, at least implicitly, what the developer will provide.

The client or customer representative group reviews the document and, if in agreement with its specifications, signs it. This process (called *signing off*) is intended to ensure that customer representatives or clients have agreed—in writing—on the specifics involved.

Almost inevitably, however, once the design and development process is underway, customers or clients think of changes or embellishments they would like, a phenomenon known as the phenomenon of "requirements creep" or "feature creep". This, if not managed with a firm hand, requirements/feature creeps can result in lost time and money and either a project far beyond the scope of what was originally foreseen, or a failed project.

Figure 8 shows an example of the total number of requirements, the cumulative number of requirements changes, and the number of remaining TBDs over time. It may be desirable to also show the number of added, modified and deleted requirements over time.

As a concluding remark, we note that requirements stability is related to size stability. This is because, size stability, which is derived from changes in the size estimate as time goes on, provides an indication of the completeness and stability of the requirements, the understanding of the requirements, design thoroughness and stability, and the capability of the software development staff to meet the current budget and schedule. Size instability may indicate the need for corrective action.

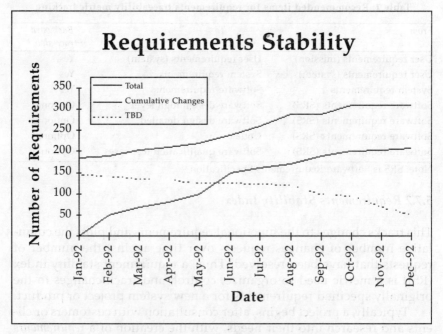

Figure 8: Requirements Stability Indicator

5.8 Measurements and Process Improvement

Having discussed the role of measurement in the software life cycle and classification of software metrics, let us now discuss role of metrics in process improvement. Process Improvement is a cyclical change process (depicted in Figure 9) in which particular process changes are introduced in order to remedy specific process defects in an environment of continuous process evolution. In this context, measurement is a means of assisting diagnosis of process problems, and of monitoring the effect of process change. Measurement, by itself, will not tell you what changes you need to make in order to improve your process. However, it can help to identify the most significant areas of weakness (even in a 'healthy' process) and allow you to decide whether a process change has the desired effect.

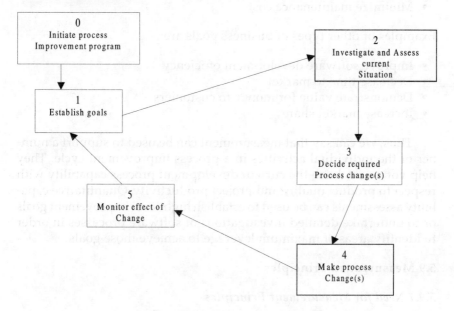

Figure 9: Process Improvement Cycle

As shown in figure 9 above, process improvement can be viewed as a cyclical set of activities consisting of 5 main stages:

1. Establishing the strategic goals of a process improvement activity
2. Investigating the current situation to set tactical goals for process improvement
3. Investigating process change options that could deliver the required improvements
4. Making the agreed process change(s)
5. Monitoring the effects of the change(s) to assess whether the desired process improvement has been delivered.

After stage 5, the cycle starts all over again, if necessary. However, before an organization can initiate a rolling cycle of process improvement, it must be clear on what its current stage is and where it wants to reach i.e. its ultimate target for a cycle. This is where data collected (from process observations) in form of measurement helps. Thus, it is important to appreciate that it is difficult to define process improvement goals without the real idea of what your problems are. *If you don't know where you are, it's pretty difficult to work out how to get where you want to be.*

Let us consider some examples of goals. For example, here are a number of goals, which relate directly to the software maintenance process:

- Maximize customer satisfaction
- Make maintenance work more predictable
- Minimize maintenance cost

Examples of other types of business goals are:

- Improve software development efficiency
- Decrease time to market
- Demonstrate value for money to customers
- Increase market share

Thus, we can say that measurement can be used to support a number of the individual activities in a process improvement cycle. They help you to establish the current development process capability with respect to product quality and project productivity. Quantitative capability assessments can be used to establish high-level improvement goals or to undertake detailed investigations of software processes in order to identify areas of maximum leverage to achieve those goals.

5.9 Measurement Principles

5.9.1 Need for Measurement Principles

In this section, we discuss the technical issues associated with software measurement and the types of measures that are available to support the goals of an organization. Once you have defined your metrics requirements (by planning out a process improvement cycle) you may find you need to obtain metrics your organization does not normally collect. In such cases, you will need to know whether existing measures meet your requirements and, if they do not, how you can adapt metrics or develop them yourself. This is the most difficult and controversial aspect of software metrics. For this reason, in this section, we review, in some detail, the theoretical aspects of what we mean by measurement. This provides the context for the discussion of practical data collection issues covered later in this chapter.

5.9.2 Structural Model for Measurement

We'll first introduce a "structural model for software measurement" (Figure 10) for our conceptual clarity. Then we'll give some examples of what can be measured and what are the issues to deal with in the real world scenario of software projects.

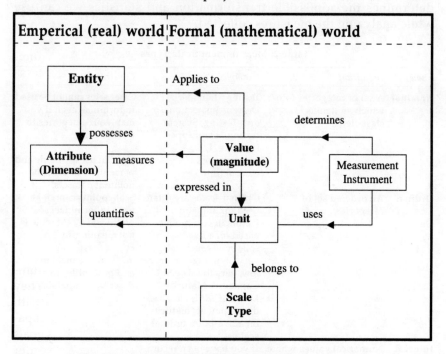

Figure 10: A Structural Model for Software Measurement

Attributes are the properties that an entity possesses. For a given attribute, there is a relationship of interest in the "real" world that we want to capture formally in the mathematical world. For example, if we observe two people, we can say that one is taller than the other. A measure of height allows us to capture the "is taller than" relationship and map it to a formal system, enabling us to explore the relationship mathematically. As Figure 10 above suggests, an entity possesses many attributes, while an attribute can qualify many different entities. For example, consider a computer program to be a software entity, which can exhibit attributes such as *length, structure and correctness*.

A measurement unit determines how we measure an attribute. The model depicted in Figure 10 above implies that an attribute may be measured in one or more units. The term 'metric' is often used for software units. For example, code length might be measured by counting the lines of code or the lexical tokens in a program listing.

5.9.3 Measurement Scales

When we consider *measurement units*, we need to understand the different measurement scale types implied by the particular units. The most common scales are: **nominal**, **ordinal**, **interval** and **ratio**. (See the Table 2 below on "Measurement Scale Types") A unit's scale type determines the admissible transformation and statistics we can use while analyzing the measures collected.

Table 2: Measurement Scale Types

Name	Definition	Examples	Constraints
Nominal	A set of categories into which an item is classified	Testing Methods: Designs Inspections, unit Testing, System testing, Error types: interface, I/O, computation, control flow	Categories cannot be used in formulae even if you map your categories to the integers. You can use the mode and percentiles to describe nominal datasets.
Ordinal	An ordered set of categories	Ordinal scales are often used for adjustment factors in cost models based on a fixed set or *scale points* such as very high, high, average, low, very low. The SEI Capability Maturity Model (CMM) classifies development/maturity on a five-point ordinal scale	Scale points cannot be used in formulae: so 2.5 on the SEI CMM scale is not meaningful. You can use medians and percentiles to describe ordinal dataset
Interval	Numerical values where the difference between each consecutive pair of numbers is an equivalent amount but there is no 'real' zero value. On an interval scale 2-1 = 4-3 but 2 units are not twice as much as 1 unit	If you have been recording information at six-monthly intervals since 1990, you can measure time since the start of the measurement program on an interval scale starting with 01/01/1990 as 0, followed by 01/06/1990 as 1, and 01/01/1991 as 2 and so on. Degrees Fahrenheit and Celsius are interval scale measurement of temperature	
Ratio	Similar to interval scale measure but including an absolute value zero. On a ration scale, 2 units are equivalent to twice the amount of 1 unit.	The number of lines of code in a program is a ratio scale measure of code length. Degrees Kelvin is a ratio scale measure of temperature	You can use the mean and standard deviation to describe ratio scale datasets

A measure is a mapping from the attribute box to the value box as shown in Figure 10. When we measure an attribute, we do so by applying a specific measurement unit to a particular entity to obtain a value. This value is often numerical, but it does not have to be. For example, a code module can be labeled 'inspected' or 'not inspected', or a defect found in a code review can be categorized as 'requirements error', 'design error', 'code error' or 'documentation error'. A measured value cannot be interpreted unless we know to what entity it applies, what attribute it measures and in what unit.

5.9.4 Measurement Principles: Summary

Having discussed the essential principles of measurements, let us now summarize for a quick re-cap. From the discussion of the structure of measurement; we can identify a number of principles to follow when we define software measures:

- We need to *specify the entities* to which the measures apply. This is essential to ensure comparability of measures.
- We need to *define the attribute* we are measuring. This is essential to ensure that we can interpret and use our results.
- We need to *define the unit* we are using. This is essential to ensure that we understand the values we obtain.
- We need to *specify the measurement* instrument we are using. Instruments are nothing but mechanisms to collect measures.

In addition, we may also need to define a *measurement protocol*. Protocols are set of rules that help in bringing consistency in measurements. They help us measure a specific attribute for a specific entity consistently and repeatably, independent of the measurer and the environment in which measurements are done. To illustrate the importance of measurement protocols, consider this example: A protocol for measuring the height of adult humans in meters might be:

- The person must be standing (not bending over)
- Measurement must start at the top of the head (not from the tip of up-stretched arms)
- The person must remove his/her foot ware
- The person must stand on the soles of the feet (not on tiptoe)

This example makes it clear that a measurement protocol is not simply derived from a definition of the measurement unit or the attribute. It is associated with obtaining a measurement value and can therefore be defined only when you have decided to measure a specific attribute on a specific entity using a specific measurement unit using a suitable (an preferably a calibrated) instrument. Unless these protocols are specified, it may not be possible to replicate the measurement and replication is the basis of scientific validation.

In view of above discussion some fundamental measurement principles emerge. A measurement process can be characterized by the following activities:

- **Formulation:** The derivation of software measures and metrics that is appropriate for the representation of the software that is being considered.
- **Collection:** The mechanism used to accumulate data required to derive the formulated metrics.
- **Analysis:** The computation of metrics and the application of mathematical tools.
- **Interpretation:** The evaluation of metrics results in an effort to gain insight into the quality of the representation
- **Feedback:** Recommendations derived from the interpretation of technical metrics transmitted to the software team.

This, in turn, results in the following associated principles:

- The objectives of measurement should be established before data collection begins
- Each technical metric should be defined in clear terms.
- Metrics should be derived on a basis that is valid for the software application domain (for example if a metrics is designed on the design principle of "cohesion" then, a metric that measures module cohesion should increase in value as the level of cohesion increases)
- Metrics should be tailored to best accommodate specific products and processes.

Collection and analysis are the next important activities in a metrication program of an organization. In this regard, the following guiding principles should be remembered:

- Whenever possible, data collection and analysis should be automated
- Valid statistical techniques should be applied to establish relationships between internal product attributes and external quality characteristics (for example: a possible correlation between the architectural complexity of a software product and the number of defects reported during the production use)
- Interpretative guidelines and recommendations should be established for each metric

Finally, as with any new initiative, management support, adequate funding, and adequate awareness etc. are crucial for successful implementation of metrics program in an organization.

5.10 Identifying Appropriate Measures and Metrics for Projects

In a project scenario, you will need to measure the five main dimensions of software production and maintenance—*COST, QUALITY, EFFORT, SIZE* and *SCHEDULE*. There is usually conflict and overlap between these dimensions, when software producers have to balance the requirements for cost, quality and timeliness within the constraints of the required functionality. Readers should note that the new *integrated CMM* (Capability Maturity Model discussed in Chapter 9) looks for "prioritization of the goals based on the project dimensions mentioned above. Attempts to control only dimension are likely to lead to imbalances in the other. Therefore the metrics to be collected should provide indicators that help track ongoing project progress, software products, and software development processes in a balanced way. As said in the beginning of this chapter, the term *indicator* is used to denote a representation of metric data that provides insight into an ongoing software development project or process improvement activity. The defined indicators shown in the table on the next page are consistent with the Software Engineering Institute's Capability Maturity Model (CMM).

Table 3 shows the recommended metrics set for a project. It shows the indicator categories, the management insight provided, and the specific indicators for recommended metrics.

From a measurement viewpoint, the *size* of the software product is an element, which influences all dimensions. It allows us to 'normalize' measures in each dimension to enable cross-project comparisons. The term 'normalize', in this context means converting a measure into a rate or percentage. As an example for how "normalization" helps interpret the data, consider this—suppose there are two programmers 'A' and 'B'. Suppose further, that as per past experience 'A' can write on an average about 150 lines of code per pay while 'B' can about 120 lines of code per day as an average. With this data can we really conclude, who is a more productive/better programmer? Perhaps not; for that, we'll need an additional piece of information—namely, the number of defect free lines delivered by each of them. With this information we can certainly normalize by comparing the two programmers on the basis of their percent defect free line of code delivered.

Similarly, as far as the EFFORT is concerned, each project will need to monitor itself against its designated monetary budget, but for comparison purposes, we also need to measure staff EFFORT. In most software projects, the main element of costs is staffing COSTS. Since there are problems using monetary values to compare projects, we use measures of staff effort as well as monetary costs to represent the cost dimensions.

As discussed in Chapter 4, there are two main facets of quality: *process quality* and *product quality*. In addition, there are two viewpoints on

Table 3: Recommended Metrics Set for a Project

Indicator Category	Management Insight Provided	Indicators
Progress	Provides information on how well the project is performing with respect to its schedule.	Actual vs. planned task completions Actual vs. planned durations
Effort	Provides visibility into the contributions of staffing onproject costs, schedule adherence, and product quality.	Actual vs. planned staffing profiles
Cost	Provides tracking of actual costs against estimated costs and predicts future costs.	Actual vs. planned costs Cost and schedule variances
Review Results	Provides status of action items from life-cycle review.	Status of action items
Trouble Reports	Provides insight into product and process quality and the effectiveness of the testing.	Status of trouble reports Number of trouble reports opened, closed, etc. duringreporting period
Requirements Stability	Provides visibility into the magnitude and impact of requirements changes.	Number of requirements changes/clarifications Distribution of requirements over releases
Size Stability	Provides insight into the completeness and stability of the requirements and into the ability of the staff to complete the project within the current budget and schedule.	Size growth Distribution of size over releases
Computer Resource Utilization	Provides information on how well the project is meeting its computer resource utilization goals/requirements.	Actual vs. planned profiles of computer resource utilization
Training	Provides information on the training program and staff skills.	Actual vs. planned number of personnel attending classes

product quality: the internal characteristics of the product such as structure and modularity, and the external characteristics of the product during operation, such a reliability and usability. In the light of the discussion so far and Table 3, we can say that minimum attributes of a project measure are:

- Total project COST
- Staff EFFORT for development and maintenance
- Other costs (tools, training, travel etc.)
- Project DURATION (calendar time)

- Post-release DEFECTS and the origins of those defects (each defect must be classified as to WHERE (in the product it is) FOUND and WHEN (in the process it was) INTRODUCED.
- Product SIZE
- COST of RE-WORK before and after product release
- PRODUCT CHARACTERISTCS in its operational environment (e.g. time between failures; time to correct defects; speed of execution; learning time; positive and negative responses to user/customer satisfaction surveys)

The Table 4 expands on the types of attributes that can be measured in each of the dimensions mentioned above. Its purpose is to provide an overview of useful measures but is not in itself a full definition. For the complete treatment of the subject "Software Measurement and Metrics" readers are referred to [1] at the end of this chapter.

Table 4: Attributes and Measures

Dimensions	Attribute	Measures	Issues to consider
COST	Development Effort	Staff effort in hours, days, months or years	Do you include overtime?
			Which activities are project related and which are overheads?
	Maintenance Effort	Same as above	Do you separate ADAPTIVE, PREVENTIVE and CORRECTIVE maintenance effort?
	Staffing level	Max. Staffing level	How do you count part-time staff members?
		Average Staffing level	How do you count part-time staff members?How do you count people who work full time but only for part of the project?
	Training costs	Cost of training event	Do you include general train ing or project-specific train ing?
		Nonproductive staff effort	For each member of staff or all members of staff?
		Cost of Training	Is training a corporate over head or a project overhead?
		Loss of staff effort during training	As above

Dimensions	Attribute	Measures	Issues to consider
Cost *(contd.)*		Loss of staff effectiveness (learning curve effects)	How is this measured or assessed?
	Tool costs	Cost of Tools	Is this discounted across all projects that use the tools?
ELAPSED TIME	Duration	Elapsed time in days/ months/years	Do you count working time or calendar time? Do you exclude holidays (those in your country, clients' countries or both?)
	Time-scale compression	Difference between estimated time-scale and planned time-scale	How are your estimates produced? What is the accuracy of the measure?
	Scheduled Start Date	Date	What constitutes the formal start of a project?
	Scheduled End Date	Date	What constitutes the formal end of a project: customer acceptance, QA sign off or final payment?
AVAIL-ABILITY, UTILIZA-TION, PERFOR-MANCE	Staff availability	Number of staff per staff category required per week	What type of staff do you need, and when do you need them? (staff loading pattern)
	Client availability	Subjective assessment (good, average, bad)	How do you ensure different people interpret this in a uniform way?
	Resource Utilization	Staff effort per week	Is this collected per person or per project?
	Performance	Elapsed time to perform task	Which tasks are measured under what workload conditions?
QUALITY *(Customer Perspective)*	Usability	User satisfaction survey results	How do you contact your users?
		Number of usability problem reports	Over what timescale do you accumulate this count?
QUALITY *(Internal attributes.)*	Portability	Percentage of product code/modules using hardware -specific constructs	How do you identify hardware-specific constructs?
	Structure	Linearly independently paths per module (cyclomatic complexity)	How is the measure extracted—manually or using a static analyzer?

Dimensions	Attribute	Measures	Issues to consider
QUALITY (*Internal attributes*) (*contd.*)			When is the measure extracted—at the end of software development or after handover to configuration control?
		Number of linearly independent module calling paths	As above
		Maximum depth of module calling tree	As above
COST OF QUALITY (*Rework*)	Development rework effort	Staff effort	How do you define rework—do you include rework after Inspection or only rework after formal acceptance of a deliverable?
	Post-release rework effort	Staff effort	Do you need to categorize rework into maintenance types such as adaptive, corrective, perfective, preventive?
			How easy is it for your development staff to distinguish different categories of work?
			Do you need to track rework to a particular product release?
QUALITY (*Testing related*)	Testing defect rate	Defects per week during system testing	How do you ensure that the amount of testing is uniform each week, so that the defect rates are comparable?
	Reliability	Mean time between software failures	What user profile are you using to ensure that results of testing can be used to assess reliability?
			What reliability model are you using to evaluate mean time to failure?
SIZE (*Requirements, Design and Code related*)	Requirements size	Number of transactions	How do you define a transaction? Are all transactions equal in terms of record size etc.? When do you make the count (of transactions)?

Dimensions	Attribute	Measures	Issues to consider
SIZE (contd.) (*Requirements, Design and Code related*)		Number and type of requirements	Do you recount them at different stages in the projects? Do you include non-functional requirements? Do you include constraints? (see Appendix A for the meaning of "constraint) Are all requirements equal/ of similar type? When do you make the count? Do you recount at different stages in the projects?
	Specification size	Number of bubbles in Data Flow Diagram or Number of Operations in the Class Diagrams	How do you ensure bubbles/ operations are at the same level of abstraction? When do you make the count? Do you recount at different stages in the projects?
		Number of entities in the Entity-Relationship Diagrams or the number of classes in the class-association diagrams	When do you make the count? Do you recount at different stages in the projects?
		Number of attributes in the Entity Relationship model or number of attributes in the class diagrams	As above
		Number of relationships in the Entity- relationship diagram or number of Associations in the Class Diagrams	As above
	Design size	Number of modules in product	How do you define a module? When do you make the count? Do you recount at different stages in the projects?

Dimensions	Attribute	Measures	Issues to consider
SIZE (contd.) (Requirements, Design and Code related)	Code size	Number of lines of code	At what stages in the construction and testing process do you measure code size?
			What is the convention for counting code size—are comments included? Are compiler directives and declarations included?
		Number of bytes of object code	As above
SIZE (Cost Implications)	Productivity	Lines of code or Number of Function Point per staff month	When do you measure the individual elements?
		Transactions per staff hour	
SIZE (Quality Implications)	Development defect rates	Defects per thousand lines of code per development activity	When do you measure the individual elements?
	Post-release defect rate	Defects per KLOC found by users	Over what time period are the defects counted?
	Test coverage	Percentage of product successfully tested	What measure of the product size will you use? How will you measure coverage?
SIZE (Elapsed time)	Code production rate	Number of lines of code or number of function points produced per week	When do you measure the individual elements?
			Do you measure the actual product of code each week, or the total code produced at the end of the project?
SIZE (Cost and Quality)	Productivity per quality level	Average productivity for products with different quality requirements	What population of products do you use?
			When is the value calculated? Is it re-calculated as new products are completed?
SIZE (Cost and Elapsed Time)	Duration compression productivity impact	Productivity levels for projects under different levels of compression	What population of projects do you use?
			When is the value calculated? Is it re-calculated as new projects finish?
SIZE (Quality and Elapsed Time)	Impact of duration compression on quality	Quality levels for projects under different levels of compression	As above

The attributes and measures shown in Table 4 revolve around a number of specific data collection issues:

- When will the value be collected or calculated?
- If a measure changes over time, will it be reconverted (if possible)?
- How will the value be obtained, manually or by the use of tools?
- Are all the elements that contribute to the value defined? This applies not just to derived measures but also to 'simple' measures such as project effort when you need to be sure that all the activities that contribute to project costs are included and whether or not unpaid overtime is included.
- What methods are used to obtain values that are estimates rather than direct measures?
- If a measure is derived from a set of other measures, is the set of units (from which the raw measures are derived) defined?

To sum up this section, we conclude that it is not very difficult to identify measurable attributes for various dimensions for projects. Factors such as cost and duration are general project management issues that are not specific to software only. However, identifying appropriate measures for *software quality* and *software size* are more difficult.

5.11 Metrics Implementation in Projects

In section 5.8 we discussed about role of metrics in process improvement. You cannot use measures to support process improvement unless you have an on-going measurement program also known as the "metrication program" A quantitative process management means quality planning and defect estimation right at the start of a software project. In this section, we'll discuss a few aspects of this challenge. The next section will add further details on this.

As discussed earlier, quality, along with cost and schedule is a major factor in determining the success of a software project. Table 4 provides details of the measures, attributes and issues in this respect. Let us now discuss how quality activities are planned and managed. Software quality is an important activity for any project.

As we'll see in Chapter 9, the CMM model, an organization at maturity level 4 is expected to have "Quantitative Process Management". Foundations set at Level 4 then help the organization to achieve one of the KPAs at Level 5 called "Defect Prevention" (the vignette in section 5.3.3)

When planning for quantitative management of quality for a project, the key issues are: (1) setting the quality goal and (2) predicting defect levels at intermediate milestones of the projects toward the quality goals set for the project. Defects may exist at any phase of the software life cycle (SDLC). Various defect related measures and metrics were discussed in section 5.4

In section 5.2.3 (the vignette for an example) we illustrated how historical performance data from past projects from the process database or process capability baseline are used. In the process capability baseline, defect data are normalized with respect to size or effort. If information normalized with respect to SIZE is to be used for predicting defect levels, then FUNCTION POINT (FP) will be needed as a size estimate for software products. In practice, often the exact data on SIZE is not available (i.e. Exact size of the product in terms of lines of codes or function points/feature points). In such a situation, it is a common practice to use EFFORT estimate for predicting the size by using the "expected productivity level" for the project. The effort estimate can also be directly used by taking advantage of the "defect injection rate" of the software process. Needless to say, this is possible only when past data on projects' performance is available.

As a further example usefulness of the past performance data consider this—suppose that the "Quality Goal" for a project is to have a minimum number of defects in the delivered product. i.e. the quality goal is the expected number of defects during acceptance testing. The quality goal can be "set" to be what is "computed" using the past data. In this case, a standard process is used without modifications and so "standard" results will be expected for quality. Alternatively, a quality goal different from the "standard" can be set. In this case, the process must be modified according to the quality goal. Two primary sources may be used for setting the quality goal: (a) Past data on similar projects and (b) data from process capability baseline.

(a) Past data on similar project

If data on similar projects are used, then the number of defects found during acceptance testing of the current project can be estimated as the product of the number of defects found during the acceptance testing of the similar projects and the ratio of the estimated effort for this project and the total effort of the similar projects Suppose, the set of similar projects is SP and the current project is P, then the estimate for defects in acceptance testing of P is:

Estimate for Acceptance Testing Defects (P) =

[AT Defects (SP) x Effort Estimate (P)] / Actual Effort (SP)

Where AT is Acceptance Testing

This gives the number of defects that can be expected if the same process is used as in the similar projects.

(b) Use of Capability Baseline

If the data from Process Capability Baseline are used, then several methods can be used to compute this value. Table 5 shows some examples of values in process capability baseline for defect estimation.

Table 5: Parameters for Defect Estimation

Productivity	4-18 FP/person-month (Avg.: 10 FP/person month)
Delivered Defects	0.04-0.09 Defects/FP (Avg.: 0.06 Defects/FP
In Process DRE	90%-95% (Avg.:93%)
Defect Injection Rate	0.8-1.2 Defects/FP (Avg.: 0.95 Defects/FP

If the quality target is set as the number of defects per Function Point, then SIZE in Function Points is estimated by using appropriate method for counting the Function Point (beyond the scope of this chapter—see www.ifpug.org for details of Function Points). In this case, the "expected number of defects" is the product of the quality figure and estimated size. The following sequence of steps is used:

1. Set the Quality Goal in terms of Defects/Product Size (From the Process Capability Baseline)
2. Estimate the "expected productivity level" for the project
3. Estimate the Product Size (Expected Productivity x Estimated Effort)
4. Estimate the Number of Acceptance Test Defects as : Quality Goal x Estimated Size

Sometimes, it is more useful to set the quality goal in terms of the "Defect Removal Efficiency" of the software process (This term was discussed in section 5.4). In this situation, the number of defects to be expected during acceptance testing can be determined from the "defect injection rate", the target-in-process removal efficiency, and the estimated size. The following sequence of steps is used:

1. Set the Quality Goal in terms of Defect Removal Efficiency (DRE)
2. Estimate the Product Size (as discussed earlier)
3. Estimate the total number of defects (Defect Injection Rate x Estimated Size)
4. Estimate the number of Acceptance Testing Defects from the total number of defects and Quality Goal

Table 6 below shows example of typical quality goals in a software project.

Table 6: Quality Goals for a Project (An Example)

Goals	Value	Basis for setting goal	Prevailing Norms
Total number of defects injected	145	0.033 defects per person-hour (This is 10% better than Project X)	0.052 defects per person-hour
Quality (acceptances defects)	3	3% or less of total estimated number of defects (defects reported by customer after product delivery)	5% of estimated number of defects
Productivity (FP per person-month) *(It should be noted that productivity may vary depending onthe development language used)*	55	3.5% productivity improvement over Project X	50
Schedule	Delivery on Time (0% schedule slippage)		Slippage within plus or minus 10%

5.12 Benefits of Measurement and Metrics for Project Tracking and Control

The basic purpose of measurement in a project is to be able to establish and effective project control and project tracking mechanism. In this section, we discuss some concepts related to metrics and measurement and the basic metrics useful for controlling a software project. Statistical Process Control (SPC) is among the well-known approaches for effective project control; however, a discussion on that is not in the scope of this chapter. (Readers can refer Appendix C for this)

In the light of the discussion so far, we can appreciate how software metrics can be used to quantitatively characterize various quality aspects. *Process metrics* quantify attributes of the software process or the development environment, whereas *product metrics* are measures for the software products (The topic of *process quality* and *product quality* has been dealt with in Chapter 4). Product metrics remain independent of the process used to produce the product. Examples of *process metrics* include *productivity, quality, resource metrics, training metrics, defect injection rates* and *defect removal efficiency* (these were discussed in the previous sections). Examples of *product metrics* include *size, reliability, quality* (quality can be viewed as a product metric as well as a process metric), *code complexity*, and *functionality*.

The use of metrics for project tracking and control necessitates that measurement be made to obtain data. This, in turn, means that for a metrics program to be successful, one must clearly understand the goals for collecting data as the models to be used for making judgments based on the data. In general, metrics to be used and measurements to be made will depend on the project goals and the goals of the organization as a whole.

Schedule is one the most important metrics because most fixed cost projects are driven by schedules and deadlines. It is easy to measure because calendar time is usually used. *Effort* is the main resource consumed in a software project. Tracking project efforts is thus a key project management activity. For this, the technique of "earned value analysis" is very useful (it is discussed in brief in the next section). It helps to determine if the project is executing within budget. Such data helps in making statements (for example) like—"The cost of current Project Y is likely to be about 40% more than an earlier project X" which was executed with very similar parameters or "The project is likely to finish within budget".

Now let discuss how measurements and metrics help a project manager make some predictions based on the past performance data. This is because defects have a direct relationship to software quality, tracking of defects, which, in turn, critical for ensuring quality. Table 7 shows an example of a hypothetical project estimates on defects in various project phases.

A large software project may include thousands of defects that are

Table 7: Defect Estimates (An Example)

Project Phase	Estimates Number of Defects (to be detected)	% of Defects to be detected	Basis for estimation
Requirements and Design review	25	20%	Similar Project in the past and process capability baseline
Code Review	25	20%	Similar Project in the past and process capability baseline
Unit Testing	60	40%	Similar Project in the past and process capability baseline
Integration and Regression Testing	30	15%	Similar Project in the past and process capability baseline
Acceptance Testing	5	5%	Similar Project in the past and process capability baseline
Total estimated number of defects to be detected	145	100%	

found by different people at different stages. In practice, it may happen that the person who fixed the defect may not the same person who found and reported the defect. Generally, the project manager would want to remove most of the defects found before the final delivery of the software product. To do this, formal mechanisms become essential for the defect tracking and reporting process. This means that defects must be logged and their closure must be tracked.

However, mere logging defects and tracking them is not sufficient to support other desirable analysis to help the project manger. The project manager need to understand what percentage of defects are caught where, phases in which defects are detected. In order to understand the defect removal efficiency of various quality control tasks (such as reviews and testing) and thereby improve their performance, not only one must know where a defect is detected but also where it was injected (the discussion in section 5.4.4). Thus, for each defect, it is essential to provide information about the phase in which the defect was introduced.

As noted earlier, Size is another fundamental metric because many data are normalized (defect density, productivity etc) are normalized with respect to size. Without the data on size, it is very difficult to do performance prediction using the past data. Function Points/Feature Points provide the uniformity because productivity measured in lines of code, differs with programming language.

To sum up, we note that a good project planning practice requires a plan to monitor the progress of the project. Tracking the progress, in turn, requires measurements and associated goals. Having established goals, measures and suitable metrics, it becomes possible to assess project's performance against the goals. The next section shows how the "earned value analysis" technique can be used to proactively track the project

5.13 Earned Value Analysis

5.13.1 Basics of EVA

Earned value analysis (EVA) in various forms is the most commonly used method of *performance measurement*. It integrates SCOPE, COST (or RESOURCE) and SCHEDULE measures to help project teams to assess project performance. The most typical use of EVA is seen in fixed cost projects. EVA is related to EVM—in the sense that Earned Value Management (EVM) is a methodology used to measure and communicate the real physical progress of a project taking into account the work complete, the time taken and the costs incurred to complete that work. *Earned Value* helps evaluate and control project risk by measuring project progress in monetary terms.

Earned value (EV) involves calculating *three key values* for each project activity:

1. *The Planned Value* (PV): also known as the *budgeted cost of work sched-*

ule (BCWS), is that portion of the approved cost estimate planned to be spent on the project activity during a given period

2. *The Actual Cost* (AC): also known as the *actual cost of work performed* (ACWP), is the total of costs incurred in accomplishing work on the activity during a given period. This Actual Cost must correspond to whatever was budgeted for the PV and EV (example: direct efforts in hours, direct costs, or all the costs including indirect costs)

3. *The Earned Value* (EV): also known as the budgeted cost of work performed (BCWP) is the value of the work actually completed.

These three key values are used in combination to provide measures of whether or not work being done is being accomplished as planned. This way, it enables proactive project tracking. An example of EVA is provided later in this section. Having understood the three key values of EVA, let us now see how these EVA based measurement and metrics help projects to take corrective actions.

5.13.2 *Use of the three key EVA-based measures for Project Tracking*

The three key values are used in combination to provide measures of whether the project work is being accomplished as planned (this is the important aspect of metrics-based proactive project tracking). The most commonly used measures are the *Cost Variance* (CV) and the *Schedule Variance* (SV). These two values can be converted to efficiency indicators to reflect the cost and schedule performance of a project. The *cost performance index* is the most commonly used *cost-efficiency indicator*. Here is how the calculations are done:

Cost Variance (CV)　　　　　　　= EV minus AC or BCWP minus ACWP
Schedule Variance (SV)　　　　　= EV minus PV or BCWP minus BCWS
Cost Performance Index (CPI)　　= EV divided by AC or BCWP/ACWP
Schedule Performance Index (SPI)= EV divided by PV or BCWP/BCWS

The basics of Earned Value can best be shown on the ubiquitous 'S-Curve'. The S-curve in its simplest form is a graph showing how project budget is planned to be spent over time. The BCWS (or Planned Value—PV) curve is derived from the *Work Breakdown Structure*, the project budget and the Project Master Schedule. The cost of each Work Package is calculated and the cumulative cost of completed Works Packages is shown based on the planned completion dates shown in the Master Schedule. The ACWP (or the Actual Cost—AC) curve is found by actual measurement of the work completed. Actual costs recorded from invoices and project team member's time sheets. This appears a daunting task but it can be very simple with sufficient planning and organizing. The BCWP (or the Earned Value -EV) is calculated from the measured work complete and the budgeted costs for that work.

Earned Value = (Percentage project complete) X (Project Budget). Section 5.14.4 shows how conclusions can be drawn from the values calculated as above.

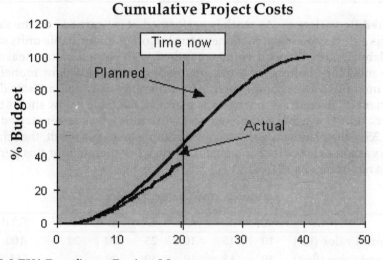

5.13.3 EVA Benefits to Project Management

The benefits to project management of the earned value approach come from the disciplined planning conducted and the availability of metrics which show real variances from plan in order to generate necessary corrective actions. However, the success of deploying EVA techniques depends of certain things (such as clarity on requirements and scope, good configuration management practices etc.). This is discussed below.

Earned value requires that the project be fully defined at the outset and then a bottom-up plan be created. This allows *measurement* to take place during the entire period of performance, from 1 percent to 100 percent of the project's lifecycle. The power in Earned Value Analysis technique is that it provides accurate and reliable readings of performance from as early as 15 percent into the project. Project manager can use these performance readings to predict how much it will cost to complete the project within a narrow band of values. If these early warning signals convey unacceptable readings to the project manager, steps can be immediately taken to avoid the undesired results. In the next section, we show how conclusions can be drawn on the basis of calculated values using the EVA technique.

5.13.4 EVA: An Illustrative Example

Baseline—The baseline plan in the table below shows that 6 work units (A-F) would be completed at a cost of Rs.100 for the period covered by a hypothetical report for the purpose of this illustration.

Baseline Plan Work Units

	A	B	C	D	E	F	Total
Planned value (Rs.)	10	15	10	25	20	20	100

Schedule variance—As work is performed, it is "earned" on the same basis as it was planned, in money terms or other quantifiable units such as labor hours. Planned value compared with earned value measures the monetary volume of work planned vs. the equivalent monetary volume of work accomplished. Any difference is called a: "schedule variance". In contrast to what was planned, the table below shows that work unit D was not completed and work unit F was never started, or Rs. 35 of the planned work was not accomplished. As a result, the schedule variance shows that 35 percent of the work planned for this period was not done.

Schedule Variance Work Units

	A	B	C	D	E	F	Total
Planned value (Rs.)	10	15	10	25	20	20	100
Earned value (Rs.)	10	15	10	10	20	-	65
Schedule variance	0	0	0	-15	0	-20	-35 = -35%

Cost variance—Earned value compared with the actual cost incurred (with information received from a formal project accounting systems) for the work performed provides an objective measure of planned and actual cost. Any difference is called a cost variance. A negative variance means more money was spent for the work accomplished than was planned. The table below shows the calculation of cost variance. The work performed was planned to cost Rs. 65 but its actual cost turns out to be Rs.91. The cost variance is 40 percent.

Cost Variance Work Units

	A	B	C	D	E	F	Total
Earned value (Rs.)	10	15	10	10	20	-	65
Actual cost (Rs.)	9	22	8	30	22	-	91
Cost variance	1	-7	2	-20	-2	0	-26 = -40%

Spend comparison—The typical spend comparison approach, whereby the party executing the contractual work reports actual expenditures against planned expenditures is not related to the work that was accomplished. The table on the next page shows a simple comparison of planned and actual spending, which is unrelated to work performed and therefore not a useful comparison. The fact that the total amount spent was Rs.9 less than planned for this period is not useful without the comparisons with work accomplished.

Spend Comparison Approach Work Units

	A	B	C	D	E	F	Total
Planned spend (Rs,)	10	15	10	25	20	20	100
Actual spend (Rs.)	9	22	8	30	22	-	91
Variance	1	-7	2	-5	-2	20	9 = 9%

Use of Earned Value Data—The benefits to project management of the earned value approach come from the disciplined planning conducted and the availability of metrics which show real variances from plan in order to generate necessary corrective actions.

Conclusions using Earned Value Analysis—*Schedule Performance Index* is a ratio of *Earned Value* and the *Planned value* of completed works. An SPI < 1 is not good. Also, Cost Performance Index is a ratio of *Earned Value* and the *Actual costs* of completed works. A CPI < 1 is not good. A lot more analysis is possible using the three key values of the EVA techniques. Interested readers may like to refer to any standard book on the subject of Project Management.

5.13.5 Essentials for EVA Success

The example above shows that the EVA technique as a tool for proactive project tracking, however appealing and powerful, is not easy to implement. It requires a considerable amount of project management discipline (such as good change control practices, project accounting control etc.). In that sense, one can say that there are "Ten Commandments" to implement Earned Value in Projects! These are summarized below:

1. Define Work Scope
2. Create an Integrated Bottom-Up Plan and Establish detailed measurement cells (called Project Accounting Systems—PAS for various aspects of projects).
3. Formally Schedule PAS
4. Assign Each PAS to an Executive for Performance
5. Establish a Baseline that Summarizes various PAS
6. Measure Performance Against Schedule
7. Measure Cost Efficiency Against the Costs Incurred
8. Forecast Final Costs Based on Performance
9. Manage Remaining Work
10. Manage Baseline Changes

5.14 Planning for Metrics Program

Like any other software or business activity, the introduction of a metrication program must be properly planned. You will need to consider the type of metrication program intended for your organization:

- One-off: this is a metrication program that has a well-defined goal, which can be addressed by performing a single data collection and analysis activity. This type of program is typical of an evaluation exercise (either a formal experiment or a case study). The important point is that once the goal has been achieved, the metrication program ends)
- On-going: this is a metrication program that is assumed to continue indefinitely. Metrication program of this type have goals related to issues such as "supporting project management and quality control as well as the SEI-CMM level achieved.
- Mixed: this is a metrication program that has some one-off goals and some ongoing ones. The distinction between the two types of goals must be made clear in the metrication plans. Your plans must also consider the stages in the metrication program to be deployed at your organization. These are somewhat similar to a software life cycle:

1. Goal setting
   - Definition of goals
   - Validating the goals
2. Data collection system specification and design
   - Formally defining all the measures
   - Defining the processes needed to extract, validate, store and analyze measures
3. Installation
   - Providing training to all concerned
   - Installing any required extraction, storage and analysis tools
4. Operation
   - Data validation—you must ensure that you have procedures for rejecting submitted data and handling re-submitted data and with valid reasons to defend rejections
   - Extracting, analyzing and reporting on data
   - Providing on-going support for software engineering staff involved with data collection system
5. Maintenance
   - Amending the data collection system if there are deficiencies
   - Enhancing the data collection system as development processes and data requirements change
6. Retirement i.e. closedown of the data collection system

5.15 Issues in Software Measurements & Metrics Program Implementation

Metrication Program in an organization is unlikely to succeed unless the software development staff who provide the raw data are committed to the cause of metrics. In practice, there are very good reasons why software development staff perceive metrication program as an unwelcome overhead and sometimes even as a major threat! Metrication program require software engineers to record information about their development activities. The information required usually includes data indicating both their own productivity and the quality of products they produce. If you introduce a system, which asks development staff to keep records of what they view as their personal limitations (e.g. the defects/faults which they introduced into their code, or the time takes them to design and code), then, it is not surprising to find that many staff are not highly motivated to keep accurate records. In addition to this, the usual project pressures take their toll on these good record-keeping habits.

Over and above this, if your staff do not know why the data is being collected or how it is going to be analyzed and used, then you are very likely to be faced with a large amount of incorrect and/or missing data. To minimize mis-recording, you must be committed enough to the data collection activity to take the time and effort needed to motivate your development staff to keep accurate records. Strategies for motivation include:

- Consultation and involvement
- User-friendly data collection systems/tools
- Awareness creation through training
- Feedback sessions
- Technical leadership
- Top Management support

5.15.1 Consultation and Involvement (Selling the Metrics Program)

If you want to introduce a metrication program in the organization, you will need to organize some consultation meetings. Consultation meetings should explain by the metrication program is needed, what it is expected to deliver, give some introduction to metrics and provide the opportunity for development staff to contribute to the program.

Mangers should tell staff why they need the data they wish to see collected. It is even more important that staff and mangers agree how the data is going to be used. If managers agree that data will not be used for personal appraisal, they must keep to that agreement whatever the temptations; otherwise the whole basis for obtaining valid data will be compromised.

It is usual to see concerns raised in these meeting about who "own" the data. This is a difficult issue to resolve. On the one hand, if you want to obtain commitment to the metrication program, development staff and/or their line managers must feel a degree of "ownership" toward the program. On the other hand, you cannot obtain the full benefit of a measurement program unless data from different projects can be collected and analyzed to provide information about the organization as a whole. Once the data are delivered from a project to another part of the organization, the originators of the data cannot realistically be allowed to assume that they still "own" all the data.

Unless you are not intending to collate data from different projects, it is better to make clear that the "company owns the data" (data as corporate asset), in the same way that the company owns the software produced by the development staff. Individual project staff and their direct line mangers should be at liberty to store, analyze and use the data they generate. In addition, they should be at liberty to collect and use data that is not needed to support corporate goals. Nonetheless, when data values are delivered to another part of the organization, they must be owned by the people who receive them.

5.15.2 User-Friendly Data Collection Systems and Tools

Every effort must be made to make data collection as easy as possible. Methods of minimizing overheads include automation and incorporating data collection into working practices of the projects. Efforts to make the system easier to use will usually reduce the incidence of deliberate mis-recording, ("cooking the metrics" for illicit purpose as it is called) as well as the amount of unintentional mis-recording. (Discussion of issues relating to automation is beyond the scope of this chapter.)

For manually collected data, in particular, the data, which depends on subjective assessment, it is vital both that data providers use well-understood definitions and that the amount of data to be collected is minimized. Information about changes resulting from defects/faults or change requests is important if you are interested in "quality of metrics" and it is important to have an appropriate classification system. The particular categories will depend on the particular development processes used in a particular environment and on the way product support is organized.

5.15.3 Training

For any non-trivial data collection process training is needed. It is the best tool for awareness creation. This should cover training in both the automated and the manual parts of the metrics system. In addition, software staff should benefit from training in software data analysis.

5.15.4 Feedback

Most metrication programs provide a set of standard reports to the management, but it is important to provide some feedback to the individuals who provide the data as well. You should report the results of data collection exercise back to staff quickly and regularly. Project staff will de-motivated if they feel that the data they collected is not being used constructively. Feedback plays an even more important role if the metrication program is itself on trial (as most programs are for the first few years). One typically used approach is to identify "metrics champions" early on, work closely with them on designing metrics suitable to their projects, win their confidence and later use these champions to act as metrics advocates. Such project mangers can be encouraged to spread success stories by word of mouth, by testimonials at carefully designed and planned workshops and by publishing articles.

5.15.5 *Technical Issues*

Technical issues to grapple with are: "operational definition of LOC (lines of Code) i.e. what basis should be used to count the number of lines of code (for example, should it include comments lines or only executable lines? Should it include compiler directives?). Extreme caution needs to be exercised when computing defect rates of two products if the operational definition of LOC, defects and time frame are not identical.

Also there are several methods to use for counting the function points and organizations need to make a careful choice by working with experts in the field. An excellent reference for a detailed discussion on this is [1].

5.15.6 *Top Management Commitment*

As said in first few chapters, like Quality Management System (QMS), metrics programs will fail without the whole-hearted support of top management. However, like quality assurance, and project management, software metrics is a "risk reduction methodology", not directly, a "cost reduction technology". This means that it may be as difficult to sell software metrics to senior management, as it is to motivate staff to collect data. In general, the following points can be made:

- Software staff already spend up-to 10 percent of their time generating data by filling in time sheets, using configuration control systems, filling in inspection reports and completing test reports. Most data collection systems do not significantly increase this burden (and good systems decrease it). Furthermore, unless this data is stored and analyzed, it is wasted.
- The largest cost associated with metrics program is the effort involved in data storage and data analysis. This can run at about 5% of project costs. However, if you are intending to obtain ISO 9001 certification, you are required to store and analyze quality records anyway, so the costs would be part of your normal QMS costs.

5.16 Object Oriented Metrics: An Overview

Object-oriented design and development is becoming very popular in today's software development environment. Object oriented development requires not only a different approach to design and implementation, it requires a different approach to software metrics. Since object oriented technology uses objects and not algorithms as its fundamental building blocks, the approach to software metrics for object-oriented programs must be different from the standard metrics set discussed so far. Some metrics, such as lines of code and *cyclomatic complexity*, have become accepted as "standard" for traditional functional/ procedural programs, but for object-oriented, there are many proposed object oriented metrics in the literature as will be seen in the next two sections. The question is, "Which object oriented metrics should a project use, and can any of the traditional metrics be adapted to the object oriented environment?" Extensive research has been done in the area of Object Oriented Metrics. A complete discussion on the topic is beyond the scope of this chapter. In the reference section some good links have been provided to the topic of OO metrics.

Object-Oriented Analysis and Design of software provide many benefits such as reusability, decomposition of problem into easily understood object and the aiding of future modifications. But the OOAD software development life cycle is not easier than the typical procedural approach. Therefore, it is necessary to provide dependable guidelines that one may follow to help ensure good OO programming practices and write reliable code. Object-Oriented programming metrics is an aspect to be considered. OO-Metrics is to be a set of standards against which one can measure the effectiveness of Object-Oriented Analysis techniques in the design of a system. As said above, the question is, "Which object oriented metrics should a project use, and can any of the traditional metrics be adapted to the object oriented environment?" In the sections that follow, we try to provide an answer to these questions.

5.16.1 Object Oriented Metrics: Details

In this section we discuss some OO metrics, which can be applied to analyze source code as an indicator of quality attributes. The source code could be any OO language.

5.16.1.1 Metrics for OO Software Development Environments

[1] Methods per Class

Average number of methods per object class = Total number of methods/Total number of object classes

- A larger number of methods per object class complicates testing due to the increased object size and complexity
- if the number of methods per object class gets too large extensibility will be hard
- A large number of methods per object class may be desirable because subclasses tend to inherit a larger number of methods from super-classes and this increases code reuse.

[2] Inheritance Dependencies

Inheritance tree depth = max (inheritance tree path length)

- Inheritance tree depth is likely to be more favorable than breadth in terms of reusability via inheritance. Deeper inheritance trees would seem to promote greater method sharing than would broad trees
- A deep inheritance tree may be more difficult to test than a broad one
- Comprehensibility may be diminished with a large number inheritance layers

[3] Degree of Coupling Between Objects

The topic "Principles of Coupling and Cohesion" is discussed in Appendix C.

Average number of uses dependencies per object = total number of arcs / total number of objects arcs = max (number of uses arcs): in an object <<uses>> network arcs—attached to any single object in a <<uses>> network

- A higher degree of coupling between objects complicates application maintenance because object interconnections and interactions are more complex.
- The higher the degree of uncoupled object the more objects will suitable for reuse within the same applications and within other applications.
- Uncoupled objects should be easier to augment than those with a high degree of 'uses' dependencies, due to the lower degree of interaction.
- Testability is likely to degrade with a more highly coupled system of objects.
- Object interaction complexity associated with coupling can lead to increased error generation during development.

[4] Degree of Cohesion of Objects

Degree of Cohesion of Objects = Total Fan-in for All Objects / Total Number of Objects (The term "Fan-in" has been discussed on page 291).

- Low cohesion is likely to produce a higher degree of errors in the development process. Low cohesion adds complexity which can translate into a reduction in application reliability.
- Objects which are less dependent on other objects for data are likely to be more reusable.

[5] Object Library Effectiveness

Average number = Total Number of Object Reuses/Total Number of Library Objects

- If objects are actually being designed to be reusable beyond a single application, then the effects should appear in object library usage statistics.

[6] Factoring Effectiveness

Factoring Effectiveness = Number of Unique Methods/Total Number of Methods

- Highly factored applications are more reliable for reasons similar to those, which argue that such applications are more maintainable. The smaller the number of implementation locations for the average task, the less likely that errors were made during coding
- The more highly factored an inheritance hierarchy is the greater degree to which method reuse occurs
- The more highly factored an application is, the smaller the number of implementation locations for the average method

[7] Degree of Reuse of Inheritance Methods

Percent of Potential Method Uses Actually Reused (PP):
PP = (Total Number of Actual Method Uses / Total Number of Potential Method Uses) × 100

Percent of Potential Method Uses Overridden (PM):
PM = (Total Number of Methods overridden/Total Number of Potential Method Uses) × 100

- Defining methods in such a way that they can be reused via inheritance does not guarantee that those methods are actually reused.

[8] Average Method Complexity

Average method complexity = Sum of the cyclomatic complexity of all Methods/Total number of application methods

- More complex methods are likely to be more difficult to maintain.
- Greater method complexity is likely to lead to a lower degree of overall application comprehensibility.

- Greater method complexity is likely to adversely affect application reliability.
- More complex methods are likely to be more difficult to test.

[9] Application Granularity

Application granularity = total number of objects / total function points

- One of the goals of object-oriented design is finer granularity. The purpose is to achieve a greater level of abstraction than possible with data/procedures-oriented design.
- An application constructed with more finely granular objects (i.e. a lower number of functions per object) is likely to be more easily maintained because objects should be smaller and less complex.
- More finely granular objects should also be more reusable. ... Therefore, each object's behavior should be more easily understood and analyzed.

5.16.1.2 Chidamber & Kemerer's Metrics Suite

Chidamber and Kemerer's metrics suite for OO Design is the deepest reasearch in OO metrics investigation. They have defined six metrics for the OO design.

[1] Weighted Methods per Class (WMC)

It is defined as the sum of the complexities of all methods of a class.

- The number of methods and the complexity of methods involved is a predictor of how much time and effort is required to develop and maintain the class.
- The larger the number of methods in a class the greater the potential impact on children, since children will inherit all the methods defined in the class.
- Classes with large numbers of methods are likely to be more application specific, limiting the possibility of reuse.

[2] Depth of Inheritance Tree (DIT)

It is defined as the maximum length from the node to the root of the tree.

- The deeper a class is in the hierarchy, the greater the number of methods it is likely to inherit, making it more complex to predict its behavior.
- Deeper trees constitute greater design complexity, since more methods and classes are involved.

- The deeper a particular class is in the hierarchy, the greater the potential reuse of inherited methods.

[3] Number of Children (NOC)

It is defined as the number of immediate subclasses.

- The greater the number of children, the greater the reuse, since inheritance is a form of reuse.
- The greater the number of children, the greater the likelihood of improper abstraction of the parent class. If a class has a large number of children, it may be a case of misuse of sub-classing.
- The number of children gives an idea of the potential influence a class has on the design. If a class has a large number of children, it may require more testing of the methods in that class.

[4] Coupling between Object Classes (CBO)

It is defined as the count of the classes to which this class is coupled. Coupling is defined as: Two classes are coupled when methods declared in one class use methods or instance variables of the other class.

- Excessive coupling between object classes is detrimental to modular design and prevents reuse. The more independent a class is, the easier it is to reuse it in another application.
- In order to improve modularity and promote encapsulation, inter-object class couples should be kept to a minimum. The larger the number of couples, the higher the sensitivity to changes in other parts of the design, and therefore maintenance is more difficult.
- A measure of coupling is useful to determine how complex the testing of various parts of a design are likely to be. The higher the inter-object class coupling, the more rigorous the testing needs to be.

[5] Response For a Class (RFC)

It is defined as number of methods in the set of all methods that can be invoked in response to a message sent to an object of a class.

- If a large number of methods can be invoked in response to a message, the testing and debugging of the class becomes more complicated since it requires a greater level of understanding on the part of the tester.
- The larger the number of methods that can be invoked from a class, the greater the complexity of the class.
- A worst-case value for possible responses will assist in appropriate allocation of testing time.

[6] Lack of Cohesion in Methods (LCOM)

It is defined as the number of different methods within a class that reference a given instance variable.

- Cohesiveness of methods within a class is desirable, since it promotes encapsulation.
- Lack of cohesion implies classes should probably be split into two or more subclasses.
- Any measure of disparateness of methods helps identify flaws in the design of classes.
- Low cohesion increases complexity, thereby increasing the likelihood of errors during the development process.

5.16.1.3 MOOD (Metrics for Object Oriented Design)

The MOOD metrics set refers to a basic structural mechanism of the OO paradigm as *encapsulation* (MHF and AHF), *inheritance* (MIF and AIF), *polymorphism* (PF) , *message-passing* (CF) and are expressed as quotients. The set includes the following metrics:

[1] Method Hiding Factor (MHF)

MHF is defined as the ratio of the sum of the invisibilities of all methods defined in all classes to the total number of methods defined in the system under consideration.

The invisibility of a method is the percentage of the total classes from which method is not visible.

Note: inherited methods not considered

[2] Attribute Hiding Factor (AHF)

AHF is defined as the ratio of the sum of the invisibilities of all attributes defined in all classes to the total number of attributes defined in the system under consideration.

[3] Method Inheritance Factor (MIF)

MIF is defined as the ratio of the sum of the inherited methods in all classes of the system under consideration to the total number of available methods (locally defined plus inherited) for all classes.

[4] Attribute Inheritance Factor (AIF)

AIF is defined as the ratio of the sum of inherited attributes in all classes of the system under consideration to the total number of available attributes (locally defined plus inherited) for all classes.

[5] Polymorphism Factor (PF)

PF is defined as the ratio of the actual number of possible different polymorphic situation for class Ci to the maximum number of possible distinct polymorphic situations for class Ci.

[6] Coupling Factor (CF)

CF is defined as the ratio of the maximum possible number of couplings in the system to the actual number of couplings not imputable to inheritance.

5.16.2 Adapting Traditional Metrics to the Object Oriented Environment

Research shows that there is considerable disagreement in the field about software quality metrics for object oriented systems. Some researchers and practitioners contend traditional metrics are inappropriate for object oriented systems. There are valid reasons for applying traditional metrics, however, if it can be done. The traditional metrics have been widely used, they are well understood by researchers and practitioners, and their relationships to software quality attributes have been validated.

Table 8 presents an overview of the metrics for object oriented systems. Traditional metrics can be aplied within the structures and confines of object oriented systems. The first three metrics in Table 8 are examples of traditional metrics applied to the object oriented structure of methods instead of functions or procedures. The next six metrics are specifically for object oriented systems and the object oriented construct applicable is indicated.

Table 8: Overview of Metrics for Object Oriented Systems

Source	Metric	Object-oriented construct
Traditional	Cyclomatic complexity (CC)	Method
Traditional	Lines of Code (LOC)	Method
Traditional	Comment percentage (CP)	Method
NEW Object-Oriented	Weighted methods per class (WMC)	Class/Method
NEW Object-Oriented	Response for a class (RFC)	Class/Message
NEW Object-Oriented	Lack of cohesion of methods (LCOM)	Class/Cohesion
NEW Object-Oriented	Coupling between objects (CBO)	Coupling
NEW Object-Oriented	Depth of inheritance tree (DIT)	Inheritance
NEW Object-Oriented	Number of children (NOC)	Inheritance

Finally, we end this section with a few concluding remarks. Researchers have found that a combination of "traditional" metrics and metrics that measure structures unique to object oriented development is most effective. This allows developers to continue to apply metrics that they are familiar with, such as complexity and lines of code to a new development environment. However, now that new concepts and structures are being applied, such inheritance, coupling, cohesion, methods and classes, metrics are needed to evaluate the effectiveness of their application. Metrics such as Weighted Methods per Class, Response for a Class, and Lack of Cohesion are applied to these areas. The application of a hierarchical structure also needs to be evaluated through metrics such as Depth in Tree and Number of Children.

Conclusion

Software metrics are numerical data related to software development. There are various ways to classify metrics. Software metrics is all about measurement, which, in turn, involves numbers; the use of numbers to improve the process of developing software. Software Metrics are applicable to the whole development lifecycle. Metrics collected from work product review help software engineers to spot error-prone components before they get as far as coding.

Measurement and Metrics can also be used to control a project as it progresses. Techniques like Earned Value Analysis provide visibility to management by generating early signals. This helps to adopt a proactive approach to project management by handling trouble areas before they become too big to manage. Thus, measurements and metrics play a significant role in effective project management. They relate to the four functions of management as follows:

1. **Planning**—Metrics serve as a basis of cost estimating, training planning, resource planning, scheduling, and budgeting.
2. **Organizing**—Size and schedule metrics influence a project's organization.
3. **Controlling**—Metrics are used to status and track software development activities for compliance to plans.
4. **Improving**—Metrics are used as a tool for process improvement and to identify where improvement efforts should be concentrated and measure the effects of process improvement efforts.

Although their usage is not as widespread as the traditional metrics, there are a number of object oriented metrics which provide valuable information to object oriented developers and project managers.

REFERENCES

[1] *Applied Software Measurement*—Capers Jones (McGraw Hill Computing Series)
[2] *Software Metrics : SEI Curriculum Module* SEI-CM-12-1.1 December 1988
[3] *Software Metrics : A Practitioner's Guide to Improved Product Development*— Moller and Paulish (Chapman & Hall)

[4] *Measuring the Software Process*—William A.Florac and Anita D.Carleton (Addison-Wesley)

[5] *The Software Measurement Guidebook*—Software Productivity Consortium (International Thomson Computer Press)

[6] IFPUG (International Function Point Users' Group)— www.ifpug.org/

[7] *Software Engineering: A Practitioner's Approach*—Roger S. Pressman (McGraw Hill International Edition Computer Science Series)

[8] An up-to-date list of World Wide Web references that are relevant to technical metrics can be found at the web-site http://www.mhhe.com/engcs/compsci/pressman/resources/tech-metrics.mhtml

[9] *Object-Oriented Design Measurement*—Scott A. Whitmire (John Wiley & Sons Inc)

[10] *Object-Oriented Metrics: Measures of Complexity by Brian Henderson-Sellers* December 4, 1995; Prentice Hall; ISBN: 0132398729

[11] *A Metrics Suite for Object Oriented Design* This paper proposes six OO design metrics that the authors (Chidamber, S.R., Kemerer, C.F.) claim are based firmly in theory of measurement and ontology of objects. Traditional metrics do not take OO notions into account.

[12] *A Validation of Object-Oriented Design Metrics as Quality Indicators* This paper presents the results of a study conducted at the University of Maryland in which the authors experimentally investigated the suite of Object-Oriented (OO) design metrics introduced by Chidamber & Kemerer.

[13] *Software Metrics : A Guide to Planning, Analysis and Application*—C.R.Pandian, Quality Improvement Consultants, Hyderabad (qic@rediffmail.com)

[14] *Software Requirements and Estimation*—Swapna Kishore and Rajesh Naik (Tata McGraw Hill)

[15] *Managing the Software Process*—Watts S.Humphrey (Addison-Wesley Publishing Company)

Chapter 6

WALKTHROUGHS AND INSPECTIONS

6.1 Overview

In this chapter we are going to discuss about the various review techniques called WALKTHROUGHS, DESK CHECKS, and INPSECTIONS. These are, "static" testing techniques. We'll discuss the, why and how of these techniques and will also present the viewpoints of various experts known to be associated with these techniques. We'll also discuss relative benefits and drawbacks of these techniques. The objective is to explain the contribution of these techniques towards ensuring the quality of product to be delivered to the customer.

6.2 Introduction

6.2.1 Why Reviews at All?

Technical work needs reviewing for the same reason that pencils need erasers: To err is human! The second reason why we need technical reviews is that although people are good at catching some of their own errors, large classes of errors escape the originator more easily than they escape anyone else. A review is a way of using the diversity and power of a group of people to:

1. Point out needed improvements in a product of a single person or team;
2. Confirm those parts of a product in which improvement is either not desired or not needed;
3. Achieve technical work of more uniform, or at least more predictable quality than can be achieved without reviews, in order to make technical work more manageable

A formal technical review (FTR) is a verification activity that is performed by software engineers. Ref [2] In a general sense of the term, a "review" is performed on any "work product"(such as a project plan, a piece of code etc). A work product is something that expends efforts and has a role in the execution of a software project. The FTR is actually a class of reviews that include *walkthroughs, inspections, and round-robin reviews* and other small group technical assessments of software. Ref [1] Each FTR is conducted as a meeting and will be successful only if it is properly planned, controlled, and attended by those for whom it is intended. In this chapter we'll discuss the various types of reviews, degree of formality involved in reviews, the various roles involved in reviews and what goes in making reviews and inspections successful as well as some typical pitfalls involved.

Another perspective on "reviews and inspection" is in terms of control. A control is anything that tends to cause the reduction of risk. Controls accomplish this either by reducing harmful effects or by reducing the frequency of occurrence. Whether Reviews and Inspections and the similar other techniques are under the realm of Quality Assurance or Quality Control is a matter of extensive debate. In this chapter, we'll bring in various perspectives on this.

6.3 Structured Walkthroughs

6.3.1 What are Walkthroughs and what they can be used for

Structured Walkthroughs, which are also known as "team debugging", "peer code reviews" etc are some review methods that have received much attention. Structured walk through technique is particularly valuable in that it can be used throughout the software life cycle. For example, customer review is one of the most widespread and apparently effective methods used for evaluating the supporting plans of commercial software projects. Walkthroughs can in fact be held of virtually any work product e.g.:

- ❑ The work assignments and schedules
- ❑ Specifications
- ❑ Data structure designs
- ❑ Program designs
- ❑ Documentation, including User Manuals
- ❑ Code
- ❑ Test plan, data and results
- ❑ Maintenance changes

They can therefore be used in the early stages of software development, such as design and planning, i.e. long before testing can begin. A variety of definitions can be given for walkthroughs

❏ A formalization of free discussion
❏ A peer group review of any work product
❏ A review session in which the originator of a work product explains it to his/her colleagues, including the intended function of the product and the reason for the method chosen for preparing/developing the work product.
❏ An in-depth technical review of some aspect of a software system

Walkthrough are therefore a static method of QA. This is also a view held by Myers, Ref [8] according to whom Walkthroughs are of equal or even more value in checking modifications to programs, as modifying an existing program or a more error-prone process than writing a new program. Walkthrough are informal meetings but with a purpose. In a way, they are similar to Japanese quality circles (see the vignette below on "*Quality Circles*").

Quality Circles

Quality Circles are groups of 4-12 people from the same work group or from within a department or sometimes from cross-departmental boundaries. The objective of the individuals united in a 'Quality Circle' is to identify local problems and recommend solutions. They meet on a voluntary basis but regularly to discuss, identify, investigate, analyze and solve their own work-related problems.

In some ways walkthroughs are similar to inspections (and hence the two terms are used interchangeably by some people) and yet in some other respects, they are different as will be discussed later in this chapter.

6.3.2 Walkthroughs—the objective and modus-operandi

As mentioned earlier, "Walkthrough" is one of the review methods and their objective is to ensure high quality, i.e. to find:

❏ Bugs, misinterpretations, omissions, inconsistencies, ambiguities, and anything that is unclear
❏ Anything that is complex or difficult to modify
❏ Deviation from standards (for simplicity, clarity, modularity, structure, documentation, external interfaces, user dialogues, exception conditions and exception handling)

It should be noted that the objective is to *find* problems and *not* correct them, because corrections are assumed to be within the province and capabilities of the developer.

Walkthroughs can be used with any of the various alternative team structures, but fit more naturally into the matrix structure because of its more democratic nature. They are less likely to be used in a rigid, bureaucratic organization. (a 'Matrix' structure is an attempt to combine the advantages of pure functional structure and the projectized organization structure)

Different authorities give different recommendations for the optimum number of participants in a walkthrough - about four persons participating in the walkthrough seems to be the generally held view. This is because, the more people there are, the greater the possibility of time-wasting due to differences of opinion, but more errors are likely to be uncovered. There are differences of opinions over *who* should attend walkthroughs, and it also depends on what type of work product e.g. specifications or code, is being walked through.

There is general agreement that the author of the product, a maintenance expert, and a member of the QA group should attend. There are both advantages and disadvantages if a manager attends a walkthrough. These are discussed later. Users (or customers) could attend specifications walkthroughs, testing walkthroughs, and possibly design walkthroughs, but not code walkthroughs. If users attend walkthroughs, designers may benefit from the increased involvement, but the users may use the walkthrough to ask for major changes. Other suggested participants include a technical secretary, a highly experienced programmer.

6.4 Inspections

Inspection as a review method was devised by Michael Fagan in IBM in 1972. As a technique they are more recent than "Walkthroughs". They are similar to walkthroughs but, there is an evidence that they are more effective. The ANSI/IEEE Std. 729-1983 IEEE Standard Glossary of Software Engineering Terminology defines inspection as

'...... *formal evaluation technique in which software requirements, design or code are examined in details by a person or group other than the author to detect faults, violations of development standards, and other problems....*'

According to Tom Gilb Ref [3] it may be wasteful to do Walkthroughs unless a document has successfully exited from Inspection. Thus, Inspection is not an alternative to Walkthroughs. In some cases it is a pre-requisite. These different review techniques have different purposes. Figure 1 shows the Inspection Process.

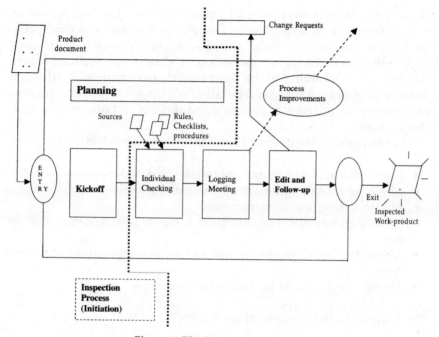

Figure 1: The Inspection Process

The various roles and responsibilities involved in Reviews and Inspections are next discussed.

6.5 Various Roles and Responsibilities Involved in Reviews/Inspections

Watts Humphrey in his book Ref [1] has talked about the various participants in the inspection meeting :

- The MODERATOR (or INPSECTION LEADER)
- The PRODUCER (or the AUTHOR)
- The REVIEWER (or the INPSECTOR)
- The RECORDER (or the SCRIBE)

Let us now understand the roles and responsibilities of these various persons involved in inspections. Of all these roles mentioned above, the *Moderator* has a key role in the Inspection Process. A capable moderator will generally produce an effective inspection, while an inexperienced or poorly qualified one often will not do so. An inspection is an interpersonal activity and the moderator's role is to ensure that the people constructively interact to produce the proper result.

The *Moderator* (also called sometimes the *'Inspection Leader'*) has the same responsibilities as in any formal technical review (FTR), but the emphasis may be more on interpersonal skills than technical skills.

Because the Inspection is more structured (following a fixed agenda of what is the scope on inspection etc) the leader may not need much technical ability. On the other hand, an inspection may consist of many more people than an ordinary review, so a good deal more conflict management may be required. For the same reason, very particular attention must be paid to the advance preparation of physical arrangements; otherwise the inspection may run aground on details of personal discussions.

In view of this, the desired attributes of a good moderator are:

- The technical ability to understand the area under review
- Ability to lead the group in effective discussions
- Ability to mediate disagreements
- Understanding of the organization and how to assign responsibilities
- Ability to identify the key issues and maintain the group's focus on them
- An unbiased view of the topics under review

The basic tasks of the moderator are to:

1. Obtain a good inspection or report to management whenever inspections could not be held along with the reasons.
2. Assist the producer in selecting the reviews and arranging for their participation.
3. Ensure that the reviewers do not have other reviews scheduled for the same day or have any other involvement that would impair their objectively.
4. Conduct a pre-inspection session for all participants and ensure that they understand both their responsibilities and the inspection process.
5. Ensure that the entry criteria for inspection are met (Refer Figure 1)
6. Make sure that the scheduled participants are present and that no mangers or observers are in attendance.
7. At the opening of the inspection, ensure that all participants are prepared or reschedule the inspection.
8. Conduct the inspection in an orderly and efficient manner.
9. Ensure that the inspection starts and ends on time.
10. Ensure that all identified problems are recorded and resolution responsibility is assigned.
11. Track each problem to resolution or ensure that it is tracked by someone else.
12. Gather the required inspection data and enter it into the process database.
13. Communicate the inspection results to all interested parties.

The *Producer* (alternatively called *'Author'*) is the one with whom the entire review is aimed. The only reward for the Reviewers, the Moderator and the Recorder is the satisfaction of helping someone do a better job and the implied promise that they will be helped in return. In spite of the critical nature of the inspection process, the producers must remember that all these people are giving their valuable time to help them. The Producer's responsibilities are thus:

1. To ensure that the work is ready to be reviewed.
2. To make the preparatory material available on time for all the participants.
3. To support the Moderator in making the meeting arrangements, providing copies for the inspection package, and helping establish schedules.
4. To promptly resolve all the identified issues.
5. To check with the participants whenever issues are not clear or when ideas and suggestions have been offered.
6. To be objective and avoid becoming defensive.

This may sound very simple but it is not. It is probably the most difficult responsibility of all. After working for months on a task the producers will have already thought through and addressed many of the issues. It will therefore seem like an enormous waste of time explaining all over again. This, however, is a necessary cost of conducting an inspection, and it invariably pays enormous dividends.

The *Reviewers* (also known as the *Inspectors*), comparatively, have the easiest job in some respects. They need only focus on the technical issues, and, when the inspection is over their work is done. The Reviewers' particular responsibilities are:

1. Be prepared for the inspection.
2. Be objective; focus on issues and not on the people.
3. Concentrate on the problems, and offer suggestions on style or problem solutions before and after the inspection.
4. Address major issues and submit minor items separately.
5. Insist on understanding issues and proposed explanations. When something is not clear, do not hesitate to stop progress until you understand.
6. When you are shown to be wrong, forget it.
7. Support the moderator.
8. Do not hesitate to praise good work.

The *Recorder's* (or the *Scribe*) responsibility includes:

1. Being generally aware of the subject matter being reviewed.
2. Recording all issues raised during the Inspection and ensuring that persons raising them agree with the way they are recorded.
3. Recording any required data on the inspection and its preparation and provide it to the moderator.
4. Producing the final inspection reporting, listing all issues, the responsible party for resolving each, and the schedule for resolution.

At the end of this chapter various checklists are provided in relation to the Inspection process.

6.6 Some Psychological Aspects of Reviews

6.6.1 Why is it Tough to Get Reviewers?

"Cost of (Poor) Quality" is the combined cost of *Prevention, Appraisal* and Failure (Figure 1 Chapter 1). Efforts spent in "Reviews" constitute "appraisal cost". Yet, in practice, it is found that instituting a review culture is not at all easy. Karl Wiegers in his article [9] provides a very interesting account of how successful reviews are a matter of Culture, Attitude, and Expression. In this section we explain the (important but often ignored) psychological aspects of conducting reviews.

In the beginning of this chapter, it was said "to err is human...." And yet, a tremendous amount of resistance is faced in making review as the regular appraisal practice. Most of the objections seem to stem from psychological reasons as will be discussed in this section. After all, asking your colleagues to point out errors in your work is a "learned"—not instinctive behaviour as some of us may think. Most of us, as human beings do not like to admit that we make mistakes! We don't like to ask other people to find them. It is important to appreciate that holding successful peer reviews (an informal review carried out by colleagues or associates who do not have reporting relationship to the author/producer) requires us to overcome this natural resistance to outside critique of our work. In a healthy software engineering culture, team members engage their peers to improve the quality of their work and increase their productivity. They understand that time spent looking at a colleague's work product/deliverable isn't time wasted, especially when other team members willingly reciprocate. In lower maturity organizations, on the other hand, "busy" practitioners are mostly reluctant to spend time examining a colleague's work. The attitude is "Anyone who needs his/her code reviewed shouldn't be getting paid as a software developer". Thus, it is often, lack of knowledge about the review process, review techniques and cultural issues and simple resistance to change that keep organization from implementing reviews as a sound appraisal mechanism.

6.6.2 Tips for the Reviewer

The dynamics between the reviewers and the author of the work product are critical aspects of peer reviews. Mutual respect is involved – the author must trust and respect the reviewers in order to be receptive to their comments. Conversely, the reviewers must respect the author's talent and efforts put in. Reviewers must focus on the work product under review and not on the producer. A review is considered as failed if the review process is not properly controlled/facilitated—as a result of which author could walk out of the review meeting frustrated. It is important equally to understand that reviews are not meant to identify scapegoats for quality problems. Having a co-worker locate a defect is regarded as a "good catch" that could prevent a fatal defect, not a personal failing. Language and expression matter too. Reviewers should keep their focus objectively on the work product being reviewed; carefully selecting the words they use to raise an issue. For example, saying "I didn't see where these variables were initialized" is likely to get a far better response than saying "how on earth you forgot to initialize the variables..? You forget such simple things...and you've been programming for how many years now...." Avoid expressions that may sound like personal attacks. As some more examples, you could raise issues by saying "Are you sure that another component doesn't already provide that service?" or identify a point of confusion: "I didn't see where this memory block is de-allocated. Thus, to reiterate an important point—direct your comments to the work product, not to the author.

6.6.3 Tips for the Author/Producer

Cultural biases run deeper than workplace attitudes. For instance, our educational system grades people primarily on their individual performance, so collaborative work is sometimes viewed as "cheating". There is an implication that if you need help, you must not be very smart. This shuns many people from asking for a formal review of their work product. We have to overcome the ingrained culture of individual achievement and embrace the value of collaboration. Then there are the excuses that people will give to avoid review of their product. This has a cascading effect—because they have "avoided" review of their work products, chances are that most likely they will not participate in reviews of work product turned out by their co-workers! Or, on the other hand, there can be "I scratch your back and you scratch mine" (reviews not done honestly for vested interests!) People who don't want to do reviews will expend considerable amount of time and energy in explaining why reviews do not fit their culture, needs or time constraints. There is the attitude that some people's work does not need reviewing (as much as some reviewers can think—"so and so is brilliant programmer....who am I to look for errors in her work?). The

Table 1: Benefits of Review

Project role	Possible benefits from peer reviews
Developer	• Less time spent performing rework • Increased programming productivity • Better techniques learnt from other developers • Reduced Unit Testing and Debugging time • Less debugging during integration and system testing • Exchanging of information about components and overall system with other team members
Project Manager	• Shortened product development cycle time • Increased chance of shipping the product on schedule • Reduced field service and customer support costs • Reduced lifetime maintenance costs, freeing resources for new development projects • Improved teamwork, collaboration, and development effectiveness • Reduced impact from staff turnover through cross-training of team members
Product Maintainer	• Fewer production support demands, leading to a reduced maintenance backlog • More robust designs that tolerate change • Conformance of work products to team standards • Better understanding of the product from having participated in design and code reviews during development
Quality Assurance Manager or Quality Control Manger	• Ability to judge testability of product features under development • Shortened system testing cycles and less retesting • Ability to use review data when making release decisions • Education of quality engineers about the product • Ability to participate quality assurance effort needed
Requirements Analyst	• Earlier correction of missing or erroneous requirements • Fewer infeasible and untestable requirements because of developer and test engineer input during reviews
Test Engineer	Ability to focus on finding subtle defects because product is of higher initial quality • Fewer defects that block continued testing • Improved test design and test cases that smooth out the testing process

other typically heard excuse is "I'm too busy fixing my own bugs to waste time finding someone else's." Other developers imagine that their software ability has moved them past the point of peer reviews. They think "Inspections have been around for twenty-five years; they're obsolete" or "Inspections work in factory/manufacturing environment; not here—software is "different"

6.6.4 Overcoming the Resistance to Reviews

It is said that you hire a person for his/her attitudes. Skills can be imparted through training but attitudes are hard to change. Lack of knowledge is easy to correct if people are willing to learn. Review workshops, wherein hands-on exercise on performing review is given, help the participants. Management attendance in these workshop helps to spread the right message ("This is important enough for me to spend time on it, so it should be important for you too" and "I want to understand reviews so I can help make this effort succeed"). Dealing with cultural issues requires that you understand your team's culture and how best to steer the team members towards improved software engineering practices.

The table 1 on the previous page shows the benefits from peer reviews to various roles in a project.

6.7 Making Reviews and Inspections Effective

According to Watts Humphrey Ref [7], there are four reasons for inspections being effective: they provide an opportunity to look at the entire work product in one go, they make use of combined knowledge and group expertise, they take advantage of different viewpoints, and they improve the odd of finding problems. In the following sections we discuss these points.

6.7.1 Inspecting the entire Work product

The main reason why review techniques like Inspections, Walkthroughs are more effective than Testing is that in an inspection or a walkthrough; you see all the cases, combinations and conditions at once (for example in case of code). With testing however, you can try only one case, with one set of data values, and under one set of conditions. Thus, with an inspection or a walkthrough you can see whether any necessary conditions are missing or whether conditions overlap or conflict. With testing, on the other hand, you must run at least a few number of tests and even then you still cannot be sure that you have covered all the potential problems. Thus, with inspections and walkthroughs or desk checks, you can look for things that are not there, whereas, with testing you test only what is there and test it only incompletely (i.e. no guarantee on completeness of testing).

6.7.2 *Using Combined Knowledge*

When several people study a single work product, they can focus their combined knowledge on finding the problems. The engineers on an inspection team usually have broader base of knowledge and experience than the authors of the product alone. Examples of problems that commonly surface in an inspection are interface conflicts, misunderstood dependencies, and errors in naming convention. Most of these problems are found because the inspection team as a group knows more about these topics than the author does.

6.7.3 *Using Different Viewpoints*

Often, developers can get into a kind of myopia; it is a sort of human psychology—we see what we know should be there and tend to overlook obvious things that conflict with our expectations (cognitive dissonance). Thus, we develop a kind of blindness to our own mistakes. Involving a number of experts to review your work product have a number of benefits; not only will they have different interests, perspectives, and varied backgrounds, but also they will provide another benefits; as you listen to your own explanation of what you were trying to do, problems that you overlooked will often become obvious. When explaining your work, you look at it from a different perspective, and often this is all it takes to help you see previously overlooked problems.

6.7.4 *Improving the Chances for Finding Errors*

When several people review the same material, even if each of them finds only a fraction of the problems, their combined reviews often find many more of the problems than any one inspector could possibly find alone. Of course, defects are not random, and some defects are much more difficult to find than others. But, particularly with hard-to-find problems, it is important to have multiple reviewers. The chance of someone finding the truly difficult problems will then be substantially better. It appears that inspection yields also decline with higher defect densities. Inspection yield measures the percentage of the defects that were in the product at the beginning of the inspection and were found in the inspection. For effective inspections, therefore, the authors must first personally desk-check their products and remove all the obvious defects. The reason is that simple defects are distracting. When reviewers see trivial errors, they are likely to concentrate on them and are less likely to see more difficult problems. Although inspections take time, effective inspection involves more than just spending enough time; you must spend that time properly. This is question of well-defined inspection methods, use of checklists and various players being well aware of their roles (The Reviewers/Inspector, The Author/Reviewee, The Moderator/Inspection Leader, the Records/Scribe as described in section 6.5). The general inspection methods are Checklists, Viewpoints and Product Concentration. Section 6.9 has discussed checklists. For discussion on Viewpoints and Product Concentration, reader are referred to [7]

6.8 Comparison of Review Techniques

Now that we've discussed various review techniques (Desk-checks, Walkthroughs and Inspections) one may wonder "which technique to use". A typically asked question is: Why do so many different people use so many different variations on the idea of Reviews? We attempt here to provide an answer to this often asked question as follows. The practice of (technical) review differs from place to place for a variety of reasons, the main ones being:

1. Different external requirements as dictated by various types of contracts
2. Different internal organizations, such as the use or nonuse of teams
3. Continuity with past practices that proved beneficial
4. The nature of work product under review itself could vary; for example reviews could be required of
   a. Functional Specification Reviews
   b. Design Reviews
   c. Code Reviews
   d. Documentation Reviews
   e. Test Plan Reviews
   f. Tool and Package Reviews
   g. Reviews of Training Materials and Plans
   h. Reviews of Procedures and Standards
   i. Operations and Maintenance Reviews

Continuity is probably the strongest reasons in most situations. When it comes to social behavior, people tend to be very conservative about changing what they already know or have done. There is nothing wrong with establishing continuity with past practices as long as the underlying task of the review is accomplished. If an organization generally has well-led, productive meetings that are regarded by everyone involved, as worth their time, it's a good idea to associate the formal technical review with this tradition. On the other hand, in an organization, where people are generally allergic to "meetings", it may prove better strategy to emphasize the formal technical review as something different from past practices.

Various experts provide their perspectives on which review technique to use. Tom Glib [3] gives a golden rule: Use Walkthrough for training, but use Inspection to improve the quality of the work product and its process. Traditionally, technical reviews and "structured walkthroughs" have been held for software development products. They have been found to be helpful in finding problems and improving the quality of software. However, these review techniques are much less formal than Inspection and much less effective at identifying according to Tom Glib [3]. They have been replaced by formal Inspection. Desk Check is an individual review technique whereas Walkthroughs are typically peer group discussion activities. Expected benefits of Inspection, when compared with other review techniques (walkthroughs and desk checks etc) are:

- Measurably high *product quality*
- Greater *productivity* from people in development and maintenance
- Shorter and more predictable *development times*

According to Freedman and Weinberg [4] "Inspection" approach tends to focus on a much narrower, much more sharply defined, set of questions. In some cases, an Inspection consists of running through a checklist of anticipated defects one after the other, over the entire work product (towards the end of this chapter, we have provided a couple of checklists.) Another way to try to cover more material is by having the product "walked through" by someone who is very familiar with it – even specially prepared with a more or less formal presentation. Walking through the product, a lot of detail can be skipped – which is good if you're just trying to verify an overall approach or bad if your objective is to find errors in detail.

In some cases, the Walkthrough is very close to a "lecture" about the product—which suggests another reason for varying the formal review approach. Reviews have educational qualities i.e. as Tom Gilb has said; Walkthroughs help towards training of new reviewers. This is a by-product of the quality assurance function. Sometimes, rapid education of large numbers of people may suggest some variation of the formal technical review. However, there may be situations where formality of reviews does not seem appropriate. For example, when members of the same team are reviewing each other's rough work (peer reviews), prior to finishing it for formal, external review, an informal version of the formal procedures may be comfortable. But there is one thing to watch against; as the review procedure gets less formal, however, there is a danger of drifting away from its central purpose. Another dimension for variation is the review team structure. At the one extreme, each review has a unique group chosen for it alone, but there are many variants that provide for some degree of permanence by having a group of people perform related reviews. At the other extreme, there are permanent review teams, devoted to specific work product, class of work product, or type of review.

IBM claims that Inspection give markedly greater productivity than Structured Walkthroughs, and result in fewer errors. Fagan listed the advantages of Inspection as:

- Inspectors have definite role to play;
- The moderator rather than the reviewee (the one whose work is under review)directs the effort
- An error checklist is used; and
- Detailed error feedback is provided to individual programmers

Inspections do not involve the members of the team which produced the work product being inspected, and so do not give the benefits of improved team communications, morale, and education of new members, provided by Walkthroughs. The key difference between Inspections and Walkthroughs is that Inspections are solely intended to detect defects. They do not have an explicit educational function, nor are they part of the design process where strategy decisions are made.

6.9 Inspection Related Checklists

Here are some useful checklists relating to Inspection as a review technique—they are:

- Checklist for the use by Inspection Moderator (Inspection Leader)
- Checklist for the Recorder (the Scribe)
- Checklists for inspection of documentation

These are presented below one by one.

Checklist for Inspection Moderator (The Review Leader)

Qualifications of the Moderator
Do you understand the purpose of the inspections in general?
Do you understand why this particular inspection is held?
Can you be objective on the subject of the inspection?
Have you ever participated in an inspection as reviewer or reviewee?
Do you have any personal difficulties with any of the reviewers that might interfere with your ability to lead the inspection objectively?

Pre-Inspection
Is the product ready for inspection?
Are all relevant materials in your possession?
Have all relevant materials been distributed on time?
Have all the reviewers received the material?
Have the reviewers confirmed their acceptance of the schedule?

Has the suitable venue been booked for conducting the inspection?
Have arrangement been made for the necessary equipment?
During the Inspection
Are all participants well prepared?
Is there agreement on the objectives of the inspection?
Are all the participants contributing?
Is the inspection well paced?
Is interest waning as the time is progressing?
Is everyone being heard?
Is anyone being tuned out?
Has someone (such as the producer/author) influenced/swayed
    participants with emotional arguments or other undue tactics?
Is there agreement on the outcome of the inspection?
Is that agreement truly understood by all participants?

Post-Inspection
Was the inspection successful?
Did the inspection reach a workable conclusion?
Was anybody responsible, if the inspection was not successful?
Is the report prompt and accurate?
Are all participants satisfied with the outcome?
Did the product get a fair and adequate treatment?
Does the producing group have a reasonable basis for clearing up
    the issues?
Have all relevant people received the appropriate information?
What can be done to improve the inspection process to make it bet-
    ter next time?
Has the required inspection data been gathered and recorded?
Have all identified problems been resolved or informed to appro-
    priate management level?

Checklist for Recorders (The Scribe)

Qualifications of the Recorder
Do you understand the purpose of inspections in general?
Do you understand why this particular inspection is being held?
Do you understand the jargon used and the formats used in this
    material?
Are you able to communicate with the type of people who will be
    in the inspection?
Have you ever participated in an inspection as a reviewer or as a
    reviewee?

Pre-Inspection
Can you identify, by name, the inspection leader and other partici-
    pants?

Have you arranged your schedule to allow time for the inspection?

Have you allowed time for the work you will have to do after the inspection?

Do you have the materials necessary for keeping an accurate record in the proper formats?

Do you have the resources available to carry out your job, during and after the inspection?

During the Inspection

Do you understand what an issue is?

Are you recording all issues?

Are you recording things that aren't really issues?

Are your notes accurate reflections of the comments received during the inspection?

Do you have copies of any supplementary material introduced as a part of any issue?

How much of your report consists of editorial commentary?

Is the outcome stated explicitly and unambiguously?

Are the issues recorded in neutral language?

Post-Inspection

Was the report promptly prepared?

Was the report accurate?

Was the report properly reviewed and signed?

Was it distributed to all relevant people including participants in the inspection?

Was all pertinent data on the inspection and its preparation gathered and provided to the moderator?

Conclusion

An inspection is a more formal review technique than Desk Check and Walkthrough. Overall, Inspections appear to provide a substantial increase in both development and particularly maintenance productivity, and also find many errors. However, since the results of Inspections (being a more formal review technique) are informed to management, people may feel threatened. There are some enthusiastic proponents of Inspections. Although Walkthroughs and Inspections have some common aspects, a disadvantage is that the Inspection process is dependent on the creation and use of less ambiguous design specification languages.

REFERENCES

[1] *Managing the Software Process*—Watts Humphrey (Addison Wesley)
[2] *Software Engineering: A Practitioner's Approach*—Roger Pressman (McGraw Hill International)

[3] *Software Inspections*—Tom Gilb and Dorothy Graham (Addison Wesley)
[4] *Walkthroughs, Inspections, and Technical Reviews*—Daniel Freedman and Gerald Weinberg (Dorset House Publishing)
[5] *Software Engineering Productivity*—C. Stevenson (Chapman & Hall)
[6] *A Discipline for Software Engineering*—Watts S. Humphrey (Addison Wesley)
[7] *Introduction to Team Software Process*—Watts S. Humphrey (Addison Wesley)
[8] *The Art of Software Testing* – Myers (John Wiley & Sons)
[9] *STQE Volume 4, Issue 2, March/April 2002* (The Software Testing and Quality Engineering Magazine)
[10] *A Slice-by-Slice Guide to Total Quality Management*—John Gilbert (Affiliated East-West Press Pvt. Ltd)

Chapter 7

SOFTWARE CONFIGURATION MANAGEMENT

7.1 Overview

"Change Management" is one of the fundamental activities of software engineering. This is because the business environments for which software applications are developed, themselves are very dynamic. Especially the rate of change in today's global economy and Internet days is beyond imagination. As a result of this, the business requirements and expectations from software applications keep changing. In fact, in the world of software project management, they say that change is the only reality. Changes to the requirements drive the design, and design changes affect the code. Testing then uncovers problems that result in further changes, sometimes even to the original requirements. Though the change process may sound simple in concept, it is quite complex in real-life large projects involving multi-teams at multi-locations. The number of communication channels in a team of the size n are: [n(n-1)/2]. The Number of co-ordination problems also increases exponentially with the project size. This is because the number of channels will rise exponentially as the team size increases. For even modest-sized projects, the number of people involved and the change volume generally require a formal change management system. That is the reason why there is a need for Software Configuration Management (SCM as popularly known). A key objective of the software process is to have change activity converge until the final product is stable enough to ship. Given this, it should be noted that management of ALL changes is important. Among change management activities, code control is typically the main focus but it is important to note that it is NOT the only activity under SCM. Control of requirements and design changes is also of critical importance. These functions are often handled as enhancements to code management system.

7.2 Configuration Management: Why and What

Before we start the discussion, here are some basic definitions pertinent to the topic of this chapter:

CONFIGURATION: *the arrangement of a computer system or components as defined by the number, nature, and interconnections of its constituent parts.*

CONFIGURATION MANGEMENT: *a discipline applying technical and administrative direction and surveillance to: identify and document the functional and physical characteristics of a configuration item, and control changes to those characteristics, report change processing and implementation status, and verify compliance with specified requirements.*

To know why configuration management, consider the following aspects of software:

- Software is Easy to Copy!
- Changes Are frequent
  - o Different Users/Customers have different Requirements
  - o Changes get clarified/known at a later date
  - o Business Environment, too, changes
  - o Technology Changes
  - o Personnel whims!
- Software Projects: Personnel Turnover
  - o Developers leave
  - o Users change
  - o Customer Single Point Contact Changes

All this further adds to the problems...already faced by the Project Main Classes of Problems Software Projects are:

- Double maintenance Problems
- Shared Data
- Simultaneous Updates
- Missing/Unknown Version Problem

For example, life of a typical project manager/project leader is full of anecdotes like the ones below:

- Listing seems OK: program does not work
- Works in Mumbai but not Chennai
- We had customized for this client. How do we install the upgrade now?
- I'd fixed this bug last month; How did it re-appear?
- I haven't changed the program. Why is it blowing up?
- Which is the latest source? I need to put a patch
- In the last month, the user asked for this change and she doesn't want it
- Where did Sunil leave the programs he was working on?

All this only means that change is inevitable when computer software is built. And change increases the level of confusion among software engineers working on the project. When change are not analyzed and documented before implementing then, confusion will result. Before making the changes, they need to be informed to those who need to know them (the testers, the end users etc). Thus, changes need to be controlled in a manner that will improve quality of the deliverable and reduce error.

.....The art of coordinating software development to minimize... confusion is called "configuration management". Configuration management is the art of identifying, organizing, and controlling modifications to the software being built by a programming team. The goal is to maximize productivity by minimizing mistakes.......

Roger Pressman [1] describes Software Configuration Management (SCM) to be an umbrella activity that is applied throughout the software process. Because change can occur at any time, SCM activities are developed to (1) identify change, (2) control change, (3) ensure that change is being properly implemented, and (4) report changes to others who may have to do with it.

It is important to make a clear distinction between software support and *software configuration management.* Support is a set of software engineering activities that occur after software has been delivered to the customer and put into operation. Software configuration management is a set of tracking and control activities that begin when a software engineering project begins and terminate only when the software is taken out of operation. Let us provide an IEEE definition of Software Configuration Management:

A discipline applying technical and administrative direction and surveillance to: identify and document the functional and physical characteristics of a configuration item, control changes to those characteristics, record and report change processing and implementation status, and verify compliance with specified requirements.

This definition of Configuration Management includes six points:

1. It is a **Management** discipline
2. It **Identifies** the proposed or implemented (actual) configuration of a system
3. This is done at discrete points in **time**
4. Systematically **records and traces** changes to all system components (conceptual and physical)
5. Provides tools for **control**ling changes; and finally
6. Allows everything happening with (and to) the system, throughout the entire life-cycle of the system, to be **verified** via auditing and reporting tools

All this is for purposes of assuring: integrity, accountability, visibility, reproducibility, project co-ordination and traceability and formal control of system/product evolution. In the context of this book, Configuration Management is a process used for efficiently developing and maintaining software. This is accomplished by improving: accountability, reproducibility, traceability and co-ordination.

"Configuration" is a list of parts and their relative arrangement. This includes the number, nature and interconnections of all constituent parts. To understand Configuration Management in the context of software systems, let us discuss what Software is:

o Structured information with hierarchical, logical and functional properties
o Created as text but maintained in several, and frequently parallel, representations during the life cycle of the product
o Machine 'processable' in its most advanced state
o Maintained in various forms, and with different tool, during development use, maintenance and operations
o Composed of parts which are themselves software
o Created via the use of tools, which are themselves also software

7.2.1 Nomenclature

Since the role of configuration management is to control the development of the system element as they are built and then combined/ integrated into a full system, it is important to establish a common system terminology before proceeding in the discussion on the topic of Software Configuration Management. This is depicted in the figure 1.

• *System* The package of all the software that meet's the user's requirements

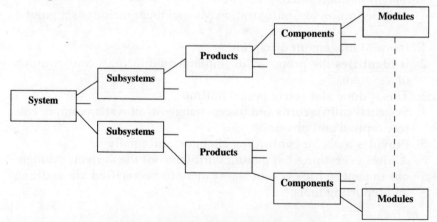

Figure 1: Software Product Nomenclature

- *Subsystem* Large systems can have many subsystems, such as communication, display and processing.
- *Product* subsystems typically contain many products. For example, an operating system might contain a control program, compilers, utilities and so forth.
- *Components* At the next level, a control program could be made up of such components of the sub-system.
- *Module* At the lowest level, components consist of a number of modules. Modules typically implement functions that are relatively small and self-contained.

7.3 Software Configuration Management Activities

The discipline of software configuration management has four major activities: **Identification, Control, Status Accounting** and **Auditing**. Here's a brief explanation to each of these activities. This will be followed by detailed treatment of each in subsequent sections.

- **Identification**: refers to the general structure of the product being produced and how the items (modules, classes etc) are to be identified
- **Control**: refers to the methods to be implemented for the management and technical control of myriad configuration items identified. (What is a "configuration item" will be defined later in this section.)
- **Status Accounting**: refers to reporting to all concerned—management, client and technical – information describing items and their status.
- **Auditing**: refers to activities, which are designed to assure the correct functioning of the SCM system, as defined.

This particular breakdown has been accepted as an industry standard. Firstly it was accepted by the IEEE as a document. Later this standard was accepted by the American National Standards Institute. The full history of IEEE is outside the scope of this book. The next sections will discuss each of the aspects of Configuration Management activities briefly.

7.3.1 Software Configuration Identification

Configuration Identification is described as: An element of configuration management, consisting of selecting the configuration items for a system and recording their functional and physical characteristics in technical documentation.

This is a formal definition as taken from part of the IEEE standard. A few points to ponder follow. The process of selecting configuration items is not quite as simple as it may seem. It is not merely a process of identifying that the system has (say) 50, or 500 files. This may be sufficient for small systems consisting of up to (say) 100 files. This begins to more complex when the system is large (several thousands files) and/or the interrelationships between the files are complex. As a hypothetical example, consider the following scenario:

A system which is composed of (say) four sub-systems, each of which is composed of several modules, each module being composed of several code units, which in turn also have several "include" files, all these contained in individual files. Also, there is a common set of 'library' routines, which everyone uses. In addition to this, we must maintain:

- Documentation
- The specifications and designs
- The test designs, data and reports
- The change and problem reports
- The 'make' files which direct and document the way the system is constructed (sometimes called 'build' files etc.)

This is a very small example of how the level of complexity rises, even for as small a system as in this example, due to both the quantities of individual items to be created and maintained and the complexities of their interrelationships. Thus, it is not just a question of simply 'selecting' the configuration items', but rather of deciding upon a general method for the process of selecting. Thus, the rules governing the process of software configuration identification (SCI) are:

- SCI defines the 'granularity' of the SCM (the concept of a generalized method for identification).
- SCI defines what is needed to be 'seen' i.e. the visibility to all those who need to know what is happening on the project.
- SCI ensures that the identification scheme selected reflects the structure of the product, the project and the organization.
- The identification process must always be coupled with a parallel process of labeling the item with a distinct and unique label.
- SCI is a critical project management task.

Let us understand what a "work product" is. Work products are tangible artifacts that are produced during the project. This includes models, reports, diagrams, plans, code and other documents, which are direct 'stepping stones' to the final deliverable. They have a specific purpose in the engagements and describe specific content using predefined semantics and syntax. Work products are produced as a result of performing one or more tasks. Some tasks produce less tangible outputs (e.g. pass or fail, trained staff) and are called 'task outcomes'.

Thus, we can say that a work product is an artifact that gets created in various phases of a (software) project. Some of the work products may undergo changes during the tenure of a project and so they need to be kept either under document control or configuration control. Thus, those work products that are likely to undergo change should be identified as "configuration item".

Thus, *Software Configuration Item* can be defined as work product or information that is created as part of the software engineering process. Given below are a few examples of work products that can be identified as configuration items. Note that there can be slightly different practices varying from organization to organization. For example, the last three work products mentioned below may be kept under document control.

- Requirements specifications
- Design Specifications
- Test Plans and Test Cases
- Source code
- Software Tools
- Software Configuration Management Plans
- Software Verification and Validation Plans
- User Manuals

Often there is confusion about what should be put under 'Document Control' v/s what should be under 'Configuration Control'. Any work product that is likely to undergo change during the tenure of the project (until the point of shipment), and forms as a deliverable to the customer and has to do with the way the customer is going to operate the given system, should be under configuration control. A work product other than this can be just under document control. This is purely author's view based on experience of practices seen adapted in the industry. The discussion of scope of a document control system is not within the scope of this chapter. Any standard reference on ISO 9001:2001 can be referred to understand the expectations from "document control".

7.3.1.1 Important Identification Principles

Now that we have gained a basic understanding of the concepts behind configuration identification, let us examine some principles that govern the process of identification of software items.

LABLES

Software items are labeled at discrete points in time. In a computerized environment, a date/time stamp is quite natural. From this we can say that *each item's label is related to labels of predecessors and siblings.* This relationship must be made obvious. It should have some logical hierarchical numbering scheme. For instance, an item labeled '2.3' clearly is later than something labeled '2.1' and earlier than '2.5'. This number is used here for illustrative purpose only. The label will usually consist of two parts; a name and a version number. The number is the time-related part, as it changes over time with each instance of the particular part being revised. The name must remain constant over time for this item.

BASELINING
The IEEE defines a baseline as:

(1) *A specification or product that has been formally reviewed and agreed upon, that thereafter serves as the basis for further development, and that can be changed only through formal change control procedures.*
(2) *A document or set of such documents formally designated and fixed at a specific time during the life cycle of a configuration item.*

Baseline through Analogy

Here is a wonderful analogy provided by Roger Pressman [1]

Consider the door to the kitchen in a large restaurant. One door is marked OUT and the other is marked IN. The doors have stops that allow them to be opened only in the appropriate directions

If a waiter picks up an order in the kitchen, places it on a tray and then realized he has selected the wrong dish, he may change to the correct dish quickly and informally *before* he leaves the kitchen through the door marked OUT

If, however, he leaves the kitchen, gives the dish to the customer and then is informed of his error, he *must* follow a procedure established by the restaurant: (1) look at the order placed to determine if an error has indeed occurred (2) apologize profusely, (3) return to the kitchen through the door marked IN, (4) explain the problem to the Chef, get the dish changed as per client specification stated on the order and so on......

Now with this analogy in mind, let us continue to discuss some more principles:

Partitioning a baseline is always subjective. So far we have discussed individual items. As shown in Figure 1, items can be aggregate of items. The topmost aggregate item is the product or system. Anytime this item (i.e. the system) is 'released', this is called a *baseline*.

Create some partition and maintain it. Whatever partition is decided upon, remember that once you have created a partitioning of the baseline, redoing it can be an enormous job. This is an early decision in the software project and all concerned must be consulted to make a 'correct' decision right from the beginning.

Baselines live forever! Once a baseline is created-defined-released for the first time, it is known as "input baseline". It (the input baseline) can never change! Subsequently, however, if a change has to be made, then it is a new baseline.

Revisions v/s Versions The difference between these two is a frequent source of confusion. This discussion refers to the numeric part of the label discussed earlier. The common industry wisdom seems to be this: 'revisions' refer to items that are 'internal' (to the developing organization) while the 'version' refers to released product out of the organization.

Visibility and Traceability.' Visibility' means permitting the software to be seen by anyone who is allowed to see it: permitting the management to 'see' what is happening and permitting the management to be seen on a project; that is, permitting them to really manage. 'Traceability' is the ability to link individual events and parts to each other in time backward as well as forward.

7.3.1.2 Configuration Identification Numbering

For the purposes of 'identification of items', a system of configuration identification numbers is both most common and most convenient. In most cases (except for very large and complex software systems) the numbering system should be kept simple. Typically, a numbering system for identifying the revisions of each item accompanied by a mnemonic is sufficient.

The most common method is the following:

- The version/revision number consists of two parts, separated by a dot
- The first part (that is, the part to the *right* of the dot) denotes the current revision from the last baseline.
- The second part (to the *left* of the dot) denotes the number of the last baseline
- Generally, the right-hand number will be fixed with each baseline

7.3.2 Software Configuration Control

We have stated that Software Configuration Management is a *discipline* intended to *facilitate the management of projects*. This means that in order to control software, the process of change must be controlled. The IEEE formal definition of the process is as follows:

Configuration Control: An element of configuration management, consisting of the evaluation, co-ordination, approval or disapproval, and implementation of changes to configuration items after formal establishment of their configuration identification.

While setting up the *configuration management scheme* for the organization of the project, the first thing will be that *levels of control* must be defined. Remember! *What you identified you must control!*

Software Configuration Control solves four of the most common problems facing software developers: the *double maintenance problem,* the *shared data problem,* the *simultaneous update problem* and the *missing/unknown version problem.* These problems are discussed in the following sections.

Double Maintenance problem is characterized by the following:

- Multiple copies of same software in use
- Fix in one—SHOULD FIX IN OTHERS
- Example
  - Same set of common routines in two systems
  - Same system installed at multiple sites
    * forgot to inform
    * sites detect bug at same time and "fix" the same bug differently!
- What is really required:
  - The Bug gets fixed in all copies
  - Fix same bug in identical manner in all copies

Shared Data Problem means:

- Changes made in one program interfere with proper functioning of other program
  - Example: subroutines, classes, DBMS definitions, header files, third party routines (DLLs/OCXs)
- Need
  - Control on modifications
  - Good communications

Simultaneous Update means:

- One module being worked on by more than one developer
  - Changes made by one developer disappear
- Need
  - Better division into modules
  - Ensure no simultaneous working

Missing/Unknown Version Problem means:

- Consciously decide which version to keep, which to destroy
- Use systematic method to identify versions and changes across versions
- Use consistent back-up procedures

7.3.3 Software Configuration Status Accounting

Basically, the main issue of Software Configuration Management is acquisition and maintenance of all information concerning a project's status and that of its parts. This status information must then be available for reporting to various levels of authority (i.e. anyone with the need to know!) Thus one needs to ask these questions: *WHAT* HAPPENED? *WHEN* DID IT HAPPEN? *WHAT* ARE THE *REASONS*? *WHO* AUTHORIZED THE CHANGE? *WHO* PERFORMED THE CHANGE? *WHAT ITEMS* WERE AFFECTED?

Time is always a critical part of status information. For each configuration item, regardless of whether the item is an individual item or an aggregate, a separate 'logical account' is maintained and transactions are recorded. Typically, a register/journal is required (either manually maintained or in form of a computer-based format) for recording these transactions. Moreover, transactions are not the only information which is recorded. In addition to the transactions, actual programming information is recorded upon the configuration item's archive. Reports are produced from the transaction log, from the archives, or from a combination of them. The section below describes the minimal list of reports that are part of the activity called "Configuration Status Accounting".

7.3.3.1 Configuration Status Accounting Reports

There are three reports, which must be called the 'most basic of reports', and must always be available. These are:

1. Transaction log
2. Change log
3. Item 'delta' report

Some other typically common reports are:

4. Resource usage
7. Stock status (status of all configuration items)
8. Changes in progress
9. Deviations agreed upon
10. Audit trail of all activities
11. File revision history
12. Traceability

The critical points to be aware of when attempting to define reporting requirements are:

- How much formality does the customer require?
- Who is audience for each report?
- Are project standards sub-ordinate to corporate standards?

7.3.3.2 *Change Control Board*

For discussion in the sections ahead, an important term needs to be described: CHANGE CONTROL BOARD (CCB) also called CONFIGU-RATION CONTROL BOARD (CCB) – *a group of people responsible for evaluating and approving/disapproving proposed changes to configuration items, and for implementation of approved changes.*

Typically, CCB members are:

- Project Managers
- User Representative
- Quality Controller
- Configuration Controller (appointed by the project manger)

In the following section, Change Log, Delta Report, Stock Status Report, Transaction Log are discussed.

7.3.3.3 *Change Log*

This log is implemented as an informal/formal notebook (the degree of formality would depend on the size and scope of the software project). However, preference in normal circumstances is to implement this log as computerized register/journal. In any case, the implementation method is always dependent upon the nature of the computing resourcing available with software project organization.

The log should contain all information relevant to, and regarding, requested changes in the system or any part thereof. The minimal distribution frequency of this report is monthly or event-driven (say a major release etc). Regardless of when the previous distribution of this report happened, this report will be (additionally) distributed before every formal review. The following minimum information is expected in the change log:

- Change number
- The change number will be assigned by the CCB (Change Control Board as described above) or the configuration controller
- Change request status type:
  o Request Opened
  o Pre-process evaluation
  o Authorized for implementation
  o In implementation
  o In pre-release testing
  o Released-originator notified of change
  o Processing suspended
  o Change request denied

- Change Request Originator details (name, designation, contact numbers, organization submitting the CR – Change Request etc)
- Impact Analysis brief– i.e. software elements or documents affected by this change request (Configuration Item number along with its version number)
- Change Request Origination date (the date the CR is first submitted)
- Change Description (A brief description of the submitted change)
- Details of the person who will carry out the Change Request when approved (the name, contact details his/her organization etc)
- Impact Analysis Details – the interfaces and impacts of the submitted change; including as applicable:
  o The impact on other systems
  o Configuration items
  o Other contractors
  o System resources
  o Training etc
  o Documentation
  o Hardware
- Follow-up action required to implement this change request (when approved by CCB)

7.3.3.4 Delta Report

This report is generated to summarize progress of the development and to compare this progress with status presented in the previous report. Also this report displays the differences between version n of a document/module and version $n + 1$. The report should include:

- Dates (the dates/reporting period of the report)
- Narrative (a summary of work performed during the reporting period including progress of each task or unit of work as of the end of the reporting period.) For example:
  Line i/module k change on dd.mm.yy
  Change resulted from change no.[_____]
  Staff Hours invested for change evaluation
  Staff Hours invested for change implementation
- Format:
  The description should be by tasks, and the breakdown of tasks and/or units of work should conform to the WBS—work breakdown structure as shown in the example below. (For basic grounding in WBS concepts and other minimal project management concepts, reader can browse through reference [2] quoted at the end of this chapter.)

Additional WBS No. affected	Additional Configuration Items affected
. . .	. . .
. . .	. . .
. . .	. . .

7.3.3.5 Stock Status Report

This report should summarize the status of each and all system changes which are in a defined state of 'OPEN'; and should indicate the following items:

- Inventory:
  A list of all the incomplete changes in the system
- Description:
  For each change, a brief description of the change should be included
- Status:
  Information related to change status
- Analyst/programmer/software engineer:
  The name, contact details and organization of the individual responsible for the change
- Completion date: the date for completing the change

7.3.3.6 Transaction Log

The transaction log is implemented as an informal notebook/register/ journal, when lack of computing resources in a software project do not allow for a better (i.e. computerized) option. Preferably, this log is implemented as a computerized register. In any case, the method of implementation would depend on the computing resources available with the software project organization.

The log contains comments of, and concerning activities, of the project with respect to Configuration Management. This report should clearly show the effect and relationships resulting from each and every event (Change Request, Change Notification etc.), which occurred during the course of the software project. At the end of this section (Table 1) we've provided a format for *Change Request*.

The purpose of Transaction Log is to provide visibility to all those concerned with the project and it should have the following minimum entries:

- Transaction number (a consecutive number for each and every entry on the log)

- Date and Time stamp (date and time of then entry and of the event)
- Originator (name of the person submitting the entry in the transaction log)
- Software element(s) or system part(s) affected
- Description of the activity (a brief description of the activity and conditions including relevant information)
- Change in Progress Report
- Participants: (the names of the persons involved in this activity)
- Impact (the impact of this activity, if any, on other planned activities of the project)
- Follow-up if required

Table 1: Change Request Form

Change Request

(To be filled in by person initiating request)

Initiated by: Date:

Project ID:

Type of Change:

Customer requirement

Review comments to be incorporated

Defects Identified

Bug Fix

Others (specify change)

Change description: (attach additional sheets, if necessary)

(To be filled in by the Project Leader/Person making the change)

Change request ID (filled in by the project leader):

Impact of change :

Sl. no.	CI s to be changed	Responsibility	Effort required

Planned start: Planned end:

Resources required:

Approver's Name: Signature:

Reason for rejection:

Change completed on: Verified by:

7.3.4 Configuration Auditing

A software configuration audit should periodically be performed to ensure that the SCM (Software Configuration Management) practices and procedures are rigorously followed. This audit can be performed directly by the specially appointed SCM staff or by some independent assurance function.

Every major baseline/release *must* be audited. For in-house systems, an informal audit is usually sufficient. Formal audit does not mean something that is unfriendly or antagonistic: the audit function is much too important for it to be relegated to someone who is not capable of performing in a manner conducive to healthy relationships. Periodic reviews *must* be held to determine progress. Of all project management functions, change control always is the most important thing to audit! Table 2 below presents a checklist for configuration audit.

Table 2: A Checklist for Configuration Audit

Sr. No	Description	Yes	No	NA
	Configuration Items (CIs)			
1.	Are the Configuration Items identified for the project?			
2.	Is the responsible person for each CI identified?			
3.	Are the CIs uniquely identified? Can changes to each CI be traced?			
	Configuration Control Board (CCB)			
4.	Does the CCB exist for the project?			
5.	Are all the activities specified in the plan carried out by CCB?			
6.	Does the Configuration Controller (CC) exist for the project?			
7.	Are the activities of CC carried out as per plan?			
	Baselining			
8.	Have the baselines identified?			
9.	Are the CIs comprising each baseline identified?			
10.	Has an input baseline established?			
11.	Are the baselines established as per plan?			
12.	Are the activities during base-lining carried out as per plan?			
13.	Is the tool to establish baseline and store and recover archive versions of configuration items identified and used?			
14.	Is the tool identified is used to establish baseline and store and recover archive versions of configuration items?			
15.	Is the integrity between the software baselines maintained?			
	Configuration Management Library System (CMLS)			
16.	Is the Configuration Management Library System established?			
17.	Does the CMLS support generation of reports?			
18.	Are the access rights on each CI for different individuals established in CMLS as per the plan?			

19. Is the Version Control procedure followed as defined in the plan?
20. Is the version numbering scheme and incremental scheme defined in the plan implemented?
21. Are the change requests handled as per the procedure defined in the plan?

Backup & Recovery

22. Has the Backup been taken as per plan?
23. Do the Backups exist at appropriate location as per plan?
24. Are the CIs recovered from archive at any time?
25. Is the recovery taken place according to the procedure defined in the plan?

Configuration Status Reporting

26. Are the status reports generated as per plan?
27. Are the status reports sent to the appropriate persons as per plan?
28. Are the status reports accessible to all affected individuals?
29. Do the reports give the proper status of the system?

Configuration Audits

30. Is the configuration audits taken place as per schedule?
31. Have the non-conformances observed during the previous audit been closed?

Synchronization (if applicable)

32. Is the code handled at multiple locations?
33. Is the synchronization of changes at the defined frequency as per plan?
34. Is the synchronization activity logged?

In this context, the term 'audit trail' is very important – let us understand what it means and why it should be a major concern. The idea is to provide as full a trace ('footprint) as possible. The intention is to provide 'project visibility'. All Software Configuration Management activities must leave some sort of residue upon the audit trail file. At the very least, all modifications to any archive (sometimes called a log file) are certainly to be reported. Audit trail information must contain four basic types of fields:

- Id of the group/individual member of the team issuing the command
- The command that was issued
- Which archive(s) have been processed
- What actions have occurred as a result of the command

Generally, configuration auditing is best performed by an external auditor i.e. someone external to the project team. Why—Because a very high degree of objectivity is required when auditing a critical management function. Figure 2 shows the audit process.

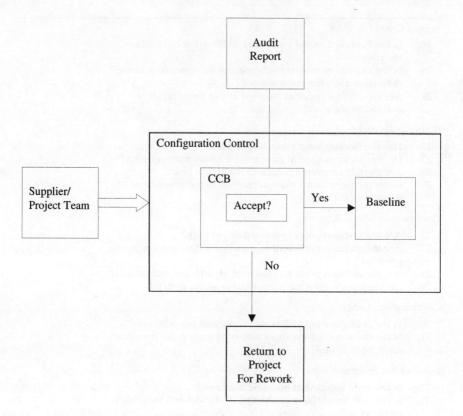

Figure 2: The Configuration Audit Process

7.3.4.1 Control over Suppliers and Subcontractors

It should be noted that the items or subsystems, which are developed by sub-contractor or supplied by vendor, must always be controlled and audited for Configuration Management. The main contractor of the project, or the customer, must be the one to determine their CM procedures.

The determination of sub-contractor Configuration Management requirements should be governed by a consistent concept of the needs of the agency issuing the contract. These requirements must be a part of the statement of work (SoW) issued to the subcontractor as part of the contract signed or work order issued. Sometime, there are 'cultural' differences in terms of maturity between the supplier/subcontractor and customer organization. The SCM requirements must be tailored to the product being developed but as a flow-down or result of those requirements governing the whole system. All SCM requirements for the subcontractor must be a result of co-ordination with the engineering functions, logistics and product/program management. Under no circumstances can the demand for a computerized SCM system be relinquished vis-à-vis the subcontractor. This is particularly true for software libraries. All issues and documentation governing the configuration identification and control of interfaces must be very well established and frequently audited.

7.3.4.2 Guidelines for Configuration Audit

With the discussion above in background, here're some general guidelines for SCM audits:

- SCM Audits are periodically needed to ensure the integrity of the software baselines.
- The SCM requirements should be adapted to the size, types and quantities of configuration items being developed.
- An audit is performed before every major baseline change or major release and non-conformances if any are tracked to closure and reported to all stake holders.
- The configuration audit team consists of qualified technical people who are not involved in the specific tasks being audited.
- The audit verifies that changes to the baseline are implemented as intended.
- The auditing function is an integral part of the SCM system.
- SCM auditing is continuous; with increased frequency and depth as development progresses.
- A documented project SCM plan is used as the basis for all SCM audits.

SCM audits are required prior to key checkpoints in each development phase. A phase review process then ensures that the proper actions are taken as follows:

1. *Requirements*—At the requirements phase review, SCM releases the software requirements and operational concept documents and places them under change control.
2. *Functional*—At the specification phase review, SCM releases the software specification document(s) and places it under change control.
3. *High-level design*—At the preliminary design phase review, SCM reviews the preliminary design documents, assigns configuration items as defined for the software components, and updates the configuration item index. SCM releases the preliminary design document, the software test plan, and the user documents, and places them under change control.
4. *Detailed Design*—At the detailed design phase review, SCM reviews the software detailed design documents, assigns configuration items according to the defined plan, and updates the configuration item

index. SCM also releases the software detailed design documents and places them under change control.

5. *Product*—SCM reviews the developed software to ensure that all programs are fully updated and have been tested and released to test and evaluation.

6. *Operational*—SCM ensures that all software components are fully updated and have passed appropriate acceptance tests.

7.4 Standards for Configuration Audit Functions

We'll discuss the standards here in three parts; ISO, CMM and IEEE.

In the older ISO standard (ISO 9000:1994) & ISO 9000-3 :1997 (Guidelines for application of ISO 9001 to the development, supply and maintenance of software), the clauses that directly address Configuration Management are:

- Clause 4.5   Document and Data Control
- Clause 4.8   Product Identification and Traceability
- Clause 4.12 Inspection and Test Status
- Clause 4.4.9 Design Changes (Design Control)
- Clause 4.13 Control of Non-conforming Products

Corresponding clauses (to those above from the older ISO standard) exist in the new ISO 9001:2000 standard as shown in the table below: We'll *not* provide here the full text of each clause. Interested readers are directed to reference [5]

Table 3: SCM and the ISO Standard (Old and New)

Clause from Old ISO Std (ISO 9000:1994)	Title	Clause from New ISO Std (ISO 9001:2000)	Title
4.5	Document and Data Control	4.2.3	Control of Documents
4.8	Product Identification and Traceability	7.5.3	Identification and Traceability
4.12	Inspection and Test Status	7.5.3	Identification and Traceability
4.4.9	Design Changes	7.3.7	Control of Design and Development Changes
4.13.1, 4.13.2	Control of Non-conforming Products	8.3	Control of Non-conforming Products

The details of the CMM are covered in a separate chapter. As far as CMM (Capability Maturity Model) is concerned, the following can be said in brief:

- Purpose
  - To establish and maintain the integrity of the products of the software project throughout the project's software life cycle
- Involves
  - Identifying configuration of software
  - Systematically controlling changes to configuration
  - Maintain integrity and traceability of configuration management
- Work Products under configuration Management
  - Software products to deliver
  - Items identified with or required to create them

CMM provides some goals pertaining to SCM; these are stated below:

- GOAL 1— Software Configuration management activities are planned
- GOAL 2— Selected software work products are identified, controlled, and Available
- GOAL 3— Changes to identified software work products are controlled
- GOAL 4— Affected groups and individuals are informed of the status and content of software baselines

CMM looks for the following *Commitments, Abilities and Activities* towards SCM in an organization:

Commitment

- COMMITMENT 1—The project follows a written organization policy for implementing software configuration management (SCM)
  - Responsibility explicitly defined
  - SCM throughout life cycle
  - For external and internal work products and designated support tools
  - Repository
  - Baselines audited periodically

Ability

- ABILITY 1—A board having the authority for managing the project's software Baselines (i.e. a software configuration control board exists or is Established
- ABILITY 2—A group that is responsible for coordinating and implementing SCM for the project (i.e. the SCM group) exists
- ABILITY 3—Adequate resources and funding are provided for performing the SCM activities

- ABILITY 4—Members of the SCM group are trained in the objectives, procedures and methods for performing their SCM activities
- ABILITY 5—Members of the software engineering group and other software related groups are trained to perform their SCM activities

Activities

- ACTIVITY 1— A SCM plan is prepared for each software project according to a documented procedure
- ACTIVITY 2— A documented and approved SCM plan is used a the basis for performing the SCM activities
- ACTIVITY 3— A configuration management library system is established as a repository for the software baselines (may have multiple control levels of SCM)
- ACTIVITY 4— The software work products to be placed under configuration management are identified
- ACTIVITY 5— Change requests and problem reports for all configuration items/units are initiated, recorded, reviewed, approved, and tracked according to a documented procedure
- ACTIVITY 6— Changes to baselines are controlled according to a documented Procedure
- ACTIVITY 7— Products from the software baseline library are created and their release is controlled according to a documented procedure
- ACTIVITY 8— The status of configuration item/units is recorded according to a documented procedure
- ACTIVITY 9— Standard reports documenting the SCM activities and the contents of the software baseline are developed and made available to affected groups and individuals
- ACTIVITY 10— Software baseline audits are conducted according to a documented procedure. It should be noted that here it is typically done in organizations by using standard checklists developed for configuration audit.

The CMM model also provides Measurement and Verification towards Configuration Management activities; however they are not discussed here. Interested readers can study the CMM model by

Visiting the site www.sei.cmu.edu

Now let us discuss about the standards produced by the Institute of Electrical and Electronic Engineers (IEEE). In 1976, a subgroup was formed under IEEE to develop a software quality assurance standard.

This has resulted in over 20+ standards and guides for related to software. The ones related to Software Configuration Management are:

- IEEE-SCM 828–1990 : Standard for SCM Plans
- IEEE-SCM 1042–1987 (r: 1993): Guide to SCM

IEEE standards do not take you towards 'certification' but this standard can be used to implement the requirements of ISO or CMM for SCM. Here is a brief overview on both the IEEE standards mentioned above:

IEEE-SCM 828-1990: Standard for SCM Plans

- Introduction
  - Purpose of the plan, scope of the SCM plan, intended use of the SCM plan, overview of the project, SCM issues and risks in project context, degree of SCM formality, limitations, assumptions, terminologies, references to other documents
- SCM Management
  - Software Project Organization structure, roles and responsibilities, directives and policies, references to (organization's or customer's) procedures and standards to be followed (in the context of SCM)
- SCM Activities
  - Configuration items identification, change management and configuration control, status accounting, configuration audits, interface and subcontractor control
- SCM Procedures
  - Sequence of SCM events, dependence between SCM activities, relationship to other key project milestones
- SCM Resources
  - Personnel, Tools, techniques, Equipments, Training, use of other personnel
- SCM Plan Maintenance
  - Responsibility, conditions for update, approvals communication of changes

IEEE-SCM 1042-1987 (r:1993):Guide to SCM

- Provides guidance in planning software configuration management practices that are compatible with IEEE 828. In Table 4 below we have provided a checklist. It can be used for evaluating the scope of system under consideration for the preparing Software Configuration Management Plan (SCMP)

**Table 4: Checklist for Evaluating the Scope of the System for
Software Configuration Management Plan**

- *Are the boundaries the system to be audited clearly delineated?*
- *Have these definitions been made a part of the systems specification?*
- *Has the purpose of the system and the function of the computers been clearly defined?*

- *Have the criteria for systems requirements allocation to the various configuration items been clearly established and made public?*
- *Is the Configuration Management system to be audited clearly defined?*
- *Have all tools to be used for the management of the system's configuration been put into place, or has a clear schedule been allocated for such?*
- *Does an organization exist for the performance of the configuration Management duties?*
- *Are the Configuration Management audits defined publicly?*

- It is intended for software developers, software management community, those responsible for preparing SCM plans
- The guide is structured as two parts:
  o Main body presents overview, principles, issues, lessons essential concepts, etc.
  o Second part contains 4 sample plans
    – For critical software for embedded systems
    – For experimental development of small systems
    – For a software maintenance organization
    – For a product line system

Figure 3 presents a snapshot for IEEE standard towards Software Configuration Management.

Define Organization's Standard SCM Process		
SCM Planning Procedure	SCM Plan Template	
Change Management Procedure	Change Request Form	Tailoring Guidelines
SCM Audit Procedure	Configuration Audit Checklist	

Guidelines for Repository Structure	Guidelines for SCM Accounting & Reporting	Guidelines for selection And Use of SCM Tools
	Guidelines for SCM Training	

Figure 3: IEEE: SCM Snapshot

7.5 Personnel in SCM Activities

As in any management discipline, it is critical to question *who is to perform the task of configuration management*. Characteristics of personnel needed for efficient performance of Software The organization must give close attention to Configuration Management tasks. This section describes some of this information in a summary manner. In principle, there are five information items concerning the 'people-ware' that must be examined in detail.

1. The **number of personnel** needed for each software configuration management task (the tasks of SCM have been discussed in the previous sections of this chapter)—this will form an important consideration for project budgeting. Usual rule of thumb is that, once the system has been set up, we should need one person per project group, for about five percent of their professional time on core project job.
2. The **expected skill levels** for all those involved—the professional to set up the system up must be at a very high skill level. The person to run the configuration management system can be at a much lower level.
3. The **job titles** of those who perform the tasks are significant but these can vary depending on the project organization, degree of formality required, which in turn is dictated by the scope and complexity of the software project at hand.
4. **Geographic locations**—are all the people co-located at one geography/city/building/site, or are some of them located at a remote site. While using a client/server based SCM tools this factor plays a critical role in setting up the computer-based Configuration management tools.
5. Are any special **security** clearances needed? This does not only refer to 'military' kinds of security! Many commercial organizations have security issues to deal with (they have their internal audit programs to audit those who audit!). Certainly, all organizations must, at very least, have back-ups to prevent loss in case of hardware failure.

7.6 Software Configuration Management: Some Pitfalls

So far, we have discussed the ideal situations for Software Configuration Management i.e. how things should be with respect to SCM. However, life in not known to be simple and as a result, SCM situations to transgress from' ideal' to something far less than ideal. Of course, like for most things in life, many factors contribute to this and the idea in this section is to discuss them so that we can understand how to avoid them. These anti-patterns can be summarized as indicated below. A full discussion on each of them is not within the scope of this book; the interested readers can visit reference [6]. Before that, let us have a quick discussion on the notion of 'anti-pattern'. Anti-Pattern is defined as "a commonly occurring solution to a problem that generates decidedly negative consequences; in other words, an Anti-Pattern is generally a commonly repeated practice in industry that is flawed in some manner and that causes symptoms that are more undesirable than whatever positive results were sought. In sum, 'anti-patterns' are the syndromes to be watched for.

- *Silver Bullet*—the mistaken belief that a tool can solve all your configuration management problems.
- *CM Takeover*—situation where configuration management becomes an all-consuming task; an end unto itself.
- *Developer-Software Configuration Management*—what happens when configuration management is left to the development team rather than an independence configuration management organization.
- *Decentralized Configuration Management*—insight into the value of centralized repository for performing development and configuration management.
- *Failure to Audit*—team fails to implement one of the fundamental aspect of configuration management; performing configuration audit.
- *Object Oriented Configuration Management*—Criticality of configuration management to object-oriented projects, which have varying levels of granularity and degree of complexity introduced by object-oriented development.
- *Software Configuration Management Expert*—those instances where unqualified individuals are given project configuration management responsibilities, and who don't know that they are not qualified.
- *Postmortem Planning*—importance of planning, and follow-through for configuration management, and results you get if you don't.

Conclusion

Software Configuration Management (SCM) is an all too important activity throughout a software project. When the project is large and complex, it requires an SCM control over requirements and specifications to ensure that the product is build and tested as per expressed requirements of the customer. SCM is an umbrella activity and as such, it should be maintained over the design of an application throughout the software development life cycle (SDLC) to ensure its integrity and maintainability. For this, requirements baselines, specification baselines, design baselines etc are established and maintained at appropriate points throughout the development cycle.

As a first step towards establishing the SCM, a software configuration management plan should be developed. Project naming conventions are established and a family of forms and procedures is provided to ensure that every change is recorded, reviewed and tracked. The software requirements specification (SRS) document is used as a basis for the design and development work and further up to acceptance testing stage.

During the design phase, SCM maintains control over the design. As changes are made, the appropriate design document is updated correspondingly. SCM facilities are also required to record all change to the code. For large projects and for all projects during the maintenance phase, procedures are needed to handle the development of simultaneous versions of the same program. The tools used to design, implement, test and maintain the software must also be maintained under configuration control as these, two may undergo versions change; especially in case of long running projects.

Software Configuration status accounting is aimed at maintaining a continuous record of the status of all base-lined items. Software configuration audits are periodically performed to ensure that the SCM practices and procedures are followed as per SCM plan.

REFERENCES

[1] *Software Engineering: A Practitioner's Approach*—Roger Pressman (McGraw-Hill International)
[2] *Effective Project Management*—Robert K. Wysocki, Robert Beck Jr., David B. Crane (Wiley Computer Publishing)
[3] *The Capability Maturity Model : Guidelines for Improving the Software Process* (Carnegie Mellon University—Software Engineering Institute)
[4] *CMM in Practice*—Pankaj Jalote (Addison Wesley)
[5] *Implementing ISO 9001:2000 : The Journey from Conformance to Performance*—Tom Taormina (Prentice Hall PTR)
[6] *Anti-Patterns and Patterns in software Configuration Management*—William Brown (Wiley Computer Publishing)

Chapter 8

ISO 9001

8.1 Overview

In Chapter 2, we had an extensive discussion on Quality (Management) System—the QMS. ISO 9001 is a well-conceived *standard* to achieve continual improvement. In normal language, *quality* is often linked to an idea of "excellence". Excellence can be achieved through continuous focus on "process improvement. In Chapter 9, we have discussed, a number of models for Process Improvement. ISO 9001:2000 is mentioned there. In this chapter, our focus is only ISO 9001.

The discussion in this chapter is broadly divided into three parts; the structure of ISO, its working (these are the lesser known details of ISO) and its brief history. Then there is a discussion about the 2000 revision of ISO giving an overview of the clauses in this new revised ISO 9001:2000 standard. Preparing for ISO Audits/Assessments and use of consultants etc. is also discussed briefly.

A couple of points to be noted—although many people believe this to be so, the word "ISO" is not the acronym for the organization but is derived from the Greek word "isos" meaning equal; as in isobars (equality of laws), isonomy (people before the law). Often ISO 9000 and TQM get mentioned together. The concept of delighting customers leads into *Total Quality Management* (TQM), which is considered a step beyond what can be achieved by putting in an effective *quality management system* (QMS) such as through use of ISO 9000 as a framework for *process improvement*. However, the difference between fully meeting customer requirements and delighting them, is in practice slight, possibly more semantic than real.

8.2 What is ISO 9000

The International Organization for Standardization (ISO) is a worldwide federation of national standards bodies, one from each from over one hundred and forty countries. The table below shows the details regarding member constitution of ISO. (The data is as of January 2003).

Table 1: Member Constitution of ISO

Members	146	National standards bodies, comprising
	94	Member bodies (P-Members)
	37	Correspondent members (O-Members)
	15	Subscriber members
Technical Committee	2 937	Technical bodies, comprising
Structure	188	Technical committees
	550	Subcommittees
	2 175	Working groups and
	24	Ad hoc study groups
Staff Technical	36	Member bodies provide the administrative and technical services for the secretariats of technical committees (TC) and sub-committees (SC) These services equal a full-time staff of
	500	Persons
Secretariats		
Central Secretariat	163	Full-time staff from
in Geneva	25	Countries coordinate the worldwide activities of ISO
Financing	140	Million CHF per year is estimated as the operational expenditure for the ISO work, of which
	80%	Is financed directly by
	36	Member bodies holding TC and SC secretariats, and
	20%	Through member body subscriptions and publications income, covering the costs of the Central Secretariat

ISO is a non-governmental organization, which sees its mission as the promotion of the development of standardization and related activities in the world. Its work results in international agreements, which are published as International Standards. Figure 1 shows the structure of ISO.

ISO is made up of three categories of members as you can see in Table 1 above. *Member Body of ISO* is the national body most representative of Standardization in its country and as such there is only one such body admitted to membership. They have full voting rights and are known s "P-Members".

Correspondent member is usually an organization in a country, which does not yet have a fully developed national standards activity. They do not participate in policy or development work but are entitled to be kept fully informed concerning relevant issues. They are known as "O-Members"

Subscriber membership is for countries with very small economies and as a result they pay reduced membership fees. However, this membership does enable them to maintain contact with international standardization work.

8.3 The Origins of ISO 9000

The origins of ISO 9000 lie in wartime and the defense industry. The problem of defects in ammunition and the need for reliability in equipment on which survival might depend, moved the focus to controlling how the work was done. Eventually this led to defined standards for quality management to which defense contractors were expected to work. As the concept of *quality management* and *quality systems* became known, buyers in non-defense industries started to demand that their own suppliers of technical products adopt quality systems.

Thus, it all started in the electro technical field and its forerunner was the IEC—the International Electro-Technical Commission, which was created in 1906. In addition, the International Federation of the National Standardizing Associations (ISA), which was created in 1926, undertook other pioneering work, primarily in mechanical engineering.

The Second World War interrupted their work and subsequent to a meeting of twenty-five countries in 1946, a new international organization was created with the objective of "the facilitation of the international co-ordination and unification of industrial standards". With this, ISO was duly formed and began its official functions on 23rd February 1947.

8.4 How Does ISO (as an organization) Carry Out Its Work?

The work of ISO is carried out by a hierarchy of "technical committees (TCs) sub-committees (SCs) and working groups (WGs) as shown in Figure 1.

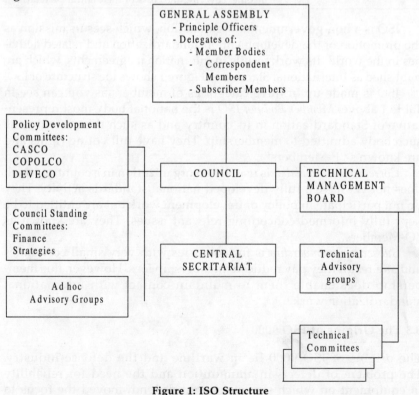

Figure 1: ISO Structure

All these TCs, SCs and WGs total up to more than 2500 groups. With these committees there are qualified industry representatives, research institutes, consumer bodies, government authorities and world wide international organizations whose objective is the resolution of global standardization issues. They are all of equal status within a group and it is estimated that more than 30,000 experts participate in meetings each year.

The Central Secretariat of ISO, located in Geneva, co-ordinates the dissemination of documentation; facilitates clarification with chairmen and the agreement of technical content by committees; co-ordinates meetings and generally provides overall support.

ISO issues a publication, *ISO Memento*, which provides information on the scope of responsibility, organizational structure and secretariats for each ISO Technical Committee. Detailed rules of procedure for technical work are given in ISO/IECC directives and are beyond the scope of discussion in this chapter.

8.5 ISO Standards Development Process

An International Standard is the result of an agreement between the member bodies of ISO through the development process of the technical committees (TCs) and the sub-committees (SCs). The process has six stages as shown below:

- Stage 1   Proposal Stage
- Stage 2   Preparatory Stage
- Stage 3   Committee Stage
- Stage 4   Enquiry Stage
- Stage 5   Approval Stage
- Stage 6   Publication Stage

Brief details on each of the stages mentioned above are provided below.

Stage 1 (Proposal)

The first step is to ascertain the need for a proposed standard. To evaluate the proposed standard, a new work item is submitted for vote by the members of the relevant TC/SC to determine if the item is to be added to the work program. The proposal is accepted only if a majority of the P-Members (refer section 8.2) of the relevant TC/SC vote in favour and that at least five P-members declare that they are committed to participate in the project actively. This normally results in the appointment of a project leader.

Stage 2 (Preparatory)

Typically, a group of experts, together with the project leader (appointed at the end of Stage 1), is established and they prepare a working draft. Successive drafts are potentially possible until the group is satisfied that the best technical solution has been developed. At this point, the draft is released as a "Committee Draft" and passed to the group's parent committee for the next consensus building stage.

Stage 3 (Committee)

Upon creation of the first draft it is registered by the ISO Central Secretariat (refer Figure 1) and distributed for comment by P-Members of the TC/SC. Successive committee drafts may also be considered until consensus is reached on the technical content. Once the consensus has been reached, the text is finalized for submission a "Draft International Standard" (DIS).

Stage 4 (Enquiry)

The DIS (Draft International Standard) is circulated to all the ISO member bodies by the ISO Central Secretariat for voting and comment within a period of five months. It is approved for submission as a "Final Draft International Standard" (FDIS) if a two-thirds majority of the P-members of the TC/SC are in favour and not more than one quarter of the total number of votes cast are against. In the event that the text is unapproved, it is returned to the originating TC/SC for further evaluation and study and revised document is then subjected to the above approval process.

Stage 5 (Approval)

The FDIS (Final Draft International Standard) is circulated to all ISO member bodies by the ISO Central Secretariat for a final Yes/No vote within a two month period. If technical comments are received at this stage, they are registered and held over to the next revision of the International Standard. If two thirds of the P-members of the TC/SC are in favour and not more than one quarter of the total number of votes cast are against, the FDIS text is approved. However, if these criteria are not fulfilled, the standard is referred back to the originating TC/SC for re-consideration of the technical reasons submitted supporting the negative votes.

Stage 6 (Publication)

Once the FDIS has been approved, no other amendments are allowed other than minor editorial changes. The text is then passed to the ISO Central Secretariat who then publish it as the "International Standard".

8.6 How the ISO 9000 Family of Standards Wok

With this background, let us now understand how the ISO 9000 family of standards works. Although the requirements for a quality system are standardized—most of us like to think our business is unique. So how does ISO 9000 allow for the diversity of say, on the one hand, a small enterprise, and on the other, to a multinational manufacturing company with service components, or a public utility, or a government administration? The answer is that ISO 9000 lays down *what* requirements your quality system must meet, but does not dictate *how* they should be met in your organization—which leaves great scope and flexibility for implementation in different business sectors and business cultures...as well as different national cultures. Thus, ISO 9000 does not take a 'prescriptive' approach; it is a *'normative'* standard.

The ISO 9000 family includes standards that give organizations guidance and requirements on what constitutes an effective quality management system. ISO 9004-1 (and the other parts of ISO 9004) are the standards giving guidelines on the elements of quality management and a quality system. The family also includes models against which this system can be audited to give the organization and to its clients assurance that the system is operating effectively. As with the previous version (ISO 9000:1994), three quality assurance models are ISO 9001, ISO 9002 and ISO 9003 (the new revision is discussed in the next section). Lastly, the family includes a standard on terminology, and other standards, which can be described as "supporting tools", that give guidance on specific aspects, such as auditing quality systems.

8.7 ISO 9001:2000

Figure 3 in Chapter 2 shows the diagrammatic overview of the concept behind the 2000 revision of ISO. Readers may find it of interest to know that the first revision to ISO 9000:1987 came in 1994. This resulted in ISO 9000:1994. It was a combination of minor enhancements and classification of ambiguities. The year 2000 revision (known as the ISO 9001:2000) is a "total re-write" of the 1994 standard. The twenty elements of the ISO 9000:1994 (some people refer to them as the "20 clauses") have been replaced by the clauses summarized below.

- Quality Management System (with 2 sub-clauses within it)
- Management Responsibility (with 6 sub-clauses within it)
- Resource Management (with 4 sub-clauses within it)
- Product Realization (with 6 sub-clauses within it)
- Measurement, Analysis and Improvement (with 5 sub-clauses within it)

(For a detailed mapping between the older ISO 9000:1994 and the new ISO 9001:2000 standard readers can refer to ref [3].

It should be noted that although all 20 of the elements/clauses of the older version of ISO (ISO 9000:1994) are contained in the 5 clauses of the current version of the ISO Standard (ISO 9001:2000), there are substantial changes and new requirements have been laid down. They include the following (Major and Minor changes):

- *Elimination of ISO 9002 and ISO 9003*
- The ability to exclude sections of ISO 9001 that do not apply to your organization
- Redefinition of ISO 9000 to "Fundamentals and Vocabulary", which eliminated ISO 8402
- Redefinition of ISO 9004 to "Guidelines for Performance Improvements"
- Commonality of the formats of ISO 9000, ISO 9001, and ISO 9004
- Change from "Quality Assurance System" to "Quality Management System" (QMS)
- Encouragement of using "the *process approach*" (Ref Figure 3 in Chapter 2)
- The use of the term "organization" rather than "supplier"
- The use of term "records" instead of "quality records"
- *Enhancing the scope of the term 'Product* " to mean hardware, software, services, and processed materials.
- Reduction in the number of documented procedures required (from 18 to 6)
- Slight increase in the number of required records (from 17 to 21)
- Identification of processes, their sequences, and interaction
- Establishing the need for criteria and methods for effective operation and control of processes
- Evidence of management commitment to QMS
- Establishment of *measurable quality objectives*
- Opening channels of *internal communications*
- Addressing and measuring *customer satisfaction* with focus on meeting customers' needs and expectations
- Identifying *competency needs*
- Evaluating *training effectiveness*
- Making employees aware of how their work affects the QMS
- Managing the *human and physical work environment*
- Communicating awareness of customer requirements
- Communicating with customer at all levels
- Expanding monitoring and measuring activities to run the QMS
- Controlling processes as well as products
- Expanding statistical techniques to *data analysis* and taking action on the data

- Building a *continual improvement* model

Thus, in summary, the ISO 9001:2000 is now structured in following sections (Refer Figure 2.)

Foreword
0 Introduction
1. Scope
2. Normative Reference
3. Terms and definitions
4. Quality Management System
5. Management Responsibility
6. Resource Management
7. Product Realization
8. Measurement, analysis and improvement

Those who are quite familiar with the older version (ISO 9000:1994) may like to note that sections 4-8 (indicated above) contain the clauses 4.1 to 4.20 together with additional requirements (indicated through the major and minor changes already discussed). With this in the background, let us discuss the organizational need for the ISO Standard.

8.8 Why do Organizations Need ISO 9000?

The ISO 9000 family of standards represents an international consensus on good management practices with the aim of ensuring that the organization can time and time again deliver the product or services that meet the client's quality requirements. These good practices have been distilled into a set of standardized requirements for a quality management system (QMS), regardless of what your organization does, its size, or whether it's in the private, or public sector.

There is a business case for the need for the ISO Standard. Often, people ask 'Why Should my organization implement ISO ? The answer is really simple! The existence of an organization without customers, or with dissatisfied customers, is in peril! To retain customers—and to keep them satisfied—your product (which may, in fact, be a service) needs to meet their requirements. ISO 9000 provides a tried and tested framework for taking a systematic approach to managing your business processes (your organization's activities) so that they consistently turn out product conforming to the customer's expectations. And that means consistently happy customers! This aspect of ISO is represented well in Figure 3 of Chapter 2. (We have repeated this figure below for readers' quick reference—see Figure 2 on the next page)

8.9 ISO Certification

8.9.1 Importance of the Certification

The organization should carry out auditing of its ISO 9000-based quality system itself to verify that it is managing its processes effectively—or, to put it another way, to check that it is fully in control of its activities. In addition, the organization may invite its clients to audit the quality system in order to give them confidence that the organization is capable of delivering products or services that will meet their requirements.

Lastly, the organization may engage the services of an independent quality system certification body (the Registrars) to obtain an ISO 9000 certificate of conformity. This last option has proved extremely popular in the market place because of the perceived credibility of an independent assessment (the topic of assessment has been covered in great details in a later section of this chapter). It may thus avoid multiple audits by the organization's clients, or reduce the frequency or duration of client audits.

The certificate can also serve as a business reference between the organization and potential clients, especially when supplier and client are new to each other, or far removed geographically, as in an export context. In a way, it is a risk-mitigation exercise (the risk is not being able to meet quality requirements in the product/service to be purchased by the customer and to be supplied by the vendor.)

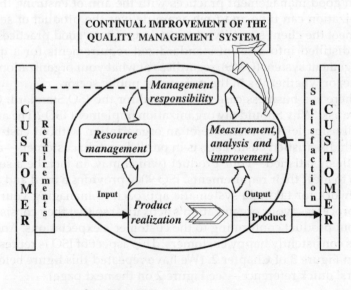

Legend: ⟶   **Value adding**
       - - ▸   **Information**

Figure 2: Conceptual Presentation of the QMS Model

8.9.2 Getting Ready for ISO Certification

From the discussion so far in this chapter, and Chapter 2, it should become apparent that the quality (management) system or the *QMS* requirements and *procedures* (they are the heart of the QMS) developed to implement them all closely lock together. The quality triangle illustrated in Figure 3 represents this concept.

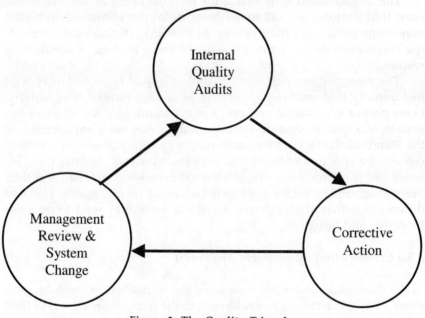

Figure 3: The Quality Triangle

Clause 8.2.2 of ISO 9001:2000 is stated below. As per that, a process for internal (quality) audit is required. Such audits must be carried out by trained staff (suitable training can be provided internally).

Clause 8.2.2: Internal Audit

The organization shall conduct internal audits at planned intervals to determines whether the quality management system

a) *conforms to the planned arrangement to the requirements of this International Standard and to the quality management system requirements established by the organization and*

b) *is effectively implemented and maintained.*

An audit program shall be planed, taking into consideration the status and importance of the processes and areas to be audited, as well as the results of previous audits. The audit criteria, scope, frequency and methods

---

> *shall be defined. Selection of auditors and conduct of audit shall ensure objectivity and impartiality of the audit process. Auditors shall not audit their own work.*
>
> *The responsibility and requirements for planning and conducting audits, and for reporting results and maintaining records shall be defined in a documented procedure.*

The management responsible for the area being audited shall ensure that actions are taken without delay to eliminate detected non-conformities and their causes. Follow-up activities shall include the verification of the actions taken and the reporting of verification results.

The management personnel planning a quality system may well feel initially that auditing appears to be a dull, bureaucratic activity. Done properly, it is none of these, and is essential for the effective operation of a quality system. Even if *auditing* was not a requirement of the Standard (ISO 9001:2000), any quality system will almost certainly cease to be effective without this important process. Furthermore, *internal audits* mirror the work of external assessors/auditors and thus prepare a company for the final (external) assessments/audits. The only difference is that often-internal auditor's work may tend to be more thorough and 'tougher'.

8.9.3 Certification, Assessment and Audit

In the discussion above we have used the terms "audit" and "assessment". We also have made a reference to the term *certification*. We now spend some time of these terms. Often people ask if there is any difference between the terms *Assessment* and *Audit*. Various opinions exist on this. In one of early works on software assessment, Roger Pressman (the author of the well known book "Software Engineering: A Practitioner's Approach) defines the *assessment* as 'a structured investigation of the current state of the software engineering practice'. Pressman relates the two terms by stating that *audit* is a primary mechanism for the *assessment*.

The IEEE has a specific definition of an audit: 'Audit—An independent examination of a work product or set of work products to assess compliance with specifications, standards, contractual agreements or other criteria' (IEEE STD-610). In reality, the term 'audit' is associated with more formal inspections and certifications performed by external resources (like a financial audit). Using the word 'audit' to refer to *software process assessment* can create a mental barrier between the assessment team and the assessment participants.

ISO documents define the concepts of *certification* and *audit* as follows: *Certification* or *third-party assessment* (referred to as 'registration' in some countries—including India), is carried out by an independent organization against a particular standard (ISO being one of them). Watts Humphrey's view (he is the author the of the world famous book "Managing the Software Process") is that 'a software process assessment is not an audit but a review of a software organization to advise its management and professionals on how they can improve their operation.

There are some more expert views on these terms [4]. *'Certification'* is the procedure by which a third party gives written assurance that a product, process or services conforms to specified characteristics. *'Assessment'* is the process of comparing the actual *measurements* (topic of measurements is discussed in detail in Chapter 5) of the characteristics of interest with the specifications of those characteristics. The most common perception of 'certification' is that it gives some form of 'guarantee' generally of quality and dependability in their widest senses. At least it is assumed that the risks of failure are reduced because certification involves some form of independent assessment.

Having discussed the terms—audit assessment and certification, let us now turn to the various types of audits and assessments.

8.9.4 Types of Assessments

Generally, there are three different types of assessments depending on who plays the main role in an assessment.

- *Self-Assessment*: Also known as *'first-party assessment'*. This refers primarily to a situation where the assessment is performed internally inside the software development organization; mainly by its own personnel. The main objective is to identify the organization's own *software process capability* and initiate an action plan for *software process improvement*. First party assessment can also be performed as guided first-party assessment where external assessors act as assessment methodology facilitators and coaches for the internal assessment team.
- *Second-party Assessment:* Also known as *'capability determination'*. This is an assessment where external assessors are used to perform the assessment. The main objective is to evaluate the organization's capability to fulfill specific contract requirements.
- *Third-party Assessment:* Also known as 'capability determination'. This is performed by an independent third-party organization. The main objective is to verify the organization's ability to enter contracts or produce software products, and sometimes to provide the fulfillment of certification according to a selected standard.

8.9.5 Types of Audits

The classification provided below is consistent is consistent with the British Standard Institution's classification of an audit.

- *First-party Audit:* When an organization carries out an *internal audit,* the procedure is referred to as *'first-party' audit.* This is done by organizations to check its quality procedures before any third party is invited to carry out a formal *compliance audit* (compliance means adhering to something specified as standard). An internal audit is equivalent to self-assessment.
- *Second-party Audit:* A *second- party audit* is an audit of an organization' relevant products and processes by a customer (acquirer). The product or quality system standards are typically selected by the customer and specified as a part of the contract. Second-party audits may be relatively narrow in scope because the purchasing organization examines only those elements and activities that relate to the products and services being purchased/acquired. The pre-contract survey is an example of a second-party audit.
- *Third-party Audit:* This is an audit of an organization at its own request and expense carried out by an external, impartial body referred to as a *certification body,* which is not a direct customer. The third-party audit is invariably performed against the requirements of a national or international standard such as ISO 9001.

8.10. Assessment/Audit Preparation

A quality (management) system cannot be realistically assessed until it has operated for some time. The assessment process involves the 'hard' evidence of completed records required by the procedures/processes. It should be noted that assessment, like 'internal auditing' can also include observing and talking to the staff. To build up an adequate body of such data takes time and until this is sufficient, a meaningful assessment cannot be carried out. It is for this reason that most assessment bodies will insist on a certain preparatory period. Sometimes the consultants play this role of assessment body. (The next section has discussion on the role of ISO consultants)

8.10.1 Gestation Period

How long is this period? Most assessors/consultants are likely to require a minimum of about three months, but longer may well be appropriate, depending on many aspects of the aspirant organization, its internal structures, business processes, nature of products/services etc. There are arguments against being 'over-cautious" and waiting too long for assessment. (Readers should keep in mind the "types of assessments" discussed in section 8.9.4)

8.10.2 Importance of Internal Audit

Internal auditing is especially vital from this perspective. The aim of internal audit should be to cover the whole system between implementation and final assessment. In this way, problems and gaps should be identified and dealt with before an assessor picks them up. In short, the importance of effective internal auditing cannot be over-emphasized.

An option before full assessment is a pre-assessment audit. This is in effect a dummy run of the real thing and unlike routine internal audits, it is carried out by outsiders. An ISO consultant involved (much more on this in the next section) throughout the project (of getting the organization ISO certified) can be considered for this work. However, it should be noted that if the same individual is involved, certain "independence" is lacking. Although there are many freelances and other independent organizations offering this service, (as we'll see in section 8.13.1) the obvious choice for pre-assessment is the external body that will carry out the final assessment. This way, at least you learn how the particular body carries out the assessment process.

Pre-assessment is particularly appropriate for organizations with little of no outside help. In such cases, it (the pre-assessment) may identify areas of the quality (management) system which are weak, or do not fully match up to ISO 9001 requirements.

8.10.3 Cost and other strategic considerations

If an organization is concerned to keep costs down then it as well may trust its own judgment on the effectiveness of its QMS (quality management system) and go straight for the final assessment. If the first attempt is unsuccessful, then little is lost since the money saved (assuming that the organization did not hire external consultant help!) will cover a second full assessment. However, there is a counter to this argument too—what about the staff de-motivation upon having "failed" the assessment and also the top management disappointment as well as "loss of faith"? Also, a fact remains that a pre-assessment may have a larger "diagnostic" element than a full assessment (where how to put right a problem may not get fully addressed). Finally, another argument against spending money on pre-assessment is that it may be better to invest more in training your own staff as internal auditors who will then be able to carry out their own equivalent of a pre-assessment. With this approach, the benefits are long term; your own trained people are going to be with you (assuming no attrition!)

8.11 The Assessment Process

Once a contract is signed with the chosen body, the details of the assessment process will get agreed with the management representative—the MR (person appointed by the client organization to liaise with the external assessors). Now the schedule for the assessment gets decided. On-site assessment is the second stage of this process and in the intervening period, a "desk investigation" is carried out.

Assessors may vary in their approach to and detailing of work carried out during desk investigation. Some do it off-site and others make a "special visit". Whatever the approach, the objective is always restricted to establishing whether the documented quality system meets the requirements of the ISO Standard (indicated in the 8 clauses—refer end of section 8.7). As a result of the desk investigation, the assessor may very well raise a number of queries and these must be dealt with. The MR (Management Representative) is involved all through and the discussions with the assessor should resolve what is required. If the assessors consider that the QMS (quality management system) is not up to the mark (as demonstrated through the major gaps found during desk investigation), then there is no point in going for the final assessment until these are put right.

The on-site assessment process is in principle the same as internal audit work (assuming it is done properly) except that the whole QMS is covered at one go. The duration of on-site assessment would depend on the manpower allocated by the assessors and the size and complexity of the client organization's business operations, software life cycles etc. During the on-site assessment, a systematic checking is done whether each element of the QMS is being implemented effectively and the procedures/processes followed. This is done through the method of "internal audit" mentioned earlier (section 8.9.5). The areas typically examined are records of internal auditing, corrective actions, and management review, including a check on changes to the QMS since the desk investigation.

Most organizations and their staff are likely to find assessment an ordeal however well prepared they are. Although generally the assessment body's outlook is positive (they want to find the evidence to award ISO certification), non-conformities (NCs) cannot be ignored. Non-conformities raised are of two kinds—*Minor NC* and *Major NC*. Minor Non-conformities are some defects in the Quality Management System (for example, some records are found to be incomplete while the majority are proper). Major non-conformities are a serious matter. These are raised if the assessor considers that a whole area of the QMS (quality management system) is no being implemented effectively. Also, a number of Minor Non-conformities may be considered to add up to a major one, particularly if a consistent theme in them is apparent. The consequence of Major Non-conformity is that ISO certification cannot be awarded until a further re-assessment visit (at an extra cost) has been made. Under such situations, organizations do feel a great disappointment but it would be wrong to dwell on this as a permanent failure—remember the whole journey is supposed to be towards "process improvement".

8.12 Surveillance Audits/Re-Certification/Re-Assessment Audits

If all goes well at the assessment visit, the organization will be awarded ISO certification. Mostly the assessors/external-auditing agency (who visited you for the final assessment) would announce this in the closing meeting. However, there is often a few weeks' delay until the certificate arrives and it is official. This is when the 'joyous' moment arrives and organizations go in spate of public announcements and celebration of its success after all the hard work done.

However, this is not the end of assessment forever. Every six months or so there is a follow-up *surveillance* visit to check that the QMS (quality management system) is still working and continues to meet the requirements of the ISO 9001 Standard. The approach is in principle much the same as adopted during the initial assessment. The only slight difference is that less time is spent (typically one to two person days on the organization's site) because only part of the whole QMS will be covered (i.e. a sampling approach is taken). A review of internal audit, corrective action and management review etc. is usually the starting point of all such visits. As in the full assessment, Minor or even Major Non-conformities can be raised. The first surveillance visit is likely to focus on whether any Non-conformities raised at the assessment have been dealt with adequately. In principle, the consequence of Major Non-conformity would be revocation of the ISO certification, although in practice this is unlikely without some warning given during previous surveillance audit visit based on deficiencies found in that visit.

A few points to consider—assessment bodies vary in their practice on re-assessment frequency. Some work to a three-year cycle with a full assessment repeated at the end of this three-year period (and a new contract agreed). The argument for this policy is that after three years, it is likely that the business circumstances of the already certified organization may have changed so much that only a full-assessment is appropriate. Considering the revision cycles by the ISO organization (section 8.5) this also happens to match well to take account of any revisions to the ISO Standard itself. Normally a previous surveillance audit would address this if such a change is in the offing. Due to this, in most circumstances, assessment bodies consider continuous surveillance to be adequate rather than a full re-assessment. In this there is a point to be noted for the client organizations—they should consider re-evaluating the quotations of the external assessors. For example, "Assessor A" may be cheaper than "Assessor B" but over five years more expensive if "B" does not require full re-assessment.

8.13 ISO Consulting Services and Consultants

So far, we have discussed about the types of assessments and audit, preparing for the assessment, the assessment process. It may have made readers aware that there are essentially three 'players' or entities involved in the implementation of the ISO based quality management system; Organization of the *user/customer*, the registrars (the external body who award the ISO Certification) and the ISO 9001:2000 Standard. Now is the time to note the forth important player; the 'consultant". In this section, we wish to give a general overview of types of consulting services available.

8.13.1 Types of Consulting and Services

There are several types of consulting services as described below:

- **Management or Accounting Firms** who have added ISO 9000 consultancy to their list of expertise. This is usually achieved by simply hiring an expert' or acquiring a consulting firm which might already have the relevant expertise.
- **Consulting Firms** which have seen the need to upgrade and expand their practice.
- **Universities and Allied Institutes** who also wish to join in the ISO 9000 market. This is usually achieved via the extended education program of the universities.
- **Individual Consultants** with varying degrees of expertise who either directly contract their skills or sub-contract to one of the above institutions.
- **Product Inspection/Testing Organizations** who have upgraded their services by including a division in charge of quality system inspection. These organizations, of which there are generally very few, usually advertise their services as facilitating the ISO 9000 implementation process (i.e. they will write and organize your quality system to suit your needs!)
- **Organizations that specialize ISO 9000 Lead Auditor or similar courses.** These organizations invariably have their head quarters in the U.K. or a commonwealth member nation.
- **Third-party Registrars** who, after much soul searching, have finally decided to join the ranks of consultants. Some registrars achieve this delicate act by creating a 'separate' consulting branch within their organization.
- **Finally,** there are consulting firms whose members usually are ex-ISO 9000 auditors/assessors. Most of these firms, offer seminars on lead auditor training and internal auditor training.

All of the above agencies will generally offer all or some of the following services or combinations thereof:

- In-house or public seminars
- Lead Auditor training courses (typically of five days duration)

- Internal Auditing courses
- Pre-assessment audit
- Third party audits (only registrars)
- Quality Manual writing
- Executive seminars for management awareness

Faced with the plethora of options, what should you do as an organization going in for ISO 9000 Certification? This leads us to the question of 'role of consultant' or 'should you hire a consultant/do you really need a consultant etc. Let us discuss this.

8.13.2 Using Consultants

Opinions on this topic vary from one extreme to another. We'll discuss both and try to present a balanced viewpoint that lies somewhere between the two extreme opinions heard. We'll also discuss what approach to take/questions to ask if you decide to hire the services of an ISO Consultant.

An extreme opinion is that the ISO Consultants are by no means essential. It is felt that if expertise is lacking in an ISO 9000 project, there are other ways of bringing it in apart from by using consultants (such as getting in your own identified persons trained on requirements of the ISO standard etc). However, the major argument in favour of consultants is that this is an effective route to buying in knowledge about the requirements of the standard and its application. The practical value of this expertise is guidance; there are real dangers of going off at a tangent and developing a system, which is either impractical, non-auditable, or simply does not meet the ISO Standard. Also, without expert guidance, the system may end up over-elaborate and far more than is truly required.

Another potential benefit of consultants is that they are outsiders and as such they can cast a fresh eye on the organizational practices and advise and recommend accordingly to bring in the quality management practices in order to meet the requirements of the Standard. However, these benefits depend on certain open-mindedness by the client organization.

Consultants can also take on a specific tasks required in building a quality (management) system—the QMS; drafting the quality manual is a good example. Here the skills and experience of a consultant may enable the job to be done more efficiently than by internal staff who generally are pre-occupied with their own high priority tasks.

However, there is also a danger in hiring the services of an ISO Consultant. It should be clearly understood (an expectations be set accordingly) that the consultants should be used primarily as facilitators and not 'doers'. This is because the ownership for the QMS should be felt by the client organization and not by the consultant. After all, consultant is not supposed to be writing the quality manual for himself/herself. This necessitates that most of the work that goes into it has to come from internal staff. At the same time, there are 'consultants' around, who after a short briefing, will sit in a corner and draft a' full quality system'! The result may just get the company through ISO 9000 but will otherwise be no good. Without considerable involvement by staff and commitment by the top management of the client organization, the quality management system (QMS) will not be 'owned' and consequently not effectively implemented.

8.13.3 Approach to Selecting ISO Consultants: Benefits and Disadvantages

The discussion in the previous section is not to mean that an organization should blindly accept ISO consultants. Nor does it mean that you should shun them; ISO consultants literally come 'cheaper by the dozen' as the expression goes—some really good and some very mediocre ones. In summary, there is no shortage of quality/ISO consultants to choose from having made such a decision. The choice ranges from independent freelancers to the large partnership of management consultants (in section8.13.1, we discussed about the several types of consulting services available)

Before selecting a consultant or a consulting organization, you should ask a few questions that help you to:

- Assess the consultant's area(s) of expertise
- Determine the number organizations where he/she has provided assistance (i.e. client referral check) and
- Perform a check on a couple of references

In author's opinion, organizations should only sub-contract for certain types of ISO 9000 consulting services. There are basically two things that a hiring organization *should not* ask consultant to do:

- Writing quality manual
- Writing Quality Assurance Processes

The reasons should be obvious—in the light of discussion in the previous section. If a consultant is hired to put a QMS (quality management system) in place, then the consultant better be present on the days of the third party audit for he will likely have become the one expert with the most knowledge about "your" quality assurance system. In such cases, your chances of passing a third party audit are actually significantly reduced.

Another disadvantage of hiring a consultant to document your quality assurance system is that it usually is somewhat expensive.

Naturally, this is good for the consultant! When you hire a consultant to document your processes, including your quality manual, you must pay him/her to first understand the "ins and outs" of your industry; thus the consultant is actually "learning" at your cost!! Depending on the complexity of the business operations of your organization, this may easily take as much as a couple of weeks even if the consultant is highly experienced and has a sharp grasp to understand the subtleties and complexities of your organization's business operations and software life cycles. Besides, why would you want to pay someone to tell him/her what and how you do something, so that he/she can write it down for you? You, in turn, will have to edit what has been written down to ensure that it is correct! Would you indeed want to pay for this "service" simply because you do not have the time to do it? This is a serious question to consider while making a decision about hiring an ISO consultant. What if your management is willing to allocate adequate time or resources to ensure that your ISO implementation process will succeed?

Having discussed the pros and cons of involving ISO consultants, this section cannot be concluded without offering some positive comments regarding their role. Consultants can be most effective in a variety of roles. For example, they can:

- Offer training
- Offer recommendations based on their varied experience
- Act as a catalyst to motivate and direct people
- "Float" across departments as "neutral agent". This can be particularly helpful in situations where inter-departmental rivalries are strong. (But then also remember that many times management hires an ISO consultant to keep their gun on his/her shoulder to shoot at their own people! That is, they get their "hidden agendas" settled through the consultant. Be aware of this "game" and avoid getting into that tango).
- Act as an interface (similar to the above point)
- Guide and help monitor efforts via carefully planned periodic visits. This activity ensures that the overall implementation plan is kept 'under control'.
- Answer "difficult" questions.
- Review and edit but NOT write documentation (quality manuals etc.)
- Conduct pre-assessment audits and offer unbiased constructive opinions/suggestions.

8.13.4 Consultation Charges and Fees

Having discussed all this about the ISO Consultants, next, the readers may have a question about the fees charged by these consultants. Well, this varies considerably depending on the mode of work and the expertise. The rates can be daily or a lump sum fee based on the tasks to be accomplished within the time schedules laid down by the client organization. To the best of author's knowledge, there are no legal guidelines on this and as a result, the consultants are free to charge fees in their own way. However while paying them some factors should be kept in mind. Some consultants may like to divide their period of professional association with the client organization in three to five broad areas and then charge differently for each phase or charge one large amount for an end-to-end involvement with their client organization. Generally, however, if an assessment body is used, their charges for pre-assessment are likely to be close to those made for the assessment itself.

As an example, we have shown below some typical phases of association with the ISO consultants (if readers recollect, section 8.13.1 indicates the types of services offered by consultants). The fees charged depend on the extent of involvement with each phase indicated below.

- "Awareness phase" (here, an awareness about quality systems is created in the client organization) based on invitation by the client
- Documentation Review
  - Identify Documents to be covered under the review
  - Gather Documents & information for review
- Assessment Planning
  - Identification of the Scope, Sponsor, Assessment and Team etc for the assessment
  - Identify "gaps" and risks based on this and establish expectations accordingly
  - Development the Assessment/Internal Audit program
  - Conduct the executive overview for the plan chalked out
- Training in Assessment/Internal Auditing Skills
  - This training is a pre-requisite for any member of the assessment team. The focus of this training is building a team during this training.
- Visit to Client organization site
  - Talk to the key members of the organization (who would be the decision makers/opinion makers and influencers)
  - Consolidate findings
  - Prepare and present draft findings
  - Prepare and deliver final findings

Prior to the phases indicated above, the organization may have already completed the following with the help from a suitable ISO consultant:

- Preparation of Draft Quality Manual (major inputs and involvement by the staff or the client organization)

- Adequacy check on the draft manual prepared
- Identify additional gaps identified, modifications to processes accordingly and revision of the Quality Manual
- Decision of the number of Internal Audit cycles as required
- Identify the third party certification agency for the client organization

The ISO consultants are expected to do handholding with the client organization until a dialogue is generated between the client organization and the third-party final auditing/assessment agency (the registrar organization). As discussed towards the end of section 8.12, client organizations should consider re-evaluation of assessment body's quotation.

8.14 ISO 9000: Some FAQs

Finally, let us look into some 'frequently asked" questions regarding ISO (though we have already dealt with some of them so far).

What does 'international standardization"mean?

When the large majority of products or services in a particular business or industry sector conform to International Standards, a state of industry-wide standardization can be said to exist. This is achieved through consensus agreements between national delegations representing all the economic stakeholders concerned—suppliers, users and, often, governments. They agree on specifications and criteria to be applied consistently in the classification of materials, the manufacture of products and the provision of services. In this way, International Standards provide a reference framework, or a common technological language, between suppliers and their customers—which facilitates trade and the transfer of technology.

What benefits does international standardization bring to businesses?

For businesses, the widespread adoption of International Standards means that suppliers can base the development of their products and services on reference documents, which have broad market relevance. This, in turn, means that they are increasingly free to compete on many more markets around the world.

What benefits does international standardization bring to customers?

For customers, the worldwide compatibility of technology, which is achieved when products and services are based on International

Standards, brings them an increasingly wide choice of offers, and they also benefit from the effects of competition among suppliers.

What is 'ISO Memento'?

This was addressed in section 8.4

Is ISO planning to do something in the prominent area of 'e-Business'?

This is addressed in the next section.

8.15 e-Business and ISO

e-business (Electronic Business) is becoming a cornerstone of the world economy. Full benefits for consumers, industry and government demand a coherent set of Information and Communication Technology standards which are:

1. Open
2. Interoperable
3. Internationally accepted

To serve this aim, a Memorandum of Understanding (MoU) on electronic business in support of e-commerce has been signed by the four main organizations which develop international standards in this area: ISO, IEC, ITU, UN/ECE, with full participation from international user groups.

The MoU establishes a coordination mechanism under a unique cooperative model to produce mutually supportive standards required in business transactions (data interchange and interoperability) as well as products design and manufacturing to meet the urgent needs of both the industry and the end-users. Electronic business covers the information definition and exchange requirements within and between enterprises, including customers. Given that it provides the vital framework for e-commerce, it is intended that this MoU will support this rapidly changing and fast growing business sector.

The purpose of the MoU is to minimize the risk of divergent and competitive approaches to standardization, avoid duplication of efforts and avoid confusion amongst users. The MoU is open to other international, regional, governmental, industry and consumer organizations whose core mission involves standards setting. The MoU vision is to offer the environment in which all key international organizations can cooperate and contribute to the delivery and promotion of the evolving set of e-business standards, and maximize their contribution to global commerce

The objective of the MoU is to encourage inter-operability by:

* Recognizing the risk of divergent or conflicting approaches to standardization
* Avoiding duplication of efforts and, therefore, confusion amongst users
* Ensuring inter-sectoral coherence

More information may be obtained from the MoU site at:

http://www.itu.int/itu-t/e-business/mou/

Conclusion

The aim of this chapter was to expose readers to many known as well as not-so-well-known aspects of ISO 9001. ISO as an organization is a very large body with international membership spread across countries. The revision process of ISO is an elaborate one wherein its members get the opportunity to express their opinions. This is because all strategic decisions are referred to the "ISO Members" who meet for an annual General Assembly.

With ISO 9001, organizations get a framework for their endeavour toward continual improvement. The new ISO 9001:2000 has come up with some additional requirements. It has ingeniously combined the scattered clauses of the older version into fewer but well organized newly titled clauses. This gives it a structure in line with most eminent process improvement models.

Opinions on utilizing the services of ISO consultants vary widely but both the extremes have their own justifications. The nature of consultants' involvement with client organizations can take many forms and the professional engagements depend on the ultimate objective of the client organization.

ISO has turned its attention to the upcoming area of e-Business and a MoU has been formed towards serving this end. ISO will continue to remain one of the most popular standard for process improvement and quality management system.

REFERENCES

[1] *Getting ISO 9000 for Software Organizations*—Rajnish Kapur (BPB Publications)
[2] *ISO 9000:Preparing for Registration*—James L. Lamprecht (ASQC Quality Press)
[3] *Implementing ISO 9001:2000*—Tom Taormina and Keith Brewer (Prentice Hall PTR)
[4] *Software Evaluation for Certification*—Andrew Rae, Philippe Robert and Hans-Ludwig Hausen (McGraw Hill International)

Chapter 9

SOFTWARE CMM AND OTHER PROCESS IMPROVEMENT MODELS

9.1 Overview

In previous chapters we have mentioned about the Software Engineering Institute (famously known as SEI) at Carnegie Mellon University, USA. As readers may be aware, their site address is www.sei.edu.cmu. By visiting this, readers can get details about the work carried out by SEI. In this chapter, our objective is to provide an overview of the *process improvement models* in general and particularly about the ones from the SEI. In doing this, we will be making a passing reference to the P–CMM model only for completeness. This is because P-CMM is a model for *"people maturity"* related practices in organizations and not about *"software maturity"* related practices. As a background to this, it is important to discuss the term *"maturity"* as it found that at times, there is some confusion about this term. This will be discussed in the context of the *"Capability Maturity Model"*. We'll also provide some insights into what are the practices followed at "mature organizations". We'll also discuss about benefits of CMM-Based Software Process Improvement. As the ISO model also is quite popular, we'll provide a comparison of the SW CMM model with the ISO models. (Chapter 8 is devoted to discussion on the ISO 9001:2000 model). We now start with discussion of some basic terms.

9.2 The Capability Maturity Model for Software: An Overview

The Capability Maturity Model for Software (SW-CMM) developed by the Software Engineering Institute (www.sei.cmu.edu) has had a major influence on software process and quality improvement around the world. Although the SW-CMM has been widely adopted, there remain many misunderstandings about how to use it effectively for business-driven software process improvement. The SW-CMM defines a five-level framework for how an organization matures its software process. These levels describe an evolutionary path from ad hoc, chaotic processes to mature, disciplined software processes. Table 2 shows the five levels, and the 18 *key process areas*. Figure 1 depicts the structure of the SW-CMM Framework. The five levels can be briefly described as shown in Table 1.

Table 1: Description of Software CMM Maturity Levels

Software CMM Maturity Level	Description of Software CMM Maturity Levels
1) *Initial*	The software process is characterized as ad hoc, and occasionally even chaotic. Few processes are defined, and success depends on individual effort and heroics.
2) *Repeatable*	Basic project management processes are established to track cost, schedule, and functionality. The necessary process discipline is in place to repeat earlier successes on projects with similar applications.
3) *Defined*	The software process for both management and engineering activities is documented, standardized, and integrated into a standard software process for the organization. All projects use an approved, tailored version of the organization's standard software process for developing and maintaining software.
4) *Managed*	Detailed measures of the software process and product quality are collected. Both the software process and products are quantitatively understood and controlled.
5) *Optimizing*	Continuous process improvement is enabled by quantitative feedback from the process and from piloting innovative ideas and technologies.

The key process areas are satisfied by achieving goals. Goals are described by key practices, sub-practices, and examples. The rating components of the SW-CMM are maturity levels, key process areas, and goals. The other components are informative and provide guidance on how to interpret the model. Appendix A has information on the Indian Software Organizations that have been assessed at maturity levels 4 and 5.

Except for Level 1, each maturity level is decomposed into several *key process areas* that indicate the areas an organization should focus on to improve its software process. The description of key process areas in Version 1.1 of the Software CMM is shown in Table 1. For convenience, the key process areas are internally organized by *common features*. The common features are attributes that indicate whether the implementation and institutionalization of a key process area is effective, repeatable, and lasting.

The five *common features* are *Commitment to Perform, Ability to Perform, Activities* Performed, *Measurement and Analysis,* and *Verifying*

Implementation. General practices that apply to every key process area at every maturity level are categorized by the *common features*. For example, establishing policies is a common practice in Commitment to Perform and providing training is a common practice in Ability to Perform. Each key process area is described in terms of the key practices that contribute to satisfying its goals and that are allocated to the common features. The key practices describe the specific infrastructure and activities that contribute most to the effective implementation and institutionalization of the key process area. For a full description of the SW CMM Model version 1.1, readers are directed to [2].

It is important to note that while the SW-CMM has been very influential around the world in inspiring and guiding software process improvement (SPI), it has also been misused and abused by some and not used effectively by others.

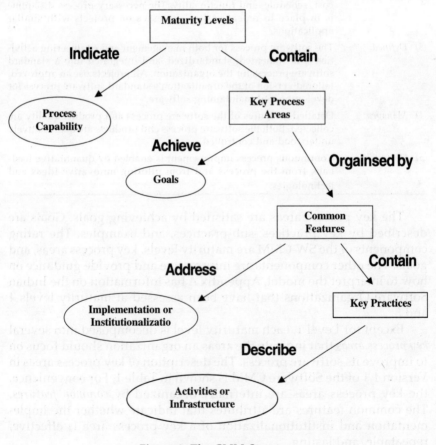

Figure 1: The CMM Structure

Table 2: The Key Process Areas in the SW-CMM version 1.1

Level	Focus	Key Process Areas
5 **Optimizing**	Continuous Process Improvement	• Defect Prevention • Technology Change Management • Process Change Management
4 **Managed**	Product and Process Quality	• Quantitative Process Management • Software Quality Management
3 **Defined**	Engineering Processes and Organizational Support	• Organization Process Focus • Organization Process Definition • Training Program • Integrated Software Management • Software Product Engineering • Inter-group Coordination • Peer Reviews
2 **Repeatable**	Project Management Processes	• Requirements Management • Software Project Planning • Software Project Tracking & Oversight • Software Subcontract Management • Software Quality Assurance • Software Configuration Management
1 **Initial**	Competent people and heroics	

9.3 Practices Followed at "Mature Organizations"

Having discussed, what "maturity" means in terms of "software processes", it will now be interesting to understand the practices followed in mature organizations. Over the last few years the Software Engineering Institute has participated in several workshops and site visits with maturity level 4 and 5 software organizations. A detailed discussion on this is provided in Appendix A. A net summary based on SEI's survey shows that the following factors/approaches are found to be present in "high maturity organizations":

• Quality Culture and Process Orientation
• Commitment to TQM
• ISO 9001 certification
• Effective Addressing of people issues
• Data-driven decision making
• Customer education when working with lower maturity customers

9.4 CMM and ISO (A Comparative Analysis)

"How does ISO compare with the CMM?"—this is one of the most frequently asked questions. People wish to know which model should an organization choose. Another question that people often come up with is "if an organization has the ISO certification, then at what (SW) CMM maturity level does this correspond to. In this section, we'll take up a discussion towards this. We'll provide a comparison analysis but we'll not make any prescriptive statement; we prefer to leave it to the reader to draw his or her own conclusions based on the analysis provided here.

9.4.1 CMM and ISO 9001

The Capability Maturity Model for Software, developed by the Software Engineering Institute, and the ISO 9000 series of standards, developed by the International Organization for Standardization, have the common concern of quality and process management. The two are driven by similar issues and are intuitively correlated, but they differ in their underlying philosophies: ISO 9001, the standard in the 9000 series that pertains to software development and maintenance, identifies the minimal requirements for a quality system, while the CMM underlines the need for continuous process improvement. This statement is somewhat subjective, of course (especially, as we'll see in the Chapter on ISO, that the new revised year 2000 release of ISO talks about "Continual Improvement). Some members of the international standards community maintain that if you read ISO 9001 with insight, it does address continuous process improvement. Corrective action, for example, can be construed as continuous improvement. Nonetheless, according to Marc Paul of the SEI [7] the CMM tends to address the issue of continuous process improvement more explicitly than ISO 9001. For a complete discussion on this topic, readers should refer [7] wherein a complete comparative analysis is provided between the CMM model and the ISO standard by taking up each clause of the ISO. Table 3 provides the summary of Marc Paulk's mapping between ISO 9001 and the CMM. However, this analysis has been extended by adding the additional column to show the mapping of SW CMM to the new ISO 9001:2000.

Table 3: Summary Mapping Between ISO 9001 And The CMM

ISO 9001:1994 Clause	ISO 9001:2000 Clause	Strong Relationship with CMM	Judgmental Relationship with CMM
4.1: Management Responsibility	4.1: General Requirement	Commitment to perform	• Ability to perform
	4.2.1: General	Software project planning	• Verifying Implementation
	5.1: Management Commitment		
	5.3: Quality Policy	Software project tracking and oversight	• Software quality management
	5.4.1: Quality Objectives	Software quality assurance	

ISO 9001:1994 Clause	ISO 9001:2000 Clause	Strong Relationship with CMM	Judgmental Relationship with CMM
4.2: Quality system	**4.1:** Quality Management Systems: General Requirement	Verifying implementation Software project planning	• Organization process definition
	4.2.1: Documentation Requirements: General	Software quality assurance	
	4.2.2: Quality Manual	Software product engineering	
4.3: Contract review	**7.2.3:** Customer Communication	Requirements management Software project planning	• Software subcontract management
4.4: Design control	**7.3.1:** Design and Development Planning	Software project planning	• Software quality management
	7.3.2: Design and Development Inputs	Software project tracking and oversight Software configuration management	
	7.3.3: Design and Development Outputs	Software product engineering	
	7.3.4: Design and Development Review		
	7.3.5: Design and Development Verification		
	7.3.6: Design and Development Validation		
	7.3.7: Control of Design and Development Changes		
4.5: Document and Data control	**4.2.3:** Control of Documents	Software Configuration Management Software Product Engineering	——-
4.6: Purchasing	**7.4.1:** Purchasing Process	Software subcontract management	——-
	7.4.2: Purchasing Information		
	7.4.3: Verification of Purchased Product		

ISO 9001:1994 Clause	ISO 9001:2000 Clause	Strong Relationship with CMM	Judgmental Relationship with CMM
4.7: Control of Customer-Supplied Product	7.5.4: Customer Property	——-	• Software subcontract management
4.8: Product Identification and Traceability	7.5.3: Identification and Traceability	Software configuration management Software product engineering	——-
4.9: Process control	6.3: Infrastructure 6.4: Work Environment 7.5.1: Control of Production and Service Environment 7.5.2: Validation of Processes for Production and Service Provision	Software project planning Software quality assurance Software product engineering	• Quantitative process management • Technology change management
4.10: Inspection and Testing	7.5.3: Identification and Traceability 8.2.4: Monitoring and Measurement of Product	Software product engineering Peer reviews	——-
4.11: Control of Inspection, Measuring, and Test equipment	7.6: Control of Monitoring and Measuring Devices	Software product engineering	——-
4.12: Inspection and Test Status	——-	Software configuration management Software product engineering	——-
4.13: Control of Nonconforming Product	——-	Software configuration management Software product engineering	——-
4.14: Corrective and Preventive Action	8.5.2: Corrective Action 8.5.3: Preventive Action	Software quality assurance Software configuration management	• Defect prevention
4.15: Handling, Storage, Packaging, Preservation, and Delivery	7.5.5: Preservation of Product	——-	• Software configuration management • Software product engineering

ISO 9001:1994 Clause	ISO 9001:2000 Clause	Strong Relationship with CMM	Judgmental Relationship with CMM
4.16:Control of Quality Records	4.2.4: Control of Records	Software configuration management Software product engineering Peer reviews	————
4.17:Internal Quality audits	8.2.2: Internal Audit	Verifying implementation Software quality assurance	————
4.18:Training	6.2.2: Competence, Awareness and Training	Ability to perform Training program	————
4.19: Servicing	————	————	————
4.20:Statistical Techniques	8.2.4: Monitoring and Measurement of Product 8.4: Analysis of Data		• Organization process definition • Quantitative process management • Software quality management

9.4.2 CMM and 15504

This section provides an overview of the Software CMM and ISO/IEC 15504, discusses the similarities and differences between them, and speculates how they may influence each other as they both continue to evolve. ISO/IEC 15504 is a suite of standards for software process assessment currently under development as an international standard. ISO/IEC 15504 has been published as a type 2 technical report, which is a stage in the development of a standard. Of the nine parts to ISO/IEC 15504, the parts directly relevant to the Software CMM are ISO/IEC 15504-2, the reference model, and ISO/IEC 15504-5, which provide an example model. As an international standard, ISO/IEC 15504 can be expected to affect the continuing evolution of CMM-related products. ISO/IEC 15504 is being developed by working group 10 (WG10) under the software engineering subcommittee (SC7) of the information technology joint committee (JTC1) established by the International Organization for Standardization (ISO) and the International Electro-technical Commission (IEC). For a detailed discussion on this, reader should refer to [8].

ISO/IEC 15504 is intended to harmonize the many different approaches to software process assessment. It has nine parts:

Part 1 : *Concepts and introductory guide*
Part 2 : *A reference model for processes and process capability*
Part 3 : *Performing an assessment*
Part 4 : *Guide to performing assessments*
Part 5 : *An assessment model and indicator guidance*
Part 6 : *Guide to competency of assessors*
Part 7 : *Guide for use in process improvement*
Part 8 : *Guide for use in determining supplier process capability*
Part 9 : *Vocabulary*

The reference model in Part 2 documents the set of universal software engineering processes that are fundamental to good software engineering and that cover best practice activities. It describes processes that an organization may perform to acquire, supply, develop, operate, evolve and support software and the process attributes that characterize the capability of those processes. The purpose of the reference model is to provide a common basis for different models and methods for software process assessment, ensuring that results of assessments can be reported in a common context. The reference model architecture is two-dimensional. The *process dimension* is characterized by process purpose statements, which are the essential measurable objectives of a process. The processes are listed in Table 4.

Table 4: Mapping Between ISO/IEC 15504-2 Processes and Software CMM Key Process Areas

(Note: For full description of each of the Activities of Software CMM v1.1, readers should refer to Ref [2].

ISO/IEC 15504 Processes Software CMM v1.1		Software CMM v1.1
CUS.1	Acquisition Software Subcontract Management	Software Subcontract Management
CUS.1.1	Acquisition preparation	Software Subcontract Management, *Activity 1*
CUS.1.2	Supplier selection	Software Subcontract Management, *Activity 2*
CUS.1.3	Supplier monitoring	Software Subcontract Management, *Activities 5 and 7-11*
CUS.1.4	Customer acceptance	Software Subcontract Management, *Activity 12*
CUS.2	Supply	(Software Project Planning; Software Project Tracking & Oversight; Software Product Engineering)
CUS.3	Requirements elicitation	——-
CUS.4	Operation	——-
CUS.4.1	Operational use	——-
CUS.4.2	Customer support	——-
ENG.1	Development	Software Product Engineering

ISO/IEC 15504 Processes Software CMM v1.1		*Software CMM v1.1*
ENG.1.1	System Requirements Analysis and Design	———
ENG.1.2	Software requirements	Software Product Engineering, *Activity 2*
ENG.1.3	Software design	Software Product Engineering, *Activity 3*
ENG.1.4	Software construction	Software Product Engineering, *Activity 4*
ENG.1.5	Software integration	Software Product Engineering, *Activity 6*
ENG.1.6	Software testing	Software Product Engineering, *Activity 7*
ENG.1.7	System integration and Testing	(Software Product Engineering, *Activities 6 and 7*)
ENG.2	System and software Maintenance	———
SUP.1	Documentation	Software Product Engineering, *Activity 8*
SUP.2	Configuration management	Software Configuration Management
SUP.3	Quality assurance	Software Quality Assurance
SUP.4	Verification	(Peer Reviews; Software Product Engineering, *Activities 5 and 6*)
SUP.5	Validation	Software Product Engineering, *Activity 5*
SUP.6	Joint review	Software Project Tracking & Oversight, *Activity 13*
SUP.7	Audit	(Software Quality Assurance)
SUP.8	Problem resolution	Software Configuration Management, *Activity 5*
MAN.1	Management	(Software Project Planning; Software Project Tracking & Oversight; Integrated Software Management)
MAN.2	Project management	Software Project Planning; Software Project Tracking & Oversight; Integrated Software Management
MAN.3	Quality management	Software Quality Management
MAN.4	Risk management	Software Project Planning, *Activity 13*; Software Project Tracking & Oversight, *Activity 10*; Integrated Software Management, *Activity 10*
ORG.1	Organizational alignment	———
ORG.4	Infrastructure	Organization Process Definition
ORG.2	Improvement	Organization Process Definition
ORG.2.1	Process establishment	Organization Process Definition
ORG.2.2	Process assessment	Organization Process Focus, *Activity 1*
ORG.2.3	Process improvement	Organization Process Focus; (Process Change Management)
ORG.3	Human resource management	Training Program
ORG.4	Infrastructure	———
ORG.5	Measurement	Measurement and Analysis (common feature)
ORG.6	Reuse	Requirements Management Inter-group Coordination Peer Reviews Quantitative Process Management Defect Prevention Technology Change Management Process Change Management

The mapping in Table 4 shows how the topics in ISO/IEC 15504 relate to the equivalent topics/*key process areas* in the Software CMM. Topics are typically not isomorphic but are highly correlated. Anyone adequately implementing, for example, the Configuration Management Process in ISO/IEC 15504 could reasonably expect to have satisfied the Software Configuration Management key process area in the Software CMM. Topics are not usually isomorphic because of extensions that may have been added or different levels of abstraction that may have been chosen (e.g., the Development Process in ISO/IEC).

9.5 Types of Capability Maturity Models (CMMs)

The Software Capability Maturity Model is the most famous one. However, the fact that there are a number of other Capability Maturity Models not known to many people. In this section, we have compiled such information on other CMM products (Table 5). The source of this data is ftp:// ftp.sei.cmu.edu/public/documents/ or http:// www.sei.cmu.edu/

Table 5: Types of Capability Maturity Models (CMMs)

Type of CMM	Description	Documents
Software CMM (the original CMM)	*Key Practices of the Capability Maturity Model*	CMU/SEI-93-TR-025
	Capability Maturity Model for Software (SW-CMM)	CMU/SEI-93-TR-024
	Personal Software Process (PSP)	Published books
Software Acquisition CMM	*Software Acquisition Capability Maturity Model (SA-CMM)*	CMU/SEI-99-TR-002
	Software Acquisition Improvement Framework (SAIF) Definition	CMU/SEI-98-TR-003
CMM-Based Assessment	*CMM Appraisal Framework (CAF)*	CMU/SEI-95-TR-001
	Software Capability Evaluation (SCE) Method Description	CMU/SEI-96-TR-002
	CMM -Based Appraisal for Internal Process Improvement (CBA IPI): Method Description	CMU/SEI-96-TR-007
CMM Framework	*Software Process Framework for the SEI Capability Maturity Model*	CMU/SEI-94-HB-001
	Software Process Framework for the SEI Capability Maturity Model: Repeatable Level	CMU/SEI-93-SR-007
	How to Use the Software Process Framework	CMU/SEI-97-SR-009
	Common CMM Framework	———

Type of CMM	Description	Documents
Personnel Management	*People Capability Maturity Model (P-CMM)*	CMU/SEI-95-MM-002
	Overview of the People Capability Maturity Model, Version 1.1	CMU/SEI-95-MM-001
	People CMM-Based Assessment Method Description	CMU/SEI-98-TR-012
Systems Engineering	*Systems Engineering Capability Maturity Model (SE-CMM)*	CMU/SEI-95-MM-003
	Description of the Systems Engineering Capability Maturity Model Appraisal Method	CMU/SEI-96-HB-004
	Integrated Product Development CMM (IPD-CMM)	None—product cancelled
Integrated CMM	*SEI Integrated CMM (CMMI) FAA Integrated CMM (FAA-iCMM)*	
	Federal Aviation Administration Integrated Capability Maturity Model (FAA-iCMM) Appraisal Method Available from http://www.faa.gov/ait/ait5/ FAA-iCMM.htm	Not public
Security	*Security Systems Engineering CMM (SSE-CMM)*	Not public
	Trusted CMM (T-CMM) (Replaces some KPA's from the SW-CMM; not a stand-alone CMM)	Not public
Related International Standards (available from IEEE Standards site)	*ISO/IEC DTR 15504—Software Process Assessment*	———
	ISO/IEC 12207—Software life cycle processes	———

9.6 The CMM-Integrated Model (CMM-I)

9.6.1 What is CMMI?

In this section, we'll discuss the overview and model structure of the Integrated Capability Maturity Model, famously known as the CMMi. Then we'll discuss the two representations available for this model. Next we'll provide a discussion on comparative differences between the Software CMM model vis-à-vis the Integrated CMM model.

CMMI (Capability Maturity Model—Integrated) is the newest process capability model to be provided by the Software Engineering Institute. It is a model, which integrates and replaces multiple CMMs (we discussed some of this in section 9.5) into a single model in order to reduce duplication and eliminate redundancy. Common terminology and components provide a consistent style. It provides guidance on Systems and Software Engineering and encourages process improvements in organizations of any structure.

The SEI, government and multiple industries and organizations built the CMMI. It was sponsored by the Department of Defense as the CMMI Integration Project. The CMMI incorporates models for systems engineering, software engineering, software acquisition, workforce practices and integrated product and process development.

9.6.2 The Background to the CMM-I Model

The CMMI Integration Project was formed to sort out the problem of using multiple CMMs. The initial mission of the project was to combine three source models into a single model for use by organizations pursuing enterprise-wide process improvement.

- CMM for Software (SW-CMM V2.0 draft C)
- Electronic Industries Alliance/Interim Standard (EIA/IS) 731 (the Systems Engineering standard)
- Integrated Product and Process Development Capability Maturity Model (IPD-CMM) V 0.98

The following diagram (Figure 2) shows the evolution of multiple process models into the CMMI model. As seen in the diagram, the resulting framework accommodates multiple disciplines and is flexible enough to support two different representations:

- Staged
- Continuous

It supports future integration of other discipline-specific CMMI models and is consistent and compatible with the ISO/IEC 15504 technical report for software process assessments. The integrated model can be adopted by those currently using other CMMs as well as those new to the CMMI concept. Figure 3 depicts the components of the Integrated CMM Model (*Ref. CMMI SE/SW/IPPD, Version 1.1 page 10*)

9.6.3 Types of CMM-I Models

The URL to the CMMi official website by the SEI (Software Engineering Institute) is www.sei.cmu.edu/cmmi/ and we urge the readers to visit this site. A number of latest products and services by the SEI are listed here. This site mention the four models of the Integrated CMM, each with two kinds of representation:

- CMMI-SE/SW/IPPD/SS, V1.1 (Continuous Representation)
- CMMI-SE/SW/IPPD/SS, V1.1 (Staged Representation)

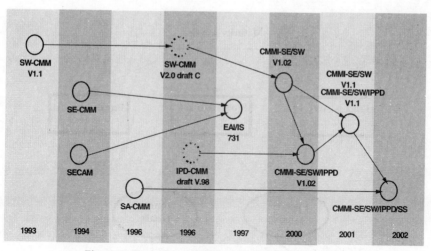

Figure 2: Evolution of CMM-I From Source Models

Source: CMMIsm—The Evolution Continues (SEI Abstract September 2001)
Pamela Curtis, David Michael Phillips, and Joan Weszka

- CMMI-SE-SW-IPPD V1.1 (Continuous Representation)
- CMMI-SE-SW-IPPD V1.1 (Staged Representation)

- CMMI-SE-SW V1.1 (Continuous Representation)
- CMMI-SE-SW V1.1 (Staged Representation)

- CMMI-SW V1.1 Continuous Representation)
- CMMI-SW V1.1 (Staged Representation)

Readers will note that each CMMI model is given a name consisting of "CMMI-" followed by the abbreviation for the disciplines selected for that model. Where more than one discipline is modeled, the disciplines are listed with a slash (/) between them. This is as follows:

- CMMI-SE/SW is the name given to the *systems engineering* and *software engineering integrated model.*
- CMMI-SE/SW/IPPD is the name given to *the systems engineering, software engineering, and integrated product and process development integrated model.*
- CMMI-SE/SW/IPPD/SS is the name given to the *systems engineering, software engineering, integrated product and process development, and supplier sourcing integrated model.*

Which model to choose and with which representation can be a very involved decision requiring pondering by all the relevant stakeholders. At times an organization may need involvement of an external consultant to help make the decision. One such article that discusses some of these aspects is "CMMI Myths and Realities" by Lauren Heinz available at ref [10]. In that article he has discussed the often-made

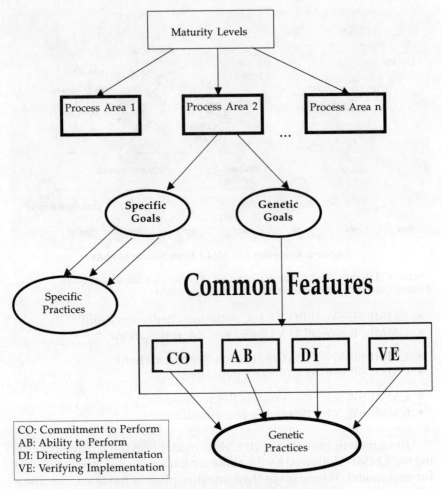

Figure 3: CMM-Integrated Model Components

remarks: *CMMI is too big and complex, A CMMI appraisal takes longer and costs more* and *CMMI is for large organizations.* In the next section, we have provided a brief discussion on "Choosing a Representation" for a CMM-I Model.

9.6.4 Transitioning to CMM-I Model

A large number of organizations worldwide are already assessed to be at the various levels of SW CMM. Some organizations may be making the decision to transition to the CMM-Integrated model as the current SW CMM model is to sunset soon. (For exact details of this, readers can visit site www.sei.cmu.edu. We recommend readers to have a look at the CMMI White Paper quoted under reference [12]

In general, while making the transition decision, a number of factors need to be considered; they are listed below:

- Size of organization in terms of total number of employees
- Type of organization (in terms of software business conducted)
- Whether the organization is into pure product development activities or service providing
- The complexity of organizations products and services
- The Process Improvement Models already adopted by the organization (if any)
- Organization's familiarity with the CMM-Integrated Model
- What information the organization has used to aid the decision of transitioning to CMM-Integrated Model
- The type of CMM-I model representation the organization intends to use and the reasons behind
- People, Technology and Process related support needed by the organization to transition to the Integrated CMM model

This is why we said earlier that the decision to make a transition from SW CMM to CMM Integrated model depends on a number of factors and being a decision with long term implications, involves all the relevant stakeholders and at times, also the services of an external consultant.

9.6.5 Process Maturity Levels in CMM-I Model

The staged representation of the CMM-I is the same representation used for the Software CMM. It provides 5 levels of process maturity:

1. Initial
2. Managed
3. Defined
4. Quantitatively Managed
5. Optimizing

These are shown in Figure 4.

Each *maturity level* contains a predefined set of *Process Areas*. In order to achieve a specific maturity level, all *goals* within the set of process areas for that maturity level must be attained. The *staged representation* provides a predefined road map for process improvement, each level building on the maturity of the previous level. The staged representation allows comparison of process maturity levels across organizations. Figure 5 (Chart-A) shows the grouping of Process Areas into the 5 levels of the *Staged Representation*.

The continuous representation is the same representation used for the systems engineering model (EIA/IS 731) and the organization of the Process Areas is derived from ISO/IEC 15504. It groups the process areas by categories of common disciplines:

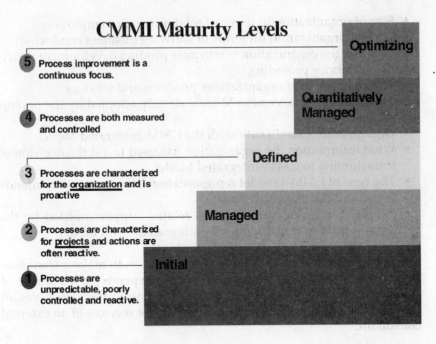

CMMI Maturity Levels

5 Process improvement is a continuous focus.

Optimizing

4 Processes are both measured and controlled

Quantitatively Managed

3 Processes are characterized for the <u>organization</u> and is proactive

Defined

2 Processes are characterized for <u>projects</u> and actions are often reactive.

Managed

1 Processes are unpredictable, poorly controlled and reactive.

Initial

- Process Management processes
- Project Management processes
- Engineering processes
- Support processes

Figure 5 (Chart B) shows the grouping of Process Areas into the Continuous Representation process categories.

9.6.6 Choosing a CMMI Model Representation

As mentioned earlier, there are two "representations" of each CMMI discipline: *staged* and *continuous*. A representation reflects the organization, use, and presentation of model elements. Both representations contain essentially the same information. Each representation consists of process areas that contain a purpose statement, introductory text, *specific goals*, *specific practices*, *generic goals*, and *generic practices*. For more information about these components, refer to Figure 3, "Model Components" of the CMMI model.

Staged—The *staged representation* offers a roadmap to approach *process improvement:* one predetermined step at a time. *Process areas* (The PAs) are grouped at *maturity levels* that provide organizations with a proven approach for process improvement. The staged representation prescribes the order of implementation for each process area according to maturity levels. Achieving each maturity level ensures that an adequate

	Causal Analysis Resolution (CAR)
LEVEL 5	Organizational Innovation and Deployment (OID)

	Quantitative Project Management (QPM)
	Organizational Process Performance (OPP)

	Organizational Environment for Integration (OEI) (IPPD)
	Decision Analysis and Resolution (DAR)
	Integrated Teaming (IT) (IPPD)
	Risk Management (RSKM)
	Integrated Project Management (IPM) *(2 additional goals for IPPD)*
	Organizational Training (OT)
LEVEL 3	Organizational Process Definition (OPD)
	Organizational Process Focus (OPF)
	Validation (Val)
	Verification (Ver)
	Product Integration (PI)
	Technical Solution (TS)
	Requirements Development (RD)

	Configuration Management (CM)	
	Process and Product Quality Assurance (PPQA)	PAs equivalent to SW CMM KPAs
	Measurement and Analysis (M&A)	*Systems Engineering Support*
LEVEL 2	Supplier Agreement Management (SAM)	*IPPD Process Support*
	Project Monitoring and Control (PMC)	**Enhancements to SW-CMM KPAs**
	Project Planning (PP)	
	Requirements Management (REQM)	

Chart A: Staged Representation

	Causal Analysis Resolution (CAR)
	Organizational Environment for Integration (OEI) (IPPD)
	Decision Analysis and Resolution (DAR)
SUPPORT	**Measurement and Analysis (M&A)**
	Process and Product Quality Assurance (PPQA)
	Configuration Management (CM)

	Validation (Val)
	Verification (Ver)
	Product Integration (PI)
ENGINEERING	*Technical Solution (TS)*
	Requirements Development (RD)
	Requirements Management (REQM)

	Quantitative Project Management (QPM)
	Integrated Teaming (IT) (IPPD)
	Risk Management (RSKM)
PROJECT	Integrated Project Management (IPM) *(2 additional goals for IPPD)*
MANAGEMENT	Supplier Agreement Management (SAM)
	Project Monitoring and Control (PMC)
	Project Planning (PP)

	Organizational Innovation and Deployment (OID)	
PROCESS	Organizational Process Performance (OPP)	PAs equivalent to SW-CMM KPAs
MANAGE-	Organizational Training (OT)	*Systems Engineering Support*
MENT	Organizational Process Definition (OPD)	*IPPD Process Support*
	Organizational Process Focus (OPF)	**Enhancements to SW-CMM KPAs**

Chart B: Continuous Representation

Figure5: Grouping of Process Areas

improvement foundation has been laid for the next maturity level, thus minimizing the organization's process improvement investment and risk while maximizing the benefits to the organization.

Continuous—The *continuous representation* offers a more flexible approach to *process improvement*. It is designed for organizations that would like to choose a particular *process area* or set of process areas based on trouble spots in the organization or a set of process areas that are closely aligned to the organization's business objectives. Process-improvement objectives are mapped to process areas in the model to identify the process areas to be implemented. As a process area is implemented, the *specific practices* and *generic practices* are grouped into capability levels. These *capability levels* enable the organization to implement the chosen process area(s) incrementally. The continuous representation also allows an organization to implement different process areas at different rates.

Readers might wonder as to what are the differences between the two representations. The table 6 outlines the differences between the two representations. Various factors affect the decision to choose an appropriate representation. They are discussed next. First we should carefully study Table 6 to understand the differences between the two representations.

Table 6:Differences between Staged and Continuous Representations of CMM-I

Continuous Representation	Staged Representation
Process areas are organized by process area categories.	Process areas are organized by maturity levels.
Improvement is measured using capability levels that reflect incremental implementation of a particular process area.	Improvement is measured using maturity levels that reflect the concurrent implementation of multiple process areas.
There are six capability levels, 0-5.	There are five maturity levels, 1-5.
There are an N+ number of practices because there are two types of specific practices: base and advanced.	There are an N number of practices because there is only one type of specific practice. The concept of advanced practices is not used, but is addressed through other means.
Capability levels are used to organize the generic practices.	Common features are used to organize the generic practices.
All generic practices are listed in each of the process areas.	Only the generic practices that are applicable to that maturity level are listed in the process areas at that level.
Generic practices exist for capability levels 1-5.	Generic practices exist for maturity levels 2-5. A subset of generic practices used in the continuous representation are applied to each process area based on its maturity level.
Overview text is written to describe the continuous representation.	Overview text is written to describe the staged representation.

An additional appendix describing equivalent staging is included, which allows a translation of a target profile into a maturity level.	There is no equivalence concept that allows a translation of maturity levels into a target profile.

Choosing the representation certainly requires some thought; in fact many find this rather perplexing and so a brief discussion on this should be in order. According to the Software Engineering Institute (SEI), three categories of factors may influence your decision- business, cultural, and legacy:

Business Factors: An organization with mature knowledge of its business objectives is likely to have a strong mapping of its processes to its business objectives. An organization such as this may find the continuous representation more useful to assess its processes and to determine how well the organization's processes support and meet business goals. The staged representation is widely used and maturity level ratings are often published. If your organization is concerned about benchmarking with your competitors and/or publishing results, the staged representation might be selected.

Cultural Factors: Cultural factors to consider when selecting a representation have to do with an organization's ability to deploy a process improvement program. For instance, an organization might select the continuous representation if the culture is experienced in process improvement or has a specific process that needs to be improved quickly. An organization that has little experience in process improvement might choose the staged representation, which provides additional guidance about the order in which changes should occur.

Legacy: Organizations with a strong systems engineering culture might be more familiar with the continuous representation, whereas software organizations may be more accustomed to a staged representation. If an organization has experience with a staged representation, it may be wise to continue with the staged representation of CMMI, especially if it has invested resources and deployed processes across the organization that are associated with a staged representation. The same is true for an organization that has experience with a continuous representation. Both staged and continuous representations were made available so that the communities that have used the different representations successfully could continue in a manner that is comfortable and familiar to them.

It should be noted that an organization isn't forced to select one representation over another. In fact, an organization may find utility in both representations. It is rare that an organization will implement either representation exactly as prescribed.

9.7.7 Comparison: SW CMM v/s CMM-Integrated

"Key Process Areas (KPAs)" will now be called "Process Areas (PAs)". The software CMM has 18 KPAs. CMMI has 24 PAs. The software CMM KPAs have goals and key practices which support those goals. Key practices are composed of Common Features and Activities Performed (AC). Common Features consist of Commitment to Perform (CO), Ability to Perform (AB), Measurements and Analysis (ME), and Verifying Implementation (VE).

There are many similarities across the common features in the software CMM KPAs, however, they are not exactly the same for all KPAs. In the CMMI model, each process area has goals, but they are comprised of General Goals and Specific Goals. General practices support the General Goals, which consist of Commitment to Perform (CO), Ability to Perform (AB), Directing Implementation (DI), and Verifying Implementation (VE). Directing Implementation replaces the Measurements and Evaluation key practice of the software CMM model. Generic Goals apply to all process areas, so there is one consistent set of practices across all process areas. This is equivalent to and an improvement to the "similar" Common Features in the software CMM. Specific Goals consist of Specific Practices, which are equivalent to the Activities Performed in the software CMM.

A frequently asked question is "How do the software CMM KPAs relate to the CMMI PAs?" The chart showing the mapping is given in Figure 6.

9.7 Other Models for Software Process Improvement and Performance Excellence

Having done extensive discussion on the SW CMM model and the Integrated CMM model, we are now going to list down the other "software improvement models" that are available. We have already mentioned the various types of "Capability Maturity Models" (CMMs) available. We explained the ISO 9001 standard as compared to the SW CMM model. We also discussed the ISO 15504 in relation to the CMM. The ISO standard will be discussed in a separate chapter.

9.7.1 TickIT

TickIT is about improving the quality of software and its application. TickIT is supported by the UK and Swedish software industries. An important purpose of TickIT has been to simulate software system developers to think about:

- What quality really is in the context of the processes of software development,

A comparison shows differences and similarities...

SW-CMM (18 KPAs)

Maturity Level 2
- Requirements Management
- Software Project Planning
- Software Project Tracking & Oversight
- Software Subcontract Management
- Software Quality Assurance
- Software Configuration Management

Maturity Level 3
- Organization Process Focus
- Organization Process Definition
- Training Program
- Software Product Engineering

- Peer Reviews
- Integrated Software Management
- Intergroup Coordination

Maturity Level 4
- Quantitative Process Management
- Software Quality Management

Maturity Level 5
- Defect Prevention
- Technology Change Management
- Process Change Management

CMMI (24 PAs)

Maturity Level 2
- Requirements Management
- Project Planning
- Project Monitoring and Control
- Supplier Agreement Management
- Process and Product Quality Assurance
- Configuration Management
- **Measurement and Analysis**

Maturity Level 3
- Organizational Process Focus
- Organizational Process Definition
- Organizational Training
- ***Requirements Development***
- ***Technical Solution***
- **Product Integration**
- **Verification**
- **Validation**
- **Integrated Project Management** *(IPPD)*
- **Risk Management**
- *Integrated Teaming*
- *Organization Environment for Integration*
- **Decision Analysis and Resolution**

Maturity Level 4
- Quantitative Project Management
- Organizational Process Performance

Maturity Level 5
- Causal analysis and Resolution
- Organizational Innovation and Deployment

Process Areas equivalent to SW-CMM KPAs, *Systems Engineering Support*, *IPPD Support*, **Enhancements to SW-CMM KPAs**

Figure 6: SW CMM and CMM-I: Comparison

- How quality may be achieved, and
- How quality management systems may be continuously improved

Although certification of compliance to ISO 9001 is a contractual requirement for software suppliers in certain market areas, it should be a by-product of the more fundamental aims of quality achievement and improvement, and the delivery of customer satisfaction. With regard to the certification itself, the objectives of TickIT are to:

- Improve market confidence in third party quality management system certification through accredited certification bodies for the software sector,
- Improve professional practices amongst quality management system auditors in the software sector,
- Publish authoritative guidance material (the TickIT Guide) for all stakeholders

TickIT applies to all types of information systems supply which involve software development processes. Typical systems suppliers include system houses, software houses and in-house developers. TickIT disciplines are also relevant for the development of embedded software. In the UK, TickIT is recognized by all Government departments and major purchasers and it is compatible with European requirements for accredited quality system certification. According to a statistics, world-wide, more than 1400 TickIT certifications have been issued so far. TickIT is managed and maintained by DISC, the department within BSI (British Standards Institute) with responsibility for all aspects of standardization in information systems and communications.

9.7.2 ISO 12207

ISO 12207 offers a framework for software life-cycle processes from concept through retirement. It is especially suitable for acquisitions because it recognizes the distinct roles of acquirer and supplier. In fact, the standard is intended for two-party use where an agreement or contract defines the development, maintenance, or operation of a software system. It should be noted that ISO 12207 is *not applicable* to the purchases of "commercial-off-the-shelf (COTS) software products.

ISO 12207 provides a structure of processes using mutually accepted terminology, rather than dictating a particular life-cycle model or software development method. It describes five **"primary processes"**—ACQUISITION, SUPPLY, DEVELOPMENT, MAINTENCNE and OPEERATION. It divides these five processes into "activities", and the activities into "tasks", while placing requirements upon their execution. ISO 12207 also specifies eight **"supporting processes"**—DOCUMENTATION, CONFIGURATION MANAGEMENT, QUALITY ASSURANCE, VERIFICATION, VALIDATION, JOINT REVIEW, AUDIT, and PROBLEM RESOLUTION. It also describes four **"organizational management processes"**—MANGEMENT, INFRASTRUCTURE, IMPROVEMENT, and TRAINING.

Since it is a relatively high-level document, 12207 does not specify the details of how to perform the activities and tasks comprising the processes. Nor does it prescribe the name, format or content of documentation. It expects organizations to tailor the seventeen processes mentioned above (5 primary processes, 8 supporting processes and 4 supporting processes.) to fit the scope of their particular projects by deleting all inapplicable activities. It defines 12207 compliance as the performances of those processes Considering this, organizations seeking to apply 12207 may want to use additional standards or procedures that specify those details.

9.7.3 IEEE 1074

The name of this process improvement framework is "IEEE Standard for Developing Software Life Cycle Processes. The standard describes the responsibilities associated for developing a software life cycle:

- Available life-cycle models (prototyping, spiral, waterfall etc.)
- One life-cycle model is selected for a project, or set of projects
- The activities described in IEEE 1074 are mapped, in time order, onto the life-cycle model. Owners and a schedule are assigned to each activity. The activities described in IEEE 1074 are a minimum set of mandatory activities.

This standard is primarily written for a process architect, the individual responsible for establishing the software life cycle to be followed on projects. By now IEEE must have revised this standard to harmonize it with ISO 12207.

9.7.4 Malcolm Baldrige National Quality Award (MBNQA)

The Malcolm Baldrige National Quality Award (MBNQA) is an annual *award* to recognize United States companies for performance excellence (not necessary restricted to software processes related excellence).

The MBNQA is a "Total Quality Management" (TQM) often referred to as a framework. The model is made of 7 elements (shown below in *italic*) under four basic principles (shown below in **bold**):

i. **Driver:** The 1.0 *Leadership* element of MBNQA drives the system by
  - Setting directions
  - Creating values, goals and systems
  - Guiding the pursuit of customer value and company performance improvement
ii. **System:** Composed of processes for meeting the company's customer and performance requirements – elements, include:
  - *2.0 Information and Analysis*
  - *3.0 Strategic Planning*
  - *4.0 Human Resource Development and Management*
  - *5.0 Process Management*
iii. **Measures of Progress:** These measures provide a result-oriented basis for channeling actions to delivering ever-improving customer value and company performance. These measure are addressed in element 6.0 *Business Results*, and include:
  - Product and Service quality
  - Productivity improvement
  - Waste Reduction/Elimination
  - Supplier Performance
  - Financial Results

iv. **Goal:** The basic aims of the system driver to deliver the ever-improving customer values and company performance. These goals are addressed in *7.0 Customer Focus and Satisfaction*, and include:
   - Customer satisfaction
   - Customer satisfaction relative to competitors
   - Customer retention
   - Market Share Gain

Other countries award equivalent to the MBNQA are:

- The Canada Award of Excellence (discussed briefly in the next section)
- The Business Excellence Award of Europe

Comparing MBNQA against ISO 9001 and SEI SW-CMM v1.0

Each standard and model emphasizes different aspects of TQM (Total Quality Management). All the three (MBNQA, ISO and SW CMM) standards and models have an overlapping focus on *process management*. A study was done by Michael Tingey to focus on the types of activities emphasized by each of the three models mentioned above. The study showed that the MBNQA model puts a large emphasis on *improving* and then *planning*. In comparison, the ISO 9001 standard puts its highest emphasis on *managing* and then on *implementing*. The SEI SW-CMM model is the reverse of ISO 9001—its largest emphasis is on *implementing* then managing.

9.7.5 Canada Award for Excellence

We had mentioned about this award in the section on MNBQA. The Canada Award for Excellence (CAE) is an annual award to recognize Canadian companies for performance excellence. It is a Total Quality Management (TQM) model. It is made up of 7 elements (shown below in *italic*).

1.0 Leadership element of CAE focuses on those who have primary responsibility and accountability for the organization's performance; this element's primary focus is on the organization's

- Strategic direction
- Leadership involvement
- Outcomes
- Continuous improvement

2.0 Planning element of CAE pertains to the planning process in regards to improvement, the linkage of planning to strategic direction/ intent, and the measurement of performance to assess progress; this element's primary focus is on the organization's

- Development and content
- Assessment
- Outcomes
- Continuous improvement

3.0 Customer Focus element of CAE pertains to the organization's focus on customer driven innovation and on the achievement of customer satisfaction; this element's primary focus is on the organization's

- Voice of the customer
- Management of customer relationships
- Measurement of customer satisfaction
- Outcomes
- Continuous improvement

4.0 People Focus element of CAE pertains to the development and deployment of a human resource plan for meeting the goals of the organization, and achievement excellence through resource plan for meeting the goals of the organization, and achieving excellence through people. In addition, the element pertains to the organization's efforts to foster and support and environment that encourages people to teach their full potential; this element's primary focus is on the organization's

- Human resource planning
- Participatory environment
- Continuous learning
- Employee satisfaction
- Outcomes
- Continuous improvement

5.0 Process Management element of CAE pertains to how work is organized to support the organization's strategic direction, with a specific focus on quality assurance practices, as well as continuous improvement; this element's primary focus is on organization's

- Process definition
- Process control
- Process improvement
- Outcomes
- Continuous improvement

6.0 Supplier Focus element of CAE pertains to the organization's external relationships with other organizations, institutions and/or alliances that are critical to it meeting its strategic objectives; this element's primary focus is on the organization's

- Partnering
- Outcomes
- Continuous improvement

7.0 Organizational Performance element of CAE pertains to the outcomes from the overall efforts for improvement, and their impact on organizational achievement; this element's primary focus is on the organization's

- Service/product quality
- Operational results
- Customers and marketplace
- Employee satisfaction and morale
- Financial performance

9.7.6 The EFQM Excellence Model

The EFQM Model is a "non-prescriptive framework" that recognizes there are many approaches to achieving "sustainable excellence". The Model has **9 criteria** depicted in Figure 7. Five of these criteria are called "**Enablers**" and four are "**Results**". The "Enabler" criteria cover what an organization does. The "Results" criteria cover what an organization achieves. "Results" are cause by "Enablers" The model is based on the premise that: **Excellent results with respect to *Performances, Results*, Customers, *People* and *Society* are achieved through *Partnerships & Resources*, and *Processes*.**

The 9 boxes of the EFQM Excellence Model, depicted in Figure 7, represent the criteria against which to assess an organization's progress towards excellence. Each of the nine criteria has a definition, which

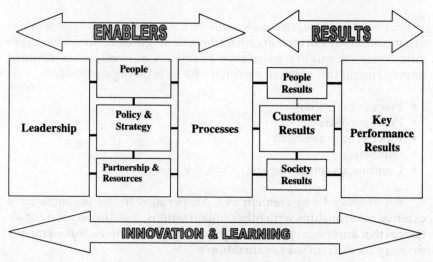

Figure 7:The EFQM Excellence Model

explains the high level of meaning of that criterion. To develop the high level meaning further, each criterion is supported by a number of sub-criteria. Sub-criteria pose a number of questions that should be considered in the course of an assessment. Finally, below each sub-criterion are list of possible areas to address. The areas to address are not mandatory nor are they exhaustive lists but are intended to further exemplify the meaning of the sub-criterion. (For additional details on this, users can refer to model.info@efqm.org)

Within this non-prescriptive framework approach there are some "Fundamental Concepts", which underpin the EFQM Model. These are expressed below. There is no significance intended in the order in which the concepts are presented below. The list (Fundamental Concepts of EFQM Excellence Model) is not meant to be exhaustive and they will change as excellent organizations develop and improve. Fundamental Concepts of EFQM Excellence Model are described below:

Results Orientation—Excellence is dependent upon balancing and satisfying the needs of all relevant stakeholders (this includes the people employed, customers, suppliers and society in general as well as those with financial interests in the organization).

Customer Focus—The customer is the final arbiter of product and service quality. Customer loyalty, retention and market share gain are best optimized through a clear focus on the needs of the current and potential customers.

Leadership & Constancy of Purpose—The behaviour of an organization's leaders creates a clarity and unity of purpose within the organization and an environment in which the organization and its people can excel.

Management by Processes and Facts—Organizations perform more effectively when all inter-related activities are understood and systematically managed and decisions concerning current operations and planned. Improvements are made using reliable information that includes stakeholder perceptions.

People Development & Involvement—The full potential of an organization's people is best released through shared values and a culture of trust and improvement, which encourages the involvement of everyone.

Continuous Learning, Innovation & Improvement—Organizational performance is maximized when it is based on the management and sharing of knowledge within a culture of continuous learning, innovation and improvement.

Partnership Development—An organization works more effectively when it has mutually beneficial relationships, built on trust, sharing of knowledge and integration, with its Partners.

Public Responsibility—The long-term interest of the organization and its people are best served by adopting an ethical approach and exceeding the expectations and regulations of the community of large.

9.7.7 Other Not-so-Well Known Models for Process Improvement

So far, we discussed some of the most popular and established approaches —CMM, ISO 9000 and ISO/IEC 15504 etc. In this section, we provide an overview of other models, which may not be so known, to most readers. This is not an exhaustive list but gives some idea to the reader as to what the other process improvement models are. To start with, there is *Engineering Maturity Model (EMM), Software Development Capability/Capacity Review (SDC/CR), Systems Security Engineering (SSE), Software Technology Diagnostic (STD), Self-Assessment Method (SAM), Quantum.* Apart from these, there are some more—brief information on those is provided in the table 7.

9.8 The People Maturity Model (P-CMM)

The People Maturity Model (P-CMM) is of a different genre altogether. Whereas the focus of Software CMM and the Integrated CMM is on the maturity of software related practices, the focus of P-CMM is on the maturity of *the people related practices* (in the software organizations). Details of this model are available at the SEI site www.sei.cmu.edu. Here, we present only an overview for the sake of completeness in the discussion of process improvement models discussed in this chapter.

9.8.1 Need for the People Capability Maturity Model

In order to improve their performance, organizations must focus on three interrelated components—*people, process,* and *technology.* With the help of the Capability Maturity Model for Software (discussed in section 9.2), many software organizations have made cost-effective, lasting improvements in their software processes and practices. Yet many of these organizations have discovered that their continued improvement requires significant changes in the way they manage, develop, and use their people for developing and maintaining software and information systems—changes that are not fully accounted for in the CMM. To date, improvement programs for software organizations have often emphasized process or technology, not people. This is the main motivation for the *People Capability Maturity* (P-CMM) model.

The P-CMM describes an evolutionary improvement path from ad hoc, inconsistently performed practices, to a mature, disciplined, and continuously improving development of the knowledge, skills, and motivation of the workforce. The P-CMM helps software organizations:

Table 7: Other Models for Process Improvement

Name of the Model	Purpose	Yr Estd.	The People Behind	Remarks
The Trillium Model—8 Capability Areas: • Organisational Process Quality o Human Resource Development and Management • Process • Management • Quality System • Development Practices • Development Environment • Customer Support	Describes a telecommunications product munications product development and support capability To be used in a number of ways: –To benchmark an organization's product development and support process capability against the best practices in the industry –In self-assessment mode, to help identify opportunities for improvement within a product development organization –in pre-contractual negotiations, to assist selecting a supplier	1994	Bell Canada, Northern Telecom and Bell-Northern Research	Can also be used as a reference benchmark in an internal capability improvement program
Bootstrap	Bootstrap Methodology with the following objective to help increase process effectiveness, to support improvement planning etc.	–	Participating partners in the Esprit project	Bootstrap Process Model has the following capability levels: **Level 0:** Incomplete Process **Level 1:** Performed Process **Level 2:** Managed Process **Level 3:** Established Process **Level 4:** Predictable Process **Level 5:** Optimizing Process
Ideal Model	Serves as a roadmap for initiating, planning and implementing improvement actions	–	Software Engineering Institute (SEI)	Ideal has five Phases: *Initiating, Diagnosing, Establishing Acting Learning*

- Characterize the maturity of their workforce practices
- Guide a program of continuous workforce development
- Set priorities for immediate actions
- Integrate workforce development with process improvement
- Establish a culture of software engineering excellence

The P-CMM is designed to guide software organizations in selecting immediate improvement actions based on the current maturity of their workforce practices. The benefit of the P-CMM is in narrowing the scope of improvement activities to those practices that provide the next foundational layer for an organization's continued workforce development. These practices have been chosen from industrial experience as those that have significant impact on individual, team, unit, and organizational performance. The P-CMM includes practices in such areas as:

❑ work environment
❑ communication
❑ staffing
❑ managing performance
❑ training
❑ compensation
❑ competency development
❑ career development
❑ team building
❑ culture development

Figure 8 shows the Five Maturity Levels of the P-CMM. Each maturity level provides a layer in the foundation for continuous improvement of an organization's workforce practices. In maturing from the *Initial* to the *Repeatable level*, the organization installs the discipline of performing the basic practices. In maturing to the *Defined level*, these practices are tailored to enhance the particular *knowledge, skills*, and *work methods* that best support the organization's business. In maturing to the *Managed* teams and empirically evaluates how effectively its workforce practices are meeting objectives. In maturing to the *Optimizing level*, the organization looks continually for innovative ways to improve its workforce capability and to support individuals in their pursuit of *professional excellence*.

Conclusion

There are a number of frameworks available for "process improvement"; some very well known like the SW Capability Maturity Model (SW CMM) and the ISO 9001, while others not so known. This chapter considered most of them.

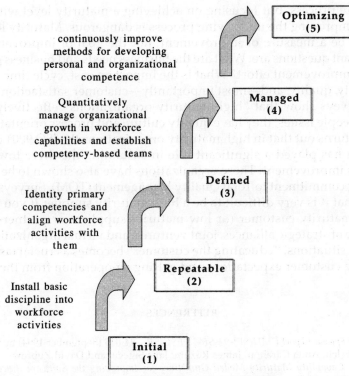

continuously improve
methods for developing
personal and organizational
competence

**Optimizing
(5)**

Quantitatively
manage organizational
growth in workforce
capabilities and establish
competency-based teams

**Managed
(4)**

Identity primary
competencies and
align workforce
activities with
them

**Defined
(3)**

Install basic
discipline into
workforce
activities

**Repeatable
(2)**

**Initial
(1)**

Figure 8 Maturity Levels of P-CMM

The SW-CMM represents a "common sense engineering" approach to software process improvement. Its maturity levels, key process areas, goals, and key practices have been extensively discussed and reviewed within the software community. While the SW-CMM is neither perfect nor comprehensive, it does represent a broad consensus of the software community and is a useful tool for guiding Software Process Improvement efforts.

ISO 9001 has a high acceptance level and that can be traced directly to the simple elegance of its fundamental tenets: Document what you do, Do what you documented and Verify that you are doing it.

One of the objectives of ISO/IEC 15504 is to create a way of measuring process capability, while avoiding a specific approach to improvement such as the SEI's maturity levels, so that the many different kinds of assessment, model, and their results, can be meaningfully compared to one another.

The focus of the P-CMM model is on the maturity of the workforce related practices. Its brief overview is included in this chapter for the sake of completeness of the discussion on improvement frameworks.

It is easy to get overwhelmed by all these process improvement frameworks and models. But never forget why process improvement is important. Standards and models can help organizations improve their software process, but focusing on achieving a maturity level without really improving the underlying process is dangerous. Maturity levels should be a measure of improvement, not the goal of improvement. Important questions are: What are the business needs and business goals of the improvement effort? What is the impact on cost, cycle time, productivity, quality, and—most importantly—customer satisfaction?

Surveys show that "high maturity organizations" effectively address people issues; they have quality culture and process orientations. Also it turns out that in high maturity organizations the ISO 9001 certification has played a significant role in sustaining the drive towards process improvement. These organizations have also shown to be supporting commitment to Total Quality Management (TQM). Surveys also show that it is very difficult to be a high maturity supplier if you have a low maturity customer (or low maturity suppliers or partners—in the case of strategic alliances, joint ventures, and virtual organizations). In such situations, "educating the customer" becomes a crucial task for shaping customer expectations and getting co-operation from them.

REFERENCES

[1] *SEI Special Report CMU/SEI-94-SR-13 ESC-SR—94-013* (September 1994) by James Hebsleb, Anita Carelton, James Rozum, Jane Sigegel and David Zubrow
[2] *The Capability Maturity Model: Guidelines for Improving the Software Process* by Carnegie Mellon University
[3] *Software Process Improvement: Practical Guide for Business Success* by Sami Zahran (Addison-Wesley)
[4] *CMM Implementation Guide* by Kim Caputo (Addison-Wesley)
[5] *Introduction to the Personal Software Process* by Watts S. Humphrey (Addison Wesley)
[6] *Introduction to the Team Software Process* by Watts S. Humphrey (Addison-Wesley)
[7] *HOW ISO 9001COMPARES WITH THE CMM*—Marc C. Paulk (Software Engineering Institute 1995)
[8] *Analyzing the Conceptual Relationship Between ISO/IEC 15504 (Software Process Assessment) and the Capability Maturity Model for Software*—Mark C. Paulk (Software Engineering Institute)
[9] *Practices of High Maturity Organizations*—Mark C. Paulk Software Engineering Institute (1999 SEPG Conference, Atlanta, Georgia, 8-11 March 1999)
[10] www.sei.cmu.edu/cmmi/adoption/adoption.html for a number of interesting articles on CMM-Integrated Model
[11] *Choosing a CMMI Model Representation*—Sandy Shrum Software Engineering Institute
[12] *Transitioning Your Organization from Software CMM Version 1.1 to CMM- I SW Version 1.0*—A CMM-I White Paper at www.sei.cmu.edu/cmmi/publications/white-paper.html)
[13] *Overview of the People Capability Maturity Model*—Bill Curtis, William E. Hefley Sally Miller (published by Software Engineering Institute at Carnegie Mellon University

Chapter 10

SOFTWARE TESTING

10.1 Overview

Testing is an organizational responsibility. The focus of this chapter is on some important aspects of software testing. Delivering quality products is sill a problem in the IT (Information Technology) industry. Testing is not a solution for this. Testing is just one instrument that can contribute to the quality enhancement of the IT systems/software products. Testing should be embedded in the overall quality management of an organization. As such, *Testing Policy* should be defined and documented and Testing Strategy should be evolved.

Often, quality assurance gets confused with testing. Sometimes people combine both terms to mean "QA". This is not correct.

- The goal of software tester is to find bugs and find them as early as possible and notify the same to developers so that they get fixed.
- A software quality assurance person's main responsibility is create and enforce standards and methods to improve the development process/testing process so that bugs can be prevented.

Thus, QA is separate from QC and deals with the overall management of quality. At times, due to budget resource constraints a slight overlap can happen between these two roles. Confusion among the team members about who is testing and who is not has caused lots of "process pain" in many projects. It must be remembered that essentially, (software) testing is a quality control (QC) activity. In Chapter 1 we discussed the difference between QA (Quality Assurance) and QC (Quality Control).

In this chapter, Software Testing as a topic is discussed for the completeness of discussion on quality, which is the theme of this book. The following aspects with regard to software testing are covered:

- Purpose of Testing
- Inspection versus Testing
- Testing versus Debugging
- Testing Life Cycle
- Roles and Responsibilities involved in Testing
- The Test Plan
- The V Model for Testing
- Testing Techniques (Testing of Functional and Non-functional attributes)
- Test Metrics
- Risk Based Testing
- Test Automation and Test Tool Selection
- Extreme Testing concept
- Human Issues and Challenges in Testing
- TPI (Test Process Improvement and Test Maturity) Framework
- Software Testing Careers and Testing Competence through professional certifications

Before proceeding further, two important terms: *Verification* and *Validation* are explained below.

Verification and Validation

Verification ensures that various work products (requirement specification document, design document code, test plan etc) are complete and consistent with respect to the other related work products and customer needs

Validation is concerned with assessing the quality of a software system in its actual operating environment. As per IEEE, Validation is the process of evaluating the software at the end of software development process to determine compliance with the user requirements.

Verification: Are we building the product right?

Validation: Are we building the right product?

High quality cannot be achieved through testing of source code alone and so reviews are important (various review techniques were discussed in Chapter 6)

10.2 Purpose of Testing

Very simply, testing is an activity associated with any process that produces a work product. It is used to determine the status of the product during and after the build. Role of testing changes as the type of process used to build the product changes. Basically, testing is the process of executing a software program/segment of code with the intent of finding errors. This implies that testing is a "destructive process". From a practitioner's view point, testing has the following roles:

Primary Role

- Determine whether system/software application meets specification (VERIFICATION)
- Determine whether system/software application meets users' needs (VALIDATION)

Secondary Role

- Instill confidence about the product developed
- Provide insight into the software development process
- Continuously improve the testing process

The IEEE definition of testing is: *Testing is the process of exercising or evaluating a system of system component by manual or automated means to verify that it satisfies specified requirements.*

Industry experience shows that testing consumes at least half of the effort expended in producing a working program. In terms of "Cost of Quality" (which comprises of Prevention, Appraisal and Failure), Testing is the appraisal effort. Not many programmers like testing and even fewer like *test design*—especially if test design and testing take longer than program design and coding. There is another problem with testing and it is related to why we do it. It's done to catch bugs. There is a myth that if we were really good at programming, there would be no bugs to catch. Boris Beizer in his famous book [6] provides a very interesting philosophical discussion on this point in terms of the "myth" just mentioned. He says:

"..........There are bugs, because we are bad at what we do; and if we are bad at it, we should feel guilty about it. Therefore, testing and test design amount an admission of failure, which instills a goodly dose of guilt. And the tedium of testing is just punishment of our errors. Punishment for what?- For being human? Guilt for what?—For not achieving inhuman perfection?.........."

Testing should focus on bug identification. To the extent that testing and test design do not prevent bugs, they should be able to discover symptoms caused by bugs. Finally, test should provide clear diagnoses so that bugs can be easily corrected. Bug prevention is the final goal based on analysis of past defect data collected by the testing process. A prevented bug is better than a detected and corrected bug because if the bug is prevented, there is no code to correct. Moreover, no re-testing is needed to confirm that the correction was valid, no one is embarrassed, no memory is consumed. More than testing, designing effective test cases is one of the best prevention actions.

The most important considerations in testing, according to Myers [11] are psychological in nature. He puts forth a set of vital testing principles or guidelines, which are summarized below:

1. *A necessary part of a test case is a definition of the expected output or result*
2. *A programmer should avoid attempting to test his/her own program*
3. *A programming organization should not test its own programs*
4. *Thoroughly inspect the results of each test*
5. *Test cases must be written for invalid and unexpected, as well as valid and expected, input conditions*
6. *Examining a program to see if it does not do what it is supposed to do is only half of the battle. The other half is seeing whether the program does what it is not supposed to do*
7. *Avoid throw-away test cases unless the program is truly a throw-away program*
8. *Do not plan a testing effort under the tacit assumption that no errors will be found*
9. *The probability of the existence of more errors in a section of a program is proportional to the number of errors already found in that section*
10. *Testing is an extremely creative and intellectual challenging task*
11. *Testing is the process of executing a program with the intent of finding errors*
   <u>A good test case</u> is one that has a high probability of detecting an as-yet undiscovered error
   <u>A successful test case</u> is one that detects an as-yet undiscovered error

10.3 Differences Between Inspection and Testing

Having discussed the purpose of testing, now let us understand the difference between Testing and Inspection, which is a typically asked question. In Chapter 6 we discussed *Reviews* and *Inspection*. We discussed there that *Verification* is a "human" examination or review of the work product. There are various types of reviews as discussed in Chapter 6(Inspections, Walkthrough, Technical Reviews).

Inspection can be used long before executable code is available to run tests. Thus, *Inspection* can be applied much earlier than testing the executable code and can be used to "verify" the requirements as well as the design. Tests to be run can be defined along with requirements and design specification process. This is because specification is the source for knowing the expected result of a test execution.

The one thing, which Testing does and Inspection does not, is to evaluate the software while it is actually performing its function in its intended/simulated environment. Inspection can only examine static documents and models; testing can evaluate the product working. To this extent, it can be said that Inspection is a *static testing* technique, The figure below shows the relationship between Testing and Inspection.

Inspection (among other verification techniques) is concerned with removal of any possible defects that may exist prior to the coding phase. The information gained from defects found by running test could be used in the same way, but this is rare in practice.

It should be noted that *Testing* and *Inspection* are NOT mutually exclusive alternatives. Test documentation is just as prone to defects as any other document, so it is essential that test documents be inspected. Inspecting the *Test Plan* can help bring out potential defects in the test plan itself which is the basic guiding document to execute tests. Thus, both *Inspection* and *Testing* aim towards establishing confidence in the work product. Both have different but complementary objectives and must be used appropriately to achieve maximum benefit.

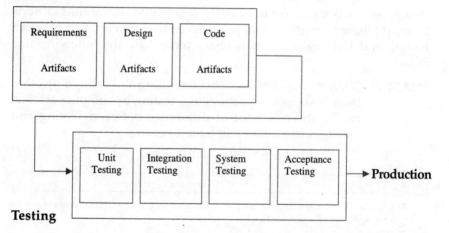

Figure 1: Testing vis-à-vis Inspection

Professional software testing practices include:

- The planning and design of testing from the beginning of the software development life cycle (Life Cycle Testing concept)
- Acceptance tests criteria defined by users at the same time as user requirements are defined
- Systems test cased identified during requirements analysis—integration test cases identified during architectural design
- Unit tests cases identified during detailed design

- Execution of unit tests, integration tests, system tests, acceptance tests
- Evaluation of test effectiveness

The advantage of early test planning is that Inspection can be effectively used to improve the quality of the test planning documents and the test planning process at early stages of a project. This will help avoid "last minute before deadline" problems in pushing the deliverables successfully out of the door.

In summary, we should note that Inspection *does not* replace Testing. They both perform some unique functions, which neither can replace for the other. What Testing *could* find later, Inspection could find *earlier,* and *probably* provides saving in correction effort. Defects injected *after* Inspection must also be found during Testing. Thus, Inspection, in a way, is form of (static) Testing and is a human intensive activity in the sense that automation is not used here. It should be noted that Inspection and Testing in combination is typically more effective than either of these techniques alone.

10.4 Testing v/s Debugging

Often these two terms are not clearly segregated. According to Boris Beizer [6] there is an attitudinal progression in differentiating between Testing and Debugging. This is characterized by the following five phases:

PHASE 0—There's no difference between testing and debugging other than in support of debugging, testing has no purpose. Actually, there is a lot of difference between Testing and Debugging as shown in table 1 below.

Table 1: Testing and Debugging

Testing	Debugging
1. Starts with known conditions, user predefined procedures, predictable outcomes	Unknown initial conditions, end cannot be predicted
2. Should be planned, designed, scheduled	Cannot be constrained
3. Is a demonstration of error/apparent correctness	Is a deductive process
4. Proves a programmer's "failure"	Vindicates a programmer
5. Should strive to be predictable, dull, constrained, rigid, inhuman	Demands intuitive leaps, conjectures, experimentation, freedom
6. Much can be done without design knowledge	Impossible without design knowledge
7. Can be done by outsider	Must be done by insider
8. Theory of testing is available	Only recently have theorists started looking at it
9. Much of test design and execution can be automated	Automation is still a dream

PHASE 1—The purpose of testing is to show that the software works.

PHASE 2—The purpose of testing is to show that the software doesn't work.

PHASE 3—The purpose of testing is not to prove anything, but to reduce the perceived risk of not working to an acceptable value ("Risk-based Approach to Testing")

PHASE 4—Testing is not an act. It is a mental discipline that results in low-risk software without testing effort.

The debugging process is depicted in Figure 2 below in reference to Table 1 above. A point to ponder is that there appears to be some evidence that "debugging prowess" is an innate human trait; some individuals are good at it, others are not. In fact, large variances in debugging ability have been reported for programmers with the same educational experience background.

Debugging Process

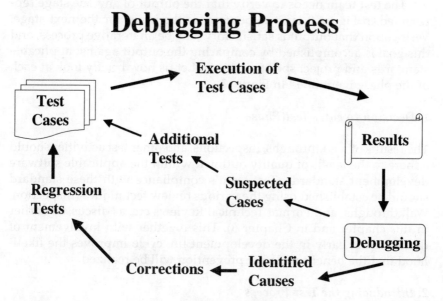

Figure 2: Debugging Process

In the words of Scheiderman:

Debugging is one the more frustrating parts of programming. It has elements of "problem solving" or "brain teasers", coupled with the annoying recognition that you've made a mistake. Heightened anxiety, and the unwillingness to accept the possibility of errors, increases the task difficulty. Fortunately, there is a great sigh of relief and a lessening of tension when the bug is ultimately corrected........

With this backdrop, we'll discuss "human issues and challenges" in testing, towards the end of this chapter. For now, let us turn to understand the testing life cycle.

10.5 Testing Life Cycle

Successful completion of work product verification activities through review techniques (such as Walkthroughs and Inspections as discussed in section 10.2 of this chapter and Chapter 6) should be the only approved gateway to proceed to the next phase of activities. Figure 3 depicts typical quality gates that apply during the *testing life cycle.*

It shows the testing life cycle sequence starting with the decision to enter the test phase and quality gates before proceeding to the next phase. It should be noted that quality gates exist throughout the entire project life cycle.

The test team needs to verify that the output of any one stage represented in Figure 3 is fit to be used as the input for the next stage. Verification that output is satisfactory may be an iterative process, and this goal is accomplished by comparing the output against applicable standards and project specific criteria. Let us now briefly look at each of the phase mentioned in Figure 3.

1. Decision to enter Test Phase

The results of walkthroughs, inspections, and other test activities should adhere to the levels of quality outlined within the applicable software development standards. Test team's compliance with these standard should be established using the various review techniques (Inspection, Walkthroughs, and Formal Technical Reviews etc. as discussed earlier in this chapter and in Chapter 6). This together with involvement of the test team early in the development life cycle improves the likelihood that the benefit of defect prevention will be realized.

2. Introducing the Test Process

This is formal announcement to the project team that the test phase is now to commence. Roles and Responsibilities are established at this stage and expectations set accordingly. Section 10.6 has a detailed discussion on this.

3. Test Plan Preparation

Test plan is the basic guiding document to carry out the testing phase. You need this to successfully manage the testing project. Writing a test plan allows you to collect your thoughts, your ideas and memories. In short, writing a thorough test plan givens you a chance to crystallize your testing knowledge and experience into a concrete way of tackling the test tasks ahead. It is your opportunity to communicate with your test team. Section 10.8 has a discussion on the *test plan*

4. Test Case Development

This is an extremely important activity whose roots lie in the requirements analysis itself. Aim should be to develop re-usable test cases, which could save a lot of efforts in the next similar project. Careful and methodical planning for test cases is important for their organization, repeatability, tracking and generating proof of testing.

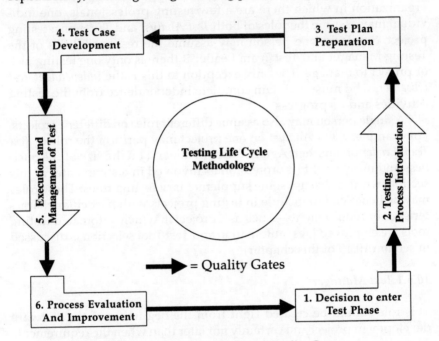

Figure 3: Testing Life Cycle and Quality Gates

5. Executing and Managing the Test Plan

The main activities involved during this are assigning the test cases to testers, gathering the test results, collecting the test process metrics (section 10.11), preparing bug reports etc.

6. Test Process Evaluation and Improvement

Testing belongs to the detective measures of a quality system. At the end of the testing phase, it is important to analyze the effectiveness of the testing process and introduce improvement measures as required. The purpose of improvement is to be able to carry out the process with less effort and budget next time (In section 10.11 we have discussed some test metrics that help improve the testing process)

10.6 Roles and Responsibilities in Testing

This section describes the roles involved in the testing process, their individual responsibilities, and their requirements for reporting and liaison. It is important to note when reading this section that it is possible for a single person to assume more than one role within any testing process. The number of roles simultaneously existing would depend on the size and scope of the testing activity. For example, in a small organization in which there are a few testing professionals, one individual may assume the roles of both *Test Analyst* and *Tester* on a testing project. Similarly, one person may assume the responsibilities of the Testing Manager and Test Team Leader if there is only one testing task or project to manage. The only exception to this is the *Independent Test Observer*, who must maintain complete independence from the testing activities and its progress.

A single person may also assume different roles on different projects. For example, a *Test Analyst* on one project may perform the role of *Test Team Leader* on another. Again, this will depend on the size of the business and number of test professionals involved in testing. Later in this section, we also discuss some supplementary testing roles. These roles may be beneficial to include in testing projects with particular characteristics or requirements—such as a project in which automated testing tools are employed (Test automation and Test Tool selection is discussed in section 10.13 of this chapter)

10.6.1 Test Manager

This role should be created right from the beginning of the software development project and certainly not later than when the requirements gathering phase is over. The Test Manager has the responsibility to administer the organizational aspects of the testing process on a day-to-day basis and is responsible for ensuring that the individual testing projects produce the required products (i.e. the outputs from the testing phases, including the fully tested AUT—application under test) to the required standard of quality and within the specified constraints of time, resources and budget.

Where appropriate, the Test Manager is also responsible for liaison with the development teams to ensure that they follow the Unit Testing and Independent Testing approach documented within the process. The Test Manager will also liaise with the Independent Test Observer(s) to receive reports on testing activities that have failed to follow the testing process appropriately.

The Test Manager reports to a senior management or director within the organization, such as the *Quality Assurance (QA) Manager* or *Information Technology Director*. In large organizations, and particularly those following a formal project management process, the Test Manager may also report to a Testing Program Board, which is responsible for the overall direction of the project management of the testing program.

10.6.2 *Test Team Leader*

In small testing projects the Test Manager himself may play this role. In larger projects this role needs to be created separately. This role should be in place after the test plan is ready and test environment is established. The **Test Team Leader** is given the responsibility to carry out the day-to-day testing activities. His or her responsibilities assigning tasks to one or more testers/test analysts, monitoring their progress against agreed upon plans, setting up and maintaining the testing project filing system, and ensuring the generation of the test artifacts as described in section 10.7.

One or more *Test Analysts* and *Testers* report to the Test Team Leader, who, in turn, reports to the Test Manager. The Test Team Leader will liaise with the Independent Test Observer (to discuss availability to attend a particular test, for example), and, where appropriate, to the *Development Team Leader* (to undertake early planning of the testing project and preliminary test design and to determine the availability of the AUT for testing). During *Acceptance Testing* the *Test Team Leader* is responsible for liaising with the User Representative and Operations Representative to obtain one or more users to perform *Acceptance Testing*, which is the responsibility of the customer.

10.6.3 *Test Analyst*

The *Test Analyst* is responsible for the design and implementation of one or more *Test Scripts* (See Table 3 for the format), which will be used to accomplish the testing of the AUT. It should be noted that if the scope of testing activity is small, the test lead might end up doing many of tasks described here. The *Test Analyst* may also be called upon to assist the *Test Team Leader* in the generation of the *Test Specification Document*. During the design of *Test Case* (see section 10.7 on *Test Artifacts*), the Test Analyst will need to analyze the *Requirements Specification* for the AUT to identify specific requirements that must be tested. During this process the Test Analyst will need to prioritize the Test Cases to reflect the importance of the feature being validated and the risk of the feature failing during normal use of the AUT. At the completion of the testing project, the Test Analyst is responsible for the back-up and archival of all testing documentation and materials, as well as the creation of a testing re-use pack. The Test Analyst is also responsible for completing a Test Summary Report briefly describing the key points of the testing project.

10.6.4 *Tester*

The *Tester* is primarily responsible for the execution of the Test Scripts created by the Test Analyst and for the interpretation and documentation of the results of the Test Case Execution (Table 4 shows the format for a *Test Script*). During the test execution, the *Tester* is responsible for filling in the Test Result Record Forms (Table 4) to document the observed result of executing each Test Script (Table 3) and for co-signing the bottom of each from with the *Independent Test Observer* to confirm that the Test Script was followed correctly and the observed result recorded accurately. The *Tester* is also responsible for the recovery of the test environment in the event of failure of the system.

10.6.5 *Independent Test Observer*

In general terms, the *Independent Test Observer* is responsible for providing independent *verification* that correct procedure (as per the testing process for the organization) are followed during the testing of the AUT. Sometimes this can be contractual requirement stipulated by the customer. Specifically during testing, the *Independent Test Observer* is responsible for ensuring that the *Tester* executes the tests according to the instructions provided in the *Test Scripts* (Table 3 has the format) and that he or she interprets the observed result correctly according to the description of the expected result. In organizations in which there is a formal *Quality Assurance Group*, *Independent Test Observers* may be drawn from the ranks of the Quality Assurance Representative. In smaller organizations or where there is not such a strong quality culture, the Independent Test Observer may be a staff member drawn from another group or project within the organization. The key criterion in selecting a Independent Test Observer is that she or he must be impartial and objective.

10.6.6 *Supplementary Testing Roles*

As said earlier, depending on the specific testing requirements of a particular testing project, it may be appropriate to include a number of additional testing roles. These are summarized below:

Table 2: Supplementary Testing Roles

Name of the Supplementary Role	Responsibilities
TEST AUTOMATION ARCHITECT	• Definition of the test automation architecture • Specification of all hardware and software configurations added • Assisting the *Test Team Leader* to plan any programming and set-up tasks needed to install a new automation environment, including deploying the testing tools and environment-specific support code.
TEST AUTOMATION ANALYST	• Implementing automated tests a specified in the *Test Specification Document* and any supplementary design documents • Implementing test support code required for efficiently executing automated tests • Setting up and executing automated tests against the AUT • Reviewing the automated test log following testing to identify and report on defects found within the AUT during testing
EXPLORATORY TESTER	• Autonomous testing of a product without following a specified set of Test Cases • Focusing on finding the highest severity defects in the most important features of the system using a risk-based testing approach

10.7 Test Artifacts

In section 10.6.2 we mentioned that the Test Team Leader is responsible for the various test artifacts. Test artifacts are work products that get created as part of numerous activities carried out during the testing phase of a software development project. In this section we have provided brief description of the test artifacts. IEEE definitions are also provided for some important terms in the context of testing. In addition to this, we have also provided some useful formats (Table 3: Test Script, Table 4: Test Results/Execution Table, Table 5: Test Plan Template).

- *The Test Plan Document,* which will be used as the basis of project management control throughout the testing process. (The Test Plan will be discussed in a separate section in this chapter). This document is produced by the Test Team Leader and is approved by the Testing Manager
- *The Test Specification Document,* which outlines in detail the approach to testing the AUT (Application Under Test), the resources needed, the testing environment, the evaluation criteria and acceptable defect rates /frequencies, exit criteria, and so on. At the minimum, the test specification document should include the following:

    o Introduction
       – Background
       – Scope
       – Structure of the Document
       – References
    o Test Requirement
       – Introduction
       – Test Philosophy (Overview, Functional Areas, Test Result
         Categories, Exclusions)
    o Test Environment
       – Overview
       – Hardware
       – Software
       – Test Data
    o Staff Roles and Responsibilities
    o Test Identification
       – Test Scripts
       – Result Reporting
       – Acceptance Criteria
       – Test Error Clearance
       – Test Documentation
    o Test Procedure
       – Introduction
       – Pre-Test Activities
       – Concluding the Test
       – Post-Test Activities
    o Test Case
    o Test Suite
    o Test Harness
    o Test Bed

**Some IEEE Definitions
(IEEE Std. 610.12)**

Test

An activity in which a system or component is executed under specified conditions, the results are observed or recorded, and an evaluation is made of some aspect of the system/component

Test Documentation

Documentation describing plans for, or results of the testing of a system or components

Test Bed

An environment containing the hardware, instrumentation, simulation, software tools, simulators and other support elements needed to conduct a test

Test Case

A set of test inputs, execution conditions, and expected results, developed for a particular objective such as to exercise a particular program, path or to verify compliance with a specific requirement

Test Coverage

The degree or extent to which a given component must meet in order to pass a given test.

Test Driver (synonymous with Test Harness)

A software module used to invoke a module under test and often, to provide test inputs, control and monitor execution, and report test results.

Test Case Generator

A software tool that accepts as input source code, test criteria, specification, or data structure definitions; uses these inputs to generate test input data, and sometimes determines expected results (synonymous with *Test Data Generator, Test Generator*)

Test Case Specification (synonymous with Test Description, Test Specification)

A document that specifies the test inputs, execution conditions, and predicted results for an item to be tested.

Test Report

A document that describes the conduct and results of the testing carried out for a system or component.

Acceptance Criteria

The criteria that a system/component must satisfy in order to be accepted by a user, customer or other authorized entity.

Table 3: Test Script

Project ID AUT Title Testing Phase	Version Test Date	Script Author

Test ID
Purpose of Test

Test Environment

Test Steps

Expected Results

Table 4: Test Result Record

Project ID AUT Title Testing Phase Test Case Id Testing Cycle No	Effort Spent (Hrs) AUT Version Test Date Tester Name	

Test ID
Test Execution Steps
Actual Test Results Observed
Defect Id *

Test Result Category **

Test Error Description

Tester Signature

Reviewer Signature

---

* *This gets logged into the Defect Tracking System*
** *Test Result Categories* (indicated on the next page)

Test Result Categories (Ref. Table 3)

PASS	observed test result conforms to the expected result
FAIL	**observed test result does not conform to the expected result at all**
ACCEPTABLE	observed test result indicates that the system differs from the agreed specification but is acceptable, requiring no change to the AUT, but requiring a change to the Functional Specification
TOLERABLE	observed result is incorrect; the AUT is workable and will be accepted but the defect must be rectified within an agreed-on time period
INTOLRABLE	observed result is incorrect and the defect must be corrected before the AUT passes this testing phase (Quality Gate)
TEST ERROR	observed result is correct, but the expected result is incorrect (e.g. a typographical error in the test script)
BREAK	test stopped because of some reasons

10.8 The Test Plan

Given that exhaustive testing is impractical, except in the most critical of the systems, the project team must design and plan a testing strategy (commonly known testing strategies are *White Box Testing* and *Black Box Testing* although these days with Web Applications a third tem called *"Gray Box Testing"* is also heard) that utilizes a balance of testing techniques to cover a representative sample of the system. The test planning process is a critical step in the testing process. Without a documented test plan, the test itself cannot be verified, coverage cannot be analyzed, and the test process is not repeatable.

In section 10.7, we have provided definitions of common test terminology. Reader should keep this in mind while reading this section. A document that defines the overall testing objectives and approach is called a *Test Plan* while a document that defines what is selected to test, and describes the expected results is called a test design. Test plans and designs can be developed for any level of testing, and may be combined in the same document.

Test Planning should begin at the same time requirements definition starts. The plan will be detailed in parallel with application requirements. During the analysis stage of the project, the Test Plan defines and communicates test requirements and the amount of testing needed so that accurate test estimates can be made and incorporated into the test plan.

Why write a Test Plan? Writing a test plan allows you to collect your thoughts, your ideas, and your memories. Writing a thorough test plan gives you a chance to crystallize that knowledge into a concrete way to tacking the tasks ahead. Basically, a test plan is also an opportunity to communicate with your test team, your development team and your project management.

Thus, documented tests are **REPEATABLE, CONTROLLABLE,** and ensure **ADEQUATE TEST COVERAGE** when executed.

Good testing requires thinking out an overall approach, designing tests, and establishing expected results for each of the chosen *test cases*. Since exhaustive testing is usually impractical, the test team must select a sample of tests that will provide the appropriate confidence level in the application. The planning and care extended on marking this selection and planning it, is the difference between a good test process and a poor one.

There are standards in the industry that define hierarchies of test documentation. In section 10.7, we had discussed a few key terms as defined in the IEEE standard. Here, we have repeated some terms for quick handy reference to the reader.

- The *Test Plan* is defined as an overall document providing direction for all testing activity
- The *Test Design Specification* refines the test approach and identifies the features to be covered by the design and its associated tests
- A *Test Case Specification* documents the actual values used for input along with the anticipated outputs
- The *Test Procedures Specification* identifies all steps required to exercise the specified test cases

The standard also addresses documents to be used in test reporting. Test plans and formats vary from organization to organization. A typical Table of Contents of a test plan is indicated below:

Table 5: Test Plan Template

Overview
Bounds
    Scope and Objectives
    Definitions
    Setting
    Assumptions
Quality Risks
Proposed Schedule and Milestones
Transitions
    Entry Criteria
    Discontinuation Criteria
    Exist Criteria
Test Configurations and Environment
Test Design and Test Tools (Automation Strategy)
Test Execution
    Resources
    Tracking and Management of Tests and Bugs
    Bug Isolation and Classification
    Release Management
    Test Cycles
Test Data Management
Risks and Contingencies
Change History
Referenced Documents

10.9 The V-Model for Testing Phases

The V-Model shown in figure 4 is software development and testing model, which helps to highlight the need to plan and prepare for testing early in the development process. The left-hand descending arm of the "V" represents the traditional Waterfall development phases, whereas the ascending right-hand arm of the "V" shows the corresponding testing phase. In the V-Model, each development phase is linked to a corresponding testing phase. We'll discuss each of theses briefly in this section. As work proceeds on a particular development phase, planning and some preliminary design work is performed for the corresponding testing phase.

The benefits of the V-Model are the following:

- The testing phases are given the same level of management attention and commitment as the corresponding development phases in terms of planning and resourcing. This allows risks to be addressed early in the development cycle
- The outputs from the development phases (such as specification and design documents) can be reviewed by the testing team to ensure their testability
- The early planning and preliminary design of tests provides additional review comments on the outputs from the development phase

We'll now discuss each of the testing phases briefly as shown in the right hand arm of the V-Model depicted in Figure 4.

10.9.1 Unit Testing

Unit Testing is also referred to as "software component testing". It represents the lowest level of testing that the AUT undergo. It is conducted to ensure that reliable program units (software components) are produced that meet their requirements. Unit testing is typically conducted by the *Development Team* and specifically by the programmer who coded the unit, the person responsible for designing and running a series of tests to ensure that the unit meets its requirements. It is unlikely that the Development Team Leader will need to produce detailed Test Plan and Test Specification documents for Unit Testing. The results of Unit Testing should be formally documented using a Test Result Record Form (such as the one shown in Table 4 in the earlier section.

10.9.2 Integration Testing

The objective here is to demonstrate that the software modules, which comprise the AUT interface, interact in a correct, stable and coherent manner. The Development Team typically conducts Integration

Testing, with responsibility for managing the testing resting with the Development Team Leader. In large organizations with well-established quality and/or mature software development and testing process, Integration Testing is conducted by a dedicated Testing Team. This team typically comprises of development team members and testing team members. The team is responsible for all aspects of testing. The results of Integration Testing should be formally documented using a suitable form for Test Result Record, which is filed by the Development Team Leader at the end of the testing phase. Another key issue to consider is the need to manage the user expectations regarding the look and feel and the operation and performance of the AUT.

10.9.3 System Testing

The fundamental objective of *System Testing* is to establish confidence that the AUT will be accepted by the users—i.e. that it will pass its *Acceptance Test*. System Testing is typically conducted as an independent testing project by a dedicated testing team, with responsibility for managing the testing falling to the Test Team Leader. For small organizations, it is possible that the development team will conduct System Testing. During System Testing, it is essential that truly independent observation of the testing process be performed. The *Independent Test Observer* may be drawn from another development project, or from the Quality Assurance group if the organization has one. As with Integration Testing, the Test Team Leader should consider inviting the User

The V Model for Testing

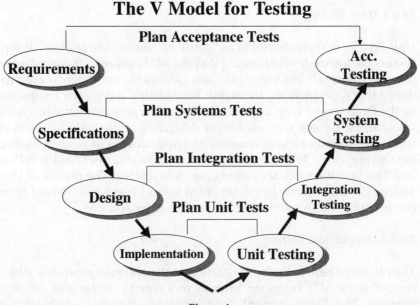

Figure 4

Representative to the System Test in an informal capacity to observe the testing process in order to manage the users' expectations of the AUT prior to formal Acceptance Testing.

10.9.4 Acceptance Testing

The purpose of Acceptance Testing is to confirm that the system meets its business requirements and to provide confidence that the system works correctly and is usable before it is formally "handed over" to the end users. Customer is responsible for ensuring this. Acceptance Testing is sometimes divided into *User Acceptances Testing* (involving the business or end users of the AUT) and *Operations Acceptance Testing* (involving the administrative/support staff of the AUT). Acceptance Testing is performed by nominated user representatives under the guidance and supervision of the testing team. During Acceptance Testing it is very important that independent observation of the testing process be performed, particularly where the user representatives are not so IT-savvy.

10.9.5 Alpha and Beta Testing

Before we move on to the next section, it is important to discuss these two important terms for the sake of completeness. In a way, the two terms are connected with *acceptance testing*. The testing ideas talked so far have been "internal"; in the sense that the people involved are from the developers' organization. Alpha and Beta testing involves "others" (external to the developers' organization) to validate that the software is working as intended.

Alpha Testing

Let us first discuss the scenario for alpha testing. However much a thorough plan may exist with the development team of the supplier organization, the fact remains that it is virtually impossible to "foresee" how the customer will "really" use a program/module/system. Operating manuals and user manual may be written and get reviewed before giving it to the customer as a part of agreed deliverables but sill there is always a possibility that instructions for use may be misinterpreted. Also, strange combination of data may happen, business rule may change subtly and the outputs produced actually under operational environmental may not be understood by the end user though the tester may have found it to be ok when he/she checked it.

When custom software is produced for one particular customer, a series of acceptance tests are conducted which helps customer to validate all requirements. Acceptance testing can be conducted over a period of weeks/months so that cumulative errors can be uncovered. If the software is developed as a product to be used with varied types of customers (typically this happens with utility software), formal acceptance testing may not feasible or practical. In such situations, a process called *alpha testing* and *beta testing* is used to uncover errors that are likely to be found only by the end users.

A customer conducts the alpha test at the developer's site. The software is used in its intended operating environment. The developer assumes the role of an "invisible observer" noting and recording the errors/usage problems as the end user interacts with the system/software

Beta Testing

Now let us understand the scenario for *beta testing*. Beta testing is the term used to describe the "external testing process" wherein the software is sent out to a select group of potential customer who use it in a "real-world environment". Beta test takes place when the developer is confident that the software is ready for the final delivery from the development organization side. Its purpose is to validate that the software is ready to release to "real customers". Some key points about beta testing are given below:

- "Know" your beta testers—since a beta test can have different goals, it is important to understand in advance who is going to participate in it: are they experienced "techies" or novice users? How useful/user-friendly the software is perceived depends really on this. If the beta testers are too advanced users, then they may not be interested in the lower details, which may really concern the novice users. So the selection of people in the best testing activity is important.
- Are you sure that the beta testers really used the software? You may have signed up with hundreds of beta tester and for months they may not report anything. Does that mean that there are "no bugs"? It is important to ensure that there is adequate follow-up happening with the beta testing participants.
- Beta tests can be a good way to find compatibility and configuration bugs; especially with the web-based applications.
- For usability issues, signing up beta testing makes a lot of sense provided the selection of participants is made carefully.
- With beta testing a risk is that only obvious, superficial problems may get reported. To motivate beta testers to spend adequate time on trying out the system, innovative schemes can be designed. If beta testers report the already known bugs to the developers then it does not serve the purpose. It is a good idea to provide a list of already found bugs to the beta testers so that they can focus on other areas.

Finally, in summary, we note that beta test is conducted at one or more customer sites by the end user(s) of the software/system. Unlike alpha testing, the developer is generally not present. Therefore, the beta test is a "live" application of the software in an environment that cannot be controlled by the developer. The customer records *all* the problems encountered and is expected to report these to the developer. This interaction of reporting problems at regular intervals may continue for quite some time. Based on the reported problems, the developer makes modifications and then prepares the software for further releases (by giving "fixes" and "patches" etc.) for the entire customer base.

10.10 Testing Techniques

Broadly speaking testing techniques can be divided into two major categories: Functional Testing and Non-Functional Testing.

[A] **Functional Testing Techniques** such as:
- Equivalence Partitioning
- Boundary Value Analysis
- Intrusive Testing
- Random Testing
- State Transition Analysis
- Static Testing
- Thread Testing

[B] **Non-functional Testing Techniques** such as:
- Configuration/Installation Testing
- Compatibility and Interoperability Testing
- Documentation and Help Testing
- Graphical User Interface (GUI) Testing
- Fault Recovery Testing
- Performance Testing
- Reliability Testing
- Security Testing
- Stress Testing
- Load/Volume Testing
- Usability Testing

We'll discuss each of these only very briefly in the following sections.

10.10.1 Functional Testing Techniques

Equivalence Partitioning

Selecting test data and designing "appropriate" test cases is the single most important task that software testers do and equivalence partitioning (also

(turn to page N)

known as equivalence classing), is the means by which this is done. Basically, an equivalence class or equivalence partition is a set of test cases that tests the same thing or reveals the same bug. Equivalence Partitioning relies on the fact that inputs and outputs from the AUT can be grouped or partitioned into coherent groups or classes and that all instances of these classes will be treated in the same manner by the system or application under test. The principal assumption of this technique is that testing one instance of the class is equivalent to testing all of them. The skill in using this technique lies in identifying the partition of values and selecting representative values from within this partition, and in deciding how many values to test.

Steps in Equivalence Partitioning are:

- Identify all inputs
- Identify all outputs
- Identify equivalence classes for each input
- Identify equivalence classes for each output
- Ensure that test cases test each input and output equivalence class at least once

As an example of Equivalence Partitioning technique, consider the following:

Example

A subroutine takes in **Marks**, **Student Type** and returns the **Grades** for the student in that subject

Inputs are:
Marks   :   (0-100)
Student Type   :   First time/Repeat

Outputs are:
Grade   :   F,D,C,B,A

Rules   :
Student Type First Time
0-40 = F, 41-50 = D, 51-60 = C, 61-70 = B, 71-100 = A
Student Type Repeat
0-50 = F, 51-60 = D, 61-70 = C, 71-80 = B, 81-100 = A

Some Test Cases to be considered:
Marks 30 and First Time Student   (Expected Output is 'F')
Marks 40 and Repeat Student   (Expected Output is 'F')
Marks 65 and First Time Student   (Expected Output is 'B')
Marks 85 and First Time Student   (Expected Output is 'A')
Marks 0 and First Time Student   (Expected Output is 'F')
Marks 0 and Repeat Student   (Expected Output is 'F')

Boundary Value Analysis

The best way to describe the concept behind this is through an analogy: If you can safely and confidently walk along the edge of a cliff without falling off, you can almost certainly walk in the middle of a field! If software can operate on the edge of its capabilities, it will almost certainly operate well under normal conditions.

Boundary (Value) Analysis is a technique related to Equivalence Partitioning and relies on the same underlying principal: that inputs and outputs can be grouped into classes and all instances of these classes can be treated similarly by the system. Whereas Equivalence Partitioning deals with selecting representative values from within the class, Boundary Value Analysis forces on the testing of values from the boundary of the class. Specifically, the technique will design a Test Case for the boundary value itself, plus a Test data for one significant value on either side of the boundary.

Thus an additional step involved for constructing test cases based on Boundary Value Analysis is that *for each input equivalent class, ensure that test cases include:*

- *One Interior Point*
- *One Extreme Point*
- *All Epsilon Points (close the either end of the range of inputs)*

Extending the example in the previous section (Equivalence Partitioning), some Test Cases for Boundary Analysis would be:

- Marks 99 and First Time Student (Expected Output = 'A')
- Marks 101 and First Time Student (Expected Output should be a suitable 'Error Msg")
- Marks negative and either First Time Student or Repeat Student (Expected Outcome should be a suitable 'Error Msg")

In conclusion, it is to be noted that boundary conditions are special because programming, by its nature, is susceptible to problems at its edges.

Intrusive Testing

As the name suggests, Intrusive Testing involves the deliberate modification of the AUT or its behaviour for the purpose of testing. For example, where the result of a test would not be visible to the tester (such as the modification of the value of a variable that would not be displayed to the user during the execution of the AUT), the Test Analyst may introduce additional statements into the application to display the value of the variable. Other examples include directly setting the values of variables using symbolic debuggers or deliberately triggering error conditions within the AUT

Clearly, any modifications made to the system for the purpose of testing must not be delivered to the customer/user of the system. Therefore rigorous change control and configuration management is essential. This technique should be used with extreme caution because there are many examples of systems that have been released containing changes introduced during Intrusive Testing that have manifested themselves during normal operation of the system.

Random Testing

This is one of the very few techniques for automatically generating Test Cases. This is because, although automating the process of providing inputs and stimulating the AUT is relatively straightforward, automating the process of checking the outputs is difficult. Depending on the approach employed, it may also be difficult to reproduce the results of a particular series of random tests. As a result of all this, it is not a commonly used technique.

State Transition Analysis

This is in terms of the states the system can be in, the transition between those states, the actions that cause the transitions, and the actions that may result from the transitions. For designing Test Cases, State Transition information can be derived from the requirements document or may be documented in the design of development methods that support State Transition Notations (for example as supported by UML—Unified Modeling Language). This technique is also useful in Negative Testing whereby the tester can cover issues that either got overlooked or poorly specified in the specification document.

Consider the example below, which illustrates the principle behind State Transition Analysis

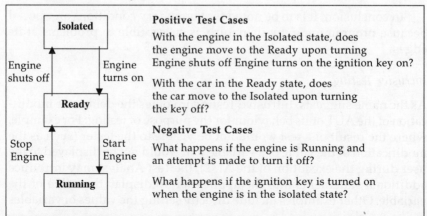

Static Testing

This does not involve executing or running the AUT but deals with inspection in isolation. We discussed this at the beginning of this chapter. Typical examples of Static Testing are: Code review and inspection, Code Walkthrough, Static Analyzers etc.

Thread Testing

The purpose here is to test the business functionality or business logic flow of the Application under Test (AUT) in an end-to-end manner, as if a user or an operator might interact with the system during its normal mode. Basically, in thread testing one tests the transactions processing as they are going to take place in the system/application designed.

As an example suppose we are doing thread testing of a student examination system, one particular thread could be processing the marks of a particular student. The thread testing process might involve the following steps:

- The operator logging onto the system
- Validation of the operator privileges
- Entry of the details of the student being processed
- Validation of the mark details
- Access the student database to verify the student
- Modification of the database to show that the student marks have now been processed
- Printing of the appropriate mark sheet to conclude the marks processing transaction

A point to be noted is that this technique contrasts with earlier testing phases (such as Unit and Integration testing) where the tester is likely to have been more interested in the correct functioning of the object under test rather than on its business logic

10.10.2 Nonfunctional Testing Techniques

First let us understand what do we mean by "nonfunctional requirements". Non-functional requirements are properties or qualities that the product must have (For example, *efficiency, integrity, reliability, usability, correctness, maintainability, expandability, flexibility, portability, re-usability* etc.) in order to enhance its "appeal". If not stated in the Software Requirements Specifications, these are generally the "nice to have" features of the software that the user is expecting.

Think of these properties or characteristics or "*software quality factors*" that make the product attractive, or usable or fast or reliable. For example, you may want your product to respond within a specified time, or display the calculated figures in certain colours and font. As another example, the product is expected to have a particular

...earance (i.e. the splash screen that comes upon starting the software, must use the standard company logo) etc. Thus, these properties of the product are not required because they are the functional requirements of the product (i.e. even without these, the software will work)—but they are there because the client wants the delivered software to operate in a certain manner. The vignette below further helps us understand "non-functional requirements".

Non-Functional Requirements

"Look and Feel" requirements—*the intended appearance*

Based on intended user (level of comfort with software)—*Usability Requirements*

Performance Requirements—*how fast, big, accurate, safe, reliable* etc.

Social, Cultural and Political Requirements—*human factors, usability by handicapped people*

Legal Requirement—*conformance to applicable laws*

Security Requirement—*the security, confidentiality and integrity of the product*

Maintainability and Portability Requirements—*how changeable the product must be*

With this understanding, now let us have a brief look at what is involved in each of these non-functional testing.

Installation Testing

This is used to ensure that hardware and software have been correctly installed, all necessary files and connections, have been created, all appropriate data files have been loaded, system default settings have been correctly set, and interfaces to the other hardware systems/components or peripheral devices are all working fine. One also needs to ensure that the already installed software does not get affected due to additional installation of the hardware components.

Compatibility and Interoperability Testing

The purpose here is to verify that when the AUT runs in the live environment, its operation does not impact adversely on other systems, and vice versa. It is often required when a new system replaces an existing system that had previously interacted with one or more other systems. Interoperability Testing verifies that when the AUT runs in the live environment it is able to communicate successfully with other specified systems (such as invoking other systems, passing data to other system and receiving data from other systems etc.)

Document and Help Testing

This is a frequently overlooked aspect. The testing of documentation of help facilities is often omitted from the testing plan; typically due to lack of time or resources. It is thought to be outside the scope of the testing process or through sheer carelessness. Contrary to the popular belief, these aspects of the AUT may be vital to its successful operation and use of the system, particularly for new or naïve users. User documentation and help system information should be checked for conformance to the requirements specification document. Specific testing techniques involve documentation review, cross-referencing checks (e.g. against the document contents and index sections), and Thread Testing of typical user help scenarios.)

(Graphical) User Interface Testing

Sometimes, this may be clubbed with Usability Testing (discussed earlier). UI (User Interface) Testing evaluates how intuitive a system is from usage point of view. Issues pertaining to navigation, usability, commands and accessibility are considered. User interface functionality testing examines how well as UI operates to given specifications. Main areas covered in UI Testing are:

- Look and feel
- Navigation controls/navigation bar
- Navigation Branching
- Instructional and technical information style
- Images
- Tables and Forms

Fault Recovery Testing

Fault Recovery Testing verifies that following an error or exception (such as a system crash caused by loss of power) the AUT can be restored to a normal state, such as the initial state of the application when it is first executed, and that the AUT can continue to perform successfully. Fault Recovery Testing may also be used to verity the successful rollback and recovery of the data used or manipulated by the AUT following an error or exception.

Performance Testing

Performance Testing is a problem area because system performance is often poorly specified. Systems performance can be measured using a variety of different criteria, including:

- System response time
- External interface response time
- Central processor unit (CPU) utilization
- Memory utilization

The primary goal of Performance Testing is to develop effective enhancement strategies of maintaining acceptable system performance. Performance testing is an information gathering and analyzing process in which measurement data are collected to predict when load levels will exhaust system resources.

In conducting Performance Testing it is essential to have a suitable performance model that specifies what aspect of the system is being tested, what the performance requirements are, how they can vary under typical system usage, and how they will be tested.

Another challenge in Performance Testing is the difficulty in accurately representing the test environment. For example, if there are likely to be a large numbers of concurrent users and/or large amounts of data, it may be impractical or infeasible to set up and conduct realistic performance testing. Because of this and similar other difficulties, testing tool support is essential for Performance Testing, Stress Testing and Load (Volume) Testing. It should be noted that *the terms performance testing, stress testing and load/volume testing* are related.

Reliability Testing

This involves tests to ensure the robustness and reliability of the AUT (Application Under Test) under typical usage. It typically includes integrity tests and structured tests. Integrity tests focus on verifying the AUT's failure frequency and compliance to language, syntax, and resource usage. For example, a particular unit could be executed repeatedly using a test harness (this term was introduced in section 10.7) to verify that there are no memory leak problems. These tests can be designed, implemented, and executed during any testing phase. Some related IEEE definitions are provided below in reference to *reliability testing* and *performance testing* (previous section).

Mean time between failure (MTBF) The expected or observed time between consecutive failure in a system or component

Up Time The period of time during which a system or component is operational and in serviced; that is, the sum of *busy time* and *idle time*

Busy Time In computer performance engineering, the period of time during which a system or component is operational, in service, and is use.

> **Idle Time** The period of time during which a system or component is operational and in service but not in use.
>
> **Mean time to repair (MTTR)**
>
> The expected or observed time required to repair a system or component and return it to normal operation
>
> **Down Time** The period of time during which a system or component is not operational or has been taken out of service

Another important point to note is "Quality and Reliability". Dictionary meaning of quality is "a degree of excellence" or "superiority of mind". If a software product is of high quality, it will meet the customer's needs ("Fitness for use" viewpoint of quality). The customer will feel that the product is excellent and superior to his other choices. Here is where the hitch comes! Software testers often fall into the trap of believing that *quality and reliability* are the same thing. They feel that if they can test a program until it is stable, dependable, and reliable, they are assuring a high quality product. Unfortunately, that is not necessarily true. Reliability is just one aspect of quality.

> **The User's mind**
>
> A software user's idea of quality may include much more than just reliability. He is thinking of the breadth of features, the ability of the product to run on his/her older version of hardware, the software supplier's post sale support, may be even the colour of the packaging! Reliability, or how often the product crashes or trashes his data, may be important but not always

Thus, to ensure that a software program is of high quality and reliable, a tester must both verify and validate throughout the product development process.

Security Testing

Security issues are of the highest concern to many organizations especially those with Web-based products and services. Despite this fact, security testing is often the least understood, and least well-defined test type. Security testing efforts require domains of expertise beyond traditional software testing. Depending on the intended role of the AUT, there may be requirements that specify the need to ensure the confidentiality, availability and integrity of the data and software. Security testing is intended to test whether the features implemented within the AUT provide this required level of protection. Security testing is mainly concerned with establishing the degree of traceability from the requirements through to implementation, and in the validation of those requirements. For rigorous security testing, dedicated test teams with expertise in the security areas are required. Security tests can be designed, implemented, and executed within any testing phase but are typically conducted at System Test and re-run during User Acceptance Testing.

Next, we discuss *stress testing*, *load testing* and *volume testing*. Often the three terms get mixed up. It should be noted that these terms are related but not the same.

Stress Testing

The purpose of this is to examine the ability of the system to perform correctly under instantaneous peak loads with the aim of identifying defects that appear only under such adverse conditions. For example, if the specification for the AUT states that the system should accept 40 concurrent users, what happens if a 42nd user attempts to log on? Similarly, what when 40 users attempt to log on simultaneously? Thus, Stress Testing evaluates the behaviour of system that is pushed beyond their specified operational limits (this may well be above the stated requirements). It evaluates responses to bursts of peak activity that exceed system limitations. As said above, determining whether a system crashes or recovers gracefully from such conditions is a primary goal of Stress Testing. Simulation is frequently used method in Stress Testing. It is also worth considering commercial tool support for Stress Testing.

Load Testing/Volume Testing

Load Testing (also known as Volume Testing) evaluates system performance with pre-defined load level. Load Testing measures how long it takes a system to perform various program tasks and functions under normal, or pre-defined conditions. Bugs are reported when tasks cannot be executed within the time limits (as defined by the product management or marketing group). Because the objective of Load Testing is to determine if a system performance satisfies its load requirements, it is pertinent that minimum configuration and maximum activity levels be determined before testing begins.

As said at the start of this section, the three terms: Performance Testing, Load (Volume) Testing and Stress Testing are often used interchangeably; each of them addresses a different objective as explained on the next page.

Stress testing is running the software under "less-than-ideal conditions" – low memory, low disk space, slow CPUs, slow modems and so on. The goal is to starve the software for the resources it is looking for. **Load Testing** is the opposite of stress testing. With Load testing, instead of starving the software, you feed it all that it can handle - operate the software with the largest possible data files. If the software system operates on peripherals such as printers or communication ports, connect as many as you can. If you are testing an Internet server that can handle thousands of simultaneous connections, do it. The idea is to max out software system's capabilities by loading it down. To this extent, sometime people like to use the terms Performance Testing and Load (Volume) Testing interchangeably. A load test is done to determine if the system performance is acceptable at the "pre-defined" load level; a Performance Test is done to determine the system performance at various load levels.

Usability Testing

Specific techniques employed in Usability Testing include:

- Conformance checks—testing the application against agreed user interface standards
- User-based surveys—psychometric testing techniques to analyze user perceptions of the system
- Usability Testing—where users are asked to perform a series of specified business tasks with the AUT under controlled conditions in order to test the usability goals or requirements of the AUT

10.11 Test Metrics

Having discussed various testing techniques, now let us turn our focus to test measures and metrics. (The topic of software measurement and metrics has been discussed in detail in Chapter 5. The meaning of terms *measures* and *metrics* has been explained there.) Test measures and metrics are important for improving the testing process. Basically the measures and metrics for testing can be divided into the following broad categories:

[A]
- Extent of testing
- Testing effectiveness
- Assessment of testing
- Resources consumed in testing

[B]
- Testability measures
- Test control metrics
- Test Result Metrics

The table below explains category [A]. The list below is only an illustrative list and not an exhaustive one. There are many more measures and metrics that can be constructed. For a detailed discussion of terms *path coverage* and *statement coverage* etc., readers may like to refer [10] in the reference list at the end of this chapter.

Table 6: Test Metrics Category 1

Measure/Metric	What is shows	Description
Statement Coverage (Instructions Exercised)	**Extent of Testing**	Number of instructions in the program that were executed during the test process
Number of tests		Number of tests required to evaluate a module
Path Coverage (Number of paths tested)		Number of logical paths that were executed during the test process
Detected production errors (errors found after the software has been moved in the production environment)	**Testing Effectiveness**	Number of errors detected in the application when deployed in the end use environment
Defects uncovered in testing		——
Business value of testing		Money saved by uncovering defects early
Re-run analysis		Re-run hours associated with undetected defects (system down time)
Cost of testing	**Resources consumed in testing**	Ratio of cost of testing to the total system cost. Amount of resources (humans, equipment etc.) deployed for testing activity and their notional cost
Average cost of locating a defect		Cost of testing versus the number of defects located in testing
The extent of adherence to testing budget		Planned cost of testing v/s actual cost of testing
Loss value of test	**Assessment of testing**	Effect of testing in reducing losses as related to the resources processed by the system
Scale of ten		People's assessment of effectiveness of testing on a 10-point scale (1 = POOR, 10 = OUTSTANDING)
Requirement coverage		Monitoring and reporting on number of requirements exercised and tested

10.11.1 Testability measures

In practice, commercial projects are always under tremendous pressure of delivery dates. Although life cycle testing (testing throughout the development life cycle) is a good concept, most of the time test teams have to struggle to draw management attention to provide them adequate testing time and testing resources. Being able to predict the testability of the software and estimating the testing effort early in a project comes in handy in such circumstances. Testability metrics can play a significant role in this perspective. The discussion that follows is from this point of view.

Testability metrics measure features of a test item, which are likely to make the item easy (or difficult) to test. Testability metrics are useful to assess the ease of all testing phases (unit testing, integration testing, system testing). Useful testability metrics are those that can be derived from requirements and design documents. This way one can use them to assess future testability during early stages of systems development.

Testability metrics for integration testing may be based on module linkage metrics such as *fan-in* (number of modules calling a module), *fan-out* (number of modules called by a module), and counts of reads and writes to common data items. *Testability metrics for code* include metrics based on module control flow such as McCabe's *cycomatic complexity number* (refer Chapter 5. For a detailed discussion on the topic of "Cyclomatic Complexity" reader can have a look at [15] quoted in the reference list at the end of this chapter). *Cyclomatic Complexity* identifies the number of independent control flow paths.

In summary, testability metrics are usually size or structure measures used for the purpose of assessing ease of testing. They are used:

- To identify potentially un-testable (or difficult to test) components at an early stage in the development process. In this context, poor testability is equated to a large number of control flow paths. This provides the opportunity to redesign components and/or provide additional testing effort.
- To assess the feasibility of test specifications in terms of the provision of adequate test cases and appropriate test completion criteria.
- To estimate the effort and schedule of test activities. This assumes that predictive models are available to relate testability metrics to testing effort and duration.

10.11.2 Test control metrics

These are of three main types:

1. Test Resource Metrics (see Table 6 in the previous section)
2. Test Coverage Metrics (see Table 6 in the previous section)
3. Test Plan Metrics

Test Resource Metrics

These are measures of effort, time-scale and staffing levels, and other cost items such as tool purchase, special test equipment, training etc. Test resource metrics are used for planning monitoring testing activities.

Test Coverage Metrics

These are among the most useful testing measures. They measure the amount of the product that has been tested at different levels of granularity. You need to identify the total set of features associated with aspect of a program/software module and measure the percentage of those features tested. In terms of "risk based approach to testing" discussed in the next section, this means prioritizing these features depending the importance of those to the customer. These features are often code features such as the number of logical paths or statements in a piece of software.

Test coverage statistics identify what percentage of the available paths or statements have been executed by a set of tests. You can set standards for test coverage metrics, such as a minimum 90 percent of branches and 100 percent of statements executed per module, which allows you to control the testing process. Test coverage of code is usually part of a white box testing regime for unit testing. However, test coverage measures can reference module-calling paths as part of integration testing or reference requirements as part of functional system testing.

In general, low test coverage values for a module are an indication of incomplete/poor testing of a specific component. Test coverage values should be checked when modules with unusually high or low defect rates are identified.

Test Plan Metrics

These indicate the amount of testing to be performed and the effectiveness of test plans. Examples of such metrics are the number of test cases planned and run vis-à-vis the number of unplanned test cases run. Like testing resource metrics, testing plan metrics are used for planning and monitoring testing activities.

10.11.3 Test Result Metrics

These are usually based on defect counts. Such counts can be related to the test item and the test activity in terms or error rates (e.g. defects per 100 lines of code and defects found per 100 testing hours respectively).

Defect counts can also be made in terms of various defect categories. A useful defect classification scheme would identify the phase and/or activity during which the error was introduced, the phase/activity during which the error was detected, and the type and severity of the error. This would eventually help move towards *orthogonal defect classification* famously known as ODC (readers are urged to use the web for ODC as the discussion on this topic is beyond the scope of this chapter).

Defect rates are often used to identify the pass and fail criteria for test item (refer Table 4—Test Results in section 10.7). For example, a module may be may be rejected if its defect rate exceeds some pre-determined limit (organizations find out the upper and lower limits based on their capability baseline which in turn is established using past performance data of their software projects.) System testing might be required to continue until the defect rate per test hour drops below some predetermined level. Defect classification is used to investigate process efficiency and to identify potential weakness in the process.

10.12 Risk-Based Testing

Basically, "Risk-based Testing" is an approach to developing a test strategy. We'll mention about the famously known *White Box Testing* and *Black Box Testing* strategies at the end of this section, along with the new term "Gray Box Testing.

Test strategies are adopted in recognition of the fact that there are a number of strategic risks associated with the development and installation of a computer-based system can be [1]:

- Incorrect results will be produced
- Unauthorized transactions will be accepted by the system
- Data integrity will be lost
- Processing cannot be reconstructed
- Continuity of processing will be lost
- Service provided to the user will degrade to an unacceptable level
- Security of the system will be compromised
- Processing will not comply with organizational policy of statutory and regulatory/legal requirements
- Results of the system will be unreliable
- System will be difficult to use
- Programs will be un-maintainable
- System will not portable to other hardware and software
- System will not be able to interconnect with other computer systems
- Performance level will be unacceptable
- System will be difficult to operate

Each of these risks can affect the proper functioning of a computer-based application. If any of any of these risks materialize, the result may be substantial loss to the organization using the system. In the section of this chapter testing techniques –we discussed how most of the above risks are addressed while testing " non-functional requirements".

The Test Plan should be in line with the organization's testing strategy. In forming a test strategy, indemnification of the "risk factors" is an important step in determining the objective of testing. This is the basis of "risk-based approach to testing". We have enumerated some of the *test factors*. Detailed discussion is not within the scope of this chapter. Interested readers can refer [1] in the reference section: *Correctness, File Integrity, Authorization, Audit Trail, Continuity of Processing, Service Levels, Access Control, Compliance, Reliability, Ease of Use, Maintainability, Ease of use, Portability, Performance, Coupling, Ease of operations.*

Developing a Test Strategy involves carrying out the following steps:

1. Identify and rank test factors
2. Identify the system development phases
3. Identify the business risks associated with the system under development
4. Place the risks in the matrix

This results in Test Factor/Test Phase Matrix as shown in Figure 5 below. This matrix is an important input to developing a Test Strategy. A detailed testing plan is required to ensure that the *test factors* have been adequately addressed. While the factors are common to the entire testing life cycle, the concerns vary according to the phase of the life cycle.

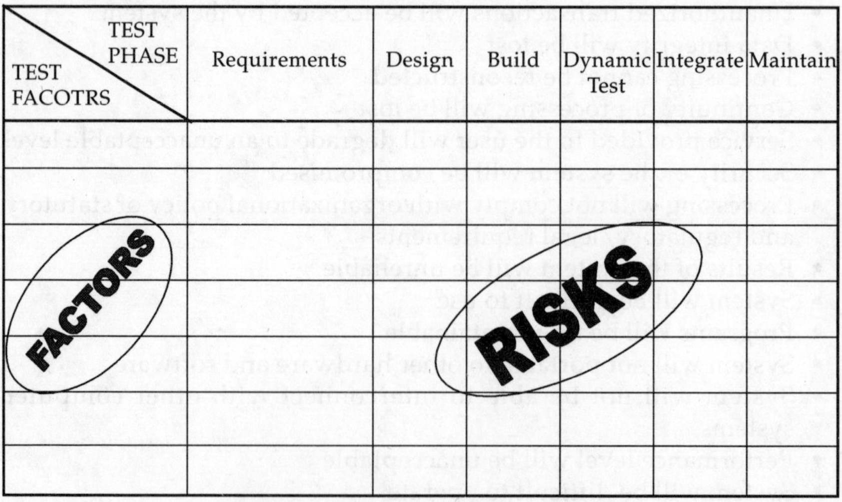

TEST FACOTRS \ TEST PHASE	Requirements	Design	Build	Dynamic Test	Integrate	Maintain

Figure 5: Test Factor/Test Phase Matrix

Earlier in this section, we mentioned that there are three important terms—*White Box Testing* (also known as "Glass Box Testing"), *Black Box Testing and Gray Box Testing* (a relatively new term). These are basically the commonly known *"testing strategies"*—a brief description is provided below.

White Box Testing (Also called "Glass Box Testing"): This is a totally logic driven testing and permits one to examine the internal structure of a software code/program. In using this strategy, the tester derives *test data* from an examination of program's logic (and often, unfortunately at the neglect of the specification!) White Box Testing considers close examination of procedural details. Executions of logical paths are considered by providing test cases that exercise specific set of conditions and/or loops. The status of program may be examined at various points in execution to determine if the expected or asserted status (for example some compilers provide "tracing" utilities to check if the control points are being reached) corresponds to the actual results.

Black Box Testing: We had said earlier exhaustive testing is virtually impossible i.e. you cannot find *all* errors even for the most trivial programs. It is highly impractical too. Black Box Testing is used as one way to examine this issue. This is completely data-driven or input/output driven. In using this strategy, the tester is not at all concerned with the internal behaviour/structure/working of the software code. Rather, the tester is only interested finding the circumstances in which the program/software code does not behave according to its specification. Thus, Black box testing refers to tests that that are conducted at the software interface. Black Box tests are generally used to demonstrate that software functions are operational. For a very exhaustive treatment of this topic of Black Box testing, reader may like to see Ref [7].

Gray Box Testing: as said earlier, this is a relatively new term coming up due to the rise of web-applications. This is mixture of White Box Testing and Black Box Testing. With Gray Box Testing, you straddle between the two. Your strategy will be to test the software as black box but you supplement the work by taking a peek (not a full look inside as in case of White Box testing) at what makes the software work. Web pages lend themselves nicely to Gray Box Testing. Web pages are created mostly using HTML. This is suitable for using Gray Box testing Strategy because HTML is not a full-fledged programming language; it is a mark-up language.

Having discussed *White Box Testing, Black Box Testing* and *Gray Box Testing*, we now turn our attention to another important term—*Regression Testing*. As you'll see in Chapter 5, while discussing *software maintenance metrics*, we have made a reference to this term. In this section, we add a discussion on regression testing to bring in completeness to the topic of testing addressed by this chapter.

What is Regression Testing?

Regression testing has a specific purpose; it is to ensure that the *Application Under Test* (AUT) still functions correctly even after carrying out the required modification or extension of the system (such as enhancements or upgrades). Typically, the modifications or extensions will be tested to make sure that they meet their requirements, after which a series of tests will be run to confirm that the existing functionality still meets its requirements.

Strictly speaking, regression testing is not a testing phase and as such, the V-Model for testing does not mention it. Rather, regression testing is a *testing technique* that can be used with any of the testing phases described in the previous sections. Regression testing can also be employed following changes to the operating environment of the AUT; such as the installation of the new version of the operating system, changes to the hardware platform, or a particular event external to the AUT. A very well known example of this is what happened when the world entered the famous year 2000! *Millennium Testing* can be considered to have been a special case of Regression Testing. During a typical millennium test, the AUT would not have been altered, but it would still be necessary to ensure that the previously designed applications performed correctly following a particular event (in this case the year 2000 date change).

Typically, Regression Testing is employed in the context of System and Acceptance Testing. Generally, Testing experts are of the opinion that Regression Testing *should* use the Black Box testing strategy to test the high-level requirements of the AUT without considering the implementation details of the system.

Regression Testing is a particularly appropriate candidate for support by means of an automated testing tool, especially if frequent new builds and releases of the AUT are anticipated. The advantages of using test automation during regression testing are:

- The ability to run the regression tests "unattended" i.e. without the need for the testing staff to be present

- The ability to rerun all the automated test scripts or selected subset of scripts against which the new build or release as required to provide maximum confidence in the software

- Establishing a high degree of confidence that the modifications or extensions to the system have not impacted unduly on its functionality

10.13 Test Automation and Test Tool Selection

In this section, we are going to have a general discussion on how to go about selecting a test automation tool. Automation is one of the factors promoting higher productivity. It is a fact that often testing is perceived as a boring job and this feeling of "boredom" (whether perceived wrongly or not) can leave to a loss of productivity. The other problem is that in an attempt to do more with less, organizations want to test their software adequately, but within a minimum schedule! Manual testing is labour-intensive and error-phone. It is impractical given the complexity of design architecture of today's software solutions. The automation of test activities provides its greatest values in instances where *test scripts* are repeated or where test scripts sub-routines are created and then invoked repeatedly by a number of test scripts. Thus the payoff from automated testing is greatest when the testing tasks are repetitious.

To understand the context of automated testing, it is necessary to understand the kinds of test, which are typically performed during the various application development life-cycle stages. Within a client-server or Web environment, the target system spans more than just a software application. Indeed, it may perform across multiple platforms, involve multiple layers of supporting applications, involve interfaces with a host of commercial off-the-shelf (COTS) products, utilize one or more different types of databases, and involve both front-end and back-end processing. Tests within this environment can include Functional Requirements Testing, Server Performance Testing, User Interface Testing, Unit Testing, Integration Testing, Program Module Complexity Analysis, Program Code Coverage Testing, System Load Performance Testing, Boundary Testing, Security Testing, Memory Leak Testing, and many more types of checks. In Figure 3, the overall Testing Life Cycle was depicted. Figure 6 details out the Test Tool selection aspect.

The *decision to automate test* represents an important decision during the testing activity.

Test Tool Acquisition is the next important activity. The process of *Introducing Automated Testing* to a new project comes next. Refer Figure 3—tool selected forms an important part during the preparation of the Test Plan. With this background, now let us discuss *Automated Test Tool Selection Process* (Figure 6). The person involved in this activity needs to develop a *test tool proposal* for management—the proposal outlines the test tool requirement and the justification for the tool. Test tool proposal development and its acceptance by management are intended to secure management's commitment for the resources needed to properly implement the test tool and support the automated testing process. To conclude this section, Table 7 presents a summary of Test Life-Cycle Tools.

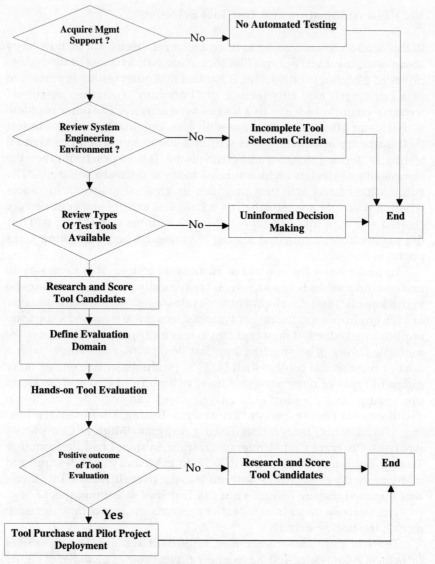

Figure 6: Automated Test Tool Selection Process

Table 7: Test Life-Cycle Tools

Life Cycle Phase	Type of Tool	Tool Description
Business Analysis Phase	• Business Modeling Tool	Allow for recording definitions of user needs and automating the rapid construction of flexible, graphical, client-server applications
	• Configuration Management Tool	Allow for base-lining of important data repositories
	• Defect Tracking Tools	Manage system life-cycle defects
	• Technical Review Management	Facilitates communication and automates the technical review/inspection process
	• Documentation Generators	Automate Document generation
Requirements Definition Phase	• Requirements management tools	Manage and organize requirements; allow for test procedure design; allow for test progress reporting
	• Requirements verifiers	Verify syntax, semantics, and testability
	• Use case generators	Allow for creation of use cases
Analysis and Design Phase	• Database Design Tools	Provides a solution for developing second-generation enterprise client-server systems
	• Application Design Tools	Define software architecture; allow for object oriented analysis, modeling, design, and construction
	• Structure charts, flowcharts, and sequence diagrams	Help manage process
	• Test procedure generators	Generate test procedures from requirements or design of data and object models or cause-effect diagrams
Programming Phase	• Syntax checkers/debuggers	Allow for syntax checking and debugging and debugging capability; usually come with built-in programming language compilers
	• Memory leak and runtime error detection tools	Detect runtime errors and memory leaks
	• Source code testing tools	Verify maintainability, portability, complexity, cyclomatic complexity, and standards compliance
	• Static and dynamic analyzers	Depict quality and structure of code

Life Cycle Phase	Type of Tool	Tool Description
	• Various code implementation tools	Depending on the application, support code generation, among other things
	• Unit test tools	Automates the unit testing process
Metrics Tools	• Code (test) coverage analyzers	Identify untested code and support dynamic testing
	• Metrics reporters	Read source code and display metrics information
	• Usability measurements	Provide user profiling, task analysis, prototyping, and user walkthroughs
Testing Phase	• Test management tools Network testing tools	Allow for test management Allow for monitoring, measuring, testing and diagnosis of performance across the entire network
	• GUI testing tools (capture/playback)	Allow for automated GUI tests; capture/playback tools record user interactions with on-line systems, so they may be replayed automatically
	• Non-GUI test drivers	Allow for automated execution of tests for products without GUIs
	• Load/performance testing tools	Allow for load/performance and stress testing
	• Environment testing tools	Testing tools for various testing environments

10.14 Extreme Testing

This is relatively new concept and becoming quite popular. Its roots are in the fact that requirements keep changing and that the delivery life cycles are shorter especially in the web world. Kent Beck is considered to be the father of "*Extreme Programming*" concept which has given rise to this new philosophy to testing called: *Extreme Testing*". The basic idea is: testing the system on the fly! The analogy given below by Kent Beck will help understand the philosophy in the Extreme Testing approach.

Kent Beck compares programming to driving a car. If you are driving a car, you don't simply point in the general direction of your destination and hold down the gas until you get there. Good, safe driving consists of making continual corrections until you reach your destination. If the road turns, you turn the steering wheel. If traffic is slowed to a crawl, you ease up on the accelerator. Extreme Testing takes the same approach from a development point of view. It is believed that change is not "bad," it's just part of the journey, and you cope with it continually along the way. (As said above, extreme testing approach is in realization of the fact that "change" is the only reality about requirements!)

One of the basic principles of extreme programming is unit testing. In fact, extreme programming suggests that even before developers start writing code they should first design an automated unit test that will fail unless the coding task is implemented successfully. Once the unit test is created, the developer writes code until the unit test stops failing, at which point the task should be successfully finished.

Extreme Programming/Extreme Testing: A Manner of Thinking

Every good tester knows that unit testing is important. So why is unit testing considered "extreme programming?" If you think of extreme as meaning "risky" or "unproven" then no, unit testing is not extreme. However, if you think of extreme as meaning "nobody else does it" then yes, unit testing is extreme. If every developer implemented unit testing then it could no longer be called extreme In fact, programmers who didn't write unit tests would be considered extreme!

A word of caution: Neither *Extreme programming* nor *Extreme Testing* claim to have the solution to every problem. You may be familiar with the phrase, "Our product variables are cost, time, and quality—choose any two." If you can decide to keep costs low and still deliver a product in a short time, quality will naturally suffer. Or if you choose to have high quality in a short delivery time, the development costs will skyrocket. However, as a philosophy, Extreme Testing is a good concept to keep the morale of the testing high throughout the project even in the face of continuously changing requirements.

10.15 Test Process Improvement Framework

We'll now discuss about "test process improvement" in the spirit of "continuous improvement"—the cornerstone of famous SW CMM (Capability Maturity Model for Software: details available at http://www.sei.cmu.edu/). For this discussion we'll use the *Test Maturity Model* (TMM). The TMM is a testing maturity that was developed by the Illinois Institute of Technology; it contains a set of maturity levels through which an organization can progress toward greater test process maturity. As shown in Figure 7, this model lists a set of recommended practices at each level of maturity above Level 1. The purpose of TMM is to promote greater professionalism in software testing, similar to the intention of the CMM for software that was developed by the Software Engineering Institute (SEI) at Carnegie Mellon University.

Interestingly, the TMM was developed as a complement to the CMM. It was envisioned that organizations interested in assessing and improving their testing capabilities would likely be involved in general software process improvement. To have directly corresponding levels in both maturity models (SW CMM and TMM) would mean to have these two process improvement drives in parallel. This parallelism is not entirely present, however, because both the CMM and the TMM level structures are based on the individual historical maturity growth patterns of the processes they represent. The testing process is a subset of the overall software development process; therefore, its maturity growth needs support from the key process areas (KPAs) associated with the general process growth. For this reason, any organization that wishes to improve its testing process throughout implementation of the TMM (and the Testing Life-cycle) should first commit to improving its overall software development process by applying the CMM guidelines.

Research shows that an organization striving to reach a particular level of the TMM must be at least at the same level of the CMM. In many cases, a given TMM level needs specific support from KPAs in the corresponding CMM level and the CMM level beneath it. The KPAs should be addressed either prior to or in parallel with the TMM maturity goals.

The TMM model adapts well to automated software testing, because effective software verification and validation programs grow out of development programs that are well planned, executed, managed, and monitored. A good software test program cannot stand along; it must be an integral part of the software development process. In Table 7, we have depicted the TMM levels together with corresponding automated software testing levels 1 through 5 in the second column as a part of TMM.

The test team must determine, based on the company's environment, the TMM maturity level that best fits the organization and the applicable software application or products. The level of testing should be proportional to complexity of design. And in general, the testing effort should not be more than the development effort. For readers interested in more details on the Test Maturity Model, we urge them to refer the information available on the internet for additional details on Test. One recommended site is: www.stsc.hill.af.mil/crosstalk/1998/nov/burnsetin.asp (It has an article by Ilene Burnstein, Ariya Homyen, Robert Grom, C.R.Carlson of Illinois Institute of Technology)

Table 8 ahead depicts the levels 1 through 5 of the TMM in the first columns, along with corresponding automated software testing levels 1 through 5 in the second column. Column 2 addresses test maturity as it pertains to automated software testing. (Refer Figure 7 for Testing Maturity Model).

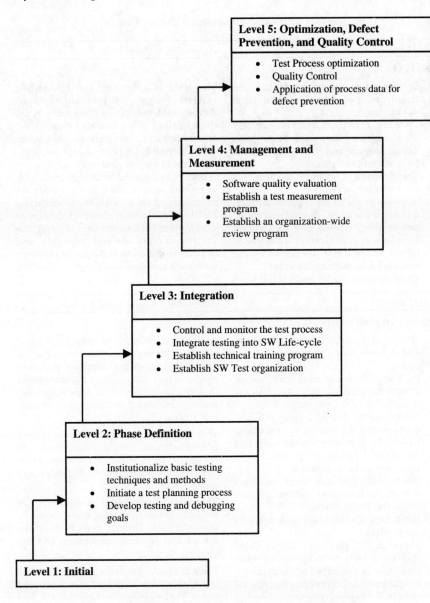

Level 5: Optimization, Defect Prevention, and Quality Control
- Test Process optimization
- Quality Control
- Application of process data for defect prevention

Level 4: Management and Measurement
- Software quality evaluation
- Establish a test measurement program
- Establish an organization-wide review program

Level 3: Integration
- Control and monitor the test process
- Integrate testing into SW Life-cycle
- Establish technical training program
- Establish SW Test organization

Level 2: Phase Definition
- Institutionalize basic testing techniques and methods
- Initiate a test planning process
- Develop testing and debugging goals

Level 1: Initial

Figure 7: The 5-level Structure of the TMM

Table 8: TMM and Automated Software Testing

TMM Level 1	*Automated Software Level 1*
INITIAL • Testing is a chaotic process; it is ill-defined and not distinguished from debugging. • Tests are developed in an ad-hoc way after coding is completed. Testing and debugging are interleaved to get the bugs out of the software. • The objective of testing is to show that the software works. • Software products are released without quality assurance. Resources, tools, and properly trained staff are lacking. • This type of organization would be at level 1 of the CMM developed by the Software Engineering Institute • There are no maturity goals at this level	This level of automated software testing is referred to as *"accidental automation"*. At the first level, automated testing is not done at all or only on an ad-hoc basis. An automated test tool might be used on an experimental basis. With a capture/playback tool, automated test scripts are reported and played back with only tool-generated scripts being used. Scripts are not modified for re-usability or maintainability. No automated script design or development standards are followed. Resulting scripts are not reusable and difficult to maintain and must be repeated with each software build.

TMM Level 2	*Automated Software Level 2*
PHASE DEFINITION • Testing is separated from debugging and is defined as a phase that follows coding. Although it is planned activity, test planning at level 2 may occur after coding for reasons related to the immaturity of the test process. • For example, at level 2 there is a perception that all testing is execution-based and dependent on the code, and therefore it should be planned only when the code is complete • The primary goal of testing at this level of maturity is to show that the software meets its specifications • Basic testing techniques and methods are in place • Many quality problems at this TMM level occur because test planning takes place late in the software life cycle • In addition, defects propagate into the code from the requirements and design phases, as not review program addresses this important issue. • Post-code, execution-based testing is still considered the primary testing activity	At this level, testing is becoming a planned activity. This implies a commitment to the completion of testing activities. A project planning tool will aid the project manager in defining test activities, allocating time, money, resources, and personnel to testing process. This level of automated software testing is referred to as *"incidental automation"*. At the second level, automated test scripts are modified but no documented standards or repeatability exists. The types of tools used at this level can included project planning tools, capture/playback tools, simulators and emulators, syntax and semantic analyzers, and debugging tools. The introduction automated of automated test tools to a new project is not planned and a process is not being followed. Test design or development standards do not exist. Test schedules or test requirements are not taken into consideration or are not reliable when contemplating the use of an automated test tool. As with Level 1, this type of test automation does not provide much return on investment can actually increase the testing effort.

TMM Level 3	*Automated Software Level 3*

INTEGRATION

- Testing is no longer a phase that follows coding; rather it is integrated into the entire software life cycle.
- Organizations can build on the test planning skills they have acquired at level 2.
- Unlike level 2 (planning for testing at TMM), level 3 begins at the requirements phase and continues throughout the life cycle supported by a version of the V model (Figure 4)
- Test objectives are established with respect to the requirements based on user and client needs and are used for test-case design and success criteria
- A test organization exists, and testing is recognized as a professional activity.
- A Technical training organization

This level of test maturity is referred to as *"intentional automation"*. At the third level, automated testing becomes both well defined and well managed. The test requirements and the test scripts themselves proceed logically from the software requirements specifications and design documents.

Automated test scripts are created based on test design and development standards, yet the test team does not review automated test procedures. Automated tests become more reusable and maintainable. At this level of automated testing, the return on investment is starting to pay off and a break-even point can already be achieved. The types of tools used at this level include requirements management tools, project planning tool, capture/playback tools, simulators and emulators, syntax and semantic analyzers, and debugging tools.

TMM Level 4	*Automated Software Level 4*

MANAGEMENT & MEASUREMENT

- Testing is a measured and quantified process.
- Reviews at all phases of the development process are now recognized as testing and quality control activities.
- Software products are tested for quality attributes such as reliability, usability, and maintainability.
- Test cases from all projects are collected and recorded in a test-case database to test case reuse and regression testing.
- Defects are logged and given a severity level.
- Deficiencies in the test process now often follow from the lack of a defect-prevention philosophy and the porosity of automated support for the collection, analysis, and dissemination of test-related metrics.

This level of test maturity, referred to as *"advanced automation"*, can be achieved when adopting many aspects of the Automated Test Life-cycle management.

This testing maturity level represents a practiced and perfected version of level 3 with one major addition – "post release defect tracking". Defects are captured and sent directly back through the fix, test creation, and regression test processes.

The software test team is now an integral part of the product development, and test engineers and application developers work together to build a product that will meet test requirements.

Any software bugs are caught early, when they are much less expensive to fix. In addition to the tools mentioned at the previous testing levels, defect and change tracking tools, test procedure generation tools, and code review tools are used at this level.

contd. ...

... contd.

TMM Level 5	Automated Software Level 5
OPTIMIZATION, DEFECT PREVENTION AND QUALITY CONTROL • Because of the infrastructure provided by the attainment of maturely goals at levels 1 through 4 of the TMM, the testing process is now said to be defined and managed and its cost and effectiveness can be monitored. • At level 5, mechanism fine-tune and continuously improve testing. • Defect prevention and quality control are practiced • Statistical sampling and measurements of confidence level, trustworthiness, and reliability drive the testing process. • An established process exists for the selection and evaluation of testing tools. • Automated tools totally support the running and re-running of test cases, providing support for test-case design, maintenance of test-related items, defect collection and analysis, and the collection, analysis, and application of test related metrics.	When incorporating the guidelines of the Test Life cycle described in this chapter, and using the applicable tools in an efficient manner, a TMM Level 5 maturity can be achieved. Tools used at this highest level include the ones mentioned within the previous level plus test data generation tools and metrics collection tools, such as complexity and size measurement tools, coverage and frequency analyzers, and statistical tools for defect analysis and defect prevention.

10.16 Human Issues and Challenges in Testing

Those who have spent considerable amount of time in the software industry managing either development projects or testing projects would vouch for the fact the world is replete with love-hate relationship between the developers and the testers! Testing is often not considered a "respected" job. If one thinks what could be some barriers for effective testing, the following factors come to one's mind:

- Optimism: *Belief that the system works*
- Negative attitude towards testing: *a belief that testing is "destructive", testing is equivalent to "fault finding"!*
- Ego: *if "we/I" have coded, it must be perfect!*
- One does not want to fail: *Feeling that the testers will "get" me and prove me wrong!*
- Conflict between testers and developers: *"they versus we" attitude*
- Testing is least structured: *the belief that testing does not require any planning!!*
- The notion that Testing is "expensive": *the belief that testing necessarily requires fancy tools, which cost a lot!*

- Time pressures due to delivery commitments: *we got to deliver first! There is no time for testing—the customer is waiting!*
- Management attitude: *sometime, management does not have the patience; push the product out seems to be the aim!*

While all these are the feelings of people and some of them could be wrongly set pre-conceived notions, one needs to understand that the primary role of testing is to determine whether the AUT meets specification and whether the AUT meets the needs of its users. The secondary role of testing is to instill confidence in the producer of the software system, as well as to provide insight into development process and to continuously improve the testing process.

There are some political (or let's call them "human issues") aspects too. For example—for every software project, there is an interest of conflict that occurs as testing begins (assume that there is no separate test group in case of a small organization and not so large project); the same persons who have built the software are now asked to test the software. This approach, prima-facie looks "harmless" i.e. after all, who "knows" the program better than its original developers? Unfortunately, these developers have a vested interest in demonstrating that the software is "error-free", that it "works" according to customer requirements, that it will be completed on schedule and without exceeding the budget and so on…Each of these "vested interests" militates against thorough testing. Unfortunately, in reality, testing occurs at that point of project when deadline pressures begin to rise, progress must be measurable and defects must surface as soon as possible!

There are few more "psychological" aspects that create challenges in the testing activity. Analysis and Design are perceived as "constructive" tasks while Testing gets looked at as a "fault finding" task! This is how it is typically thought: The software engineer creates the software system, its documentation and the related data structures. The software engineer, as a creator, is proud of what has been built through his/her constructive efforts. Come testing and the picture changes—after all, testing is a "destructive" act. Developers feel that in testing, there is a subtle yet a defying attempt to "break" the thing that they have so fondly built i.e. the software developers/programmers tend to have "emotional attachment" to what they have created. So, what happens is (in case the developer is entrusted with the task of testing what he or she had created) that such test cases are designed so as to prove that "it all works"! Actually, what is needed is a third party, independent and "ruthless" approach to testing. While forming the testing teams, all these aspects should be kept in mind. It is worth reading the references [3] and [12] quoted at the end of this chapter; this topic is handled at length by the authors.

10.17 Software Testing Careers and Testing Competence Through Professional Certifications

Software test engineering can provide for an interesting and challenging work assignment and career. In addition, there is high demand in the marketplace for test engineering skills. More specifically, the evolution of automated test capabilities have given birth to many new career opportunities for software engineers. This trend is further boosted by international quality standards and software maturity guidelines that place a greater emphasis on software test and other product assurance disciplines. The aspiration of a person looking for tester's job is best expressed as:

"......I like to perform a variety of different work, learn a lot of things, and touch a lot different products. I also want to exercise my programming and database skills, but I don't want to be off in my own little world, isolated from others, doing nothing but hammering out code. I have an aptitude for working with software tools ......"

Many software engineers are choosing career in the test arena for two main reasons: (1) the different kinds of tasks involved and (2) the variety of applications for which they are introduced. How does one know whether he/she will make a good test engineer? Good software developers have been trained and groomed to have a mindset to make something work and to work around the problem if necessary. The test engineer, on the other hand, needs to be able to make things fail! At the same time, however, he/she needs to possess a developer's mentality to develop workaround solutions, if necessary, especially during the construction of test scripts. Test engineers need to be structured, attentive to detail, and organized, and, given the complexities of automated testing, they should possess a creative and planning ahead type of mindset. Because testers need to work closely with developers, they need to have the co-operative attitude, high emotional intelligence, be both assertive and poised when working through trouble reports and issues with developers.

Given the complexities of the test effort associated with a client-server or multiple environments, test engineer should have a broad range of technical skills. In addition to this, in an automated test environment, the test engineer needs to know the script programming language of the primary automated test tool. Table 8 outlines a series of progressive steps possible for an individual performing in a professional test engineering capacity. For international certifications in Software Testing, reader may like to visit www.softwarecertifications.com for the details of Quality Assurance Institute's (QAI) CSTE (Certified Software Test Engineer) Professional certification, which is widely recognized. One can appear for this certification examination in India. The examination is designed to evaluate the knowledge of both the principles and practices of software testing. The URL mentioned above can be visited for information about the knowledge domains covered for the CSTE Certification examination. The table below provides a summary of various roles available for testing professionals.

Table 9: Test Career Progression

Career Progression	Description
Junior Test Engineer	An entry-level position for an individual with a computer science degree or an individual with some manual testing experience. Develops test scripts and begins to become familiar with the test life cycle and testing techniques.
Test Engineer/Programmer Analyst	A test engineer or programmer who has three to four years of experience. Helps to develop or maintain testing or programming standards and processes, leads peer reviews, and acts as a mentor to other, more junior test engineers or programmers. Continues to develop skills in programming languages, operating systems, networks, and databases.
Team Lead	A test engineer or programmer who has four to six years of experience. Responsible for the supervision of one to three test engineers or programmers. Has some scheduling and effort size/cost estimation responsibilities. Technical skills become more focused.
Test/Programming Lead	A test engineer or programmer who has six to ten years of experience. Responsible for the supervision or four to eight personnel. Responsible for scheduling, size/cost estimation, and delivery of product within schedule and budget targets. Responsible for developing the technical approach to the project. Provides some customer support and presentations. Develops technical expertise in a few specific areas.
Test/QA/Development (Project) Manager	Ten-plus years of experience. Responsible for eight or more personnel performing on one or more projects. Full development life cycle responsibility within this area (test/QA/Development). Provides some customer interaction and many presentations. Has cost, schedule, planning, and staffing responsibility.
Program Manager	Fifteen-plus years of development and support (test/QA) activity experience. Responsible for personnel performing on several projects and full development life cycle responsibility. Assumes project direction and profit/loss responsibility.

Conclusion

This chapter discussed some important aspects of software testing. Typically, 25-50% of the total costs of developing a software system are spent on test activities. This figure is likely to be significantly larger for high reliability, business critical and safety critical systems. Testing is an organizational responsibility. Therefore an appropriate Testing Policy should be defined and documented and Testing Strategy should be evolved. Testing process has its own life cycle. The testing process begins along with the requirements phase of development life cycle and from there runs parallel with the entire development life cycle phases. There are number of testing techniques and testing strategies for the testers to deploy. Extreme testing is a relatively new technique coming up and gaining fast popularity. Towards the end, we've also considered the test process improvement model.

REFERENCES

[1] *Effective Methods for Software Testing* by William Perry (Wiley)
[2] *Testing Applications on the Web* by Hung Q. Nguyen (Wiley)
[3] *Surviving the Challenges of Software Testing* by William Perry and Randall Rice (Dorset House)
[4] *Software Testing Techniques* by Joe Abbot (NCC Publications)
[5] *Test Process Improvement* by Tim Koomen and Martin Pol (Addison-Wesley)
[6] *Software Testing Techniques* by Boris Beizer (Dreamtech Publication)
[7] *Black Box Testing Techniques* by Boris Beizer (Wiley)
[8] *Software Testing in the Real World* by Edward Kit (ACM Press—Pearson Education)
[9] *Software Testing* by Ron Patton (SAMS Techmedia)
[10] *The Art of Software Testing* by Glenford Myers (Wiley)
[11] *Automated Software Testing* by Dustin, Rashka and Paul (Addison Wesley)
[12] *Managing the Testing Process* by Rex Black (Microsoft Press)
[13] *Testing Object Oriented Systems* by Robert Binder (Addison Wesley)
[14] *Software Testing & Quality Engineering* (March/April 1999) issue at www.stqemagazine.com
[15] *Software Engineering: Design, Reliability and Management* by Martin L. Shooman (McGraw Hill International Ed.)

Chapter 11

CAREERS IN QUALITY

11.1 Overview

In the chapter on *Software Testing*, towards the end, we discussed career progression for a Software Tester. In this chapter we want to discuss career paths available to quality professional. While doing that, a discussion on some people issues is important as it helps us understand how we "grow". As we have seen so far, Quality (Assurance) is a vast field. It comprises of multiple challenges demanding diverse skills. The professional opportunities are either in "process consulting" (software process improvement initiatives, Auditing and Assessments) or in the area of Testing. Quality Professionals can be deployed in various roles and responsibilities, as we'll see in this chapter. We'll start the discussion with some general issues and then move on to discuss the various roles that quality professionals can play. Each of the roles would demand a certain skill sets. We also provide some useful site references on "quality certifications" at the end of this chapter. Role of a mentor is crucial in helping you develop your career and so we've taken up some discussion on this topic.

11.2 Introduction

An interesting thing to note is how people grow and mature in their professional life. Have a look at where you stand currently as software professional or a quality professional (if you are one). You'll realize that as people mature, they gain a better understanding of themselves and learn to appreciate their own strengths and weaknesses. Having matured, they can set more realistic goals than they were younger, and can adjust career objectives to better fit their potentials and talents.

Initially, we tend to be overtly concerned about status and job titles and we tend to make fuss about the size of our office, cabin, the style of its furniture etc. We tend to frown on this "external motivators" even when we know in the minds of our mind that these are really not the things that should be make any difference; but we do sulk about all these things.

Throughout their careers, professionals learn from their successes and failures. Successes build self-confidence but defeats also teach you a lot and it is ok to have a few of them. They provide us evidence of our shortcomings and limitations. In the famous book "Personal Software Process", Watts Humphrey says: *"........ as they debug their programs, software engineers constantly face the consequences of their own fallibility. When engineers learn to realistically accept themselves, they are better able to establish rewarding career goals......"* This is very well holds for the quality professionals as well.

11. 3 P-CMM and Careers

One point to note is that the People Capability Maturity Model (famously known as the P-CMM model) is not going to be discussed here. It is a generic framework for improving people related practices in organizations. It has a number of Key Process Areas that have to do with career development, empowerment etc. The interested readers are directed to SEI's site www.sei.cmu.edu to get overview and other details of this model. However, since we are discussing careers of software quality professionals in this chapter, it would be pertinent to talk about some people issues. Some of the top people issues as perceived by the industry are the following:

- Enabling people to deal with continual change in the organization
- Managing skills and career growth
- Ensuring consistent communication between managers and staff
- Providing clear performance feedback
- Overcoming low morale & burnout
- Subjective or inappropriate measuring
- Identifying competencies
- Defining roles and responsibilities
- Motivating personal goals to align with organizational goals
- Reducing turnover

11.4 Some Important "People Issues"

Each of the issues mentioned above is important for an organization to manage if high turnover of people is to be helped. For example, let us take the issue of "low morale & burnout": it is the phenomenon of job withdrawal. An employee's feeling of being helplessly trapped in a meaningless job generally causes burnout. It is not caused by age, overwork, or exhaustion but is more a defense against the loss of self-esteem caused by an apparent lack of personal value. Routine jobs with little challenge evoke reduced performance; one dull task inexorably follows anther. Other people issues are: Age and Creativity, Age and Performance, Age and Motivation. Interested readers are referred to [2]

11.5 Finding a Mentor to Shape Your Career

We'd like to start this section by making a note that "Mentoring" is one of Key Process Areas in the P-CMM model from Software Engineering Institute (the SEI—for additional details, visit the site quoted in section 11.3 www.sei.cmu.edu).The word "mentor" comes from the mythical character *Mentor*, wise man and trusted friend of Odysseus in Homer's *Odyssey*. A mentor provides advice based on experience, helps you navigate around personal and professional obstacles, and acts as a mirror to enable you to see yourself more clearly. A true mentor is honest and would tell you what he/she frankly thinks whether or not the protégée (the person under mentoring) wants to hear it. At times, a mentor would raise protégée's self-confidence by asking his advice. The most effective mentors encourage you to test your wings and fly. They cheer your success and introduce you to others who might be able to help you soar to higher levels. Most importantly, they tell you what you *need to hear* and not what you *want to hear*.

It is worth noting that it takes a secure person to be a good mentor, someone who can honestly say. "I taught her/him everything I know" instead of "I taught her everything she knows." It is important to understand that being a mentor is a very tough mantle and not all managers are capable of providing mentorship. A common mistake is to assume that the mentor has to be a technical expert in your area of work; this is not true. Good mentors are special people—as said earlier they help to protégé to fly. So look everywhere, not just in the obvious places like your workplace. You may find potential mentors at work, in your family, or in your community. Look for people with complementary skills to yours. For example, if you are new test lead, maybe you'd benefit from a mentor with extensive experience as test manager. If you're a fresh tester, perhaps someone with contrasting test skills could help you expand your range of testing skills. Someone can be a good mentor on a single subject; mentors don't need to know more than you do about all aspects of your job.

Beware of choosing mentors only for the power they wield. It is far better to spend time with an individual contributor who possesses a great deal of wisdom than a VP whose only attribute is the influence she could use to get you a promotion. What you learn from a wise person will last a lifetime! What you get from a powerful person will only last as long as their influence on your career lasts. Search for people with whom you have something in common, whether it is shared values, gender, ethnic background, or sense of humour. Having a connection to your mentor beyond your desire to learn from him/her will help establish and sustain the mentoring relationship. To summarize, a mentoring relationship is about spending time getting to know someone who has the wisdom and experience that can help you in the long term. It is not about just finding a job; it is about shaping a career.

11.6 Roles for Quality Professionals

At the outset, we would like the readers to once again note difference between Quality Assurance and Testing. Quality Assurance often gets mixed with testing, which is essentially "quality control" (QC). William Perry (author of the famous book—"Effective Methods for Software Testing") provides a correct viewpoint; "*...the role of QC (Quality Control) is to measure product against a standard or attribute....*" Thus, according to William Perry, the purpose of QC is to identify defects (for the developers to correct) so that a defect-free product or a product within acceptable quality can be produced. Quality Assurance (QA) is separate from QC and deals with the overall management of quality. Often, we hear the statement that the product is in QA—this can be misleading. In this context, QA is projected as quality control or testing. This error is not limited to day-to-day users or developers but even to people dealing with processes. For a more detailed discussion on this, readers can refer to [3].

With this important point in the background, presented below is the list of roles/jobs typically available for quality professionals'; followed by brief discussion on each of them. Sine these roles require you to work with the developers, management teams within your organization as well as the customer, you'll find that good communication skills become an essential skill requirement in all these roles discussed below. It is to be noted that the following are only representative and not exhaustive titles for the typical roles available for Quality professionals in the Information Technology/Software industry. Also, please note that the following roles are not necessarily hierarchical.

- System Tester
- Software Quality Tester
- Quality Assurance Engineer
- Process/Quality Engineer
- Quality Control Analyst
- Quality Assurance Auditor
- Quality Control Manager
- Software Quality Assurance Manager
- Senior Product Verification Specialist
- SEI CMM Lead Assessor
- Director, Software Quality Assurance

11.6.1 System Tester

Sometimes such a role is offered on a contract basis and could be of short duration. Such a role may come into existence when multiple software applications are in various stages of development and require functional as well as data and database integrity testing prior to implementation. Functional and database integrity testing is generally automated through appropriate test software. This kind of role calls upon a number of corporate and external relationships:

- Daily contacts with development and services groups
- Report Regular contact with customers and audit agencies
- Daily involvement with staff
- Reporting to the Operations and Services group

Your responsibilities in this role is mainly to work under the direction of the Project Lead and with additional assistance from the Software Quality Assurance Lead and project development teams to undertake the following tasks:

- Writing or assisting in writing the Test Plan
- Creating test cases for all identified components
- Automating test cases using suitable tool(s)
- Executing test scripts using suitable tool(s)
- Providing written test results

As a System Tester, you're expected to provide the following deliverables

- Provide Test Cases stored as a Test Suite
- Provide Test scripts that are modular and maintainable
- Provide written test results that are reproducible

To perform this role effectively, you should have at least 2–4 years of experience in planning and organizing testing efforts for large systems in GUI and non GUI environments including the execution of systems integration tests and specialized tests (i.e.) stress tests etc., experience in planning, organizing and implementing testing efforts at the specified levels of proficiency, possess knowledge of structured methodologies for the development, design, implementation and maintenance of applications, knowledge and experience in the use of case tools and data query tools to aid in the development of test cases. Experience in the use of automated test tools and version control systems on one or more platforms, excellent analytical, problem solving and decision-making skills; organizational, creativity and perseverance skills; verbal and written communication skills; and interpersonal skills are also required. You should be a team player with a track record for meeting strict deadlines.

11.6.2 Software Quality Tester

Most software companies have a QC group whose job is to test the software for bugs and incompatibilities with specifications. QC professionals are responsible for designing testing strategies that will ensure a quality product, and for implementing these strategies.

For performing this kind of role effectively, some programming experience is necessary, but not as much as with traditional programming. Many companies hire entry-level people into QC, as a way for them to get to know the product and the working environment. Communication skills, teamwork abilities, and problems solving skills are important. Such candidates are thoroughly groomed into organization's testing procedures

A position like this, is often a stepping stone to other positions in the company, such as technical support or programming. Apart from this, an aspiring candidate should note that QA is related to the Total Quality Management (TQM) movement, and there is a lot of literature written about various QA strategies. People who become heavily involved in QA and knowledgeable about it are highly valued in a company.

11.6.3 Quality Assurance Engineer

This job would require demonstrated experience in writing and performing detailed reviews of procedures and instructions. The person is expected to be experienced in the review of technical procedures required to perform and control activities associated with design, procurements, of QC Tools, inspection and testing of items and systems associated with Codes and standards.

11.6.4 Senior Quality Assurance Engineer

Responsibilities include participating in high-level design reviews; developing test specifications, test plans, test cases and automation scripts for new product functionality; functional, integration and regression testing of the modules and identifying and documenting product effects. Additional experience in developing a QA infrastructure, methodology, and process are crucial to this role. This position would typically require at least 4+ years of industry experience, working in positions of increasing responsibility. Test automation experience is mandatory, in particular the execution of tests using some test automation tools. These days, experience in testing Web applications and knowledge of Web technologies, such as HTTP/HTML and XML is an asset, and so is understanding of RDBMS and SQL. The persons should have excellent written and verbal communication skills and the ability to work independently as well as in a team environment.

11.6.5 Process/Quality Engineer

In this role you will identify, lead and support process improvement activities leading to performance improvement and customer satisfaction. Hands on application of process map and effectiveness of the quality system in the development process improvement methods, structured problem solving and statistical analysis techniques will direct your focus. You will also play a key role in transition from ISO9001 to other quality models as required by your client's evolving business and other requirements. A strong belief in teamwork, commitment to continuous improvement, previous experience with quality systems and related technical education will help you meet the interesting and challenging nature of this position.

11.6.6 Quality Control Analyst

As a Quality Control Analyst, you will ensure product quality by testing its security features as well as it's interoperability with the various security providers. In this job, you'd need strong technical skills, you should also have a working knowledge of security technologies and enjoy working closely with development to produce a quality product. You'd be working with Development and Product Management to understand testing requirements. You'd also develop and execute manual and automated test packages. As your additional responsibilities, you would be required to report and follow up on product issues and also assist with development testing activities. The skill requirements for this role would be college diploma OR university degree in Computer Science or equivalent, minimum of 2 years testing experience, demonstrated experience testing product security and excellent communications skills (oral and written).

11.6.7 Quality Assurance Compliance Associate

In this role, responsibilities would include: ensuring that development processes, specifications, product packaging and product release program remain consistent with the Product Registration procedures in the region of work where employed. Quality professional in this role is also expected to advise the product development organization on expectations regarding validation, assisting in the resolution of product-specific process issues. Additional responsibilities would include participating in corporate audits and providing status reports as required, maintaining quality metrics for the product development organization, encouraging continuous improvement, assisting in the management of the change control program, assuring Product Complaints are investigated in a timely manner, participate in new product introductions.

Employer would look for a person with a university degree in a relevant scientific discipline, superior English communication skills, working knowledge of standard development practices with a minimum 5 years of experience in the industry, ability to work effectively with regulatory agencies, technical and non-technical personnel to provide products of superior quality.

11.6.8 Quality Assurance Auditor

Experienced Internal (or external) QA Auditors in utility, process or manufacturing environments familiar with one or more of the standard QA programs like ISO 9000. Interpersonal skills and judgment for dealing with senior management would be considered important aspect of the job.

11.6.9 Quality Control Manager

In this role, your responsibilities include reporting to the Director of Quality, assisting the organization in achieving corporate objectives through the effectiveness and cost-efficiency of product quality controls to ensure on-going compliance to product performance parameters, including regulatory and contractual requirements, ensuring that product Quality Control requirements are defined and controlled by driving the evolution of applicable systems, in a multi-site ISO 9001 environment, and coaching cross-functional personnel on product assurance.

11.6.10 Senior Product Verification Specialist

As a Senior Product Verification specialist, you will be expected to have over 5 years of experience in Software Verification. You should possess excellent knowledge of the design life cycle and extensive expertise in software verification practices. As an experienced tester, your duties will include designing test plans and executing test cases as well as contributing to the overall test strategy for the product. You will be expected to act as a resource person for the group reporting to you. This includes training and mentoring newcomers, providing support to team members, assisting your manager in planning overall resources and tracking projects. As a key member of the Product Verification Team, you will require self-direction, good multi-tasking abilities, excellent troubleshooting and reporting skills.

This role calls upon some personal qualities like the ability to work independently; flexibility and ability to adapt to a new environment; excellent communication skills (verbal and written). Team orientation;

taking initiative; being a quick learner; solid knowledge of and experience with: Product Verification Methodologies (Strategy, Test plan, Test cases writing/execution, problem reporting), overall Software Development process and life cycle; Black box, load, installation and performance testing are also the essential skills.

11.6.11 Software Quality Assurance Manager

For this position, the employer organization typically looks for enthusiastic Software Quality Assurance Manager to lead their QA/Test group in the delivery of software of the highest caliber. As QA Manager your mandate is to evaluate the performance, interoperability and reliability of developing organization's software and ensure that product specifications and customer requirements are met. As a QA Manager, you will lead the planning and development of your organization's ongoing test automation effort; manage the development and implementation of test plans and test cases; form SQA plans, processes and procedures and advise the development team of quality issues. This job would typically insist on the following minimum skill requirements on part of the candidate:

- Minimum of 4 years QA Management experience in the software industry
- Degree in Computer Science/Mathematics/Engineering or related discipline.
- Must possess experience with software quality assurance tools, methods, automation and performance testing.
- Knowledge of eminent tools (for example Winrunner, SILK)
- Exceptional written and oral communication

11.6.12 SEI CMM Lead Assessor

This is a fairly senior role. You're expected to be a talented and team oriented professional to lead a group towards process improvement/maturity practices, act as a mentor and a leader who drives the initiative across the organization in close coordination with the SEPG/Software Process Improvement group. The individual must have successful previous implementation and assessment experience. In this role, your typical responsibilities include: Preparing the detailed Software Process Improvement (SPI) plan with associated risk and opportunities, Conducting organizational assessment of current maturity level, Facilitating organizational change management through SPI, Defining and driving SEI CMM assessment plan for the organization that enables SEI CMM level 2-5 compliance to the required level of the SEI CMM Model (details of this and other process improvement frameworks are discussed in a separate chapter devoted to this topic), Defining metrics and processes necessary for measurements of SEI CMM compliance as an organization, Performing SEI CMM assessments for IT organizations required level of compliance, Performing SEI CMM audit functions to insure continued compliance.

To fit well in this demanding senior role, you need to be (preferably) a SEI Certified CMM Lead Assessor having the experience of assessing both large and small organizations for SEI CMM compliance. The role expects you to have solid knowledge of Capability Maturity Model. It is essential to have project leadership experience in IT organization and also experience with software development methodologies. Since quantitatively managing the software process is the crux of the requirement of the SEI CMM model, you must have experience in establishing metrics for SEI CMM organization measures. In this role, SEI CMM audit experience for IT organizations and needless to say like all QA responsibilities, you should also have excellent communication and interpersonal skills.

11.6.13 Director, Software Quality Assurance

A QA Director is expected to lead the Quality Assurance group/department. Past experience with SQA stints helps to guide the Software Quality Assurance professionals that form the QA group in the organization. In some organizations dealing with e-Business applications, a person in this position is expected to be a hands-on manager of software quality assurance for large-scale high volume web sites. The successful candidate must have a proven track record in building a software quality assurance group. Practical experience with industry leading tools, writing and executing test plans is a must. This position would typically report to the VP—Software Development. Minimum skill requirements for this job would be: at least 2 years experience building and managing a software quality assurance department, 5 years in a practical hands-on software quality assurance role, experience with a few industry standard tools, experience in stress testing Internet sites, some good degree in software technology.

11.7 Quality Certifications

In this section, we'll discuss the various international level certifications available to persons who wish to work as quality professionals. It should be noted that these certifications are only meant to endorse your proficiency in the concerned area. However, in themselves, they are not a substitute to work experience in quality profession. It is the experience that can really build the knowledge skills and competency. While Certifications help you to gain the conceptual knowledge, it is the field experience that makes you a real practitioner/SME (subject matter expert). This happens when you get the opportunities to apply the knowledge gained through certification. Needless to say, however, that these certifications go a long way in bringing in the required conceptual framework which you can hope to apply in your working situations if you have not already got the opportunity to do so. Pl keep this in mind while you read ahead.

We are going to discuss the certifications available from two well-known international level organizations; ASQ (American Society for Quality) and QAI (Quality Assurance Institute—USA). At the end, we've provided the URLs from where the interested readers can seek further details.

11.7.1 Certification Benefits

Certification is a mark of excellence that:

- Provides verification of an individual's knowledge
- Is recognized by several organizations
- Is maintained through demonstrable professional practice
- Ensures continuing education
- Is reinforced through use of designator letters.

Certification has a certain impact on the individual who undergoes the certifications and on the organizations that sponsor individuals for the said certification and the professional community around. Impact on the person is high immediate and on-going professional growth. Impact on the organization is that it highlights interest in Quality, infects colleagues and creates ground swell of professional activity. Impact on our community is that of heightened professionalism that spills over to other organizations. Thus, there is no doubt that Professional certification has long been a way to advance one's career independent of industry and political constraints.

11.7.2 Certifications from American Society for Quality (ASQ)

An ASQ Certification is a peer recognition program indicating proficiency in a designated subject area. These programs are independent of employers and hence portable. Certification is indicated by using the appropriate letters after the person's name e.g. Ninad Deshpande, CQE. Table 1 provides a summary of quality related Certifications available from ASQ. For those who'd be interested, we've provided below a brief history of certifications from the American Society for Quality.

History of ASQ Certification Programs

Table 1: ASQ Certifications

ASQ Designation	Designed For ...
Certified Quality Engineer (CQE)	... those who understand the principles of product and service quality evaluation and control.
Certified Quality Auditor (CQA)	... those who understand the standards and principles of auditing and the auditing techniques of examining, questioning, evaluating, and reporting to determine quality systems adequacy.
Certified Quality Manager (CQMgr)	... those who understand quality principles and standards in relation to organization and human resource management.
Certified Software Quality Engineer (CSQE)	... those who have a comprehensive understanding of software quality development and implementation, have a thorough understanding of software inspection, testing, verification, and validation; and can implement software development and maintenance processes and methods.
Certified Reliability Engineer (CRE)	... those who understand the principles of performance evaluation and prediction to improve product/systems safety, reliability, and maintainability.
Certified Quality Technician (CQT)	... those who can analyze quality problems, prepare inspection plans and instruction, select sampling plan applications, and apply fundamental statistical methods for process control.
Certified Mechanical Inspector (CMI)	... those who, under professional direction, can evaluate hardware documentation, perform laboratory procedures, inspect products, measure process performance, record data, and prepare formal reports.
Certified Quality Improvement Associate (CQIA)	... those who have a basic knowledge of quality tools and their uses and are involved in quality improvement projects but do not necessarily come from the traditional quality area.
Six Sigma Black Belt Certification	... those who have a comprehensive understanding of Six Sigma and its methodologies.
Quality Auditor Certification-Biomedical (CQA-Biomedical)	The ASQ Board of Directors and the Certification Board with sponsorship from the Biomedical Division approved this most recent "Add-On Certification" to the Certified Quality Auditor exam. Note: You must be an ASQ Certified Quality Auditor and have two years of experience working with Biomedical auditing. This two-year requirement can be part of the eight-year requirement used for the CQA exam.
Quality Auditor Certification-HACCP (CQA-HACCP)	In November 1999, the ASQ Board of Directors and the ASQ Certification Board, with sponsorship of the Food, Drug, and Cosmetic Division, approved the first "Add-On Certification" to the Certified Quality Auditor exam. Note: You must be an ASQ Certified Quality Auditor and have two years of experience working with the HACCP standards. This two-year requirement can be part of the eight-year requirement used for the CQA exam.

The certification program was first developed to serve three industries; Nuclear, Consumer and Automotive. Certification programs are established to meet specific quality focus areas and are typically developed over a 2–3 year period in consultation with recognized industry experts, for example:

- Certified Quality Engineer (CQE) was started in 1966.
- Certified Quality Auditor (CQA) was started in 1987.
- Certified Quality Manager (CQMgr) was started in 1995.
- Certified Software Quality Engineer (CSQE) was started in 1996.
- Certified Quality Improvement Associate (CQIA) was started in 2001.

11.7.3 Certifications from Quality Assurance Institute

11.7.3.1 *Certified Software Quality Analyst*

Acquiring the designation of Certified Software Quality Analyst (CSQA) indicates a professional level of competence in the principles and practices of quality assurance in the IT profession. CSQAs become members of a recognized professional group and receive recognition of their competence by business and professional associates, potentially more rapid career advancement, and greater acceptance in the role as advisor to management.

11.7.3.2 *Certified Software Test Engineer*

The Certified Software Test Engineer (CSTE) certification is intended to establish standards for initial qualification and provide direction for the testing function through an aggressive educational program. Acquiring the designation of Certified Software Test Engineer (CSTE) indicates a professional level of competence in the principles and practices of quality control in the IT profession. CSTEs become members of a recognized professional group and receive recognition of their competence by business and professional associates, potentially more rapid career advancement, and greater acceptance in the role as advisor to management.

Conclusion

In this chapter, our aim was discuss about growth path for quality professionals. Broadly speaking, as a quality professional, you can grow either in the process side (Quality Assurance) or testing side (Quality Control). To shape your career you need good planning as well as a strong mentor. Armed with appropriate certifications your path to upward mobility can be fuelled for a faster growth. Though there is no substitute for hard work and field experience, certifications can help you expand your vision; they also help you with the right conceptual framework.

REFERENCES

[1] *Surviving the Challenges of Software Testing: A People-oriented Approach* by William Perry (Dorset House Publishing)
[2] *Managing Technical People* by Watts Humphrey (Pearson Education)
[3] *Process Quality Assurance for UML-Based Projects* by Bhuvan Unhelkar (Addition-Wesley)
[4] www.softwarecertifications.com for information on certifications CSQA and CSTE
[5] asq0407@quality.org for the details of ASQA Certification Programs

Appendix A

PROCESS IMPROVEMENT RELATED MISCELLANEOUS TOPICS

A.1 Some Basic Terms

In this section, we have discussed some fundamental terms that were mentioned in Chapter 9 (*Process Improvement Models*)

A.1.1 Process

The term "process" can be defined in a variety of ways; here are a few acceptable definitions:

'a course of action or proceeding, especially, a series of stages in manufacturing or some other operation'

'a system of operations in producing something...a series of actions, changes or functions that achieve an end result'

'a sequence of steps performed for a given purpose, for example the software development process'

'a collection of activities that takes one more kinds of input and creates an output that is of value to the customer'

'a set of actions, tasks, and procedures that when performed or executed obtain a specific goal or objectives. More specifically, a software process is a software development procedures'

'the set of activities, methods, and practices used in the production and evolution of software' [SEI CMM]

The three important aspects of Process are shown in Figure 1. Next, we discuss about symptoms and behaviours of "process orientation". This discussion is important for understanding the patterns the *"High Maturity Organizations"*. (In Chapter 9, there is a discussion on "practices followed at *"Mature Organizations"*.)

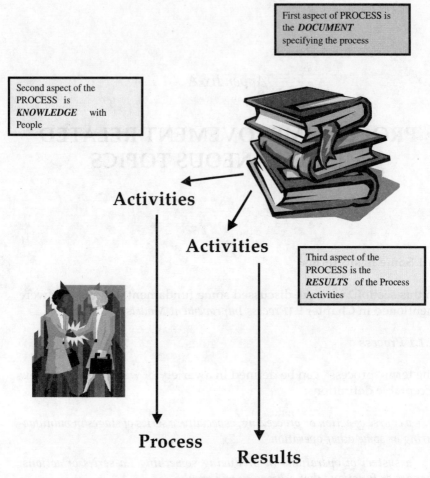

First aspect of PROCESS is the *DOCUMENT* specifying the process

Second aspect of the PROCESS is *KNOWLEDGE* with People

Third aspect of the PROCESS is the *RESULTS* of the Process Activities

Activities

Activities

Process

Results

Figure 1: Process Aspects

A.1.3 Maturity

Readers must understand that throughout the discussion of the term "process improvement" and related topics, the term "maturity" is used in the context of "process maturity". Organizations at various levels of process discipline are like people at different stages of maturity (obtained out of the process of living which provides experiences and lessons!). The difference between and immature process and a mature process is like the difference between a young child and a mature adult. Process thinking has an impact on behaviour. For illustrations of this point see Table 1 (adapted from [3]). Also another good reference is [5] for concepts on "discipline"—applicable to Software Engineering Profession" as provided by Watts Humphrey.

Table 1: Process Focus

Parameter	Without Process Focus	With Process Focus
Process Discipline	Processes are improvised by the staff and their management on the fly (in the course of performing the activities)	Processes are defined and followed by staff as well as by management; process discipline is the un-questioned norm
Organization	Functions are roles do not necessarily align with the process requirements	Functions and roles are defined in support of the process
Management	Staff performance is measured in terms of the number of work hours (irrespective of whether they were productive or not) Managers are usually focused on solving immediate crises (fire-fighting approach)	Staff performance is measured in terms of process performance and results rather than merely focusing on activities. Such measurements are defined and agreed Managers focus on the quality of processes as well as quality of products
Skills and Training	Training is *ad hoc,* and oriented towards personal inclinations	Training is a planned activity, subject to periodic reviews by all concerned
Tools and Technology	Tools & Technology are acquired as *ad hoc* point solutions without an overall plan and strategy	Tools & Technology acquisition involves all stakeholders (in cognizance to organizations vision and mission) Selection is made in support of the end-to-end process and the automation of process activities with a view to obtain higher productivity in the long run

A.1.4 Process Orientation

An effective process environment is characterized by an existence of process feedback mechanisms in order to collect data on process performance. This feedback data collected and stored in process data becomes organization's memory ("Lessons learnt") wherein the organization stores experiences and results of its process performance. This can then be used to improve processes (for example improving the performance of another similar projects executed next time.) Such information should be available to all those in the organization who are involved in performing process activities (say software engineering). Table 2 shows symptoms and behaviour in the context of process orientation.

Table 2: Process Orientation

Key Term	Description of symptom/behaviour
Process Visibility	The process definition and process responsibility are visible to everybody in the organization
Process Discipline	Following the process is the norm, and acting outside the process is the exception
Process Institutionalization	Following the process is "second nature" to the people in the organization i.e. following the process is engraved into the organizational policies and procedures, and supported by the management
Management Commitment to Processes	The processes are supported by top management of the organization as well as all other levels of management and staff
Process Enforcement	Process enforcement is evident and is in force
Process Ownership	The process is owned, maintained and continuously improved and supported by an organizational infrastructure
Process Feedback	Feedback on the process effectiveness is practiced by every one in the organization, and is enabled by appropriate feed back mechanism
Performance Assessment	Measurement and evaluation of staff and team performance is tightly linked to the process performance (i.e. achieving the process goals)
Process Training	Process Awareness and training mandatory for all staff, and process induction is mandatory for new recruits (for that matter for anyone who is engaged in software engineering activities)
Process Improvement	Process Improvement in planned and implemented through the participation of all the staff involved in software engineering activities as well as relates support processes (configuration management, training etc)

A.2 High Maturity Organizations (those at SW CMM Level 4 or 5)

In Chapter 9, we discussed the term "maturity" in terms of "software processes". It will now be interesting to understand the practices followed in mature organizations. Over the last few years the Software Engineering Institute has participated in several workshops and site visits with maturity level 4 and 5 software organizations. This section summarizes the lessons learned as reported by SEI based on their interactions with high maturity organizations. Specific areas of interest include *statistical process* and *quality control* and product lines/families, and several other observations made by the SEI over a variety of engineering and management practices, including issues outside the scope of the Capability Maturity Model for Software. For a detailed discussion, reader is referred to [1]. The purpose of this section is to summarize in a general way the techniques, methods, and lessons learned about getting to CMM levels 4 and 5. We do not, however, attempt to describe all good software engineering and management practices. Although these observations are specific to software organizations, it is believed that these practices, or discipline-specific variants, are valuable to any high maturity organization in any engineering discipline. The data that is summarized in this section comes from a variety of sources, including published case studies, workshops, site visits, and assessments, data collected by SEI through their surveys etc.

It turns out that *high maturity organizations* typically have a broader scope of improvement concerns than just the CMM's process issues. Some high maturity organizations were found to be doing process improvement long before the Software CMM framework was published. Others, such as Motorola India, were started with one business objective being" high process maturity." Common Practices Observed in High Maturity Organizations are described below.

A.2.1 Role of TQM in Mature Organizations

If there is a Total Quality Management (TQM) initiative within the company, the high maturity organization's software process improvement program is explicitly aligned and co-ordinated with the TQM initiative. Aligning with TQM initiatives can be a challenge for high maturity organizations. If the organization is already performing at Six Sigma levels, there is a major challenge in improving dramatically. In such cases, the alignment may be conceptual rather than quantitative.

A.2.2 Role of ISO 9001 Certification

Eleven out of thirteen of the organizations surveyed (The 1999 survey conducted by the SEI) had ISO 9001 certification. Some commented that they began their process improvement efforts using ISO 9001, then shifted to the CMM after obtaining certification. Others obtained certification as a business requirement in their market.

A.2.3 Addressing Other Issues

As mentioned earlier, surveys show that high maturity organizations address issues outside the scope of the CMM. Their improvement programs include a strong emphasis on automating the software process and addressing people issues. Processes, data collection, and statistical analysis are automated wherever practical. High maturity organizations generally emphasize openness, communication, and a commitment to quality and the customer at all levels. They appreciate the "people issues" (In this connection, it is worth visiting the SEI site (www.sei.cmu.edu) to fully understand the overview of the "People

CMM" model apart from the mention in this chapter). Thus, one can say that much of the maturity practices are to do a lot with "organizations culture".

A.2.4 Process Orientation in High Maturity Organization

Another finding of these surveys conducted by the Software Engineering Institute is that the high maturity organizations encourage a "process orientation" in their staff. Worker empowerment and participation in process definition and improvement activities are real; process improvement is part of everyone's job. Their strategic approach to quality management involves the linkage of quality with business goals and a focus on customer satisfaction and delight. (Interestingly, the "People CMM" model addresses several of these aspects.)

A.2.5 Quality Culture

There is a "quality culture" in high maturity organizations. Rewards and incentives are established for process improvement efforts, and worker empowerment and participation are more than just slogans. People believe in the process, and when mistakes happen (as they inevitably do in any human endeavor), the focus is on improving the process, not disciplining or penalizing the people, who may only be the bearers of bad tidings.

A.2.6 Approach to People Issues

High maturity organizations recognize the importance of good staff. To quote one participant in the SEI CMM 1996 workshop, "*Getting the right person into the right job on the project is still the most important aspect of project success. People are not plug-compatible. The expertise of individuals is critical. Process is an enabler; not a replacement...*". Knowledge and skills are systematically cultivated in software engineering, management, interpersonal skills, and the application domain. Another workshop participant stated, "*We have the philosophy of not assigning people to jobs they are not prepared for....*" It was also observed that not everyone needs to have deep domain knowledge so long as the key lead engineers do, although at least one member of each team needs to have the right domain expertise to support the team effort.

A.2.7 Approach to Using the CMM Model in High Maturity Organizations

High maturity organizations apply common sense in using the SW CMM. New projects are typically expected to address all 18 key process areas, but alternate implementations are used when appropriate.

When there is a controversy, (strategic) business value is the foremost factor in resolving the situation; this sometimes means going against the "letter of the CMM" or customer desires, but doing so with data to support an informed decision.

A.2.8 Customer Relationships and Customers' Maturity Levels

It is very difficult to be a high maturity supplier if you have a low maturity customer (or low maturity suppliers or partners in the case of strategic alliances, joint ventures, and virtual organizations). At higher maturity, there is a better foundation and understanding to explain to customers why you do things a certain way. The customer is usually reasonable when presented with data, facts and frequent patterns of success, e.g., delivering on schedule and budget. The general philosophy of high maturity organizations is to proactively work with the customer to gain a mutual understanding of what will be done, which often means educating the customer on how the organization usually does things, with data and results to back up the methods.

One high maturity organization provides the last two years of performance data in its proposals; although it is rarely the low bidder, consistent past performance provides credibility. In one instance, a long-term customer in a maintenance environment did not want the software development plan updated. The supplier chose to develop a separate plan that the organization uses—an example of doing the right process thing, even if the customer is uninterested (or perhaps opposed!). Another supplier, in a commercial environment, established a customer liaison engineer, separate from the systems engineer, to work the interface with the customer. The customer liaison engineer is usually on the customer's site, and change control boards include customer representatives.

The SEI 1999 survey indicates a general emphasis on proactively managing the evolution of the customer's requirements via evolutionary and incremental life cycles. Eleven of the thirteen organizations surveyed use incremental life cycles, and nine of the thirteen (with two piloting) use evolutionary life cycles.

A.2.9 Project Management (Issues for Maintenance Organizations)

A practice in the CMM's project management key process areas that requires significant interpretation for maintenance organizations is size estimating. Maintenance organizations are frequently funded as level-of-effort, and little business value may be derived from size estimating. Although size may be a useful measure for enhancements, for corrective maintenance "size" is likely to be "number of problem reports," and the variability is likely to be quite high. All thirteen organizations in the survey (conducted by the SEI in 1999) use lines of code as a size measure (and two use function points also, with two more organizations piloting them), but comments pointed out that there are instances where size estimating is not of value for maintenance—schedules and budgets may be fixed *a priori* for maintenance projects, and the variable parameter is the functionality of the update package. It is also interesting to note that only eight of the thirteen organizations surveyed use cost models in their planning process, and one maintenance organization had actively rejected them.

A.2.10 *Risk Management in High Maturity Organizations*

High maturity organizations systematically manage risks. Eleven of the thirteen organizations surveyed do "systematic" risk management. This would lay a good foundation for transitioning to the CMM-Integrated model where "Risk Management" is a separate process area at Level 3. Based on the survey the following characteristics can be noted for the high maturity organizations:

a) Operating in a high risk environment;
b) Having a profound knowledge of the risks associated with their (fairly specialized) application domains; and
c) Having internalized risk management so thoroughly—and systematically—into their processes that they no longer recognize how mature their risk management process is.

The conclusion appears to be that systematic risk management is an intrinsic characteristic of high maturity, which is integrated into the process and internalized by the staff.

A.2.11 *Roles, Responsibilities and Delegation in High Maturity Organizations*

In high maturity organizations, many traditional management responsibilities are delegated to roles specified in the process, e.g., progress tracking, day-to-day customer interfaces, and process improvement. Managers are freed to focus on longer-term strategic and operational issues. Managers can truly "manage by exception" in an open culture where the messenger is not shot and problems are identified and escalated appropriately and quickly. When roles are established, and responsibility and authority delegated, the people in the roles:

- speak for the organization
- are empowered to make commitments that will be honored
- are supported by their management

A.2.12 Measurement in Mature Organizations

High maturity organizations tend to have dedicated measurement people at the project and organization levels, although they may not be assigned full-time. They also encourage their customers to become actively involved in specifying measures and setting quality goals. Measurement in a high maturity organization can be characterized as:

- driven by business goals
- standardized across the organization for common measures
- tailored to the specific needs of the user/customer
- based on operational definitions that define how to collect consistent data
- collected as close to the point of origin as possible (primary metrics)
- involve the active participation of the affected parties, including the customer

A.2.13 Product and Process Assurance in High Maturity Organizations

Software Quality Assurance (SQA) is perhaps the most controversial key process area in the CMM. There are passionately held, opposing opinions on whether there should be an independent SQA organization or whether the SQA function should be "built into the process" as part of the quality culture that should be expected of high maturity organizations. (Reader will re-collect that the topic or how the organization and reporting of the SQA group should be was discussed in the early chapters of this book; with this background, it would be interesting to see what the survey shows about "high maturity organizations")

Questions in the survey were intended to probe this issue, but the surprising result was that all thirteen organizations indicated that they use an "independent SQA group" and embed the SQA function in the process. The SQA groups in these organizations were found to use the level 4 process and product data to identify high-leverage opportunities for auditing.

As one reviewer commented, *"I was convinced several years ago that SQA would disappear as an organization matures and software quality functions would be embedded into the software engineering functions. I viewed the CMM to have a problem, because SQA as an independent function was always required even as the organization matured (since it was a Level 2 KPA). However, I changed my opinion after our experience ... When SQA makes the appropriate transition to process audits in addition to product audits, they can become a valuable team member. We still make mistakes in a high maturity organization, and it is still valuable to have a backup to catch those. Their role in process audits is very valuable as it separates that function from the SEPG so that the SEPG does not appear to be the policeman."*

Further to this, the SEI Survey (1999) found that some high maturity organizations separate process and product assurance. The "SQA group" may focus on process monitoring, while product assurance is built into the peer reviews and configuration management system.

A.2.14 *Training and Mentoring in High Maturity Organizations*

High Maturity Organizations give extraordinary importance to Training. Some organizations have mandatory training for new hires that can last up to eight weeks, plus mandatory continuing education requirements. This training includes internally and externally developed training materials, awareness programs, and workshops. Other organizations rely heavily on formal mentoring programs to impart skills and knowledge. Most high maturity organizations have both training and formal mentoring programs. Training is tailored to the needs and experience of the students, with an emphasis on training in the application domain. High maturity organizations recognize the criticality of domain expertise; the organization may even be structured into product lines. Teams will usually have staffing requirements for expertise in the application domain as well as software engineering techniques and technologies.

A.3 Strategic Planning for Software Process Improvement

By now, readers may have appreciated the fact that "Software Process Improvement" does not occur overnight, and cannot be implemented on a "fad of the week" basis nor can the results be produced in "flash-in-the-pan" manner. If it is done that way then, it is doomed to failure. Implementing software process improvement involves the development of an overall strategy, requiring patience on the part of all parties involved: management, the developers, and the stakeholders. Many small steps are involved. If the development of the overall strategic plan is not performed judiciously, valuable time and money can be wasted.

The strategy for implementing process improvement should be addressed in a plan that accomplishes improvement actions as a series of small projects. The strategic plan should be one that is commensurate with the overall business objectives of the organization and should identify the resources (including personnel, capital outlays, and software and hardware tools) needed to execute the projects, the schedule, associated tasks, project responsibilities, and measures that will be utilized to indicate success or failure.

In developing a strategic plan, a team is organized consisting of the personnel who were trained and participated in the assessment, as well as any other personnel who have a vested interest in the outcome of the planning effort. Senior management also has an important role to perform.

As they say "there is no free lunch"! To expedite undertaking the various analyses that need to be performed and to achieve agreement on priorities, the planning process is typically conducted in a workshop mode, led by a facilitator. The approach found to most effectively lead to a sound process improvement strategy includes the following steps:

- Develop Process Improvement Proposals
- Evaluate the Proposals
- Rank the Proposed Projects
- Estimate the Implementation Schedule
- Obtain Management Commitment

In sum, we can say that successful process improvement planning is ensured when the planning process is based on key planning concepts:

- Strong linkage of processes to business objectives
- Involve the right people (People buy-in throughout)
- Using proven business planning methods.
- Facilitate productive communication and sharing of ideas among all participants (creating "process champions")
- An approach that does not loose sight of the big picture.

Author, based on her extensive experience in the Information Technology/Software Development industry (in the role of Quality Professional) finds that organizations adopting this approach have found that they can efficiently and rapidly move from assessment to implementing the needed changes with the confidence that their decisions are sound and will lead to a stronger software engineering capability.

A.4 Software CMM for Small Organizations

A frequently asked question is, "Can the Software CMM be used for small projects (or small organizations)?" However, since the definition of "small" is relative and sometimes challengingly ambiguous, we have shown this Table 3 as represented by the world famous SEI (Software Engineering Institute)

Table 3: Small Projects

Variant of "Small"	Team Size	Project Duration
Small	3–5	6 months
Very small	2–3	4 months
Tiny	1–2	2 months
Individual	1	1 week
Ridiculous!	1	1 hour

Note that small to tiny projects are in the range being addressed by Humphrey in his "Team Software Process" work [4] and the individual effort is in the range of the Personal Software Process [3]. TSP and PSP illustrate how CMM concepts are being applied to small projects. The "ridiculous" variant represents an interpretational problem.

One of the first challenges for small organizations in using the CMM is that their primary business objective is to survive! Even after deciding the status quo is unsatisfactory and process improvement will help, finding the resources and assigning responsibility for process improvement, and then following through by defining and deploying processes is a difficult business decision. The small organization tends to be victims of what is known as "Group Think Effect" and "Cognitive Dissonance"; i.e. the people in "small" organizations have a belief that: (Note that "Group Think Effect" is most often based on wrong beliefs that teams working in isolation have about themselves):

- We are all competent—people were hired to do the job, and we can't afford training in terms of either time or money
- We all communicate with one another—"osmosis" works because we're so "close"
- We are all heroes—we do whatever needs to be done, the rules don't apply to us (they just get in the way of getting the job done), we live with short cycle times and high stress

Even in "small" organizations/small projects, the following is required at a minimum:

- Documented customer (system) requirements
- Communication with customer (and end users)
- Agreed-to commitments
- Planning
- Documented processes
- Work breakdown structure

Some practices, however, deal with "large-project implementations." A small project is unlikely to need an SCM group (Software Configuration Management) or a Change Control Board... but configuration management and change control are always necessary; An independent SQA group may not be desirable, but objective verification that requirements are satisfied must be present. An independent testing group may not be established, but testing is always necessary. We thus see that it is only a question of degree of the formality involved but certainly not a complete absence of required processes!

The intent is critical even if the implementation is radically different between small organizations and large. Many of the large-project implementation issues relate to organizational structure. If one reads the CMM definition of "group," it states that "a group could vary from a single individual assigned part time, to several part-time individuals assigned from different departments, to several individuals dedicated full time," which is intended to cater to a variety of contexts. In addition to these, specific questions that arise repeatedly, especially for small organizations, relate to:

- Management sponsorship
- measurement
- SEPGs
- "as is" processes
- documented processes
- Tailoring
- Training
- Risk Management
- Planning
- Peer Reviews

In sum, we can say that Small Organizations should seriously consider PSP and TSP [3 and 4]. Taking the PSP course has shown to help building self-discipline [5]. Note, however, that the effect of reading the PSP book is not the same as taking the course and doing the work! Where the CMM addresses the organizational side of process improvement, PSP addresses building the capability of individual practitioners. The PSP course convinces the individual, based on his or her own data, of the value of a disciplined, engineering approach to building software.

A.5 Mini Assessment Process

The *Mini-Assessment Process* (MAP) was designed to provide corporate managers with accurate, detailed assessment results with minimal investment. Level 1 and Level 2 organizations that are considering starting a *process improvement* program can use it to determine their potential return-on-investment. Organizations who have started their improvement activities, and may lack focus, can use a MAP to pinpoint the areas where further improvement is most desirable and effective.

The Mini-Assessment Process includes:

- Definition of corporate appraisal objectives
- Opening briefing summarizing the process maturity concepts and the MAP methodology
- Review of corporate documents (policies, procedures, guidebooks, training materials, etc.)

- Review of project documents (software development plans, configuration management plans, specifications, quality assurance plans, etc.)
- Interviews with corporate managers and staff
- Interviews with project personnel
- Complete findings briefing

The Mini-Assessment Process typically takes one to two days. Fully authorized assessors follow a *tailored version of the assessment method* developed by the Software Engineering Institute (SEI) and used by hundreds of software companies. Results include the maturity level of your organization and how your practices compare to the industry standards, as documented in the SEI's Capability Maturity Model.

The assessment findings are presented immediately following the assessment:

- Maturity rating score for your organization;
- Detailed strengths and weaknesses against the CMM's Key Process Areas;
- Cultural barriers to improvement in your organization;
- Recommended improvement ideas for immediate action.

A complete assessment report and improvement action plan can also be produced, if desired. Many companies have benefited from the Mini-Assessment Process, and consider it an important part of their and improvement strategy.

A.6 The Integrated Capability Maturity Model (CMM-I)

A.6.1 CMM-Integrated: Myths and Realities

There are a lot of misconceptions about the new integrated capability maturity model. In this section, we wish to dispel the doubts most people may have about this new integrated model. (Readers may like to recollect that in Chapter 9 we had discussed about making a transition to CMM-Integrated model).

In this context, the most common misconceptions seem to be:

- CMMI is too big and complex.
- A CMMI appraisal/assessment takes longer and costs more than an appraisal for SW-CMM.
- CMMI is only for large organizations.

These and other myths are often heard in discussions about upgrading from the SW-CMM to a CMMI model. But those who have been using the new set of models and training materials contend that making the switch to the CMMI Product Suite is not only easier than it looks, but well worth it. For organizations already operating at a high Maturity Level, (recollect the discussion in the earlier section of this Appendix) the process of achieving CMMI is very straightforward. In fact, most organizations that have made a transition to the integrated CMM feel that CMMI validates the *best practices* already had in place due to requirements of the software CMM model. CMM-I, then, is just the matter of consolidating these practices institutionalizing them further.

CMMI enforces tying project objectives to organizational objectives, which is not only a good thing to do, but also a bad thing not to do. CMMI shows you exactly what you should be doing to improve your quality processes.

Although the CMMI models were developed in part to help larger organizations tackle complex issues across multiple disciplines, they can be tailored to meet the needs of smaller companies, especially if the companies apply the models purely for process improvement. Many smaller organizations aren't interested in using CMMI to benchmark themselves against other organizations. They don't need to commit to all the Process Areas and Practices. CMMI is designed so they can pick and choose among the *Process Areas* that have the most immediate applicability to them. The CMMI Product Suite is currently being applied across a range of organization sizes, from large to small.

A.6.2 Assessment Requirements for CMMI

First, let us understand what is "assessment". The Software Engineering Institute (SEI) defines this term as follows:

An examination of one or more processes by a trained team of professionals using an assessment reference model as the basis for determining strengths and weaknesses. An assessment is typically conducted in the context of process improvement or capability evaluation.

The Assessment Requirements for CMMI (Integrated Capability Maturity Model) comprise a set of high-level design criteria for developing, defining, and using assessment methods based on CMMI models. These requirements constitute an evolutionary progression from the CMM Appraisal Framework V1.0, which was produced originally to provide a common basis for assessment methods employing the Capability Maturity Model for Software.

There is what is known as *"Assessment Classes"*—each class is a family of assessment methods that satisfy a defined subset of requirements in the Assessment Requirements for CMMI (ARC). These classes are defined so as to align with typical usage modes of assessment. There are three classes of assessments for CMM-I: Class A, Class B and Class C. Depending on the class of assessment, the requirements vary (*Assessment Method Documentation, Plan and Preparation for the*

Assessment, Data Collection, Data Consolidation and Validation, Rating and Reporting Results)

Assessment teams use CMMI models as the basis for deriving the strengths and weaknesses of the processes investigated during an assessment. These findings, along with guidance provided by the practices in the model, are used to plan an improvement strategy for the organization.

The assessment principles for the CMMI Product Suite are the same as those for assessments using the Capability Maturity Model for Software:

- Start with an assessment reference model
- Use a formalized assessment process
- Focus the assessment on the sponsor's business goals
- Observe strict confidentiality and non-attribution of data
- Approach the assessment collaboratively
- Focus on follow-on process improvement activities

In connection with the CMM-I Assessments, various *roles and responsibilities* come into picture as defined by the SEI: (individual descriptions are beyond the scope of this appendix. The detailed description for each role is available at the SEI site www.sei.cmu.edu):

- The sponsor of the assessment
- The assessment team leader

The SEI has laid down a stringent set of requirements on the *Assessment Method Documentation*. Those descriptions too are available at the SEI site mentioned above.

REFERENCES

[1] *Practices of High Maturity Organizations*—Mark C. Paulk Software Engineering Institute (1999 SEPG Conference, Atlanta, Georgia, 8–11 March 1999)
[2] *Strategic Planning for Software Process Improvement: Techniques for Making the Hard Choices*—by Frank J. Koch and Emanuel R. Baker, Ph.D.
[3] *Introduction to the Personal Software Process* by Watts S. Humphrey (Addison Wesley)
[4] *Introduction to the Team Software Process* by Watts S. Humphrey (Addison-Wesley)
[5] *The Personal Software Process: An Empirical Study of the Impact of PSP in Individual Engineers*—Will Hayes, James W. Over (Technical Report CMU/SEI-97-TR-001 ESC-TR-97-001 December 1997)

Appendix B

INDIAN SOFTWARE INDUSTRY
IN PERSPECTIVE

B.1 Quality Certifications Scenario in India

According to Bill Curtis, Former Director of the Process Program, SEI, Author of the CMM (Capability Maturity Model):

"India is making progress on both the Software CMM and People CMM faster than any other nation. The pinnacle will be reached when Americans are seeking visas so they can learn and work in India"

According to N.R. Narayana Murthy, the CEO, Infosys Technologies:

For Quality Experts to successfully inspire everybody from top to bottom in an organization there are three basic requirements:

- *Quality has to be linked to business goals*
- *There has to be a sense of pride deeply instilled in your organization*
- *The third requisite for quality is a shared vision and commitment of top management*

With this backdrop, let is understand the Indian scenario on software practices maturity. Let us take a look at the statistics on the quality certifications scenario in India.

B.1.1 SW CMM Maturity Level 4 and 5 Organizations in India

The table on the next page presents some vital information in this context. It shows that there are quite a few Indian SW organizations that are at SW CMM maturity level 4 and 5. They are listed below in alphabetical order of their names.

Table 1

Organization	Maturity Level	Date of Appraisal
BFL Software Limited, Bangalore	4	June 1999
CG-Smith Software, Bangalore	5	Sept 1999
Citicorp Overseas Software Limited (COSL), Mumbai	4	Dec 1998
DCM Technologies, DCM ASIC Technology Limited, New Delhi	5	April 2000
DSQ Software, Chennai	4	June 1998
Future Software Private Limited, Chennai	4	June 1999
HCL Perot Systems, Noida and Bangalore	5	Feb 2000
Hughes Software Systems, Bangalore and Gurgaon	4	Jan 2000
IBM Global Services India, Bangalore	5	Nov 1999
i-flex solutions limited (formerly Citicorp Information Technology Industries Limited aka CITIL), Mumbai	4	Dec 1995
i-flex solutions limited (formerly Citicorp Information Technology Industries Limited aka CITIL) Data Warehouse Center of Excellence, Bangalore	5	Nov 1999
International Computers India Ltd (ICIL), Pune	5	Feb 1999
Motorola India Electronics Ltd. (MIEL), Bangalore	5	Nov 1993
Network Systems and Technologies (P) Ltd, Trivandrum	5	May 2000
Oracle Software India Limited, India Development Center, Bangalore	4	May 1999
Origin Information Technology (India) Ltd., Mumbai	4	May 1999
Origin Information Technology (India) Ltd., Mumbai	4	Oct 1999
Satyam Computer Services Ltd, India	5	March 1999
Silverline Technologies Limited, Mumbai, India	4	Dec 1999
Tata Consultancy Services, HP Centre, Chennai, India	5	July 1999
Tata Consultancy Services, SEEPZ, Mumbai, India	5	Aug 1999
Tata Consultancy Services, Shollinganallur, Chennai, India	5	Nov 1999
Tata Consultancy Services, US West, Chennai, India	5	April 1999
Tata Elxsi Limited, Bangalore, India	4	Aug 1999
Wipro GE Medical Systems, Bangalore, India	5	Jan 1999
Wipro Technologies, Enterprise Solutions Division, Bangalore, India	5	Dec 1998
Wipro Technologies, Global R & D (formerly Technology Solutions), Bangalore, India	5	June 1999

B.1.2 The P-CMM Scenario in India

People CMM is a process targeted at managing and developing an organization's work force and adopts the maturity framework of the Capability Maturity Model for software (CMM). The aim of PCMM is to radically improve the ability of software organizations to attract, develop, motivate, organize, and retain talent needed to continuously improve software development capability. PCMM consists of five maturity levels that lay successive foundations for continuously improving talent, developing effective teams, and successfully managing the people assets of the organization. (In Chapter 9 we had provided an overview of the P-CMM model).

For a country like India, with its large assets in the form of skilled human resources, the relevance of People CMM needs no emphasis. A large number of Indian IT software and services companies have been quick to realize this and have either implemented or initiated programs. The chart below presents the P-CMM scenario in India.

Indian Software Industry (P-CMM Scenario)	
Company	*Certified Level*
Dattamatics Ltd.	Level 2
Datamatics Technologies Pvt. Ltd.	Level 2
Intelligroup Asia Pvt. Ltd.	Level 2
QAI (India) Limited	Level 2
MASTEK Ltd.	Level 3
Future Software Limited	Level 3
R S Software (India) Ltd.	Level 3
Siemens Information Systems Ltd.	Level 3
TechSpan India Ltd.	Level 3
Tata Consultancy Services	Level 4
Wipro Technologies	Level 5
IBM Global Services India Pvt. Ltd.	Level 5

B.1.3 List of Quality Certified Organizations in India

Provided below is the alphabetical list of quality certified organizations in India (both CMM, ISO, PCMM and others).

Table 2

Company Name	Quality Certifications
A	
A G Technologies Pvt Ltd	• ISO 9001
Ace Software Exports Ltd	• ISO 9002
Aithent Technologies Pvt Ltd.	• SEI CMM Level 5
Ajuba Solutions (India) Pvt. Ltd.	• ISO 9001
Alcatel India Limited	• ISO 9001
ALSTOM Systems Limited	• ISO 9001
American Express (India) Pvt. Ltd.	• SEI CMM Level 2
AmitySoft Technologies Pvt Ltd	• ISO 9001
Aptech Limited.	• ISO 9001
Aviation Software Development Consultancy India Ltd.	• SEI CMM Level 3
AXA Business Services Pvt Ltd	• ISO 9002
Axes Technologies (I) Pvt Ltd	• ISO 9001

contd. ...

... contd.

Company Name	Quality Certifications
B	
BAeHAL Software Limited	• ISO 9001
Bangalore Software Services Ltd	• ISO 9001
Barry-Wehmiller International Resources Pvt Ltd	• ISO 9001
Bells Softech Limited	• ISO 9001
Beni Softwares Pvt Ltd	• ISO 9001
Bhari Information Technology Systems Pvt. Ltd.	• ISO 9001
Birla Technologies Ltd	• ISO 9001
Birlasoft Limited	• ISO 9001
Blue Star Infotech Ltd	• ISO 9001
BPL Telecom Ltd.	• SEI CMM Level 3
BT (Worldwide) Ltd.	• ISO 9001
C	
Canbank Computer Services Ltd.	• ISO 9001
CA-TCG Software Pvt. Ltd.	• ISO 9001
CDS International Ltd	• ISO 9001
Cellnext Solutions Ltd	• ISO 9001
Celstream Technologies Pvt Ltd	• ISO 9001
Cerebra Integrated Technologies Ltd	• ISO 9001
CGI Information Systems and Management Consultants Pvt Ltd.	• SEI CMM Level 4
CG-Smith Software Limited	• SEI CMM Level 5
CG-VAK Software & Exports Ltd.	• ISO 9001
Chandigarh Infotech Centre Ltd.	• ISO 9001
Churchill India Pvt. Ltd.	• ISO 9001
Cognizant Technology Solutions India Pvt. Ltd.	• PCMM Level 5
Compudyne Winfosystems Limited	• ISO 9001
Compulink Systems Pvt Ltd	• ISO 9001
Computer Clinic India Pvt. Ltd.	• ISO 9001
Computer Sciences Corporation India Pvt Ltd	• ISO 9001
Congruent Solutions Pvt. Ltd.	• ISO 9001
Consolidated Cybernetics Co. Pvt. Ltd.	• ISO 9001
Consulting Engineering Services (I) Ltd	• ISO 9001
Contech Software Ltd.	• SEI CMM Level 3
Convergent Software Limited	• SEI CMM Level 3
Covansys India (Private) Ltd.	• ISO 9001
Cressanda Solutions Limited	• ISO 9001
Crossword Software Pvt Ltd	• ISO 9001
D	
Datamatics Ltd.	• SEI CMM Level 5
Datamatics Technologies Pvt. Ltd.	• ISO 9001
DCM Datasystems Ltd.	• ISO 9001
DCM Technologies Limited	• SEI CMM Level 5
DDE ORG Systems Ltd.	• ISO 9001
Differential Technologies Limited	• ISO 9001
Digital GlobalSoft Ltd.	• SEI CMM Level 4
Divine India Limited	• ISO 9001
DPS Technologies India Pvt Ltd	• ISO 9002
DSL Software Ltd.	• ISO 9001
DSS Infotech International Ltd.	• ISO 9001

E

Eastern Software Systems Ltd.	• SEI CMM Level 5
Eclipse Systems Pvt. Ltd.	• ISO 9001
eFunds International Private Limited	• SEI CMM Level 3
Eonour Software Ltd.	• ISO 9001
EXplora InfoTech Limited	• ISO 9001

F

Financial Technologies (India) Ltd.	• ISO 9001
FirstApex	• ISO 9001
Future Software Limited	• PCMM Level 3

G

Gavs Information Service Pvt. Ltd.	• ISO 9001
Genisys Integrating Systems (I) Pvt. Ltd.	• ISO 9001
Geometric Software Solutions Company Ltd.	• SEI CMM Level 3
Global Business Technology Services Pvt Ltd	• ISO 9001
Global Dialnet Limited	• ISO 9001
Global Tech India Pvt. Ltd.	• ISO 9001
Globalsoft Pvt. Ltd.	• ISO 9001
Globsyn Technologies Ltd.	• ISO 9001
Godrej Infotech Ltd	• ISO 9002
Goldstone Technologies Ltd	• ISO 9001
Growth Compusoft Exports Ltd.	• ISO 9002
GTIC (India) Pvt. Ltd	• ISO 9001
GTL Limited	• SEI CMM Level 4
Gurukulonline Learning Solutions (P) Ltd	• ISO 9001

H

HCL Infosystems Ltd	• ISO 9001
HCL Perot Systems Pvt Ltd	• ISO 9001
HCL Technologies Ltd	• SEI CMM Level 5
Hewlett-Packard India Limited	• SEI CMM Level 5
Hexaware Technologies Limited	• ISO 9001
Hinduja TMT Ltd	• ISO 9001
HMA STARware Ltd	• ISO 9001
Holool E-Business Pvt Ltd	• ISO 9001
Honeywell India Software Operations Pvt. Ltd.	• SEI CMM Level 4
HTC Software Development Centre	• SEI CMM Level 3

I

i2 Technologies India Pvt. Ltd.	• ISO 9001
IBILT Technologies Ltd	• ISO 9002
IBM Global Services India Pvt. Ltd.	• PCMM Level 5
IBS Software Services (P) Ltd	• SEI CMM Level 5
ICICI Infotech Services Ltd.	• SEI CMM Level 3
Ideaspace Solutions Ltd	• ISO 9001
i-flex solutions ltd.	• SEI CMM Level 5
Indchem Software Technologies Ltd	• SEI CMM Level 4
Indus Software Pvt. Ltd.	• ISO 9001
Information Technology Park Ltd.	• ISO 9000
Infosys Technologies Ltd.	• PCMM Level 5
Infotech Enterprises Ltd.	• ISO 9002

contd. ...

... contd.

Company Name	Quality Certifications
Infozech Software (P) Ltd.	• ISO 9001
InfraSoft Technologies Limited	• ISO 9001
Integra Software Services Private Limited	• ISO 9001
Intelligroup Asia Pvt. Ltd.	• PCMM Level 2
Intergraph Consulting Private Limited	• SEI CMM Level 5
iSeva Systems Pvt Ltd	• ISO 9001
IT Solutions (India) Pvt. Ltd.	• SEI CMM Level 5
ITC Infotech India Ltd	• SEI CMM Level 5
ITTI Limited	• ISO 9001
Ivega Corporation Pvt Ltd	• ISO 9001
IVL India Pvt. Ltd.	• ISO 9001
J	
JK Technosoft Ltd	• ISO 9001
JP Mobile (India) Limited	• ISO 9001
K	
Kale Consultants Ltd.	• ISO 9001
Kals Information Systems Ltd	• ISO 9001
Kanbay Software (India) Pvt. Ltd.	• ISO 9001
Karvy Consultants Ltd	• ISO 9002
Keane India Ltd	• ISO 9001
KLG Systel Ltd.	• ISO 9001
KPIT Cummins Infosystems Limited.	• SEI CMM Level 4
L	
Lambent Technologies Pvt Ltd	• ISO 9001
Lapiz Digital Services	• ISO 9001
Larsen & Toubro Infotech Limited	• ISO 9001
Laser Soft Infosystems Ltd	• ISO 9001
LG Soft India Pvt. Ltd.	• SEI CMM Level 5
Linc Software Services Pvt. Ltd.	• ISO 9001
Live Tech Solutions (P) Ltd	• ISO 9000
M	
Majoris Systems Pvt. Ltd.	• ISO 9001
MASCON Global Limited	• ISO 9000
Mascot Systems Ltd.	• ISO 9001
MASTEK Ltd.	• PCMM Level 3
Medicom Solutions (P) Ltd	• ISO 9001
Megasoft Limited	• ISO 9001
Melstar Information Technologies Ltd	• SEI CMM Level 3
Micro Technologies (India) Ltd	• ISO 9001
Momentum India Private Limited	• SEI CMM Level 4
Motorola India Electronics Private Ltd.	• SEI CMM Level 5
Mphasis BFL Ltd.	• ISO 9001
N	
NatureSoft Private Limited	• ISO 9001
Navayuga Infotech Pvt. Ltd.	• ISO 9001
NeilSoft Limited	• ISO 9001
Network Programs (India) Ltd.	• SEI CMM Level 3

Newgen Imaging Systems (P) Ltd. • ISO 9001
NIIT Ltd. • SEI CMM Level 5
NSE.IT Ltd. • SEI CMM Level 3
Nucleus Software Exports Pvt. Ltd. • SEI CMM Level 5

O

Ontrack Systems Limited • ISO 9001
Onward Technologies Limited • ISO 9002
Oracle India Private Limited. • SEI CMM Level 4
Oracle Solution Services (India) Pvt Ltd • SEI CMM Level 4
OrbiTech Solutions Limited • SEI CMM Level 5

P

Paharpur Business Centre • ISO 9002
Paragon Solutions (I) Pvt. Ltd. • SEI CMM Level 3
Patni Computer Systems Ltd. • ISO 9001
Pentamedia Graphics Limited • ISO 9001
Pentasoft Technologies Limited • SEI CMM Level 4
Phoenix Global Solutions (India) Pvt. Ltd. • SEI CMM Level 4
Pinnacle Info Solutions Pvt. Ltd. • SEI CMM Level 4
Planet PCI Infotech Ltd • ISO 9001
PlanetAsia.com Limited • SEI CMM Level 4
Polaris Software Lab Ltd • SEI CMM Level 5
Premier Technology Group Pvt. Ltd. • ISO 9001
PSI Data Systems Ltd. • ISO 9001

Q

QAI (India) Limited • PCMM Level 2
Quinnox Consultancy Services Ltd • SEI CMM Level 5

R

R S Software (India) Ltd. • PCMM Level 3
R Systems International Limited • SEI CMM Level 4
Ram Informatics Ltd. • ISO 9001
Ramco Systems Ltd • SEI CMM Level 4
Rave Technologies (India) Pvt Ltd • ISO 9001
RelQ Software Pvt Ltd • ISO 9001
Rishabh Software Pvt Ltd • ISO 9001
River Run Software Group • ISO 9001
RMSI Private Limited • ISO 9001
Robert BOSCH India Limited • SEI CMM Level 3
Rolta India Ltd. • ISO 9001

S

SAP India Pvt. Ltd. • ISO 9002
Sasken Communication Technologies Limited • SEI CMM Level 5
Satyam Computer Services Ltd. • SEI CMM Level 5
Scicom Infotech Pvt. Ltd • ISO 9001
Siemens Information Systems Ltd. • SEI CMM Level 5
Siemens Public Communications Network Ltd. • ISO 9001
Sierra Atlantic Software Services Limited • ISO 9001
Siri Technologies Private Limited • ISO 9001
Sitel India Pvt Ltd • ISO 9000
Sobha Renaissance Information Technology • SEI CMM Level 5
Softek Limited • ISO 9001

contd. ...

... contd.

Company Name	Quality Certifications
SoftProjex (India) Limited	• ISO 9001
Solitar Systems (India) Pvt Ltd	• ISO 9001
SolutionNET India (Pvt) Ltd	• ISO 9001
Sonata Software Limited	• ISO 9001
Speck Systems Limited	• ISO 9001
SRA Systems Ltd.	• SEI CMM Level 4
Srishti Software Private Limited	• SEI CMM Level 3
SSI Technologies	• ISO 9002
Subex Systems Limited	• ISO 9001
Summit Information Technologies Ltd	• ISO 9001
Sundaram Infotech Solutions	• ISO 9001
Syntel (India) Ltd.	• SEI CMM Level 5
T	
Tasaa Netcom Private Limited	• ISO 9001
Tata Consultancy Services	• PCMM Level 4
Tata Elxsi Ltd.	• SEI CMM Level 5
Tata Infotech Ltd.	• ISO 9002
Tata Interactive Systems	• ISO 9001
Tata Technologies Limited	• ISO 9001
TCG Software Services Pvt. Ltd.	• ISO 9001
TCIL BellSouth Ltd.	• ISO 9001
TechSpan India Ltd.	• SEI CMM Level 3
Tektronix Engineering Development I) Ltd.	• ISO 9000
Telecommunications Consultants India Ltd.	• ISO 9001
Temenos India Pvt. Ltd.	• ISO 9000
Thinksoft Global Services (P) Ltd	• ISO 9001
Three S Solutions Ltd	• ISO 9002
U	
UshaComm India Pvt. Ltd.	• ISO 9001
Ushus Technologies Pvt Ltd	• ISO 9001
V	
ValueMomentum Software Services Pvt Ltd	• ISO 9001
Vision Healthsource (I) Pvt. Ltd.	• ISO 9001
Vispark Solutions (I) Pvt Ltd	• ISO 9001
VJIL Consulting Limited	• ISO 9001
VXL eTech Ltd	• SEI CMM Level 3
W	
Web Spiders (I) Pvt Ltd	• ISO 9001
Webify Services (India) Private Limited	• ISO 9001
Wipro Technologies	• SEI CMM Level 5
WNS Global Services	• ISO 9001
X	
Xansa (India) Ltd	• SEI CMM Level 5
Xcelvision Technologies Limited	• ISO 9001
Xerox Modicorp Limited	• SEI CMM Level 3
Z	
Zensar Technologies Limited	• EFQM

B.1.3 *Top 20 software companies in India*

Below is the NASCOM's list of Top 20 software companies (Software and Services Exports)

Table 3: Top 20 IT Software and Services Exporters from India

Rank	Company	Rs. crore	US$ million
1.	Tata Consultancy Services	3,882	813
2.	Infosys Technologies Limited	2,553	535
3.	Wipro Technologies	2,256	481
4.	Satyam Computer Services Limited	1,703	357
5.	HCL Technologies. Ltd.	1,319	277
6.	IBM Global Services India Pvt. Ltd.	764	160
7.	Patni Computer Systems	732	153
8.	Silverline Technologies	603	126
9.	Mahindra-British Telecom Limited	541	113
10.	Pentasoft Technologies Ltd.	459	96
11.	HCL Perot Systems Limited	449	94
12.	Pentamedia Graphics Ltd.	431	90
13.	NIIT Limited	400	84
14.	Mascot Systems Ltd.	399	84
15.	i-Flex Solutions Ltd.	392	82
16.	Digital Globalsoft Ltd.	331	69
17.	Mphasis BFL Group (Consolidated)	313	66
18.	Mascon Global Limited	307	64
19.	Orbitech	264	55
20.	Mastek Limited	259	54

Note: Companies are ranked on the basis of export revenues from India for Indian and MNC Companies
Source: NASSCOM

Table 4: Indian IT Software and Services: Export Revenues Ranking (2001-02)

Rank	Company	Rs. crore	US$ million
1.	Tata Consultancy Services	3,882	813
2.	Infosys Technologies Ltd.	2,553	535
3.	Wipro Ltd.	2,298	481
4.	Satyam Computer Services Ltd.	1,703	357
5.	HCL Technologies Ltd.	1,320	277
6.	Patni Computer Systems Ltd.	732	153
7.	Silverline Technologies Ltd.	603	126
8.	Mahindra British Telecom Ltd.	541	113
9.	Pentasoft Technologies Ltd.	460	96
10.	HCL Perot Systems Ltd.	449	94
11.	Mascot Systems Ltd.	403	84
12.	NIIT	400	84
13.	i-Flex Solutions Ltd.	392	82
14.	Mphasis BFL	313	66
15.	Mascon Global Ltd.	307	64
16.	Mastek Ltd.	259	54
17.	Birlasoft Ltd.	259	54
18.	Polaris Software Lab Ltd.	247	52
19.	L&T Information Technology Ltd.	245	51
20.	Hexaware Technologies Ltd.	241	50

Note: Does not Include MNC companies
Source: NASSCOM

Table 5

Top 20: Software exporters (MNCs) 2001-02

		(no. of employees)
1.	IBM Global Services India Ltd.	3,100
2.	Cognizant Technology Solutions	2,712
3.	Oracle India Pvt. Ltd.	2,000
4.	Hughes Software Systems Ltd.	1,500
5.	Hewlett-Packard (I) Software Operation Ltd.	1,489
6.	Digital Globalsoft	1,480
7.	Syntel	1,464
8.	Covansys (I) Ltd.	1,449
9.	PwC	1,200
10.	OrbiTech Solutions	1,191
11.	Siemens Information Systems Ltd.	1,187
12.	Xansa (India) Ltd.	892
13.	Motorola	800
14.	ST Microelectronics	800
15.	Texas Instruments India Pvt. Ltd	741
16.	Intel Tech India Pvt. Ltd.	700
17.	i2 Technologies	700
18.	Cisco	670
19.	Robert Bosch	629
20.	Huawei	500

(no. of employees as of March 2002)
Source: NASSCOM

B.2 The Indian Software Scenario in General

Global Scenario for Software Market is characterized by the following:

- Total value of software is estimated to be around $600 billion+
- About half is for general-purpose or shrink-wrapped software products
- Other half is the software services market

Given this scenario, services segment is well suited for offshore work (low risk, low capital, manpower intensive....) in which low dependence on physical infrastructure is considered ok. This makes the scheme of things well suited for country like India as the software industry is mostly in service sector.

Opening of the economy has given spurt to the Indian Software Industry, which is young.

Earlier, there were only few players, with only one big player (the TCS). Later, economic liberalization took place in 90s. As a result, computer import became easy and cheaper, tax benefits and other facilities were declared for exporting, controls and regulations were eased, making export easy.

As seen in the tables above, today, there are more than 1000 software companies of which at least 30 are with more than 1000 employees. Major Indian IT players have a global presence. Many multinationals have centers in India—IBM, Microsoft, Cisco, GE, Oracle, Novell, Sun, Hughes etc.

B.3 Cost and Quality Advantage: Indian Software Industry

In the past few years, the Indian IT industry has pursued the goal of attaining the highest international standards of quality. A World Bank funded study conducted as early as 1992 to discuss Indian software strategies had concluded that more and more vendors in the US prefer to get their software developed undertaken in India for its quality and cost advantage.

Indian players have created a strong value proposition in the IT software and services arena. India enjoys advantages of people sophistication in terms of a very large pool of English speaking scientific personnel, varied and extensive skill sets in terms of technology, and offering services at globally competitive costs. India also boasts vendor sophistication—with more than 200 companies being quality accredited and serving the needs of over 255 Fortune 500 companies. Today, the world looks towards the Indian IT software and services industry for its good quality and high price performance. This is a matter of national pride for us.

According to McKinsey & Co., India has and will continue to have a growing number of vendors successfully working on complex projects across all areas of software and services, and performing at levels comparable to those of leading global players.

In March 2002, NASSCOM conducted a survey to ascertain the adoption of international quality standards by IT software and services companies in India. An analysis of top 300 companies in India revealed some interesting statistics. NASSCOM's Survey presents the following picture on organization's quality plans.

Quality Certification	No. of Companies
Already acquired ISO 9000 or SEI and other certification	216
Companies acquired quality certification by March 2002	6
Certification expected between April-December 2002	64
Additional certification expected during 2002	70
No plans at present	22

SEI Quality Assessment	No. of Companies as on 31st May, 2002	No. of Companies by 31st March, 2003
SEI CMMi	3	5
SEI CMM Level 5	42	46
SEI CMM Level 4	22	38
SEI CMM Level 3	24	34
SEI CMM Level 2	3	16
PCMM Level 5	2	2
PCMM Level 4	1	2
PCMM Level 3	5	6
PCMM Level 2	4	12

Note: Some companies have multiple certifications.

As of 27 June 2002, India had 85 companies at SEI CMM Level 5 assessment. It is more noteworthy that worldwide, only 42 organizations have acquired such assessment. The quality maturity of the Indian software industry can be measured from the fact that already 316 Indian software companies have acquired quality certifications and more companies are in pipeline to do so.

The other heartening feature has been the growing acceptance and adoption of the newly emerging *People-Capability Maturity Model* (People-CMM) by the Indian software industry. For a country like India, with its large assets in the form of skilled human resources, the relevance of People CMM needs no emphasis. A large number of Indian IT software and services companies have been quick to realize this and have either implemented or initiated programs. (In the previous section, we have presented the statistics on the P-CMM scene in India)

During 2001-02, three Indian companies achieved notable distinctions in CMMi certification. Polaris Software Lab was assessed to SEI CMMi Level 5 (Version 1.02) in October 2001, making it the first company in the world to acquire this quality standard. Recently, both Wipro and Infosys have also been assessed to CMMi Level 5 quality standards.

B.4 the Indian Software Industry: Problems & Challenges

Indian software exports are steadily growing. The largest number of quality certified software organizations are in India as seen in the previous section. However, although all this may appear to present a rosy picture, it is not that the Indian Software Industry is without any problems and challenges In this section, we have provided a discussion on this point. The major problems and challenges seem to be:

- The Uneven Profile of the Indian Software Industry
- People Management Problems
- Infrastructure related problem
- Growing competition from other countries (especially China)

One of the major problems faced by the Indian software industry is its uneven profile. This is the point of discussion in this section. Indian software exports have shown very high growth rates for many years. Yet, behind this success lie a number of skews.

B.4.1 The Uneven Profile of Indian Software Exports

By almost any standards, the growth of India's software exports has been phenomenal. Exports began in 1974 but made limited impact until the 1980s. From that time on, growth rates have been consistently high, as the table below illustrates.

Table 6: Indian Software Exports and Growth Rates (1980-1997/98)

Year	Software Exports (US$million)	Growth Rate
1980	4.0	
1981	6.8	70%
1982	13.5	99%
1983	18.2	35%
1984	25.3	39%
1985	27.7	9%
1986	38.9	40%
1987	54.1	39%
1988/89 (Apr–Mar)	69.7	29%
1989/90	105.4	51%
1990/91	131.2	24%
1991/92	173.9	33%
1992/93	219.8	26%
1993/94	314.0	43%
1994/95	480.9	53%
1995/96	668.0	39%
1996/97	997.0	49%
1997/98	1650.0	65%

Source: Dataquest (1998)

However, all is not quite what it seems. For example, as noted, these 'headline' figures represent gross foreign exchange earnings. Net earnings (less outflow of foreign exchange from India to pay for travel and living allowances of Indian software workers who undertake their contracts overseas, marketing, multinational profit repatriation, importation of hardware and software, etc.) are now estimated to be around 40% of the gross figures. The Indian software industry has also been characterized by an uneven profile along several dimensions. These skews have important implications for both the growth and earnings potential of Indian software, as described below.

1. Uneven Output: Services not Packages

Indian software exports have been dominated by export of software services, in the form of custom software work, rather than export of software products, in the form of packages. Why have packages not taken off despite India's low labour cost advantages? Because, notwithstanding the low cost at which Indian companies can develop such packages, there are serious barriers to entry into this market which are worse than those for software services. Indian firms and their developers are not sufficiently familiar with the foreign package markets they seek to penetrate, and their distance from those markets makes it hard to keep up with changing needs and standards. The Indian domestic market is a poor guide for software developers thanks to differences in user needs, in work and hardware environments, and thanks to the generally low level of innovation.

2. Uneven Export Destination: US Domination

Indian companies have exported software to more than forty countries but there is a heavy reliance on the US market, as the table below indicates.

Table 7: Breakdown of Indian Software Exports by Destination (1997/98)

Destination	Proportion of Total Exports
US	65%
UK	10%
Other Europe	10%
Japan	5%
Other	10%

Source: Dataquest (1998)

The US market dominates Indian software exports partly because it is by far the world's largest software market, constituting around half of all software sales in the 1990s, and partly because American information technology and financial services companies have moved much more quickly than their European counterparts to take advantage of offshore programming. Until recently (till the 11/9 tragedy) the US has also had more liberal immigration rules for work or residence than most other developed countries. However, India is also more 'locked-in' to the US market than others because many Indian businesses have links through family members or friends who are US residents; because many software developers are US-trained and so understand that market best; and because there is a vast predominance of US firms in the all-important collaborations which provide so much of India's software export market.

The US-orientation of exports might present a limitation to future growth because US share of the world market is slowly declining. However, the American market is still expanding substantially in absolute terms plus, since the early 1990s, Indian software exports have shown their ability to grow in other markets, such as those of Asia and Europe.

3. Uneven Divisions of Labour: 'Body Shopping Trap'

[A] Uneven Locational Divisions: Onsite and Offshore Work

Much of India's export work developing custom software is actually carried out at the client's site overseas ('onsite') rather than offshore in India. Back in 1988, an average of 65% of export contracts were carried out wholly at the client site, while 35% contained some offshore elements. This translated into just under 75% of Indian software export development taking place overseas and only 25% in India. This was even true of work in India's export processing zones, which were intended to be bases for offshore work. Subsequent surveys have shown that the amount of work carried out offshore has increased within individual firms. The trend is particularly noticeable in the subsidiaries of multinational firms. However, a significant amount of onsite work has remained within the industry overall so that, by 1997/98, it was still true that more than half of all software services export earnings came from onsite work (Dataquest 1998). This forms the basis for an international locational division of labour within India's software export trade.

[B] Uneven Skill Divisions: Dominance of Programming

During the period 1988-1998, at least 65% of export contracts were solely for programming work billed on a 'time and materials' basis, with programming figuring strongly in the remaining one-third of contracts (Dataquest 1998). As with offshore work, there have been changes within individual client-contractor relationships, but there has been much less change within overall industry averages. So, in general terms, India's software export trade has been characterized by an international skill division of labour such that the majority of software contracts allocate only the less-skilled coding and testing stages to Indian workers. That is to say, Indian workers have far more often been used as programmers, working to requirements and design specifications set by foreign software developers, rather than as systems analysts or designers.

4. Uneven Market Share: Economic Concentration of Production

Since Indian software exports are services rather than goods, examples cannot easily be displayed to potential buyers to establish credibility. There is therefore a heavy reliance on reputation, track record, references and the skills and appearance of the marketing team, which all go together to determine the Indian firm's credibility. All these credibility-related factors, which principally hinge on track record and spending on marketing, obviously work to the advantage of larger, longer-established firms. As an example, a few firms have had to invest in export marketing for two or three years before getting their first export order.

5. Uneven Site Distribution: Locational Concentration of Production

Software companies are not distributed evenly throughout India, but are mainly located around a few major Indian cities, especially around Bangalore. The table below indicates the location of company headquarters for over 550 software companies (including a number focused on the domestic market).

Table 8: Location of Indian Software Company Headquarters

City	Number of Software Firm HQs
Bangalore	152
Mumbai (Bombay)	122
Chennai (Madras)	93
Delhi/New Delhi	86
Hyderabad/Secunderabad	34
Calcutta	27
Pune	22
Other	22
Total	**558**

Source: Dataquest (1998)

There are several factors behind this unequal siting growth of software development centers in India. (Such as skills availability, proximity to customers, quality of life, infrastructure etc).

B.4.2 People Management Problems in the Indian Software Industry

There is widespread dissatisfaction among senior managers in the software industry with the performance of software projects. This takes the form of inordinate delays, time and cost overruns, user dissatisfaction and maintenance problems. "High Burn Out" is a common problem in most Indian software companies (we discussed this phenomenon in Chapter 11). In order to overcome these problems, software companies are investing heavily to make improvements in their software processes and practices. Many of them have realized that lasting improvements require significant changes in the way they manage, develop and use people. In many software companies the work of managing people is seen as a responsibility of the Human Resources Department. The practices relating to management of people are done in an ad-hoc manner with little realization of their impact on the motivation and morale of staff. The reluctance of project leaders/managers to undertake such responsibilities is because they have not been trained to perform functions relating to management of people and also the fact that they are constantly under the pressure of delivery deadlines.

B.4.3 Infrastructure related Problems

Infrastructure consists of transport, electricity, and connectivity; land availability, quality of life, government facilities etc. In this section, we discuss issues that are considered as deterrent to foreign investors looking to India as an outsourcing destination. Seen from the eyes of a foreign investor, the perception is that at present, there are severe limitations in general and infrastructure are a primary weakness of the Indian software industry.

Good communication infrastructure is considered vital for the continued growth of the software industry. Overall, the data communication infrastructure in India is expensive and in limited supply. It appears that the problem has a significant institutional component, with government agencies like the department of telecommunication and VSNL, until recently the sole ISP in India, unwilling to give up their stranglehold on telecommunications. Clearly, the poor communication infrastructure has affected the diffusion of the Internet domestically, and through that, has discouraged the growth of new firms that could provide software services for and through the Internet.

As another example of factors that cause negative perception in the minds of foreign investors, consider this—the power grid failures for several hours at a stretch are a common feature even in the metropolitan cities of India. Tap water is contaminated in most Indian locations. The main roads get clogged very often. Traffic snarls are not well-managed Telephone connections take longer to complete than they would in most other countries. Fully half of the population is illiterate; three-fourths are rural. Village India remains the social and political anchor. There are shooting civil wars in progress in several states owing to ethnic hostilities. The Indian press is not considered friendly and developed.

There is a silver lining though—foreign investors feel that in spite of its problems, India is quietly becoming an international software giant. The Indian government appears to have taken bold steps towards providing the right combination of incentives along with a relatively low hassle support (a radical change in its policies of yesteryears.) What has evolved is something like a coordinated, rational strategy for industrial policy. The preferred strategy does not seem to be "off-shore" development (i.e., lots of cheaper body shops) but the establishment of many highly capable software product organizations that can develop and support complex systems. A concern for quality and desire to make effective use of state of the art technologies is evident. It seems the lessons of software engineering have been well studied by the Indians.

B.4.4 Growing competition from other countries

Currently India boasts more than 300,000 skilled workers work in the software industry. This makes India the second largest English speaking pool of technical manpower in the world. But India should not take a complacent view towards this, as this position may not last for too long. The global reach for software products and services from India is constantly under threat from global competition from other countries that can offer educated manpower at competitive rates. China and Russia are good examples of potential threats.

The table below presents quick comparative figures for India vis-à-vis China. The statistics speak for themselves.

Table 9

India	China	
Per Capita Income	$ 400	$ 800
Foreign Direct Investments per year	$ 3 Billion	$ 45 Billion
Exports (General)	$ 45 Billion	$ 180 Billion
Number of Internet connections	0.8 Million	22 Million
PC Sales in Yr. 2000	1.7 Million	7 Million
Cell Phones (per 1000)	2	34
Software Exports	$ 6.2 Billion	$ 0.5 Billion

According to Research Director of Gartner's Asia-Pacific operations, the entry of major Indian software firms will enable China to raise its software exports and within four years it will be able to catch up with India. From last year's $850 million, it should rise to $27 billion by 2006. Apart from this, the Indian software industry faces a number of challenges as the labour cost advantages diminish and competition from other countries with supplies of educated and under-utilized workers increases.

Interestingly enough, although competition from other countries such as Philippines and China is typically cited in the press, as the table below shows, most software exporters indicate that their main competitors are located either in the US or in India itself.

Table 10: Location of primary competitors of Indian software firms

Location of Competitors	Number of Firms	% of Firms
India	7.5	82
Israel	12	13
Ireland	12	13
USA	58	63
Singapore	19	21
Philippines	6	7
Eastern Europe/Russia	10	11

Recent trends show that programmers from China, Russia and Romania are proving to be worthy competitors in the low-end segment, for providing the programming and support services that have been the core of the Indian software exports value proposition.

There are other problems as well; walloped first by the dotcom meltdown and then by the September 11 attacks, India's software industry is now discovering new woes — visa restrictions and police raids overseas that some see as shades of protectionism. Recently, at least two well-known Indian software companies made it in the news media for a negative publicity with incidents of illicit nature taking place abroad. Apart from this, Several recent incidents, including one in which Malaysian police detained 270 Indian information technology workers on suspicion of being illegal workers, have shaken an industry that was looking at steady growth, as overseas firms move software work offshore to benefit from India's low-cost engineers.

REFERENCES

[1] *The Indian Software Industry* by Ashish Arora, V. S. Arunachalam, Jai Asundi and Ronald and Fernandes—research on the Indian software industry, carried out at Carnegie Mellon University

[2] *The People Capability Maturity Model*—Guidelines for Improving the workforce by Bill Curtis, William E.Hefely and Sally A. Miller (Pearson Education Low Price Edition)

[3] *NASCOM reports* published at various points of time.

[4] *Sustaining Growth—Indian IT Industry* (Address to the Inaugural Session of NASSCOM 2002 by S Ramadorai Chief Executive Officer at the Tata Consultancy Services)

[5] *Indian Software Industry: Prospects and Policy* (Shyam Sunder Yale School of Management ASHA, Mid-Hudson Valley and ISA, Pace University, February 21, 2002)

[6] *The Uneven Profile of Indian Software Exports* by Richard Heeks (1998) Published by Institute for Development Policy and Management—University of Manchester, Precinct Centre, Manchester, M13 9GH, UK

Appendix C

QUALITY RELATED ADDITIONAL TOPICS

C.1 Statistical Quality Control and Statistical Process Control

C.1.1 Introduction

It is important to understand the role of statistics in *Quality Assurance*. *Statistical Process Control* (SPC) and *Statistical Quality Control* (SQC) methodology is one of the most important analytical developments available in this century. Their origins are in the manufacturing industry.

SPC has come to be known as an on-line tool providing close-up views of what's happening to a process at a given moment. SQC provides off-line tools to support analysis and decision making to help determine if a process is stable and predictable. Thus, SPC and SQC are related. When SPC and SQC tools work together, users see the current and long-term picture about processing performance (the "voice of the process"). In sum:

- SPC provides on-line tools that permit a close-up view of what's currently happening to a process.
- SQC provides off-line tools to support analysis and decision-making about process stability over time.

In general, processes achieving the most benefit from SPC and SQC are products with:

- Highly repetitive processes;
- High-volume production and low margins; or
- Narrow tolerances.

To make SPC and SQC work, key parameters indicating product variations are measured and recorded.

SPC and SQC are an effective part of continuously improving a process. When measurements are accurately collected and analyzed, improvements are identified and implemented, and controls established to ensure improvements are permanent; a process is well on its way to meeting quality requirements.

Control Charts are a fundamental tool of SPC and SQC and provide visual representation of how a process varies over time or from unit to unit. *Control limits* statistically separate natural variations from unusual variations. Points falling outside the control limits are considered out-of-control and indicate an unusual source of variation (more about this in section C.1.4).

C.1.2 Process Control

The term *process* (which was discussed in Appendix A) means different things to different people. So first let us give a definition to it (Also see the various definitions given in Appendix A). Especially in the context of a software development or support environment:

A process can be defined as the logical organization of people, materials, energy, equipment, and procedures into work activities designed to produce a specified end result.

Statistical Process Control (SPC) takes advantages of the natural characteristics of any process. All business activities can be described as specific processes with known tolerances and measurable variances. The measurement of these variances and the resulting information provide the basis for continuous process improvement. We'll mention the basic tools of SPC later in this section.

"Controlled processes are" *stable processes* and stable processes enable you to predict results. *Software Process Management* (SPM) is about successfully managing the work processes associated with developing, maintaining and supporting software products and software intensive systems. "Successful management of a process" means that products and services produced by the process conform fully to both internal and external customer requirements and that processes meet the business objectives of the organization responsible for products/services.

This concept of "process management" is based on the principles of *Statistical Process Control* (SPC). These principles hold that by establishing and sustaining stable levels of *process variability*, processes will yield predictable results. We can then say that the processes are under statistical control.

Software Process Management has four key responsibilities:

1. *Define* the process
2. *Measure* the process
3. *Control* the process (ensure that variability is stable so that results are predictable)
4. *Improve* the process

C.1.3 Basic Tools of SPC/SQC

These basic tools are: (These are known famously as the "*Seven Quality Control Tools*")

- Data Tables (for Problem Identification)
- Pareto Analysis (for Problem Identification)
- Cause-and-Effect Diagrams (for both Problem Identification as well as Problem Analysis)
- Trend Analysis (for both Problem Identification as well as Problem Analysis)
- Histograms (for Problem Analysis)
- Scatter Diagrams (for Problem Analysis)
- (Process) Control Charts (for Problem Analysis)

Control Charts, are the most important tool of Statistical Quality Control (SQC). Considering their importance in Process Control, they are discussed separately in the next section.

C.1.4 Control Charts

What are Control Charts?

A control chart is a popular statistical tool for monitoring and improving quality. Originated by Walter Shewhart in 1924 for the manufacturing environment, it was later extended by W. Edward Deming to the quality improvement in all areas of an organization (a philosophy known as Total Quality Management).

The Purpose of Control Charts

The success of Shewhart's approach is based on the idea that no matter how well the process is designed, there exists a certain amount of nature variability in output measurements.

When the variation in process quality is due to "*random causes*" alone, the process is said to be in-control. If the process variation includes both random and "*special causes*" of variation, the process is said to be out-of-control. The control chart is supposed to detect the presence of special causes of variation.

In its basic form, the control chart is a plot of some function of process measurements against time. The points that are plotted on the graph are compared to a pair of *control limits* (The *Upper Control Limit* and the *Lower Control Limit*). A point that exceeds the control limits signals an alarm.

An alarm signaled by a control chart may indicate that special causes of variation are present, and some action should be taken, in order to trace and eliminate these causes. On the other hand, an alarm may be a false one, when in practice no change has occurred in the process. The design of control charts is a compromise between the risks of not detecting real changes and of false alarms (This is known as the trade-off between *Type I and Type II error*).

Assumptions Underlying Control Charts

The two important assumptions are:

1. The measurement-function (e.g. the mean), that is used to monitor the process parameter, is distributed according to a *normal distribution*. In practice, if your data seem very far from meeting this assumption, try to transform them.
2. Measurements are independent of each other.

Constructing a 3-sigma ("Shewhart-type") control chart

During a stable stage of the process (Section C.1.2 explains what a stable process is):

1. Determine the process parameter that you want to monitor (such as the process mean, or spread).
2. Create the centerline of the plot, according to the target value of your monitored parameter.
3. Group the process measurements into subgroups (samples) by time period or any other suitable parameter. The points to be plotted on the plot, are some function of the process measurements within each subgroup, which estimate the target value.
   For example, if you are monitoring your process mean, then the points on the plot should be the sample-means, computed at regular intervals. Denote the point at time t as X_t
4. Create upper and lower control limits (UCL,LCL) according to the following formula:

   UCL = CL + 3 s
   LCL = CL − 3 s

   where s is the standard deviation of X_t.

For the example above, X_t may be daily means of process measurements. If each daily sample comprises of n measurements, then the standard deviation of X_t is equal to the process standard deviation divided by the root of n

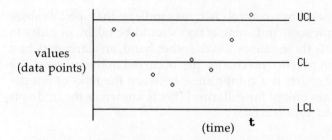

After the control limits have been set, continue to plot the points on the graph, as a function of time. When a point exceeds either of the control limits (Upper or Lower), it indicates that the process is out of control, and action should be taken (of course, there is a slight chance that is is a false alarm).

Analysis of Patterns on Control Charts

A control chart may indicate an out-of-control condition either when one or more points fall beyond the control limits, or when the plotted points exhibit some nonrandom pattern of behavior. The process is "out of control" if any one or more of the criteria is met:

1. One or more points outside of the control limits. This pattern may indicate:
   - A special cause of variance from a material, equipment, method, or measurement system change.
   - Mismeasurement of a part or parts.
   - Miscalculated or misplotted data points.
   - Miscalculated or misplotted control limits.
2. A run of eight points on one side of the centerline. This pattern indicates a shift in the process output from changes in the equipment, methods, or materials or a shift in the measurement system.
3. Two of three consecutive points outside the 2-sigma warning limits but still inside the control limits. This may be the result of a large shift in the process in the equipment, methods, materials, or worker or a shift in the measurement system.
4. Four of five consecutive points beyond the 1-sigma limits.
5. An unusual or nonrandom pattern in the data.
   1. A trend of seven points in a row upward or downward. This may show:
      - Gradual deterioration/wear in equipment/tool.
      - Improvement or deterioration in technique/method.
   2. Cycling of data can indicate:
      - Temperature or other recurring changes in the environment.
      - Differences between operators or operator techniques.
      - Regular rotation of machines.
      - Differences in measuring or testing devices that are being used in order.

6. Several points near a warning or control limit.

Limitations of Control Charts: Sensitizing rules for control charts

The American Standard is based on "three-sigma" control limits (corresponding to 2.7% of false alarms), while the British Standard uses "3.09 sigma" limits (corresponding to 2% of false alarms). In both cases it is assumed that a normal distribution underlies the relevant estimators.

It has been shown that Shewhart-type charts are efficient in detecting medium to large shifts, but are insensitive to small shifts. One attempt to increase the power of Shewhart-type charts is by adding supplementary stopping rules based on runs. The most popular stopping rules were suggested by the "Western Electric Company". These rules supplement the ordinary rule: "One point exceeds the control limits". Here are the most popular Western Electric rules:

- 2 of 3 consecutive points fall outside warning (2-sigma) limits, but within control (3-sigma) limits.
- 4 of 5 consecutive points fall beyond 1-sigma limits, but within control limits.
- 8 consecutive points fall on one side of the centerline.

There are two *types of control charts* as discussed below.

Variable Control Charts

Variable Control Charts include:
- Individual values
- Median values
- Median
- X-bar
- Range
- Standard deviation
- Cumulative sum (q-sum), and
- Exponentially Weighted Moving Average

Attribute Control Charts

Attribute Control Charts include:
- Percent defective (p-chart)
- Number defective (n-chart)
- Nonconformities per unit (u-chart), and
- Nonconformities (c-chart)

In summary, we can say that as part of the lifecycle of many systems, users need to perform *statistical analysis* of data pertaining to the operation. This function can be required at any point from being part of the initial definition process though post startup performance appraisals. As discussed so far, *Control charts* are a fundamental tool of SPC and SQC and provide visual representation of how a process varies over time or from unit to unit.

C.1.5 Process Performance Variation

Earlier we mentioned about *"special causes"* and *"random causes"*. Shewhart categorizes sources of variation as follows:

- Variation due to phenomena that are natural and inherent to the process and whose results are common to all measurements of a given attribute (random variation in the process).
- Variations that have assignable causes (also known as "special causes") that could be prevented.

In summary, Shewhart's *Control Charts* (discussion earlier) are techniques for quantifying process behaviour. Control charts and associated methods of statistical quality control (SQC) are most effective when they are used within the broader context of goals you have established and the activities you perform to achieve these goals.

C.2 Software Maintenance Models: The Evolution

C.2.1 Introduction

Software maintenance is recognized **as a**n important part of the software development life cycle (SDLC). The maintenance phase of the software development life cycle is often long and expensive and covers the areas of version upgrade, database migration, language migration, reengineering, functionality upgrades and porting. Our timely and cost-effective maintenance services include critical aspects of planning for post delivery operations, supportability and logistics determination. Maintenance is of three types:

a. Corrective

Corrective maintenance involves changing a software application to remove errors and bugs. The three main blocks of corrective maintenance are:

- Design errors
- Logic errors
- Coding errors

Examples may include, simple correction of problems such as misspelled words in the interface of your application and complex design issues relating to incorrect algorithms in your product which at its worst may damage, corrupt or destroy application data.

b. Adaptive

Adaptive software maintenance involves tasks relating to changes in your application's operating environment. These environmental modifications consist mainly of changes to the following:

- Rules, laws, regulations and localizations that affect the application
- New operating systems
- Hardware configuration changes
- Changes in data format
- Changes in supporting utilities

c. Perfective

Perfective maintenance is an activity that we undertake to improve the maintainability, performance or other attributes of your application. Furthermore, perfective maintenance includes all changes, insertions, deletions, modifications, extensions and enhancements made to the application to meet evolving and/or expanding user needs.

C.2.2 History of Software Maintenance Model Evolution

The Maintenance Cycle is related to the Development Cycle. Most readers would be familiar with the different types of models used during the development process. In this section, we intend to provide only a very brief overview of this. The *Waterfall, Incremental* and *Evolutionary* models are well known (For details of this, readers can refer to *"Software Engineering: A Practitioner's Approach"* by Roger S. Pressman— McGraw-Hill International). Many people are not aware that there are also *models used during the maintenance process*. So, the frequently asked questions are: "Is there a *maintenance model*?" "Is it similar to the development models?" "Are they the same?" "How have they evolved?" This is the reason why we included this topic in this section of this appendix. We now start with a brief discussion of the *history of development models*. This will be followed by a discussion on *history of the maintenance process*.

C.2.1.1 The Code and Fix Development Model

This is one of the early software development models—*Code and Fix*. It simply consisted of two steps: Code and then Fix the code.

This model had many difficulties. There was always a risk of code structure deterioration due to enhancements, updates and a lack of formal change standards. It then became apparent that a *Design Phase* was needed. Often the software did not match the users' needs. This resulted into the feeling that a *Requirements Phase*, too, was required. Eventually, *code quality* became a concern, and so the *Testing Phase* was developed.

C.2.1.2 The Waterfall Development Model

In the Seventies came this model very popularly known as the "Waterfall Model". The Waterfall Model refined Stage wise Model and added two primary enhancements. The first new enhancement was addressing the need to create a system of feedback between stages. The second enhancement was the initial incorporation of *prototyping* in the software life cycle. The difficulties with the Waterfall model are well known today. In the words of Bill Curtis (A key person at the SEI—Software Engineering Institute) these difficulties are:

- It requires fully elaborated documentation
- It does not work well for the end-user application
- It reflects a manufacturing orientation
- It fails to treat software development as a problem-solving process.

The result of this realization was the development of more recent models, such as the *Incremental and Evolutionary models*. The *Spiral Model* was evolved from the Waterfall Model. (For details, refer *"Software Engineering: A Practitioner's Approach"* by Roger S. Pressman—McGraw-Hill International).

In summary, we say that it is important to note—the discipline of software engineering is still relatively new. Models and processes for software engineering are evolving and will continue to evolve. With this introduction, we now turn to the discussion on the history of "Maintenance Process".

C.2.2 History of the Maintenance Process

Maintenance projects continue to be a major constituent of software related businesses worldwide. In the context of the Indian Software Industry (Refer Appendix B), Maintenance is one of the most viable businesses next to only Skills Exports (the other often used term is "Body Shopping"). Thus, the maintenance work is important to us. This is the motivation to writing this section on maintenance.

"Operations and Maintenance" is usually the last phase in a Software/System Development cycle. This last phase occurs after product delivery. Often this is understood as a single simple step at the end of the development cycle! Experts feel that "maintenance" would be more accurately portrayed as additional development stages. Basically, there is so much disagreement about what happens during maintenance and when development ends and maintenance begins! Because of this, the commonly held view is to think of maintenance as the murky, ill-remembered yucky area of the life cycle process. With this background, let us know discuss the Maintenance Models.

C.2.2.1 Early Maintenance Models

Since the 1970s, several software maintenance models have been proposed. Many of these are very similar. In general, each model has three stages:

- Understand the software
- Modify the software based on the specified requirements
- Re-validate (Test) the software

For *Corrective Maintenance*, the models focus on Problem Verification, Problem Diagnosis, Re-programming and Baseline Re-verification. Other software maintenance models propose several phases such as:

- Determine the maintenance objective
- Understand the program
- Generate a maintenance change
- Account for the ripple effect
- Conduct Regression Testing (The topic of "Regressing Testing" has been discussed in Chapter 10)

C.2.2.2 Later Maintenance Models

With the increasing realization toward the need for standardization in software maintenance, the IEEE Computer Society Software Engineering Standards Subcommittee published the "IEEE Standard for Software Maintenance" (IEEE 1219). The standard detailed an iterative process for managing and executing software maintenance activities (www.IEEE.com). The process model includes inputs, process, control and output for software maintenance. The standard states that maintenance planning should begin when planning for software development begins. However, the suggestion for planning and maintenance are just suggestions—they are not part of the standard. They are included in the standard's annex for information only.

If you were setting up a software maintenance organization and needed to implement a process model for maintenance, you would first ask, "Is there a standard or do we have to invent one?" A number of

Software Maintenance Standards do exist. The 20 most popular *software maintenance standards* are listed below:

Table 1

Maintenance Standards	Name
ISO/IEC 14764	**Software Maintenance**
ISO/IEC 12207	**Information Technology-Software Life Cycle Processes**
ISO/IEC 12207 — Amendment 1—	Amendment 1: **Information Technology-Software Life Cycle Processes**
ISO/IEC TR 15271	Guide for ISO/IEC 12207—(Software Life Cycle Processes)
ISO/IEC TR 15504-2	Guide for ISO/IEC 12207—(Software Life Cycle Processes)
IEC 60601-1-4	Medical Electrical Equipment—Part 1: General Requirements for Safety-4. Collateral Standard: Programmable Electrical Medical Systems
IEC 60880	Software for Computers in the Safety Systems of Nuclear Power Stations
IEEE 828	Software Configuration Management Plans
IEEE 1042	**Software Configuration Management**
IEEE 1219	Software Maintenance
IEEE 1540	Software Life Cycle Processes—- Risk Management
AECL CE-1001-STD REV.1	Standard for Software Engineering of Safety Critical Software
AIAA ANSI/AIAA R-013	Recommended Practice for Software Reliability
BSI BS-5760-8	Reliability of Systems, Equipment & Components—Guide to Assessment of Reliability of Systems Containing Software
BSI BS-7738	Specification for Information Systems Products Using SSADM—(Structured Systems Analysis and Design Method)
DEF 00-55 Part 2	The Procurement of Safety Critical Software in Defense Equipment-Requirements
DEF 00-56 Part 2	Safety Management Requirements for Defense Systems Containing Programmable Electronics Part 2: General Application Guidance
German Process-Model (V-Model)	Software Life-Cycle Process Model (V-Model)
ASTM E 792	Guide for the Selection of a Clinical Laboratory Information Management System
ASTM E 1578	Standard Guide for Laboratory Information Management System
RTCA DO-178B/ED-12B	Software Considerations in Airborne Systems and Equipment Certification

C.2.2.3 *The IEEE Maintenance Model*

The IEEE defines software maintenance as the "process of modifying a software system or component after delivery to correct faults, improve performance or other attributes, or adapt to a changed environment." Software maintenance is the process that allows existing products to continue to fulfill their mission, to continue to be sold, deployed, and used, and to provide revenue for the development organization. Generally speaking, *maintenance* refers to all the activities that take place after an initial product is released. However, in common usage, people apply the term *maintenance* not so much to major *evolutions* of a product, but regarding efforts to:

- Fix bugs (*Corrective Maintenance*)
- Add small improvements, or keep up with the state-of-the-art (*Perfective Maintenance*)
- Keep the software up-to-date with its environment: the operating system, hardware, major components such as DBMS, GUI systems, and communication systems (*Adaptive Maintenance*)

The figure below depicts the *IEEE Maintenance Process.*

Figure 1

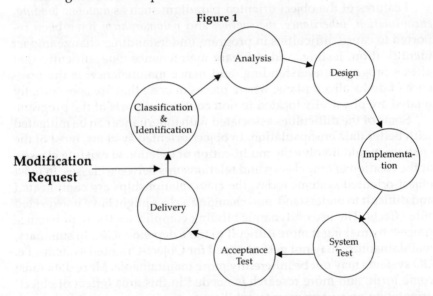

The standard starts with the software maintenance effort during the post-delivery stage, as do all other maintenance models. It does not take into account the pre-delivery activities that are critical to cost-effective support of a software system. The complete discussion on each of the activities shown in figure above is beyond the scope of this book.

C.3 OO Maintainability

Most of the systems today are built using the object-oriented technology One of the main arguments for using *object-oriented methods* is that is should reduce the amount of maintenance required on the software development (object orientation is known to promote "component reuse"). Several studies have been conducted to determine the impact of OO methods on maintainability. According to one study conducted in 1990, individual maintenance tasks are more difficult when using object-oriented software compared to the procedural software. On the other hand, there are others who support the premise that object-oriented techniques result in fewer maintenance changes and reduced maintenance effort overall (Object Oriented Effort Points or OOEP are often use in measurements related to object-oriented system).

However, there is not much empirical data upon which upon which to base claims about the effectiveness of OO as far as the maintenance effort is concerned.. According to some experts, *inheritance* makes dependencies among objects harder to find and analyze. Additionally, the greater the *depth of inheritance*, the greater the level of difficulty associated with understanding and maintaining the software. Thus, "Inheritance" is one of the key factors in determining maintainability. Greater levels of inheritance help *re-use,* but decrease maintainability.

Features of the object oriented paradigm such as *dynamic binding, encapsulation, inheritance, messaging,* and *polymorphism* have been reported to cause difficulties in program understanding, change impact identification, testing, and software maintenance One difficulty that affects program understanding, and hence maintenance, is the presence of de-localized plans: where pieces of code that are conceptually related are physically located in non contiguous parts of the program.

Some of the difficulties associated with inheritance can be mitigated with better data encapsulation. In object-oriented systems, most of the changes would involve the modification or deletion of existing classes, or the creation of new classes and relationships between classes. In most object-oriented systems today, the class relationships are complicated and difficult to understand, and changing a class might have unexpected side effects. The use of dynamic binding complicates the maintenance process by making it more difficult to trace dependencies. In summary, maintainability may not get enhanced for Object-Oriented systems; i.e. OO systems may not be inherently more maintainable. More data must come forth, and more research is needed in this area (effect of object-orientation on system maintainability).

C.4 Maintenance in e-Business Era

C.4.1 e-Business Models

In today's digital era, most businesses are done on the Web with the e-Commerce paradigm. e-Business models play a vital role. Portals and sites are the gateway to the companies and their businesses. Since they play such a crucial role in generating revenue through the e-Business, these sites/portals have to be well maintained—uptime must be very high (almost 100%). Most of the time, the activity of Web-site maintenance is outsourced mostly to off-shore partners (This counts for a big business chunk for India). The entire discussion in this section is based on this fact.

Although a full discussion on various kinds of e-Business models does not form the scope of this book, we have listed below a number of e-Business models proposed. The basic categories of business models mentioned in the table below include:

- Brokerage
- Advertising
- Infomediary
- Merchant
- Manufacturer

These e-Business models are implemented in a variety of ways Moreover; a firm may combine several different models as part of its overall Internet business strategy.

C.4.2 Web site's Life Cycle

Given the importance of the sites and portals in the e-Business era, managing the Web Sites becomes crucial. Web-site maintenance is a big time activity in the e-Business era.

At any point in time your Web site is either being planned, under development or re-development, being launched, maintained, evaluated, enhanced and promoted or being assessed with a view to undergoing a re-birth. These stages form a "life cycle" which is rather like that of a garden's life cycle: the initial planning; each section planted out according to a schedule; plantings monitored and tendered to; sections developed further to cater for growth and the emergence of new trends in gardening. Any gardener knows that this life cycle requires constant management if it is to yield rewards. This is true of web sites too.

At any point a Web site is located somewhere in the Life Cycle as illustrated below. The eight phases identified in the *Web Site Life Cycle* are independent. Acknowledgement of the Web Site Life Cycle and the need to manage it dispels the myth that developing and managing a Web site finishes on the day it is launched—the launch is simply the end of the beginning. Successful Web sites are in a state of perpetual change, which requires systematic management. The Web Site Life Cycle is depicted in the figure on the next page.

PLANNING:

- Savings & Revenues (e-Commerce, Cost Savings and Revenues)
- Promotion (search engines, the launch, advertising, portals, repeat visitors)

BUILDING:

- Engaging External Web Developers (Project Plan, Request for Proposal, Development Contract, Developer selection)

- Managing the development (Staging the Development, Managing the deliverables, Testing Procedures)

MAINTENANCE (Technical maintenance, content updating, evaluating and enhancing, resources, tool and budgeting)

MANAGEMENT (the Web Site Life Cycle, the management team, managing people, resources, budgets & risks)

END USER PERSPPECTIVE

- The Users' experience (aims, audiences, naming, content, functionality, technical issues)
- The Design (accessibility, information and graphics design, other technical issues)

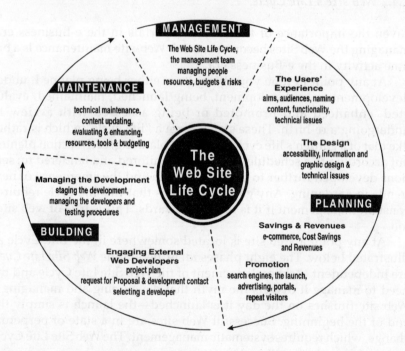

C.4.3 Why Manage the Life Cycle?

The elements that require managing will usually fall into three main categories:

- **People**—management, curators and artistic directors, marketing, education officers, IT, clerical, Web designers and authors (both in-house and external)
- **Resources**—time, hardware and office equipment, databases, space
- **Finances**—money for in-house staff salaries, fees to external designers, programmers etc, software licenses, copyright clearance

Managing all the elements of each category effectively will help to ensure that:

- What you try to achieve in each stage of the Life Cycle is realistic and achievable given the available people, resources and finances
- Each stage of the Life Cycle is completed on time and within budget
- People in your organization are not over-stretched for time nor expected to undertake tasks for which they are not qualified or skilled—all of which leads to stress and unhappy people
- Each stage of the Life Cycle is carried out in the most efficient manner leading to maximum saving of money and resources, e.g. resources and money are not wasted due to poor timing or sequencing of events
- Each stage of the Life Cycle is actually undertaken, e.g. evaluation conducted regularly
- Risks are foreseen and managed appropriately, e.g. hold-ups due to difficulty in securing reproduction rights.

C.4.4 Who Should Manage the Web-Sites

The Management Team—The team's role is to consider all matters related to the *Web Site Life Cycle*. The Management Team consists of people representing at least the following areas within the organization:

- Management, e.g. director, head curator, artistic director
- Curatorial staff / practitioners
- Marketing/promotions
- Education
- Information services/technology

The Online Manager—The Online Manager is the "head gardener" of the Web Site Life Cycle (i.e. his efforts decide how the site will "bloom"!). Issues to consider when choosing the Online Manager:

- Personal attributes
- Role and responsibilities
- Skills and knowledge

Managing the People—The Web site Life Cycle, from the planning stage through the building phase to the evaluation and maintenance stages, is demanding on your organization's staff. It requires:

- **Time**—meetings, responding to emails, design and test prototypes etc
- **Energy**—to contemplate the issues, engender enthusiasm

- **Vision**—what new ways of presenting exhibitions might be possible
- **Research**—marketing, audience needs, technology adaptation
- **Analysis**—technology platforms, usability testing
- **Coordination**—of others in the organization to gain their opinions and input; content scheduling; redirecting existing work to produce content for the site
- **Understanding**—of the internet and the expectations of the users
- **Patience**—everything takes longer than you think it will!
- **Tolerance**—of other points of view and requirements of other departments in your organization

If insufficient consideration is given to the level and kinds of input required of staff throughout the Web site Life Cycle—i.e. not merely through the building of the site—then its effectiveness will suffer, as will the people involved.

Roles in the Web-Site Life Cycle—Who is needed

These are the roles that have to be filled if the Life Cycle is to be maintained effectively:

- Project director
- Content editor
- Webmaster/technician
- Research officer
- Content technician
- Librarian
- Marketing/promotions manager
- Trainer
- Financial controller
- Legal advisor
- Graphic designer
- Web programmer

Some of these roles require full-time positions while others may only be required during certain stages of the Life Cycle. Also some of above roles may get combined (for example the Webmaster and Web Programmer, the Content Technician and the Graphic Designer). For many smaller organizations one or two people may have to undertake most of these roles.

To Outsource or not to Outsource?

How much of the Web development and management can or should be conducted in-house and how much should be outsourced? Issues to consider are:

- Keep to your core business or learn new skills?
- Skills transfer
- Training required and new job descriptions
- Time allocations

Maintaining the Right Attitude: Building a Web Culture

Possible strategies to encourage a Web culture in your organization:

- Workflow engineering
- Awareness raising
- Creating ownership
- What competitors are doing

Managing the Resources—What resource management issues will you need to address? Consider these:

- Communications, hardware and software requirements
- Time
- Office space and equipment

C.4.5 Managing the Maintenance of Your e-Business Site

C.4.5.1 The Site Maintenance Triangle

The following Site Maintenance Triangle recognizes that web-*site maintenance* consists of three principal elements: **Technical Maintenance**,

Figure 2

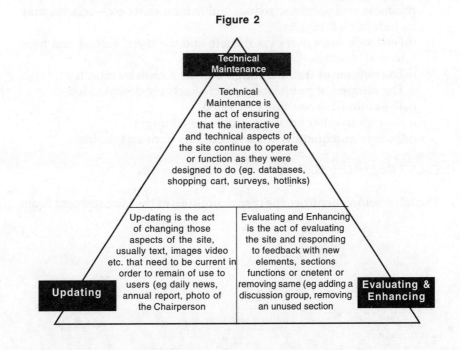

Technical Maintenance

Technical Maintenance is the act of ensuring that the interactive and technical aspects of the site continue to operate or function as they were designed to do (eg. databases, shopping cart, surveys, hotlinks)

Up-dating is the act of changing those aspects of the site, usually text, images video etc. that need to be current in order to remain of use to users (eg daily news, annual report, photo of the Chairperson

Updating

Evaluating and Enhancing is the act of evaluating the site and responding to feedback with new elements, sections functions or cnetent or removing same (eg adding a discussion group, removing an unused section

Evaluating & Enhancing

Updating, **Evaluation** & **Enhancing**. Considering site maintenance in the light of these categories encourages appropriate planning and resource allocation thereby minimizing the risk of overlooking or underestimating maintenance issues, costs, resources required and responsibilities.

Technical Maintenance is the act of ensuring that the interactive and technical aspects of the site continue to operate or function as they were designed to do.

C.4.5.2 *Managing the Maintenance of Your Site*

The Management Team established early in the life cycle should meet at least monthly after the launch of the site to:

- Review/suggest new content (where appropriate) for inclusion in the site
- Identify where Web site enhancement/development is required
- Review relevant activities of the marketing and promotions group
- Assess the statistics and feedback on the site from all sources (e.g. contact-us, Web server, questionnaires, anecdotal) and identify necessary action to remedy problems and/or highlight strengths
- Review Internet policies (including the legal aspects see [16] at the end of this appendix) and procedures and develop new ones where required
- Evaluate the success of the site against its stated aims and objectives, e.g. to improve public awareness of the organization's products and services, reduce publishing costs etc—criteria may include such things as:
  o Feedback from users via the site and the usual formal and non-formal channels
  o The volume of traffic through the site month by month
  o The number of publications, fact-sheets etc downloaded
  o The amount of revenue generated
  o Savings in other areas e.g. publishing budget
  o Quality and quantity of contributions from stakeholders

C.4.5.3 *Day-to-Day Maintenance of an e-Business Site*

The table below identifies the responsibilities of the Management Team

Table 2

Function	Twelve Month Maintenance Tasks	Estimated Working days per month	Estimated Total Days per year
Project Director	Chairs Management Committee: policy decisions and resource allocation, budgets, legal and contractual issues, overall responsibility for the site		
Manager	Responsible for all day-to-day operations of the site, oversees the Webmaster, coordinates contributions of content, implements policies and guidelines, monitors usage of the site, initiates and oversees further development		
Content Editor	Ensures integrity of content, editing, creating, collating of content, uploading new content to the site		
Site Marketer	Implements marketing strategy, develops new strategies as appropriate		
Content Contributors	Provides content to the Content Editor from their particular area of the organization, e.g. new images, exhibition		
Writer	Creates new text as requested		
Webmaster	Maintains technical functions of the site and provides assistance to Content Editor as required, maintains the database mailing lists etc, reports on hits and traffic		
Outsourced Web Developer	Incorporates new features and designs new graphical elements as directed		
Outsourced Project Advisors	Provides ad hoc online strategic advice, legal and marketing advice		

C.4.5.4 Perfective Maintenance for e-Business Web Sites

Identifying What Requires Updating on the e-Business Sites/Portals

The table below is not exhaustive in its listing of content, graphics etc. It is intended to be used as a template for Web site managers responsible for the maintenance to draw up their own list of what needs up-dating and maintaining and how frequently. It will be helpful to use the site map as a guide to ensure that all areas of the site are covered in the table.

Table 3

Maintenance Frequency	Content	Graphics	Functionality Examples	Technical Implications
Daily	Daily news items	Images from performances, galleries	Discussion groups	Monitor hits and traffic
			Contact us	Export data collected from forms to the
			Shopping cart	appropriate personnel
			Bookings for seats, events etc	Check error reports from web server
Weekly or Monthly	Bulletins	Images from performances, galleries	Links	Email list servers
	Articles	Promotional banners	Search facility	E-commerce system Database configuration
	e-newsletters			Report on hits and traffic
	Competition Tracking			Re-register with search engines
As required	Introductory text	Photographs	Post-cards	Report on data collected from surveys
	About us	Illustrations	Maps	Maintain Web server
	Contact details	Diagrams	Navigation elements	Play-back feature for audio/video
	Educative material	Logos	Password function	Auto-email back
	Audio		Animations	Ensure integrity of file naming conventions
	Video		Uploading PDFs (Portable Document Formats)	
	Prices			
	Items for sale			Maintain metadata
Annually	Annual Reports Annual events: e.g. festivals (Seasonality of Business)	Review compatibility with corporate image	Review possible new functionality	Review impact of new tools & solutions

C.4.5.5 Quality Issues in Web-Site Maintenance

Quality Control of Updating—The updating of content should not be conducted without some checks and balances in place. The Content Editor should be assigned the responsibility for verifying the quality and accuracy of new content for the site as supplied by others and for ensuring it is up-loaded to the right place and in a timely manner. Some tips for the quality assurance procedure:

- Establish a pro-forma that all contributors to the Web site use to submit new content and/or changes to existing content and/or functions, specifying such things as:
  o The format for the content
  o How to indicate requested links
  o Where in the site the new or revised content is to be placed
- Confirm that the content supplied for up-dating does not infringe anyone's copyright, IP etc
- Proofread the new content and seek approval from the author for changes prior to up-loading
- Determine whether new content should be signed-of by the Management Team
- Use the updating templates created by the Web developers and/or any necessary software as purchased for the purpose to facilitate updating

Updating Tools

There are numerous tools available on the Web free or at a very reasonable cost that will make maintenance and updating relatively easy. User-friendly HTML editors produced by some of the biggest names in the Internet that can be purchased and downloaded include:

- Macromedia Dreamweaver—http://www.macromedia.com/software/dreamweaver/
- Microsoft FrontPage—http://microsoft.com/frontpage/
- Adobe GoLive—http://www.adobe.com/products/golive/main.html

The Web developer that built the site, or other of standard competence, should be able to build various templates that can be accessed from the desktop and enable text, images, audio or video files to be inserted into the template for uploading to the site.

C.4.5.6 Evaluating and Enhancing Your Site

How do you know in what ways the site could be enhanced? Is it anecdotal evidence, personal assessment or feedback from your users or a third party engaged to evaluate your site? Each of these is a valid means of identifying how the site could be improved. The evaluation process needs to be systematic and managed as an integral part of the Web Site life cycle. Techniques that can be employed in this regard include:

- Feedback from the site
- Questionnaires
- Focus-groups
- Monitoring site activity

Monitoring can inform you as to what is working, what is popular and where the "dead" areas are that require rejuvenation or cutting. The following information can be gained from monitoring software:

- How many people access the site
- The pattern of access over 24 hours, a week etc.
- What country are the users from
- What areas of the site are visited the most and the least
- What routes users take through the site
- How long they stay in the site
- What point they exit from the site
- The existence of broken links

The following sites offer tools that can be downloaded or Web sites that offer a monitoring and reporting service:

- WebTrends—www.netiq.com/webtrends/
- Maxamine—www.maxamine.com
- Microsoft Site Server 3—http://www.microsoft.com/siteserver/site/default.htm
- My Mind-it—http://www.pumatech.com/press_releases/012202.html

C.4.5.7 Technical Maintenance

Recall the figure "Site Maintenance Triangle" in section C.4.5.1. Technical Maintenance is the act of ensuring that the interactive and technical aspects of the site continue to operate or function as intended—i.e. maintaining the technical status quo. This might include:

- Responding to faults with the database, search capacity on the site, shopping cart feature, discussion groups etc
- Ensuring online forms are working and that data from them is being passed to the correct person
- Monitoring the security of the site
- Registering and re-registering the site with search engines
- Responding to emails from users regarding technical faults on the site
- Ensuring the site works for new versions of Internet Explorer and Netscape
- Checking hotlinks to external sites to ensure they are still valid

The person assigned to the technical maintenance role requires a sound level of technical expertise and experience with the World Wide Web. This person is usually termed the "webmaster" and is an integral part of the Management Team.

C.5 Cyclomatic Complexity

C.5.1 What is Complexity?

Complexity

1. *Apparent Complexity* is the degree to which a system or component has a design or implementation that is difficult to understand and verify
2. *Inherent Complexity* is the degree of complication of a system or system component, determined by such factors as the number and intricacy of interfaces, the number and intricacy of conditional branches, the degree of nesting, and the types of data structures.

C.5.2 What is 'Cyclomatic Complexity'?

Cyclomatic complexity is a *measure of software complexity* first introduced by Thomas McCabe in 1976 and measures the number of *linearly independent paths* through a program module. A program module is generally considered to be a procedure having a single entry and exit point. Each program instruction that can potentially cause the execution path to change, such as an "If... Then" statement, increments the complexity measure.

C.5.3 How is it Different than Other Software Measures?

Software complexity is one branch of *software metrics* (The topic of Software Measurements and Metrics was discussed in Chapter 5) that is focused on direct measurement of software attributes, as opposed to indirect software measures such as project milestone status and reported system failures. There are hundreds of software *complexity measures*, ranging from the simple, such as source lines of code, to the esoteric, such as the number of variable definition/usage associations.

C.5.4 Cyclomatic Complexity: Implications for Maintenance and Testing

"Complexity" has some relation to software maintenance and to testing. For instance, research has shown that minimizing complexity is a key to writing high quality code. If the *cyclomatic complexity* of software is measured regularly during construction then complex areas of code can be identified early in the development life cycle and re-structured to improve understanding and to reduce testing and future maintenance effort.

The cyclomatic complexity measurement of a procedure equates to the number of tests required to execute all code paths through a procedure and is therefore of use to developers whilst unit testing. It is commonsense following that higher the complexity, the more difficult becomes the software to test. The cyclomatic complexity of existing software can also be measured to assess possible risk during modification and the level of testing required.

C.5.4.1 Cyclomatic Complexity as related to Software Maintenance

Maintenance is the most expensive phase of the software lifecycle, with typical estimates ranging from 60% to 80% of total cost. Consequently, maintenance methodology has a major impact on software cost. "Bad fixes," in which errors are introduced while fixing reported problems, are a significant source of error. Complexity analysis can guide maintenance activity to preserve (or improve) system quality, and specialized testing techniques help guard against the introduction of errors while avoiding redundant testing.

Complexity tends to increase during maintenance, for the simple reason that both error correction and functional enhancement are much more frequently accomplished by adding code than by deleting it. Not only does overall system complexity increase, but the complexity of individual modules increases as well, because it is usually easier to "patch" the logic in an existing module rather than introducing a new module into the system design.

Cyclomatic complexity usually increases gradually during maintenance, since the increase in complexity is proportional to the complexity of the new code. For example, adding four decisions to a module increases its complexity by exactly four. Thus, although complexity can become excessive if not controlled, the effects of any particular modification on complexity are predictable.

C.5.4.2 Complexity as related to Software Testing Effort

There is a direct relationship between the cyclomatic complexity value and the number of test cases that need to be devised and executed to fully test a procedure. Cyclomatic complexity values can therefore be used to identify which areas of the software will require greater testing effort than others. The lower the cyclomatic complexity, the easier it is to determine suitable tests and to perform them.

As cyclomatic complexity measures the amount of decision logic in a single software module, it is used for two related purposes in the structured testing methodology. First, it gives the number of recommended tests for software. Second, it is used during all phases of the software lifecycle, beginning with design, to keep software reliable, testable, and manageable.

C.5.5 Acceptable Level of Complexity

Many organizations have found it useful to set a threshold complexity value that all developers must stay within—a value less than 10 is widely regarded as an acceptable value, although research has shown that for highly skilled developers, expressing commitment to increased testing, values less than 15 may occasionally be acceptable). Studies show that the lower the cyclomatic complexity for a procedure, the easier it is for the evaluator to understand the intended purpose of the procedure.

C.5.6 Cyclomatic Complexity and Modification Risk Assessment

The cyclomatic complexity of a procedure can also be used as an indicator of the possible risk associated with modifying a procedure. Higher complexity will normally result in higher cost and risk when making modifications. The following table assesses the risk of modification to a procedure:

Table 4

Cyclomatic Complexity	Risk Assessment
1–10	Simple procedure, low risk.
11–20	More complex procedure, moderate risk.
21–50	Complex procedure, high risk.
Greater than 50	Un-testable procedure, very high risk

Cyclomatic complexity is based entirely on the structure of software's *control flow graph*.

C.5.7 Control Flow Graphs

*Control flow graph*s describe the logic structure of software modules. A module corresponds to a single function or subroutine in typical languages, has a single entry and exit point, and is able to be used as a design component via a call/return mechanism. Each flow graph consists of nodes and edges. The nodes represent computational statements or expressions, and the edges represent transfer of control between nodes.

Each possible execution path of a software module has a corresponding path from the entry to the exit node of the module's control flow graph. This correspondence is the foundation for the structured testing methodology.

Cyclomatic complexity is defined for each module to be e − n + 2, where e and n are the number of edges and nodes in the control flow graph, respectively. For more details on the topic of "Cyclmatic Complexity" readers may like to refer any standard textbook on Software Engineering.

C.6 Requirements

C.6.1 What's the big deal about 'requirements'?

One of the most reliable methods of insuring problems, or failure, in a complex software project is to have poorly documented requirements specifications. Requirements are the details describing an application's externally perceived functionality and properties. Requirements should be clear, complete, reasonably detailed, cohesive, attainable, and testable (A good standard for writing requirements specification is the *IEEE Guide to Software Requirements Specification Std 830*). A non-testable requirement would be, for example, 'user-friendly' (too subjective). Ambiguous requirements cause problems for validation i.e. testing. A testable requirement would be something like 'the user must enter their previously-assigned password to access the application'. Determining and organizing requirements details in a useful and efficient way can be a difficult effort; different methods are available depending on the particular project. Many books are available that describe various approaches to this task (one such is the [5] at the end of this appendix.

C.6.2 Requirements Taxonomy

A requirement is a specification of what a system must do—the things/ behaviour of the systems users can observe. Sometimes, this is called the *architecture* of the system. Good requirements have three primary characteristics (the IEEE Std 830 mentioned above has the details on this):

1. They are *precise*, with no possibility for misinterpretation by users or implementers
2. They specify *what* the system must do, not *how* to do it. They avoid specifying implementation details
3. They show *conceptual integrity*, building on a simple set of facilities that interact well with each other.

The figure below presents a matrix for "requirements taxonomy":

Figure 3

	Customer Doesn't Care	Customer Cares	
		Measurable	Un-measurable
Observable To Users	Requirement likely to change	*Requirement*	*Goal*
Not Observable To Users	Implementation detail	*Constraint*	

While defining the systems requirements, an architect may also define *"constraints"*(the other word for this is *"nonfunctional require-ments"*) and *goals* for the system. A constraint is a limitation on possible implementation of the system (For example, a particular implementa-tion language or a particular algorithm insisted upon). From project management point of view, it is often better to negotiate away constraints, since they limit the freedom of the implementer.

A goal is a statement that guides tradeoffs among design decisions. For example, a customer may care a lot about the maintainability of the software, but may not care so much for efficiency. A point to note is that a goal may become a requirement if you can find a way to "quantify" it. For example, "high throughput" is a goal, but "at least 50 transactions per second" is a requirement. One lesson we draw from this is that if something is not quantifiable, it may become difficult to test causing problems in the later phases of the project!

Thus, care should be taken to involve ALL of a project's significant stakeholder (mainly 'customers') in the requirements process. 'Custom-ers' could be in-house personnel or outsiders, and could include end-users, customer acceptance testers, customer contract officers, cus-tomer management, future software maintenance engineers, salespeople, etc. Anyone who could later derail the project if their ex-pectations aren't met should be included if possible. From this perspective the "requirements taxonomy" presented above is useful.

Organizations vary considerably in their handling of requirements specifications. Ideally, the requirements are spelled out in a document with statements such as 'The product shall.....'. 'Design' specifications should not be confused with 'requirements'; design specifications should be traceable back to the requirements. This is an important angle from the Integrated CMM perspective which expects something known as "bi-directional traceability" (The *Process Areas* called *Requirements Development* and *Requirements Management* of the CMMI—see Chapter 9) Readers may also like to note that the IEEE Standard 1471:2000 is about "Architecture Design for Software Intensive Systems"

In some organizations requirements may end up in high-level project plans, *functional specification documents*, in *design documents*, or in other documents at various levels of detail. No matter what they are called, some type of documentation with detailed requirements will be needed by testers in order to properly plan and execute tests. Without such documentation, there will be no clear-cut way to determine if a software application is performing correctly!

Finally at the end of this section, we present the various aspects or activities involved in "Software Requirements":

Software Requirements

- Requirements *Engineering* Process
  o Process Models
  o Processes and Actors
  o Process Support and Management
  o Process Quality and Process Improvement
- Requirements *Elicitation*
  o Sources of Requirements
  o Elicitation Techniques
- Requirements *Analysis*
  o Requirements Classification
  o Conceptual modeling
  o Architectural Design and Requirements Allocation
- Requirements *Specification*
  o Requirements Definition Document
  o Software Requirements Specification
  o Document Structure and Standards
  o Document quality
- Requirements *Validation*
  o Requirements Reviews
  o Prototyping
  o Model Validation
  o Acceptance Tests
- Requirements *Management*
  o Change Management
  o Requirements Attributes
  o Requirements Tracing

The detailed discussion is beyond the scope of this book. Some good references on the topic of "Requirements" are indicated at the end of this appendix.

C.7 Principle of COUPLING and COHESION

C.7.1 Background and Introduction

Larry Constantine and Edward Yourdon discussed *Coupling* and *Cohesion* at great length in their 1976 landmark book, *Structured Design*.

"Coupling and Cohesion" are fundamental design principles. Since these concepts have been tied to structured programming, in today's object-oriented scenario, it seems that many programmers are forgetting what they mean. In many ways, the concepts are still extremely important as fundamental design concepts. The aim of the designer or system architect is supposed to be "High COHESION and Low "COULPING".

The design of software is often depicted by graphs that show "components and their relationships". For example, a structure chart shows the calling relationships among components. *Object-oriented design* too is not an exception to this. Coupling and Cohesion are attributes that summarize the "degree of interdependence or connectivity among subsystems/modules and within subsystems/modules", respectively.

When used in conjunction with measures of other attributes, coupling and cohesion can contribute to an assessment or prediction of software quality. These measures have the properties of system-level coupling and cohesion defined by Briand, Morasca, and Basili.

Coupling is based on relationships between modules. We can have a measure for intra-module coupling based on an intra-module abstraction of the software, rather than inter-module. Intra-module coupling is calculated in the same way as inter-module coupling. We can define cohesion in terms of intra-module coupling, normalized to between zero and one.

C.7.2 Coupling and Cohesion in Measurement Context

Inter-module Coupling

It is the measure of the interdependence of one module to another. Modules should have low coupling. Low coupling minimizes the "ripple effect" where changes in one module cause errors in other modules. This helps minimize issues during Regression Testing (The topic of Testing is covered in great detail in Chapter 10).

Inter-module Cohesion

It is the measure of strength of the association of elements within a module. Modules whose elements are strongly and genuinely related to each other are desired. A module should be highly cohesive.

C.7.3 Cohesion

We will discuss cohesion first, since it is a bit easier to understand. As said earlier, "Cohesion" refers to how clearly defined a particular module or procedure is. A module with high cohesion does one or a few things exceedingly well. Let's take an example of a job description. Suppose you placed the following ad:

Wanted: Programmer with solid skills in the following areas: System analysis, design, testing methodologies, EDI, software auditing, COBOL, BASIC, PAL, SmallTalk and C++ required. Strong real-time data acquisition skills, scientific applications experience and accounting knowledge a must. Candidates must be experienced, energetic, willing to work long hours, be able to lead groups of programmers, get along with others and have the patience of Job......

If this is the way you stated the requirement, how many qualified candidates would you get? And if you found one, how long would he or she last? How many skills can one person excel in at one time?

What this means is that if a particular module is responsible for a diverse set of tasks, chances are the module will be, like our hapless candidate in the above example, a mess!

So the question that comes up is "what constitutes a module, which exhibits poor cohesion?" From this, there are a few points to note:

Concept of Cohesion goes a lot with the principle of "divide and rule" and "work-breakdown structure. As you can see, the first sign, *usually*, that a module exhibits poor cohesion is its "length". The longer a programmer rambles on in a module, the drearier and less comprehensible the module becomes (This also adversely affects *code maintainability*). The module lacks the punch, (which of course, is a good thing for keeping those who maintain the code awake and get paid for doing this!).

As an illustration to drive this point, if a program module is coded to perform too many different things: getting input from the user (on whether to continue or not, messaging the user on error conditions, performing several queries and setting up the query images and locking tables. Each of these tasks can be delegated down in the hierarchy to a specialized module. In the Object-Oriented paradigm this would mean writing short but focused methods to handle only a particular type of task. Such an approach would improve the module's cohesiveness.

In life, there are exceptions to the rule. This is true here too. It is possible for a lengthy module to still have a high degree of cohesion, *provided the module excels in one or two things only.* For example, some modules contain code, which executes a series of commands or a series of evaluations. The latter case is especially common in situations where the module needs to evaluate a list of menu choices or a list of events. For example, a long series of case statements evaluate the user's menu choice. Since this kind of a module would exactly one thing, *evaluate a menu choice*; it qualifies as a highly cohesive module.

Thus, as a good design principle, it is a good idea to decompose the programming problem into a hierarchy of cooperating procedures.

Clearly identify the job description for each module. Try to keep each module as painfully ignorant as possible of what the other modules are doing (In Object Oriented paradigm, this is the concept of "hiding").

After all, a number of programmers would be assigned various modules to code. How many times have you looked at your own code, written months ago, baffled by what it does? If you clearly identify a *narrow* job description for each procedure, the chances for confusion later are less.

It might be helpful to keep in mind the following "Rule of Module Intelligence":

Bosses are ignorant. Workers are smart

(Readers from the older SSADM—Structured System Analysis and Design days would recall the *"Functional Decomposition Diagram* or the FDD).

Just like in real life, endowing your various modules with different skill helps keep cohesion high. For example, the higher you go in a module hierarchy, the less nitty-gritty work the module actually does. In fact, higher-level modules usually bark out commands, as the module in the listing below (hypothetical):

Code Listing—High-Level Module

```
procedure BIG_BOSS()
    if UNIVERSE_CREATE_THYSELF() = false then
    return false
    endif
    PROCESS_MAIN_MENU_SELECTION()
    if UNIVERSE_GO_AWAY() = false then
    SHOW_MESSAGE("Something bad happened during universe
        shut-down")
    return false
    endif
    return true
endproc
```

In this example, BIG_BOSS() initializes the application, calls the procedure which displays the main menu and handles the user's selection and then shuts the application down. This module does very little except issue a few key commands to subordinates.

Main procedures like BIG_BOSS() are fairly easy to write without losing cohesion. The real challenge is writing in lower-level procedures properly. Often, programmers use the procedure they are working on as a sort of scratch pad to explore possible alternatives to a solution.

And often, a less experienced programmer will try to patch-up the scratch pad or cobble together the random bits and pieces of code into a working single module.

Having discussed the basic concept behind "Cohesion", let us now consider various "types of Cohesion"

C.7.3.1 Types of COHESION

As discussed above, "Cohesion" is the measure of strength of the association of elements within a module. Modules whose elements are strongly and genuinely related to each other are desired. Thus, a module should be highly cohesive. There is a "Cohesion spectrum" as illustrated below:

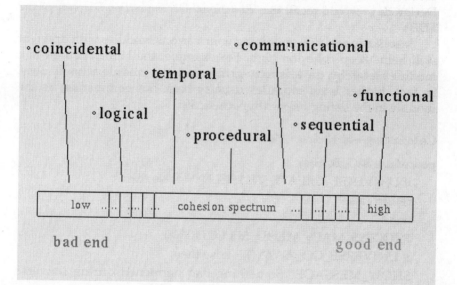

[1] Coincidental cohesion

A module has *coincidental cohesion* if its elements have no meaningful relationship to one another.

Example

A perhaps mythological story—A manager who is responsible for maintaining a largish (say, 10000 line of code) FORTRAN program reads about modularity and how helpful it is in improving programming understanding of programs.

The manager tells his chief programmer to restructure the FORTRAN program (which is a one large subprogram) into modules. He's going to get those benefits.

The chief programmer, who thinks he has better uses for his time, decides the fastest way to make modules out of the program is to take a ruler, measure down every 6 inches in the program listing and draw a line. At each line, he inserts a call to a new subprogram, and after that call creates the header for the new subprogram. With this short cut approach taken, these "modules" exhibit ultimate coincidental cohesion!

[2] *Logical cohesion*

A *logically cohesive* module is one whose elements perform similar activities and in which the activities to be executed are chosen from outside the module. See the diagram below.

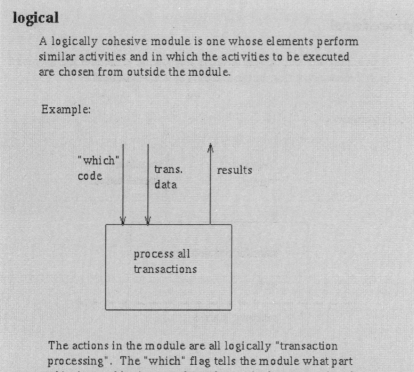

logical

A logically cohesive module is one whose elements perform similar activities and in which the activities to be executed are chosen from outside the module.

Example:

"which"
code   trans.   results
            data

process all
transactions

The actions in the module are all logically "transaction processing". The "which" flag tells the module what part of its internal logic to apply to the particular transaction data coming in for each specific invocation.

[3] *Temporal cohesion*

A temporally cohesive module is one whose elements are functions that are related in time. Example:

Consider a module called "On_Really_Bad_Failure" that is invoked when a "Really_Bad_Failure" happens. The module performs several tasks that are not functionally similar or logically related, but all tasks need to happen at the moment when the failure occurs. The module might

- Cancel all outstanding requests for services
- Cut power to all assembly line machines
- Notify the operator console of the failure
- Make an entry in a database of failure records

[4] Procedural cohesion

A *procedurally cohesive* module is one whose elements are involved in different activities, but the activities are sequential. See the diagram below.

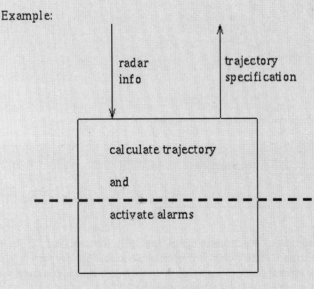

procedural

A procedurally cohesive module is one whose elements are involved in different activities, but the activities are sequential.

Example:

radar info

trajectory specification

calculate trajectory

and

activate alarms

Why might we want these as two separate modules (say, cut along the dotted line)?

Then we could calculate trajectories for other purposes without risking alarms going off... or, similarly, we could set off alarms without having to have some target to track first.

[5] Communicational cohesion

A *communicationally cohesive* module is one whose elements perform different functions, but each function references the same input information or output. See the diagram below.

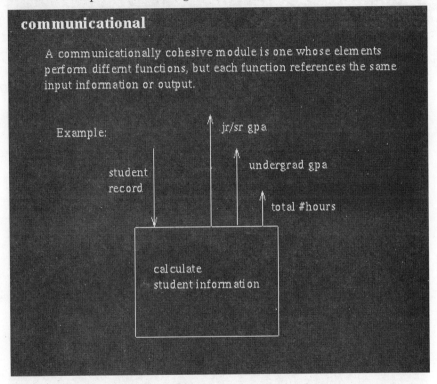

[6] Sequential cohesion

A *sequentially cohesive* module is one whose functions are related such that output data from one function serves as input data to the next function. See the diagram on the next page.

[7] Functional cohesion

A functionally cohesive module is one in which all of the elements contribute to a single, well-defined task. Object-oriented languages tend to support this level of cohesion better than earlier languages do. Examples of functionally cohesive modules are:

- Calculate Net Employee Salary
- Read a Transaction Record
- Assign seat to a passenger
- Compute point of collision of two objects
- Verify syntax

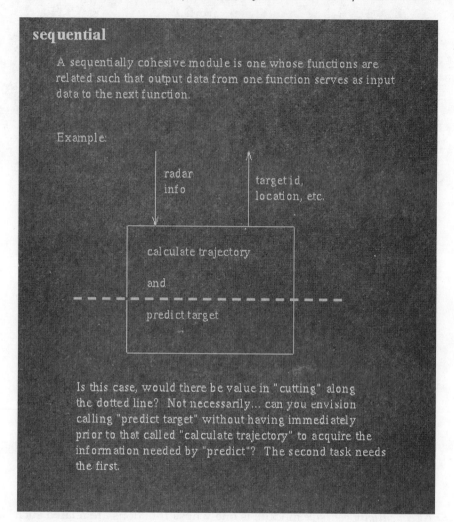

sequential

A sequentially cohesive module is one whose functions are related such that output data from one function serves as input data to the next function.

Example:

radar info

target id, location, etc.

calculate trajectory

and

predict target

Is this case, would there be value in "cutting" along the dotted line? Not necessarily... can you envision calling "predict target" without having immediately prior to that called "calculate trajectory" to acquire the information needed by "predict"? The second task needs the first.

C.7.4 Coupling

The other design issue, "Coupling", refers to what information needs to be communicated between modules. In real life jobs, most bosses prefer to have workers that can perform their duties without excessive communication, either spurious or required. The more *self-reliant* the worker, the less maintenance the worker will require.

Procedures need to communicate data between themselves. In fact, communicating data between modules is necessary to write anything other than a trivial program, such as the famous "Hello world" program shown in most textbooks on programming. Procedures transform data for the user. To do that, they must share data and COUPLING is about data sharing through parameters or messages exchanged between two or modules/classes.

Writing modules with low coupling is desirable. Why—Because a module with low coupling is more independent and usually less complex because there is less data for the module to work on. The less a module has to know about data in other modules, or in any other part of the application, the better.

Coupling, Cohesion, Span and life of a variable can be discussed in simple terms. The problem can be stated this way:

1. Smaller procedures are easier to understand because they contain less visual and hence logical information. This creates less complications..
2. The more information about a program that is immediately available to the programmer's eye at one time, the easier the program is to understand and review.
3. The more order and structure inherent in the information about a program, the easier it is to understand. The more random or chaotic the information in a program, the more difficult it is to understand, review or modify.

Having discussed the basic principle behind "Coupling" let us now consider various "types of Coupling".

C.7.4.1 Types of COUPLING

As discussed earlier, *Coupling is the measure of the interdependence of one module to* another. Modules should have low coupling. Low coupling minimizes the "ripple effect"

where changes in one module cause errors in other modules.

There is a "coupling spectrum" as illustrated in the diagram below:

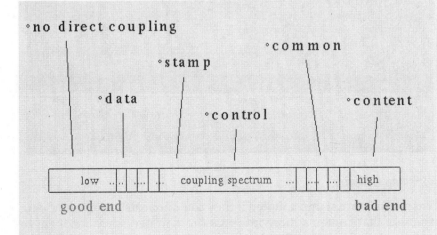

There are various *types of Coupling* as discussed below:

[1] No Direct Coupling

These are independent modules and so are not really components of a single system.

[2] Data Coupling

Two modules are data coupled if they communicate by passing parameters. This has been told to you as a "good design principle" since day one of programming instruction. See the diagram below.

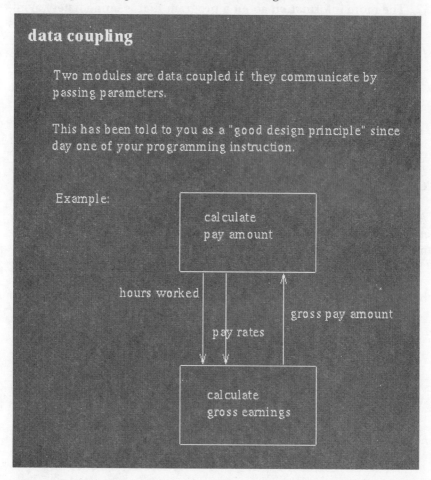

[3] Stamp Coupling

Two modules are stamp coupled if they communicate via a passed data structure that contains more information than necessary for them to perform their functions. See the diagram below.

stamp coupling

Two modules are stamp coupled if they communicate via a passed data structure which contains more information than necessary for the modules to preform their functions.

Example:

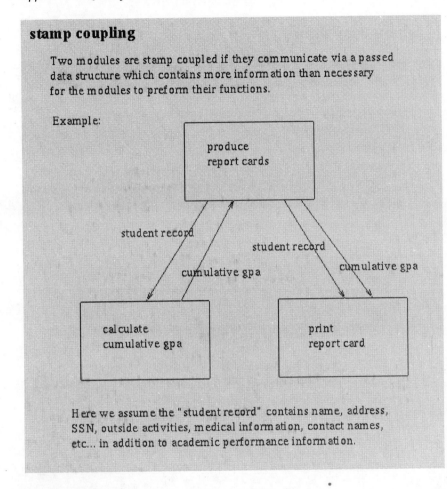

Here we assume the "student record" contains name, address, SSN, outside activities, medical information, contact names, etc... in addition to academic performance information.

[4] Control Coupling

Two modules are control coupled if they communicate using at least one "control flag". See the diagram on page 401.

[5] Common Coupling

Two modules are common coupled if they both share the same global data area. Another design principle you have been taught since day one: don't use global data. See the diagram titled 'Common Coupling' on the next page.

[6] Content Coupling

Two modules are content coupled if:

1. One module changes a statement in another (Lisp was famous for this ability)

common coupling

Two modules are common coupled if they both share the same global data area

Another design principle you have been taught since day-one: don't use global data

Example: Venn diagrams to show common global areas
　　　　　　Module group A is less tightly coupled than is group B

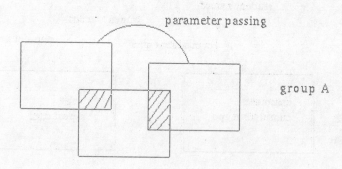

parameter passing

group A

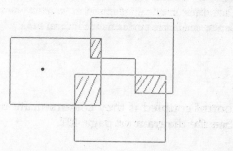

group B

2. One module references or alters data contained inside another module
3. One module branches into another module

C.7.5 Summary: Coupling and Cohesion

In the case of "poorly cohesive programs", the information in the procedure may appear haphazard and unstructured to another

control coupling

Two modules are control coupled if they communicate using
at least one "control flag"

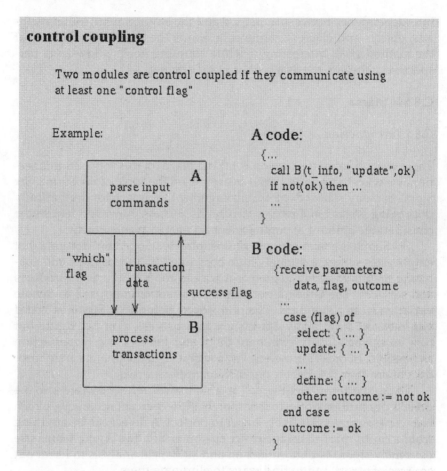

Example:

A code:
```
{...
    call B(t_info, "update",ok)
    if not(ok) then ...
    ...
}
```

B code:
```
{receive parameters
    data, flag, outcome
    ...
    case (flag) of
        select: { ... }
        update: { ... }
        ...
        define: { ... }
        other: outcome := not ok
    end case
    outcome := ok
}
```

Figure labels: A — parse input commands; B — process transactions; "which" flag; transaction data; success flag

programmer, hence the program is harder to understand. In much the
same way it is harder for us to understand what is going on in a picture
the more the picture contains random and haphazard features. Driving
home at night in a heavy rainstorm is harder than driving home on a
clear, sunny day. An obscure or complicated job description is harder
to understand than a succinct and precise job description.

In the case of "highly coupled programs/modules", the amount of
information in the program might be too high, as in the case of long
parameter lists. Or, some information may not be immediately visible
to the programmer, as in the case of global variables and tables.

If you think about programming in terms of information that is
immediately and easily discernible to the programmer, it becomes clear
that programs occupy "space" in programmers' minds. The larger and
more chaotic that space, the more difficult it is to understand the
program!

Thus, to summarize:

The main goal of design (from a low-level perspective) is to "minimize COUPLING and maximize COHESION". Coupling is the level of

interdependency between a method and the environment, (other methods, objects and classes), while cohesion is the level of uniformity of the method goal. Interestingly, while coupling needs a low-level perspective, cohesion needs a higher point of view.

C.8 Six Sigma

C.8.1 Introduction

These days, a lot of discussion is taking place on this topic. In this section, we wish to provide a brief overview on the topic of Six Sigma. Six Sigma is today's most dynamic management approach for dramatically improving *product and process quality*. Its success, however, required a considerable amount of commitment on part of management.

Six Sigma is a management philosophy developed by Motorola that emphasizes setting extremely high objectives, collecting data, and analyzing results to a fine degree as a way to reduce defects in products and services. The Greek letter sigma (σ) is sometimes used to denote variation from a standard. The philosophy behind Six Sigma is that if you measure how many defects are in a process, you can figure out how to systematically eliminate them and get as close to perfection as possible. In order for a company to achieve Six Sigma, it cannot produce more than 3.4 defects per million opportunities.

Thus, the term "Six Sigma" is a statistical term that refers to 3.4 defects per million opportunities (or 99.99966 percent accuracy), which is as close as anyone is likely to get to perfect. A defect can be anything from a faulty part to an incorrect customer bill. Six Sigma teams use extremely rigorous data collection and statistical analysis to ferret out sources of errors and to find ways to eliminate them.

There are two Six Sigma processes: *Six Sigma DMAIC* (Define, Measure, Analyze, Improve, Control) and *Six Sigma DMADV*, each term derived from the major steps in the process. Six Sigma DMAIC is a process that defines, measures, analyzes, improves, and controls existing processes that fall below the Six Sigma specification. Six Sigma DMADV (Define, Measure, Analyze, Design and Verify) defines, measures, analyzes, designs, and verifies new processes or products that are trying to achieve Six Sigma quality. All Six Sigma processes are executed by Six Sigma Green Belts or Six Sigma Black Belts, which are then overseen by a Six Sigma Master Black Belts, terms created by Motorola.

C.8.2 What is Six Sigma in the Statistical Context

"Six Sigma " is a statistical concept that measures a process in terms of defects. Achieving Six Sigma means that your processes are delivering on 3.4 defects per million opportunities (DPMO). In other words, they are working nearly perfectly. Sigma (the Greek letter σ) is a term in statistics that measures something called "standard deviation". In business context, it indicates defects in output of a process, and helps us to understand how far the process deviates from perfection. A Sigma represents 691462.5 defects per million opportunities, which translates to a percentage of non-defective outputs of 30.854%. This shows bad performance. If we have processes functioning at a three sigma level, this means we are allowing 66807.2 errors per million opportunities or delivering 93.319% non-defective production.

The central theme in Six Sigma Management is that if you can measure the defects in a process, you can systematically figure out ways to eliminate them, approach a quality level of zero defects. "Defect" is a measurable characteristics of the process or its output that is not within the acceptable customer limits i.e. not conforming to specifications. Six Sigma is about practices that help you eliminate defects and *always* deliver products and services that meet customer expectations.

So, in short, Six Sigma is several things:

- A *statistical basis of measurement*: 3.4 defects per million opportunities
- A *philosophy and a goal*: being as perfect as practically possible
- A methodology towards *achieving excellence*
- A symbol of *quality*

C.8.3 How does Six Sigma work?

Measurement & Metrics (The topic of Chapter 5) lie at the heart of Six Sigma. The basic approach is to measure performance on an existing process, compare it with a statistically valid ideal and figure out how to eliminate any variation. Project teams might speak in terms of reducing cycle time, improving customer satisfaction, cutting down on returns and improving the speed and accuracy of order fulfillment. No project is considered complete until the benefit has been shown and a team of financial auditors signs off.

In essence, DMAIC is the Six Sigma Improvement Framework There are five steps in DMAIC:

1. **Define**: A Six Sigma project team—led by a black belt—identifies a project based on business objectives as well as customer needs and feedback. The team identifies CTQs (critical to quality characteristics) that the customer considers to have the most impact on quality. It also separates the "vital few" from the "trivial many" (the projects that will have the most impact versus those that could stand improvement but are not critical).
2. **Measure:** The team identifies the key internal processes that influence critical process parameters impacting quality (the CTQs) and measures the defects currently generated relative to those processes.

3. **Analyze**: The team discovers why defects are generated by identifying the key variables that are most likely to create process variation.
4. **Improve:** The team identifies the maximum acceptable ranges of the key variables and validates a system for measuring deviations of the variables. The team modifies the process to stay within the acceptable range.
5. **Control:** Tools are put in place to ensure that the key variables remain within the maximum acceptable ranges over time.

C.8.4 Six Sigma: A Panacea for All Problems?

Six Sigma proponents claim that its benefits include up to 50% process cost reduction, cycle-time improvement, less waste of materials, a better understanding of customer requirements, increased customer satisfaction, and more reliable products and services. It is acknowledged that Six Sigma can be costly to implement and can take several years before a company begins to see bottom-line results. Motorola Texas Instruments, Scientific-Atlantic, General Electric, and Allied Signal are a few of the companies that practice Six Sigma.

If you are already operationally excellent and want to squeeze out defects and increase efficiency, Six Sigma is for you. If your business is built on intangibles—those aspects that are awfully hard to subject to statistical analysis—then Six Sigma is not for you. If you want to be a product leader competing primarily on quality—but not first-to-market—then do go for Six Sigma.

A word of caution: Data collection is the Achilles' heel of many a Six Sigma effort. This sort of woe, often caused by an amalgamation of disparate computer platforms thrown together in a merger or acquisition, is common at the large companies (several billions in revenues) that have been early adopters of Six Sigma. Making matters worse, to the best of author's knowledge, there is currently no software program that goes across a variety of computing platforms to collect data for Six Sigma analysis.

REFERENCES

[1] *Statistical Quality Control*—Eugene L. Grant and Richard S. Leavenworth (Tata McGraw Hill)
[2] *Measuring the Software Process*—William A. Florac and Anita D.Carleton (Addison Wesley)
[3] *Statistical Quality Assurance Methods for Engineers*—Stephen B. Vardeman, J. Marcus Jobe ISBN: 0-471-15937-9
[4] *The Practical Guide to Structured Systems Design*—by Meilir Page-Jones (Prentice Hall International Edition)
[5] *Software Engineering: Planning for Change*—by David Alex Lamb (Prentice Hall International Edition)

[6] *Experiments with Coupling and Cohesion Metrics in a Large System*—by Timothy C. Lethbridge and Nicolas Anquetil (School of Information Technology and Engineering University of Ottawa)

[7] *Requirements Engineering: A Good Practice Guide*—Ian Sommerville and Pete Sawyer ((John Wiley & Sons)

[8] *Software Requirements and Estimation*—Swapna Kishore and Rajesh Naik (Tata McGraw Hill)

[9] *Managing the Requirements Process*—Suzanne Robertson and James Robertson (Addison Wesley)

[10] *Software Requirements*—Karl E. Wiegers (Microsoft Press)

[11] *Object Oriented Modeling and Design*—James Rumbaguh (Prentice Hall India Ltd)

[12] *The Object-Oriented Through Process*—Matt Weisfeld (Techmedia)

[13] *Object Oriented Software Engineering*—Ivar Jacobson (Addison Wesley)

[14] *Object Oriented Analysis and Design*—Grady Booch (Addison Wesley)

[15] *Object-Oriented Design Measurement*—Scott A. Whimire (John Wiley & Sons Inc)

[16] *Legal Issues in e-Business*—Nina Godbole (December 2001 and January 2002 issues of the Information Technology Magazine: A Delhi-based Publication)

[17] *What Is Six Sigma?*—Peter S. Pande, Larry Holpp, Pete Pande, Lawrence Holpp (Tata McGraw Hill)

Index

A

Acceptance criteria, 271
Acceptance test, 37, 41, 46, 55, 267, 276, **277**
Acquiring test tools, 297
Actual Cost of Work Performed (ACWP), 138
ACWP (see Actual Cost of Work Performed), 138
Adaptive maintenance, 367
Adequacy audit, 38
Alpha testing, **277**
ANSI Standard (American National Standard)—for reviews, **60**
Anti-pattern, 198
Application architecture, 62
Application granularity, 149
Application under test (AUT), 269
Appraisal costs, **5**
ARC (see Assessment Requirement for CMM-I), 339
ASQ (American Society for Quality)
ASQ Certification Program—history, **323**
Assessment
classes of, **339**
definition, **210**
first party, second party, third party, **211**
method Documentation, 340
of software production process, 92
process of, **213**
requirement for CMM-I (ARC), 339
types of, **211**
Assessments/Audits—preparation, **212**
Attribute Control Charts, **365**
Audit

classification of (British Standards Institute), 211
definition (IEEE), **210**
first party, second party, third party, **212**
trail, **189**
types of, **211**
Auditing, 44
Audits and Assessments, **210**
gap identification through, 213
AUT—see application under test, 269
Author
in inspection process, 158
in review process, 161
Automated test packages, 317
Automated test tools—selection process, **298**
Awareness Programs, 334

B

Backlog Management Index (BMI), 112
Bad fixes, **109**
Baselines, **179**
IEEE definition, **180**
BCWP (see Budgeted Cost of Work Performed), 138
BCWS (see Budgeted Cost of Work Scheduled)
Beta testing, 277, **278**
Bi-directional Traceability, 61, 387
for requirements, 115
Black box testing, 273, 293, **295**
BMI (See Backlog Management Index)
Boehm—view of software product quality, **85**
Boundary value analysis, 281
Brief history of ISO 9001, 200

British Standards Institute—audit classification, 211

Budgeted Cost of Work Performed (BCWP), 138

Budgeted Cost of Work Scheduled (BCWS), 138

Bugs v/s Defects, **106**

Bugs, 106

Burn out problem—software industry, 357

Business Excellence Award of Europe, 247

Business value—ISO certificate, 208

C

Canada Award of Excellence (CAE), 247, **248**

Capability determination—through assessment, **211**

Capability Evaluation, 339

Capability Maturity Model
SW CMM, 93, 224
Integrated CMM-I, 235
types, **234**

CAR (see Causal Analysis and Resolution)

Career objectives, 311

Career paths—for quality professionals, 258, 311

Carnegie Mellon University, 93

Causal Analysis and Resolution (CAR), **72**

Causal Analysis, 62

CCB (see Change Control Board, Configuration Control Board)

Certification
and Assessments, 211
benefits and impact, **321**
from QAI, **323**
ISO, 201

Change control—in testing context, 282

Change Control Board (CCB), 184

Change log, 184

Change management, 173

Change Request—Format, **187**

Checklist for evaluation—SCM Plan, **196**

Chidamber & Kemerer's Metrics suite, 149

Choosing a CMM-I representation—factors to consider, **243**

Clause 8.2.2 of ISO 9001:2000, **209**

CMM (see Capability Maturity Model)

CMM and SCM, **193**

CMM-based Software Process Improvement, 224

CMM I (Integrated Capability Maturity Model), 235
Background of, 236
choosing a representation for, **243**
Components of, 236, **238**
disciplines, 236, 237
generic practices in , 242
maturity levels, 239,**241**
model evolution, 236, **237**
myths & realities, 237, **338**
process areas, 239
process area grouping, **241**
process areas selection, 339
representations of, 236, 237
representation selection—factors to consider –, **243**
specific practices, 242
staged v/s continuous representation, **242**

COCOMO (See Constructive Cost Model)

Code control, 63, 173

Code walkthroughs, 158

Coding guidelines, 94

Cognitive Dissonance, 336
effect on reviews & inspections, 166

Cohesion, **389**, **390**
as a design principle, 11, 45
types of, **391**

Common Features—SW CMM, 94

Communication skills—for quality professionals, 314

Comparison b/w SW CMM and CMM-I, **244**

Comparison between SW CMM and ISO, 227, **228**

Comparison of SW CMM Model with ISO Models, 224

Complexity
apparent, 382
inherent, 382
measure for, 18
metrics for, 18

Compliance audit, 212
Components of the CMM-I Model, 236, **238**
Configuration Audit
  guidelines for, **191**
Configuration, **174**, **176**
  board for (Configuration Control Board—CCB), 184
  control, 63, 184
  controller, 184
  identification of, 63
  in testing context, 282
  items under, 64
  management—ISO Clauses for, **192**
  management of, 41,63, **174**
  management—plan for, 59
  management—why, **174**
  process for management of, **176**
  status Accounting, 63, 183
  v/s Document Control, **179**
Conflict management—in reviews, 160
Constraint, 10
Constructive Cost Model (COCOMO), 115
Constructive Quality Model (COQUAMO), 88
Consulting services—ISO, **216**
Continual improvement, 30
Continuous (process) improvement, 29, 80, 318
Continuous Representation—Integrated CMM, 239, **242**
Contractual document, 37
Control Charts, 99, 361, **362**, 366
  limitations of, 365
  purpose of, **362**
  types of, 365
Control Flow Graphs, 385
Control Limits—Upper and Lower, **362**, 363
Control of Documents and records—ISO 9001:2000 clause, **66**
Conventions (IEEE Std. 983 definition), **83**
Corporate audits, 317
Corporate objectives—quality, 318
Corrective action, 63
Corrective maintenance, 331, 366
Correctness, **84**

Correspondent Members of ISO 9001, 201
Cost
  Estimate of, 42
  of (poor) quality, 162, 259
  Performance Index (Cost Performance Index—CPI), 138
  tracking of, **42**
  variance of(cost variance—CV), 138
Costing technique, 42
Country subscriber—membership for ISO 9001, 201
Coupling, 11, 388, 395
  types of, 397
Coupling & Cohesion, 11, **33**, 62, 388
  summary of, **400**
CSTE (Certified Software Test Engineer)
CSTE program from QAI, 308
Cultural differences—maturity (supplier and customer), 190
Cultural issues in Reviews, **165**
Customer-reported bugs and defects, 71, 108
Cyclomatic complexity, 11, 146, 291, 382
  for maintenance implications, **383**
  implications for testing, **384**

D

Database integrity testing, 315
Debugging Process, **263**
Debugging v/s Testing, **262**
Decision Analysis & Resolution (DAR), 44
Decision making rationale, **44**
Defect
  density v/s MTTF, **107**
  density, 106
  injection rate, **108**
  levels & user satisfaction—the relationship, 105
  measures and metrics, 105, 106
  prevention activities for, **71**, 104, **105**
  rate of, **106**
  removal effectiveness, **108**, **109**
  removal efficiency, **108**, **114**

severity, 71
tracking report, 113
v/s bug, **106**
Defective fix, 113
Defects—customer reported, 108
Defined software process, 67
Degree of cohesion of objects, 147
Degree of reuse—inheritance methods, 148
Delinquent fixes, 113
Delta report, 185
Design Review, 61
Design validation, **40**
Desk investigation, 214
Desk-checks, 155, 168
Development Stages of ISO 9001, **203**
Disaster Recovery Plan (DRP), 64
Document Control
   ISO expectations, 179
   v/s Configuration Control, **179**
Document of understanding (DoU), 37

E

Earned Value (EV), 138
Earned Value Analysis (EVA), 34, 35, 136, **137**
Earned Value Management (EVM), 137
e-Business
   and ISO, **222**
   models for, 372
   websites—perfective maintenance, 379
Edwards Deming, 93
Effective inspection, 166
Effective Test Case, 260
Efficiency, **84**
Effort as a measure, 136
EFQM—fundamental concepts, **250**, 251
Engineering Maturity Model (EMM), 252
Enhancement projects, 102
Entity Life History Diagram, 62
Entity Relationship Diagram (ERD), 62
Equivalence partitioning, **279**, **280**, 281
Errors, 106

Estimates, 38
EVA (see Earned Value Analysis)
EVA
   an illustrative example, **139, 140, 141**
   benefits to project management, 139
   success essentials for, **141**
   ten commandments of, **141**
EVM (see Earned Value Management)
Evolution of software systems, **81**
Evolutionary Approach to Software Product Development, 88
External assessors/auditors—ISO, 210
External attributes—software product, 83
External audits, 49
External motivators, 311
Extreme programming, 300
Extreme testing, **300**

F

Factoring effectiveness, 148
Failure costs, **5**
Failures, 106
Fan-in and Fan-out, 291
Fault recovery testing, **285**
Final/External assessments/audits—ISO, 210
First-party-assessment and audit, **211, 212**
Fish Bone Diagram, **72**
Fix Backlog, 112
Fix quality, 113
Fix-response-time, 113
Form attributes, **84**
Formal inspection, 168
Formal Notation for SRS, 18
Formal Technical Review (FTR), 155,159
Format for Change Request, **187**
Function points and feature points, **103**
Functional attributes, **84**
Functional Audit, **62**
Functional objectives, 88
Functional requirements, 116
Functional testing techniques, **279**
Functional traceability, **39**

Functionality, **83**
Function-oriented software metrics, 103

G

Gap analysis and identification—Audits/Assessments, 213
Gary box testing, **295**
Generic Practices in CMM-I, 242
Goal, 10
Goal-Question-Metric Model, 87
Gray box testing, 273, 293
Group Think Effect, 336
GUI standards, 94

H

High Maturity Organizations, 227, 325, 329
general philosophy and the SEI Survey, 331
Human issues and challenges in testing, **306**

I

IEC (See International Electro-Technical Commission), 202
IEEE—SCM snapshot, 196
IEEE—testing related definitions, **259, 270, 271**
IEEE (see Institute of Electrical and Electronic Engineers)
IEEE 1074, **246**
 audit—definition, **210**
 baseline—definition , **180**
 guide to (software) requirements specification, 61, **385**
 maintenance model, **370**
 quality metric definition, 88
 SCI—definition, **177**
 SCM—definition , **175**
 standard for software quality assurance plan, 56, **57**
 validation—definition , **258**
IEEE Standards
 Std 1061, 89
 Std. 610.12, 82—software product definition, **82**
 Std. 610.12, 82,83
 Std. 983—for Conventions, **83**

Std 828:1990—for SCM Plans, 195
Std 1042: 1987—Guide to SCM, 195
Incremental and Evolutionary models, 368
Independent SQA Group, 333
Independent test observer, 266, 267, 268
Independent test observer, 276
Indian software scenario
 exports growth, **353**
 NASCOM survey, **352**
 people management problems & challenges, 353, **356**
 quality maturity, 352
 software practices maturity, 341
 top twenty companies, **349**
Informed decision, 331
Inheritance, 372
 dependencies, 147
 tree depth, 149
In-Process Audit, **62**
In-Process-Defects, 108
Inspection
 advantages/benefits of, **168**, 169
 as a static testing technique, 261
 checklists, **169, 170, 171**
 conflict management, 160
 reasons for effectiveness, **165**
 typical problems, **166**
Inspection, 155, 158, **260**
 responsibilities of the leader -, **159**
 methods for, 166
 v/s Testing, **260**
 yield, **166**
Installation testing, 284
Institute of Electrical and Electronic Engineers (IEEE), 80
Integrated Capability Maturity Model (CMM I), **235**
 continuous representation, 239,**242**
 disciplines for, 236, 237
 generic practices, 242
 maturity levels, 239, **241**
 myths & realities, 237, **338**
 Process Area grouping, **241**
 Process Areas selection, 239, 339
 representations, 236, 237
 specific practices, 242
 staged representation, 239, **240**
 vis-à-vis SW CMM, 235
Integration testing, **42, 275**

Internal attributes of software product, 83
Internal Audit, 49, **212**, 214
International Electro-Technical Commission (IEC), 202
International Organization for Standardization (ISO), 228, 231
Inter-object coupling, 147
Intrusive testing, **281**
ISO (International Organization for Standardization), 228
ISO
brief history, 200
central secretariat, 202
document control, 179
FAQs (Frequently Asked Questions), **221**
MoU for support to e-Business, 222
standards—development process, **203**
ISO 12207, **246**
organizational management processes, **246**
primary processes, **246**
supporting processes, **246**
ISO 8402
definition of software quality, **88**
ISO 9000
need for , **207**
ISO 9000:1987
first revision to, 205
ISO 9000:1994, 205
clauses, **205**
major and minor changes, **206**
ISO 9000-3, **90**, 92
ISO 9001, 92, 200
audits/assessments, 200
continual improvement context, 200
correspondent members, 201
country subscriber membership, 201
Final Draft International Standard (FDIS), 204
member body, 201
member constitution, **200**, **201**
O Members and P Members, 201
origins of, **201**, **201**
structure of, 200, **201**
working of, 200, **205**

Draft International Standard (DIS), 204
use of consultants, 200
ISO 9001, 9002, 9003, 205
ISO 9001:2000
clause 8.2.2, **209**
clause about control of documents and records, **66**
clause about suppliers, **65**
ISO 9004-1, 205
ISO 9126
quality definition, **87**
standard quality model, **87**
ISO
and e-Business, **222**
certificate as a business reference, 208
certification, **208**
configuration management related clauses, **192**
definition of audit/assessment, **210**
mapping to SW CMM, **228**
ISO consultants
handholding with the client, 221
involvement phases, **220**
selection and usage, 213, 215, **217**, **218**, **219**
services offered, 215, **216**
ISO memento, 203
ISO registrars, 208
ISO technical committee, 203
ISO/IEC 15504, 231, **232**
ITC (See ISO Technical Committee), 203

J

Juran, 93

K

KPA (see Key Process Areas)
Key Practices—SW CMM, 225
Key Process Areas (KPAs)—SW CMM, 94, 225, 234

L

Labels—in configuration management, **179**
Lessons learnt, 38, 327

Levels of control—SCM, 182
Library function, 63,64
Life Cycle
   testing, **264**
   website, **375, 376**
Limitations of Control Chart—**365**
Linear Sequential Approach to Software Development, 88
Load testing, **288**
Low morale & burnout, **312**

M

Maintainability—object orientation context, **371**
Maintainability, **83, 85**
Maintenance
   adaptive, 367
   corrective, 366, 371
   perfective, 367
   of website, **373**
Maintenance models (for software)
   evolution, **367, 369**
   IEEE, **370**
Maintenance Projects—Project Management Issues, **331**
Major and Minor changes to ISO 9000:1994, **206**
Major NC, 214
Malcolm Baldrige National Quality Award (MBNQA), 247
Management commitment, 30
Management reviews, **62**
Managing web-site maintenance, **377, 378**
Mapping
   ISO 9001 and CMM, **228**
   SW CMM and ISO/IEC 15504, **232**
Maturity, 81, 224
Maturity levels, 93
   Integrated CMM, 239, **241**
   P-CMM, **254**
   SW CMM, 225
Mature organizations—practices followed in, 328, **329**
Maturity model, 89
MBNQA (see Malcolm Baldrige National Quality Award)
   as TQM framework, 247
   equivalent awards in other countries, 247

McCabe's cyclomatic complexity number, 291
McCall
   software product quality model, 85, 86
   factor-criteria-metric Model, **85**
Mean time to failure (MTTF), 106
Measurable objectives, 88
Measurement
   definition, **97**
   in High Maturity Organizations, **333**
   in project, 135, 136
   need for, **98**
   principles and protocols, **120, 123**, 124
   scales, **122**
   steps, **99**
   structural model for, **121**
   theory, 96
   user satisfaction context, 105
Measures v/s metrics, 96
Member Body of ISO 9001, 201
Member constitution of ISO 9001, **200, 201**
Mentor, 319
   role for quality professionals, 311
Mentoring, **313**, 318, 334
Method complexity, 148
Metrication program, **132**
Metrics
   derived, 101
   object oriented design, 151
   object oriented software development, 146
   requirements related, **115**, 116
   software maintenance, **110, 111**
   test coverage context, **292**
   test plan context, 292
   test result context, 292
Metrics program, 68, **70**, 71
   development—issues to be considered, **71**
   implementation—issues, **142, 143**
   planning, **141, 142**
Metrics-based proactive project tracking, 138
Michael Fagan of IBM, 158
Mini assessment process, **337**
Minor NC, 214

Mission statement, 25
Models for product quality and process
    quality, 80, **85**, 87
Moderator
    basic tasks, **160**
    in inspection process, **159**
Modifiability, **17**
MTTF (see Meant Time to Failure)
MTTF v/s Defect Density, **107**
Multiple reviewers—importance, 166
Myers—views on walkthroughs, 157

N

NASCOM survey—quality standards
    by Indian software and IT organi-
    zations, **352**
NC (see Non-conformities/Non-con-
    formances)
Non-conformances, 49
    major and minor, 214
Non-functional requirements, **10**, 284,
    294, 386
Non-functional testing techniques,
    279, 283

O

Object classes—coupling, 150
Object library effectiveness, 148
Object Orientation and Maintainability
    —**371**
Object oriented metrics: an overview,
    146
Objective evidence, 28
Object-oriented analysis and design
    (OOAD), 146
Object-oriented design, 11
Objects—degree of cohesion, 147
ODC (see orthogonal defect classifi-
    cation)
O-Members of ISO 9001, 201
On-site assessment process, 214
Operational integrity, **84**
Origins of ISO 9001, **201, 201**
Orthogonal defect classification
    (ODC), 293
Other process improvement models,
    253
Outsourcing, 64

P

PA (see Process Areas)
Past performance data, 136
    illustration on its use, **100**
    usefulness, 133
Path coverage, 290
P-CMM (see People CMM)
People CMM (P-CMM), 224, **252, 254,**
    255
    aim of, **342**
    maturity levels, **254**
    scenario in India, **342, 343**
    model, 312, 329, 330
People issues
    in quality assurance, 53, 311, 312
    in management problems—Indian
        software industry, 356
People maturity, 224
Perfective Maintenance, 367
    e-Business websites, 379
Performance attributes, **84**
Performance testing—**285**, 286
Personal Software Process (PSP), 336
Philip Crosby, 93
Pitfalls in Software Configuration
    Management, **197**
P-Members of ISO 9001, 201
Portability, **84**
Practices at mature organizations, 224
Pre-assessment, 213
Preparing for assessments/audit, **212**
Prevention costs, **5**
Primary metrics, 333
Priority number, 63
Problems v/s failures, **106**
Process
    capability baselines (PCB), 133
    change management (PCM), 74, **76**
    change request for (PCR)—Format,
        76
    champions for, 335
    consulting for, 311
    definition of, **325**
    important aspects of, 325, **326**
    management of, 67
    maturity of, 326
    metrics, 11, 114, 135
    quality, 92, 126
    variability, 361

Process and Product Assurance, 334
Process Areas
  for the Integrated CMM, 239
  grouping for Integrated CMM, **241**
  selection for CMM Integrated, 339
Process Engineering Group (PEG), 76
Process Focus, **327**
Process Improvement, 35, 80, 93, 200, 326, 339
  stages of, 119
  models and frameworks for, 94, 224, 319
  planning for, 335
  program, 337
  proposals, 335
Process orientation, symptoms & behaviour, 327, **328**, 330
Processes in ISO 12207, **246**
Processes-to-Business Objectives linkages, 335
Processing attributes, **84**
Producer—in the review, 161
Producer—responsibilities, **161**
Product
  assurance, 318
  attributes, 82
  certification, 49
  complaints, 318
  metrics, 11, 114, 135
  quality, 80,82,106, 126
  registration procedures, 317
Professional certifications, 321
Project
  de-briefing, **46**
  effort tracking, 136
  management Issues in Maintenance Projects, **331**
  monitoring, **39**
  productivity, 38
  S-curve, 138
  tracking—use of metrics, 138
Prototyping, 40, 368
PSP and TSP for small organizations, 337

Q

QA strategies, 316
QAI (Quality Assurance Institute), 323
  Certifications from , **323**
  CSTE program from, 308

QC group, 316
QC professionals, 316
QMS—organizational expectations, 59
QMS (See Quality Management System)
Quality—in the context of software development process, 92
Quality & reliability, 287
Quality Assurance (QA), 314
  social commitment, 55
  QA Auditor, **318**
  QA Compliance Associate, **317**
  QA Engineer, **316**
  QA Function (SQA), 19
  QA group, 268
  QA Institute (QAI), 83
  QA Plan, 56
Quality Certification, 38, 311, 320
  Indian statistics, 341
  certified Indian organizations—alphabetical list, **343**
Quality circles, **157**
Quality consultant, 44
Quality Control (QC), 318
  QC Analyst, **317**
  QC Manager, **318**
  QC Tools, 362
Quality, 1
  certifications—from ASQ, 321, **322**
  criteria for, 86
  culture, 47, 330
  definition—ISO 9126, **87**
  engineer, **317**
  factors for, 85
  gates for, 82
  goal—DRE (Defect Removal Efficiency), 134
  goal setting—sources of data, 133
  IEEE definition, **88**
  improvement program—principles, 93
  improvement program—principles, 93
  improvement, 224
  issues in Web-site maintenance, **380**
  management of—quantitative, 132, 202
  metrics for, 11, 317
  planning for—in the project, **40**

models for, 83
model—ISO 9126 Std, 87
objectives for, 56,59
of support, 18
QFD (Quality Function Deployment) , 36
QMS (Quality Management System), 25, 36, 37, 200, 214, 218
policy for, 25, 30
record for, 28
Quality Manual—contents, 25, **26**
Quality maturity of the Indian software industry, 352
Quality systems, 27, 202
effectiveness of, 40
improvement in, 40
review of, **40**
triangle of, 209
Quantitative quality management, 132

R

Random cause, 362, **366**
Random testing, **282**
Recorder—responsibilities, **162**
Regression testing, 295, **296**
advantages of test automation, **296**
Reliability, **83**
testing for, **286**
Representations for the CMM-I (Integrated CMM), 236, 237
Requirement, **9**, 10, 385
bi-directional Traceability, 115, 387
creep in, 118
specification—the IEEE guide, 385
specification for, 37, 44
stability of (relationship to size), 118
stability index for, 116, **117**
taxonomy for, **386**
traceability, **43, 117**
Re-use-Pack, 37, 43
Reviewer—responsibilities, **161**
Reviews
ANSI Standard for, **60**
compared with Audits, 60
compared with Inspections—roles and responsibilities, **159**
cultural issues in, **165**
educational qualities, **168**

need for, **155**
psychological aspects of, **162**
team structure for, 168
types of, 260
Revisions v/s Versions, 181
Re-work, 16
Risk
identification, analysis and appraisal, 40, 41
management in High Management Organizations, **332**
risk-based approach to testing, 292, 293, 294
Role of ISO consultants, **219**
Role of mentor, 311
Role of Quality Assurance function, 20
Role of testing, **259**
Ron Radice, 93
Root Cause Analysis (RCA)—concepts and template, 72, **73**, 77
Round-robin reviews, 156
Rules for software configuration items selection, **178**

S

Schedule
as a measure, 136
performance index for (SPI), 138
slippage, 38
variance for (SV), 138
SCM (Software Configuration Management)
anti-patterns, 197
checklist for plan evaluation, **196**
CMM aspects of, **193**
IEEE definition for, **175,177**
major activities in, **177**
people-ware, **197**
pitfalls in, **197**
S-curve, 138
Second-party-assessment and audit, **211, 212**
Security features testing, **287**, 317
Security technologies, 317
SEI (see Software Engineering Institute), 224
SEI
1999 Survey (High Maturity Organizations), 331
CMM compliance, 320

CMM Lead Assessor, **319**
CMM organization measures, 320
Selecting ISO consultants, **218**
Self assessment, **211**
SEPG (Software Engineering Process Group)
Severity level, 63
Shewhart-type control charts, **363**
Six Sigma, 329, **402**
Size
  and requirements stability, 118
  estimating in Maintenance Projects, 331,332
  metrics for, 11
Skill level of project staff, 35
Skills and Knowledge, 334
Skills for SQA role, 50
Small Organizations and CMM—challenges, 335, 336
Software application attributes—classification, **84**
Software attributes, **82**
Software CMM
  common features, 94
  key process areas, 94
  version 1.1 of, 225
  for Small Organizations/projects, 335
Software configuration audit, **188**
SCI (Software Configuration Item)
  identification and rules for, **177, 179, 178**
SCM (Software Configuration Management), 183
  need for, **173**
  description, **175**
Software Development Life Cycle (SDLC), **2**
Software Engineering Institute (SEI), 80, 93, 224
Software life cycles, 214
Software maintenance
  definition, **110**
  metrics for, **110**
  models evolution, **367**
Software maturity, 224
Software metrics, 11, 70, 96, 383
  classification, 97
  definition, **98**
  effectiveness attributes, **101**

Software practices maturity—Indian scenario, 341
Software process
  assessment, 210
  assets, 67
  capability, 211
  defined, 67
  engineering group for (SEPG), 47, 48
  improvement (SPI), 211, 226, 319, 334
  management of (SPM), 361
Software product
  characteristics of, **82**
  definition (IEEE Std. 610.12), **82**
  external attributes of, 83
  internal attributes of, 83
  model for quality—McCall, **86**
  quality, 83
  quality—Boehm's view, 85
Software project—umbrella activities, 102
Software Quality
  analyst (SQA), 47
  assurance for (SQA), 333
  assurance Manger, **319**
  assurance Plan—IEEE Standard, 56, **57**
  ISO 8402 definition, **88**
  metrics for, 88
  tester for, **316**
Software requirements, 387
Software standards—ISO, CMM, IEEE, 59
Software systems evolution, **81**
Software testing
  careers in, 258, **308**
  practices, **261**
Software verification, 318
SPC (see Statistical Process Control)
Special causes, 362, **366**
Specific practices in CMM-I, 242
SPI (see Software Process Improvement), 226
SQA (Software Quality Assurance)
SQA function, **19**
  benefits, **20**
  objectives, **22**
  people issues, **53**
  role and skills, **19**, 20, **23, 50**
  need, **21**

SQA plans, 319
SQA responsibilities, **23**
SRS (Software Requirements Specification)
  formal notation, 18
  IEEE Guide for, 61
Stable process, 361
Staged representation—Integrated CMM, 239,**240**
Stages v/s Continuous representation for CMM-I, **242**
Standard
  process definition, **68**
  IEEE definition, **82**
  QAI definition, **83**
  procedures, 40
State transition
  analysis, 282
  diagram, 62
Statement coverage, 290
Static testing, 283
Statistical Process Control (SPC), 135, 360, 361
Statistical Quality Control (SQC), 360, 361
Statistics on Quality Certification scenario in India, 341
Statistics on TickIT certifications, 245
Status reports, 317
Stress testing, **288**, 315, 320
Structure of the ISO 9001, 200
Structured reviews, 168
Structured walkthroughs, **156**
Sub-contractor, 65
Suppliers—ISO 9001:2000 cause, **65**
Support quality, 18
Surveillance audit, **215**
SW CMM
  Ability to Perform, 225
  Activities Performed, 225
  Commitment to Perform, 225
  Common Features, 225
  comparison with CMM-I, **244**
  comparison with ISO, 227, **228**
  General Practices, 226
  Key Practices, 225
  Key Process Areas, **227**, 234
  mapping with ISO, **228**
  maturity levels in, 225
  measurement & analysis in, 225
  structure of, **226**

Verifying Implementation, 225
  mapping ISO/IEC 15504, **231**, **232**
  v/s Integrated CMM, 235, **244**
  vis-à-vis ISO, 224
SW CMM to CMM-I transition, 238, **239**, **338**
System Integration tests, 315
System Security Engineering CMM (SSE CMM), 252
System tester, 314, **315**
System testing, 37, 41, **276**

T

Tailoring guidelines, 51, 68
Team debugging, 156
Team Software Process (TSP), 336
Technical maintenance—website, 377, 382
Technical reviews, 40, 168
Technology
  change management (TCM), 43, 74
  impact analysis, 74
  innovation, 74
  pilot—Summary Format, **75**
Test analyst, 267, 268
Test artifacts, **269**
Test automation, **297**, 319
  & Test Tool Selection, 266
  during regression test—advantages, **296**
Test bed, **271**
Testing career—progression, **309**
Test case, 37, 62, **271**, 319
  based on boundary value analysis, **281**
  effective, 260
  execution, 268
  generator, 271
  prioritization, 267
  specification, 271, 274
Test control metrics, 291
Test coverage & metrics, 271, **292**
Test design specification, 274
Test documentation, 261, 270
Test driver, **271**
Test factors, 294
Test harness, 271
Test life-cycle tools, **299**
Test manager, 266
Test maturity, 258

Test metrics, **289**
Test observer, 268
Test phase matrix, 294
Test plan—261,**269**, **273**, **274**, 294, 319
  metrics, 292
  preparation of, 264
  template for, **274**
Test procedure specification, 274
Test process evaluation & improvement, **265**
Test Process Improvement (TPI), 258, 301
Test report, 271
Test resource metrics, **292**
Test result metrics, 292
Test result record—format, **272**
Test scripts and format, 267, 268, **272**
Test specification document, 267, **269**
Test strategies, 293, 294, 318
Test strategy development—steps, **294**
Test summary report, 268
Test team leader, 267
Test tool selection and acquisition, 297
Testability, **84**
  metrics for, 291
Testing, 270, 311
  additional roles in , 268, **269**
  competence for, **308**
  documentation & help, 285
  human issues and challenges, **306**
  IEEE definition, **259**
  life cycle—**264**
  maturity model (TMM), 301
  policy for, 257
  primary and secondary role, **307**
  product security, 317
  professional certifications, 308
  related definitions—IEEE, **270**, **271**
  risk-based approach to, 292
  role of, **259**
  security features, 317
  strategies for, 257, 316
  usability, **289**
  v/s Debugging, **262**
  v/s Inspection, **260**
The need for ISO, **207**
The Structure of ISO 9001, **201**
The working of ISO 9001, **205**
Third-party-audit and assessment, **211**, **212**
Thread testing, 283

TickIT
  objectives, 245
  purpose, 245
  statistics on certification, 245
Tips for Author/Producer, **163**
Tips for Reviewer, **163**
TMM (Testing Maturity Model), 301
  and CMM connection, 302
  & automated software testing, **304**
  structure of, **303**
Tom Gilb—on Walkthroughs, **158**
Top twenty software companies in India, **349**
Total quality culture (TQM), 54, 200, 316, 329
Traceability, **17**, 62, 181
Traditional metrics—adaptation to OO paradigm, 152
Training, **42**
  responsibility of, 35
  role in quality, 27
  and awareness programs, 334
  records of, 42
Transaction Log, 186
Transformability, **16**
Transitioning from SW CMM to the CMM-I, **238**, **239**
Type I and Type II error, 363
Types of audits and assessments, **211**
Types of CMMs, **234**
Types of control charts, 365
Types of reviews, 260

U

Unit test records, **40**
Unit testing, 40, **275**
Upgrading from SW CMM to CMM-I, 338
Upper and Lower Control Limits, 59
Usability, **83**
User interface testing, **285**
User satisfaction measures, 105
Using consultants, **217**
Using the CMM—challenges for small organizations, 336

V

Validation—IEEE definition, **258**
Variable control charts, **365**
Verifiability, **16**

Verification & validation, 9, 258
Version control systems, 315
Visibility, 181
Vision Statement, 25
V-Model for testing—benefits, **275**
Volume testing, **288**

W

Walkthroughs, 155
    and organization structure, **158**
    as static QA methods, 157
    definitions, **157**
    Myers' views, 157

    objectives, **157**
    optimum number of participants, **158**
Walter Shewart, 93
Watts Humphrey, 93
WBS (see Work Breakdown Structure)
Web-site life cycle, **375, 376**
Web-site maintenance and quality issues, **373, 380**
Weighted methods per class, 149
White box testing, 273, 293, **295**
Work breakdown structure (WBS), 138
Work product, **178**
Working of ISO 9001, 200